Turning Points

Other books by Mark A. Noll

Adding Cross to Crown: The Political Significance of Christ's Passion

Amazing Grace: Evangelicalism in Australia, Britain, Canada, and the United States (editor, with George Rawlyk)

Between Faith and Criticism: Evangelicals, Scholarship, and the Bible in America

The Bible in America: Essays in Cultural History (editor, with Nathan Hatch)

Charles Hodge: The Way of Life (editor)

Christian Faith and Practice in the Modern World: Theology from an Evangelical Point of View (editor, with David Wells)

Christianity: A Social and Cultural History (with Howard Kee, Emily Hanawalt, Carter Lindberg, and Jean-Loup Seban)

Christians in the American Revolution

Confessions and Catechisms of the Reformation (editor)

Eerdmans Handbook to Christianity in America (editor, with Nathan Hatch, George Marsden, David Wells, and John Woodbridge)

Evangelicalism: Comparative Studies of Popular Protestantism in North America, the British Isles, and Beyond, 1700–1990 (editor, with David Bebbington and George Rawlyk)

The Gospel in America: Themes in the Story of America's Evangelicals (with John Woodbridge and Nathan Hatch)

A History of Christianity in the United States and Canada

One Nation Under God? Christian Faith and Political Action in America

Princeton and the Republic, 1768–1822: The Search for a Christian Enlightenment in the Era of Samuel Stanhope Smith

The Princeton Defense of Plenary Verbal Inspiration (editor)

The Princeton Theology, 1812–1921: Scripture, Science, and Theological Method from Archibald Alexander to Benjamin Breckinridge Warfield (editor)

Religion and American Politics: From the Colonial Period to the 1980s (editor)

The Scandal of the Evangelical Mind

The Search for Christian America (with Nathan Hatch and George Marsden)

Voices from the Heart: Four Centuries of American Piety (editor, with Roger Lundin)

What Is Darwinism? by Charles Hodge (editor, with David Livingstone)

Turning Points

Decisive Moments
in the History of Christianity

Mark A. Noll

Baker Books
A Division of Baker Book House Co
Grand Rapids, Michigan 49516

Leicester, England

© 1997 by Mark A. Noll

Published by Baker Books
a division of Baker Book House Company
P.O. Box 6287, Grand Rapids, MI 49516–6287

Library of Congress Cataloging-in-Publication Data

Noll, Mark A., 1946–
    Turning points : decisive moments in the history of Christianity / Mark A. Noll.
       p.   cm.
    Includes bibliographical references and index.
    ISBN 0-8010-5778-7 (pbk.)
    1. Church history. I. Title.
BR145.2N65   1997
270–dc21
                                                     97-29873

For information about academic books, resources for Christian leaders, and all new re-
leases available from Baker Book House, visit our web site:
http://www.bakerbooks.com

and

Inter-Varsity Press
38 De Montford Street
Leicester LE1 7GP
England

British Library Cataloguing in Publication Data
A catalogue record for this book is available from the British Library.
ISBN 0-85111-191-2

Third printing

Printed in the United States of America

To the Illinois Presbyterians and Transylvanian Baptists
for whom the material in this book was first prepared
and who, though students, have taught me
much more than ever I gave to them

Contents

Acknowledgments

For help on the subjects of this book, some of it going back many years, I am deeply grateful to a large group of teachers, friends, and colleagues:

- to gifted teachers with whom I studied church history, including Harold O. J. Brown, Jack Forstman, John Gerstner, Dale Johnson, H. D. McDonald, John Warwick Montgomery, the late Richard Wolf, and John Woodbridge. I hope these scholars, and especially David Wells, my first teacher in several senses of the term, will take it as nothing but a compliment if a few of their phrases or a hint of their outlines have worked their way through years of re-arranging lecture notes to the printed page. Over the past several years the influence of another kind of teaching from Andrew Walls has profoundly deepened my understanding of the history of Christianity.
- to a generation of college students, mostly in classes at Wheaton College, who through patient listening and probing questions have pushed cut-and-dried information into genuine historical engagement.
- to patrons associated with Wheaton College who generously expedited progress on this book.
- to friends joined in the work of the Institute for the Study of American Evangelicals who, by being such splendid colleagues on questions of Christian history in North America, have provided a matchless counterpoint for considering the worldwide history of Christianity.
- to family members who for several decades have encouraged, tolerated, and indulged a fascination with history that leaves me sometimes only half-present in the here and now.

- to Robert Brown, amanuensis, friend, and initial organizer of this project.
- to Estelle Berger, research associate, friend, and dedicated co-worker in finishing it off.
- to Maria denBoer, Mary Ann Jeffreys, Craig Noll, Jim Ohlson, and Jim Weaver for excellent editorial help of different kinds.
- to members and Sunday school regulars at Bethel Presbyterian and Immanuel Presbyterian churches in Wheaton and Glen Ellyn, Illinois, who have shown such eager interest in the Christian past.
- and to the Baptist theological students in Oradea and Cluj, Romania, especially to friends in Oradea who provided an opportunity in the summer of 1989 to condense notes for a two-week introduction to the study of church history onto a single 4 x 6 card, and in so doing planted the seed that has sprouted as this book.

Three kinds of notes are found in this book. Notes that explain terms or other questions in the text are marked with an asterisk and are placed at the bottom of the page. Also at the bottom of the page are reference notes to quotations and other authorities. Each of the longer quotations in the inset boxes is also provided with a note. These are gathered together consecutively at the back of the book in the section, "Box Notes," on pages 317–19.

Introduction: *The Idea of Turning Points and Reasons for Studying the History of Christianity*

Among the last words that Jesus spoke to his disciples were statements recorded in Matthew, chapter 28, and Acts, chapter 1. These words, though they are important for many other reasons, also outline a framework for the history of Christianity.

"All authority in heaven and on earth has been given to me." Nothing could now happen to the followers of Christ that lay outside the reach of his sovereignty; no experiences that the church underwent, no matter how glorious or how mundane, were irrelevant to the living Word of God.

"Therefore go and make disciples of all nations." The history of Christianity would always involve at least two related actions: a movement outward to reach places where Christ's name was hitherto not known and a movement inward to train hearts in learning more of Christ.

"[S]urely I will be with you always, to the very end of the age." However the church might wander, whatever the sins committed by Christians as individuals and as a body, the people of God would be sustained, not by their own wisdom, but by the presence of Christ.

"[Y]ou will be my witnesses . . . to the ends of the earth." The Christian faith would take root in particular cultures, and it would profoundly shape individual peoples, regions, and nations. But Christianity itself would belong to none of them. Rather, the church would exist to bear witness to God's love revealed in Christ and to bear that witness throughout the whole world.

These parting words of Jesus do not, of course, provide details about the later history of Christianity, but they do provide orientation for that history. The history of Christianity has wound its way through vast regions across vast stretches of time and in a vast variety of forms. But it

11

remains the history of those who worship the Lord of Life, who seek to serve him, and whose witnesses they are.

One of the most interesting ways to grasp a general sense of Christian history (though there are many others) is to examine critical turning points in that story. Identifying such critical turning points is a subjective exercise, for an observer's decisions about what those most important turning points are inevitably depends upon what the observer considers to be most important. Yet however subjective it is to select a limited number of turning points as *the* critical moments in Christian history, such an exercise has a number of advantages.

- It provides an opportunity to select, to extract from the immense quantity of resources available for studying the history of Christianity a few striking incidents and so to bring some order into a massively complicated subject.
- Concentrating on the turning points of church history also provides an opportunity to highlight, to linger over specific moments so as to display the humanity, the complexity, and the uncertainties that constitute the actual history of the church, but which are often obscured in trying to recount the sweep of centuries.
- Studying specific turning points more closely also provides an opportunity to interpret, to state more specifically why certain events, actions, or incidents may have marked an important fork in the road or signaled a new stage in the outworking of Christian history.

The advantages for organizing an introduction to Christian history around a series of turning points were pressed home to me over a period of several years. First was the need for a framework for organizing an adult education course at my church. Then came the opportunity on two occasions to introduce the sweep of church history in short courses for Romanian pastors and lay workers. Finally was the chance to rethink the best way of teaching a one-semester survey of the history of Christianity to students at Wheaton College. For each of these audiences, a concentration on critical turning points turned out to allow greater focus on specific episodes while also providing more opportunity for interpretive reflection than I had found when teaching such material in other ways.

This book comes directly out of those varied teaching experiences. In each case, much was sacrificed in order to concentrate on a few major turning points. But much also was gained by attempting to combine more focus than a survey usually allows, while still attending to large-scale movements of institutions, people, and doctrines in the history of the church.

The book that grows out of these teaching assignments is intentionally shorter rather than longer. It is written for laypeople and introductory students rather than for scholars. It comes from an author with Christian presuppositions (specifically of the Protestant evangelical variety), but it intends to be as fair and as nonpartisan as such presuppositions allow. It is also written with an intent to present Christianity as a worldwide religion rather than a faith for just Europeans and North Americans.

The twelve turning points singled out for special attention, as well as the potential turning points for the twentieth century discussed in the final chapter, are by no means the only ones that could have been selected. A good case could have been made for including many other events, for example (as only a partial list):

the mission of Patrick to Ireland in the early fifth century;

the foundation of the reforming monastery at Cluny in France in 909;

the arrival of Eastern Orthodoxy in Kyivan Rus in 988;

the start of the Crusades in 1095;

the revival of monasticism through the friars (especially Dominicans and Franciscans) at the start of the thirteenth century;

the fall of the Byzantine Roman Empire to Islam in 1453;

any number of significant moments in the missionary proclamation of Christianity beyond the West;

the production of important translations of the Bible (for example, Jerome into Latin ca. 400, the English translation inspired by Wycliffe at the end of the fourteenth century, Luther's translation into German of 1522, the King James Bible of 1611, or some of the many new translations of the nineteenth and twentieth centuries);

the beginning of independent churches in Africa at the end of the nineteenth century; and

the emergence of significant protest and humanitarian movements that decisively influenced the shape of later history (for example, the Waldensians in 1173, Conrad Grebel and the Anabaptists in 1525, John Smyth and the Baptists in 1609, George Fox and the Quakers in 1652, or William and Catherine Booth and the Salvation Army in 1878).

Attempting to select the twelve most important turning points in the history of Christianity is a good exercise in itself. I have chosen the turning points treated in this book primarily because I think they reveal vitally important matters about church history, but also in part because these are events I know something about from my own teaching and reading. If the book inspires others to think about why the turning points found here are not as important as other possibilities, it will have been a successful book.

Each chapter begins with a relatively detailed account of the turning point itself, since historical details remind us that "Church History" is never just the grand sweep through great eons of magisterial Doctrines, clashing Principles, or inevitable Consequences, but is rather the cumulative result of the often blurred thoughts, often hesitant actions, and often unforeseen consequences experienced by people more or less like ourselves.

Only after attempting to flesh out history in this kind of concrete way do we go on to larger, more general questions of why, how, and so what. Why was this event crucial? How did it relate to what went before and lead on to what followed? And what might those of us looking back at the end of the twentieth century learn from the event? Answers to these questions must, of necessity, be more general, but they are intended to connect, rather than disconnect, grand historical consequences with sharply focused critical events.

To provide even more context for the turning points, each chapter begins with a hymn and ends with a prayer that were written close to the time of the turning point under discussion. Each chapter also contains several longer quotations from people who took part in the turning point or who were affected by it. These materials, along with maps, charts, and illustrations, are intended in part to provide a more readable book. But they are also meant as a way for putting some flesh on the bare bones of history. The great decisions of the Christian past were made by people who sang and prayed with their fellow believers, who experienced the priceless nurture of regular worship and the disillusioning sorrows of intrachurch conflict, and who often expounded at great length on the page or in public speech. To hear their voices is not just to offer window dressing, but to show that the great events of church history always involved real people, for whom regular worship, study of Scripture, participation in the sacraments, and attention to preaching and teaching provided a foundation for what gets written up in books.

But why, the question might be raised, be concerned about church history at all? Why think that any sort of knowledge about the Christian past—which can so easily seem obscure, petty, confusing, or complex—should interest or assist Christian believers in the present?

Obviously, some people are more naturally inclined to historical study than others. But for believers at the end of the twentieth century, there are several reasons why at least some attention to the history of Christianity is valuable. Brief explanation of those reasons builds a foundation for the specific turning points that make up this book.

1. In the first instance, studying the history of Christianity provides repeated, concrete demonstration concerning the irreducibly historical character of the Christian faith. The Bible itself is rife with explicit statements of that great truth. For instance, God gave the Ten Commandments to the children of Israel in direct consequence of his action-in-history on their behalf: "I am the LORD your God, who brought you out of Egypt, out of the land of slavery. You shall have no other gods before me" (Exod. 20:2–3). The vision of the New Testament is just as fully taken up with historical realities. The narrative heart of Christian faith, as well as its central dogma, is the truth that the Word became flesh (John 1:14). The apostle John spoke further of the Christian faith in the concrete terms of that "which we have heard, which we have seen with our eyes, which we have looked at and our hands have touched" (1 John 1:1). Luke wrote at the beginning of his Gospel that the Christian message depended on "the things that have been fulfilled among us, just as they were handed down to us by those who from the first were eyewitnesses and servants of the word" (Luke 1:1–2). The apostle Paul spoke of events in Jewish history that provided "examples" for believers in the first century (1 Cor. 10:6, 11).

The message of these and many other biblical passages is summarized in the key affirmations of the Nicene-Constantinopolitan Creed of 381 concerning the historical character of Christ's work, who for the sake of humanity and our salvation "came down from heaven, and was incarnate by the Holy Ghost of the Virgin Mary, and was made man; he was crucified for us under Pontius Pilate, and suffered, and was buried, and the third day he rose again."

In a word, since Christianity is not captured simply in a set of dogmas, a moral code, or a picture of the universe—though Christianity certainly involves dogmas, morality, and a worldview—since Christianity is ultimately the acts of God in time and space, centrally the acts of God in Christ, then to study the history of Christianity is continually to remember the historical character of Christian faith.

To be sure, there are dangers in taking history seriously. Throughout the entire history of Christianity, problems have constantly arisen when believers equate the human acts of the church with the acts of God, when Christians assume that using the name of God to justify their actions in space and time is the same as God himself acting. But that danger grows from a positive reality: to be a Christian is to have an infinite stake in the events of God-in-Christ, with all that led up to the incarnation, crucifixion, resurrection, and ascension, and all that now flows from those realities in the shape of the church's history.

2. A second contribution of church history is to provide perspective on the interpretation of Scripture. In varied forms, all Christians testify to their dependence upon the Bible, yet as even the briefest reflection indicates, there are vast differences in how the Bible is understood and used. Studying the history of Christianity provides guidance in several ways for discovering the meaning of Scripture.

We may view the Christian past like a gigantic seminar where trusted friends, who have labored long to understand the Scriptures, hold forth in various corners of the room. There is Augustine discoursing on the Trinity, here St. Patrick and Count von Zinzendorf comparing notes on the power of Light over Darkness, over there Catherine of Siena and Phoebe Palmer discussing the power of holiness, across the room Pope Gregory the Great on the duties of a pastor, there the Orthodox monk St. Herman of Alaska and the first African Anglican bishop Samuel Ajayi Crowther on what it means to carry Christianity across cultural boundaries, here St. Francis on the God-ordained goodness of the earth, in a huddle Thomas Aquinas, Simeon the New Theologian, and Blaise Pascal talking about the relation of reason to revelation, there Hildegard of Bingen and Johann Sebastian Bach on how to sing the praises of the Lord, here Martin Luther on justification by faith, there John Calvin on Christ as Prophet, King, and Priest, there Charles Wesley on the love of God, there his mother, Susanna, on the communication of faith to children, and on and on.

If a contemporary believer wants to know the will of God as revealed in Scripture on any of these matters, or on thousands more, it is certainly prudent to study the Bible carefully for oneself. But it is just as prudent to look for help, to realize that the question I am bringing to Scripture has doubtless been asked before and will have been addressed by others who were at least as saintly as I am, at least as patient in pondering the written Word, and at least as knowledgeable about the human heart.

Teachers of foreign languages say that you don't really know your own language unless you have tried to learn a second or a third language. In the same way, students of the Scriptures usually cannot claim to have understood its riches unless they have consulted others about its meaning. In fact, Christians are always consulting one another about the meaning of the Bible, whether by listening to sermons, by reading commentaries, or by meeting for Bible studies of one kind or another. The dimension added by the history of Christianity is the realization that in books may be found a wondrously rich reservoir of engagement with the Scriptures from those who, though dead, still speak of what they have found in the sacred texts.

As much as church history offers this kind of direct help in understanding the Scriptures, it also offers a great caution. From the distance supplied by time, it is often quite easy to see that some biblical interpretations that once seemed utterly persuasive were in fact distortions of Scripture. When we find out, for example, that some believers once thought the Bible clearly taught that the Roman Empire was to usher in the millennium or that Christ would return in 1538 or that Africans were an inherently inferior form of humanity, then we can see the role that specific thought patterns or intellectual conventions of an age have played in interpretations of the Bible.

The benefit from noting such mistaken interpretations from the past is to raise the possibility that some of our treasured interpretations of Scripture today may be as dependent on conventions of our own era, and also as irrelevant to the actual message of the Bible as clearly deviant interpretations of former epochs were. For this problem it is difficult to provide examples from the present, since the biblical interpretations I hold most dear are likely to be precisely those that I consider to be least influenced by passing fashions. (It is much easier to see where biblical interpretations I reject are dominated by the thought forms of today.) Still, to see in the past that very godly people were able to maintain bizarre interpretations of Scripture should be a caution for us all.

3. The study of church history is also useful as a laboratory for examining Christian interactions with surrounding culture. To take one pressing, if not all-important, example, many Western churches at the end of the twentieth century struggle with questions about what kind of music to use in church. Should all the old hymns be dropped in favor of new songs of praise? Should music be provided by an organ? a combo? Should it be performed a capella? with electricity? with drums? Study of the past cannot provide easy answers on how best to use music for Christ today. But to examine periods like the first half of the sixteenth century, when, in response to the tumults of the Reformation, at least five or six different decisions were taken with respect to the use of music in church, would certainly be a help. When Roman Catholics took the path of complex music and professional performance, Calvinists of congregational Psalm-singing with straightforward tunes, the Orthodox of preserving ancient liturgies, Anabaptists of rejecting all "worldly" forms of music in favor of unaccompanied congregational song, Lutherans of combining professional music with congregational singing, and Anglicans wobbling (typically) among

Lutheran, Catholic, and Calvinist styles, there were consequences that helped shape each of these Christian traditions. To see what flowed from the decision for traditional, trendy, populist, professional, elaborate, or simple forms of music provides substantial context for trying to think through issues in the use of music today.

On a question that can have life-or-death consequences, modern Christians face weighty choices in how to live as believers in various political situations. Again, the history of Christianity cannot provide definitive answers, but it can provide a welter of contrasting scenarios. Sometimes the church has thrived under tyranny, sometimes tyranny has decimated it. In different eras the church has supported (or attacked) monarchy, democracy, and aristocracy. Churches have both upheld and resisted ruling regimes. Modern believers in Montana, Serbia, Kuwait, Russia, Rwanda, and Northern Ireland are probably going to be looking for direction of different kinds from church history, but all will be able to find some fellow believers who have gone down a road something like theirs before.

And so it is with many other circumstances: Christian engagement with science, Christian attitudes to alien ethnic groups, Christian promotion of peace or war, Christian contributions to different forms of economic organization, Christian discussion about what to eat or drink, Christian strategies for organizing the work of God, and so on.

Even a little bit of historical understanding may benefit modern believers attempting to act responsibly in any of these cultural spheres. The first reassurance is that almost all such issues have been faced before, at least in some form. The second is that believers—guided by Scripture, church authorities, sage employment of worldly wisdom, and the inner prompting of the Spirit—have often acted wisely and well on such cultural matters. The third is that, even where in retrospect it appears that Christians have blundered badly in their decisions, the Lord of the church has not abandoned them to their folly but, despite their misbegotten efforts, has remained to sustain his own.

4. This realization, which historical study fairly shouts out loud, that God sustains the church despite the church's own frequent efforts to betray its Savior and its own high calling, points to another benefit from the history of Christianity. Study of the past can be useful, that is, in shaping proper Christian attitudes. It is often easier in reviewing the past than in looking at the present to discriminate between matters that are absolutely essential to genuine Christianity and those that are either of relative importance or not important at all. If we are able to isolate from past generations what was of crucial significance in the church's mission, then we have a chance in the present to order our

emotional and spiritual energies with discrimination—preserving our deepest commitment only for those aspects of Christian faith that deserve such commitment and acting with ever greater toleration as we move from the center of the faith to its periphery.

Even more important, study of church history should increase our humility about who we are and what we believe. There is nothing that the modern church enjoys that is not a gift from previous generations of God's people. To be sure, we modify, adjust, adapt, and expand these gifts from the past, but we do not make them up. Again, if the church is always only one generation from extinction, it also enjoys a peerless inheritance. The more we know about how those gifts have come down to us, the more we may humbly thank God for his faithfulness to past generations, as well as to our own.

Even more than humility, a study of the Christian past can also engender profound gratitude. Despite a dazzling array of God-honoring triumphs and despite a wide and deep record of godliness among believers of high estate and low, the sad fact is that the church's history is often a sordid, disgusting tale. Once students push beyond sanitized versions of Christian history to realistic study, it is clear that self-seeking, rebellion, despotism, pettiness, indolence, cowardice, murder (though dignified with God-talk), and the lust for power along with all other lusts have flourished in the church almost as ignobly as in the world at large. A study of church history can be an eye-opener. The heroes of the faith usually have feet of clay—sometimes thighs, hearts, and heads as well. The golden ages of the past usually turn out to be tarnished if they are examined closely enough. Crowding around the heroes of the faith are a lot of villains, and some of them look an awful lot like the heroes.

And so along with all the positive direction and ennobling examples in church history stands also a full record of human wrongdoing. Our response? It could be to despair at the persistent human inability to act toward others and toward God as God has acted toward humanity. It would be better, however, to consider the hidden reality that the long record of Christian weakness and failure reveals, for what it shows is a divine patience broader than any human impatience, a divine forgiveness more powerful than any human offense, and a divine grace deeper than our human sin.

Despite a tangled history, the promise of the Savior concerning the church has been fulfilled: "the gates of Hades will not overcome it" (Matt. 16:18). But precisely that tangled history points to the reason why Christianity has endured: "*I will build *my* church.*"

By way of final introduction, it may be helpful to say a few last words about what follows.

Most of the chapters speak more often of "the history of Christianity" than of "church history," since "church history" entails a stronger commitment to a particular expression of the faith than does "the history of Christianity." My own conviction is that "Christianity" means something definite with boundaries that are fairly well defined by the major creeds treated in the first three chapters. Furthermore, my own evangelical Protestant convictions lead me to think that revitalized forms of Reformation faith are the truest and best forms of Christianity. At the same time, however, historical study has convinced me that confessional Protestants have sometimes honored the ideals of the Reformation more in words than in reality. Historical study also shows that believers in other Christian traditions regularly display Christ-like virtues and practice humble dependence upon God's grace more than my confessional Protestant convictions tell me they should. With these facts in mind, I have tried to write with as much respect as possible for the widely diverse forms of Christianity that have been practiced with integrity, and continue to be practiced with integrity, in all parts of the Christian church.

The pages below reflect what might legitimately be called a male bias toward the history of Christianity. In a stellar book on the religious lives of medieval Catholic women, Caroline Walker Bynum writes that "women tended to tell stories and develop personal models without crises or turning points."[1] The fact that it is mostly men who figure as the principal actors in the turning points that follow is less a statement about the intrinsic character of the faith than it is a reflection of how the church's public life has been documented through the centuries. It is gratifying indeed to see that the flourishing of scholarship over the past decades on women in Christian history is already leading to the kind of popular general studies that this one also tries to be, but written with a focus on the spheres of Christian life in which the experiences of women have figured more prominently.[2]

1. Caroline Walker Bynum, *Holy Feast and Holy Fast: The Religious Significance of Food to Medieval Women* (Berkeley: University of California Press, 1987), 25.
2. For example, Ruth Tucker and Walter L. Liefeld, *Daughters of the Church: Women and Ministry from New Testament Times to the Present* (Grand Rapids: Zondervan, 1987); Amy Oden, ed., *In Her Words: Women's Writings in the History of Christian Thought* (Nashville: Abingdon, 1994); and Margaret Bendroth and Phyllis Airhart, eds., *Faith Traditions and the Family* (Louisville: Westminster/John Knox, 1996).

Finally, it may be worth observing that the abbreviation "ca." is from the Latin *circa*, "about," and is used to designate a date concerning which there is some uncertainty.

Each of the chapters ends with a prayer taken from a figure related in some way to the turning point of the chapter. It is therefore appropriate that this introduction do the same by enlisting from the Psalms two parts of a great biblical prayer of Moses concerning the rule of God over human history:

> *Lord, you have been our dwelling place*
> *   throughout all generations.*
> *Before the mountains were born*
> *   or you brought forth the earth and the world,*
> *   from everlasting to everlasting you are God.*
> *You turn men back to dust,*
> *   saying, "Return to dust, O sons of men."*
> *For a thousand years in your sight*
> *   are like a day that has just gone by,*
> *   or like a watch in the night.*
> *You sweep men away in the sleep of death;*
> *   they are like the new grass of the morning—*
> *though in the morning it springs up new,*
> *   by evening it is dry and withered.*

> *Teach us to number our days aright,*
> *   that we may gain a heart of wisdom.*
> *Relent, O LORD! How long will it be?*
> *   Have compassion on your servants.*
> *Satisfy us in the morning with your unfailing love,*
> *   that we may sing for joy and be glad all our days.*
> *Make us glad for as many days as you have afflicted us,*
> *   for as many years as we have seen trouble.*
> *May your deeds be shown to your servants,*
> *   your splendor to their children.*
> *May the favor of the Lord our God rest upon us;*
> *   establish the work of our hands for us—*
> *   yes, establish the work of our hands.*

> *(Ps. 90:1–6, 12–17)*

Further Reading

Each of the chapters ends with a short list of books and articles that provide further reading concerning the turning point or its broader context. At the end of this introduction it is appropriate to list some of the general and reference works that were most helpful in preparing this book.

Barrett, David B., ed. *World Christian Encyclopedia.* New York: Oxford University Press, 1982.

Bettenson, Henry, ed. *Documents of the Christian Church.* 2nd ed. New York: Oxford University Press, 1963.

Bradley, James E., and Richard A. Muller. *Church History: An Introduction to Research, Reference Works, and Methods.* Grand Rapids: Eerdmans, 1995.

Clouse, Robert G., Richard V. Pierard, and Edwin M. Yamauchi. *Two Kingdoms: The Church and Culture through the Ages.* Chicago: Moody, 1993.

Cross, F. L., and E. A. Livingstone, eds. *The Oxford Dictionary of the Christian Church.* 2nd ed. London: Oxford University Press, 1974.

Douglas, J. D., ed. *The New International Dictionary of the Christian Church.* Grand Rapids: Zondervan, 1974.

Eerdmans' Handbook to the History of Christianity. Grand Rapids: Eerdmans, 1977.

The 100 Most Important Events in Church History [*Christian History,* no. 28]. 1990.

Lane, Tony, ed. *Harper's Concise Book of Christian Faith.* San Francisco: Harper & Row, 1984.

Leith, John H., ed. *Creeds of the Churches.* 3rd ed. Atlanta: John Knox, 1982.

New Catholic Encyclopedia. 17 vols. New York: McGraw-Hill, 1967–79.

The New Schaff-Herzog Encyclopedia of Religious Knowledge. 13 vols. New York: Funk & Wagnalls, 1908–14.

Schaff, Philip. *The Creeds of Christendom.* 3 vols. 6th ed. New York: Harper & Brothers, 1919.

Walker, Williston, with Richard A. Norris, David W. Lotz, and Robert T. Handy. *A History of the Christian Church.* 4th ed. New York: Charles Scribner's Sons, 1985.

1

The Church Pushed Out on Its Own: The Fall of Jerusalem (70)

The apostle Paul encouraged the church at Ephesus to "sing and make music in your heart to the Lord" (Eph. 5:19). Several of Paul's letters indicate that the singing of "psalms, hymns and spiritual songs" formed part of the earliest Christian expression of worship, an outpouring of thanksgiving and gratitude to God for Jesus' saving action on the cross (Eph. 5:19 and Col. 3:16; also 1 Cor. 14:26). Although scant evidence remains concerning the content of hymns during the first century of the church, some scholars have identified "hymnic" passages in the New Testament based on their "lyrical quality and rhythmical style," as well as their unique vocabulary and doctrinal content.[1] Drawing initially on Jewish expressions of praise, the first Christians quickly began to develop uniquely Christian hymns and their own, separate forms of liturgy.

One of the earliest accounts of the church from an outsider happens to mention hymn-singing. It is from Pliny, the Roman governor of the province of Pontus and Bithynia in Asia Minor (modern Turkey) from A.D. 111 to 112. Describing to the emperor Trajan what he has learned of Christian practice, Pliny writes that "on an appointed day they had been accustomed to meet before daybreak, and to recite a hymn antiphonally to Christ, as a god."[2]

---

1. Ralph P. Martin, *Worship in the Early Church* (Grand Rapids: Eerdmans, 1974), 48.

2. Henry Bettenson, ed., *Documents of the Christian Church*, 2nd ed. (New York: Oxford University Press, 1963), 3–4.

Later accounts testify that hymn-singing was well established in Christian worship by the second century. As it developed, believers used models from the New Testament like the following lyric passage from Colossians. In it the early Christian community declares the centrality of Jesus in creation and in the church, looking back to Christ's death and resurrection and forward to the restoration of all things in him:

> *He is the image of the invisible God, the firstborn over all creation.*
> *for by him all things were created: things in heaven and on earth,*
> *visible and invisible,*
> *whether thrones or powers or rulers or authorities;*
> *all things were created by him and for him.*
> *He is before all things,*
> *and in him all things hold together.*
> *And he is the head of the body, the church;*
> *he is the beginning and the firstborn from among the dead,*
> *so that in everything he might have the supremacy.*
> *For God was pleased to have all his fullness dwell in him,*
> *and through him to reconcile to himself all things,*
> *whether things on earth or things in heaven,*
> *by making peace through his blood, shed on the cross.*

(Col. 1:15–20)

In A.D. 66, Jewish exasperation with the insensitive rule of Rome at last came to a boil. A long history of strife lay in the background between Jews and the Roman occupiers of Judea. Jewish relations with Greek-speaking settlers, merchants, and imperial officials, who were sheltered by the Roman umbrella, were no better. Rome had frequently raided the temple treasury to make up for what it called unpaid taxes. It had sent Greek-speaking procurators as rulers to Palestine who had neither interest in nor sympathy for Judea or Judaism. It had monopolized positions of wealth and influence. It had pushed the Jewish farmers of the countryside deeper and deeper into debt.

The Jewish revolt began in Caesarea, on the Mediterranean coast about fifty miles northwest of Jerusalem. Greek-speakers celebrated a local legal victory by launching an attack on the Jewish quarters. The Roman army stood by passively as Jews were cut down. When word of these events arrived in Jerusalem, there was an immediate reaction. Although the Jews were divided into many factions, radical voices carried the day. Jews attacked the local garrison, slaughtered its defenders, and appealed for an end of the hated subjugation to Rome. When priests and other more moderate Jewish leaders stopped the mandated ritual sacrifices to the Roman empire, all-out war became inevitable.

Seven years of bloody strife followed. At first the Jewish rebels gained the upper hand. Then, under the tested veteran general Vespasian, Rome sent four legions to discipline its wayward Judean colony. Vespasian advanced cautiously, first securing the Mediterranean ports and then moving slowly against Jerusalem. The noose he was constructing for the Jewish capital relaxed in the summer of 68, when the emperor Nero died, for Vespasian himself was a candidate to succeed him. Events in Rome moved slowly, but eventually Vespasian was handed the palm, and so he left Judea. But this was only a temporary respite. To carry on the job, Vespasian left his son, Titus, who proved just as forceful as his father.

Once again the Roman legions moved toward Jerusalem. Once again the noose tightened. This time there was no relief. In April of the year 70, the siege began. The suffering of those who were trapped in Jerusalem became horrific. In September the most zealous Jewish rebels made their last stand in the temple. Fragmentary sources describing the revolt leave conflicting accounts as to Titus's intentions. Josephus, a former Jewish general who had come over to the Romans in the early days of the revolt, wrote that Titus hoped to save the temple as a gesture of Roman moderation. A later Roman authority, Sulpicius Severus, reported an account from the great Roman historian Tacitus with a different story. This report held that Titus was eager to destroy the temple. Titus's reasoning, as reported by Sulpicius Severus, is particularly noteworthy, for he wanted to eradicate the temple "in order that the Jewish and Christian religions might more completely be abolished; for although these religions were mutually hostile, they had nevertheless sprung from the same founders; the Christians were an offshoot of the Jews, and if the root were taken away the stock would easily perish."[3]

Whether or not Sulpicius Severus got the story right, his comments illuminated a crucial reality about the early history of the Christian church. Titus would go on to wipe out the last remnants of Jewish resistance, including the determined band that held the mountain fortress Masada for nearly three years after the fall of Jerusalem. Later Jewish resistance to Rome would elicit even harsher repression, espe-

3. Quoted in F. F. Bruce, *The Spreading Flame: The Rise and Progress of Christianity from Its First Beginnings to the Conversion of the English* (Grand Rapids: Eerdmans, 1958), 156.

This frieze, taken from an archway in Rome, depicts the conquering general Titus and his troops carrying away spoil from the sack of Jerusalem in A.D. 70.

Tony Lane

cially from Emperor Hadrian in response to a revolt in 135. But even before Jerusalem fell and the temple was destroyed in A.D. 70, Titus's observation about the mutual dependence of Christianity and Judaism had become ancient history. While Christianity in its very earliest years may, in fact, have functioned like an appendage of Judaism, by the year 70 it was moving out on its own. That move to independence from Judaism was greatly accelerated by Roman destruction of the Jewish temple and the cessation of the sacrifices that had played such a large role in Jewish worship.

The blows that Vespasian, Titus, Hadrian, and other Roman generals rained upon Jerusalem did not destroy the Christian church. Rather, they liberated the church for its destiny as a universal religion offered to the whole world. Yet from the perspective of the very earliest Christians, Roman decimation of Jerusalem probably seemed like an unspeakable tragedy. Christianity was born in the cradle of Judaism. As indicated by the great meeting reported in Acts 15, the early center of Christianity's communications, organization, and authority was Jerusalem. The first leaders of the church, like James the half-brother of Jesus, who presided over the council in Acts 15, functioned like presidents of a synagogue. The Gospels were written, in large part, as a demonstration of the way that Jesus brought Israel's earlier history to its culmination—Matthew to show that Jesus fulfilled the prophetic promises for the Messiah, Luke to show that Jesus fulfilled the essence of Jewish law, and John to show that the divine revelation to Abraham had culminated in Jesus Christ (John 8:58, "Before Abraham was born, I am"). Several of the early Christian writings were directed to the Jewish diaspora, such as the Epistle of James, which begins, "To the twelve tribes scattered among the nations." Other early Christian writings that would also become part of the New Testament were preoccupied with negotiating the boundaries between Judaism and Christianity. The apostle Paul, especially, argued frequently against those who wanted to maintain the Jewish rite of circumcision as a requirement for salvation. And his interpretations of the Old Testament returned repeatedly to the way in which Jesus' work climaxed God's consistent offer of grace to the Jews. In sum, as historian W. H. C. Frend has written, "All Christianity at this stage [in the apostolic period] was 'Jewish Christianity.' But it was Israel with a difference."[4]

The great turning point represented by the destruction of Jerusalem was to move Christianity outward, to transform it from a religion shaped in nearly every particular by its early Jewish environment into a religion advancing toward universal significance in the broader reaches of the Mediterranean world, and then beyond. The apostles Peter and Paul were probably martyred in Rome under the emperor Nero about the time that Titus and Vespasian were advancing on Jerusalem. Just a few decades later, Rome would replace Jerusalem as the center of Christian communications and authority. Theological discussion likewise turned rapidly away from problems posed by the system of Jewish morality to issues framed by Hellenistic philosophy or Roman conceptions of order. Already by A.D. 70 Jewish synagogues scattered throughout the Mediterranean, rather than temple worship in Jerusalem, provided the main vehicles for Christian outreach.

When the Romans conquered Jerusalem, most Christians had already left. A tradition, reported in the fourth century by the early church historian Eusebius, says that the Christians had taken refuge in Pella, a substantial town northeast of Jerusalem across the Jordan. Archaeological and later evidence has not verified Eusebius's report, but the physical fate of Jewish Christianity is not the main issue. Rather, the smashing of Jerusalem accelerated a change in perception. To Christians, to Jews, and soon to many others, it was increasingly clear that Rome's disruption of Judaism had pushed the Christian church out on its own. As the historian and biblical scholar F. F. Bruce once put it, "In the lands outside Palestine, the decade which ended with the year 70 marked the close of the period when Christianity could be regarded as simply a variety of Judaism. . . . From A.D. 70 onward the divergence of the paths of Jewish Christianity and orthodox Judaism was decisive. . . . Henceforth the main stream of Christianity must make its independent way in the Gentile world."[5]

4. W. H. C. Frend, *The Rise of Christianity* (Philadelphia: Fortress, 1984), 123.

5. Bruce, *The Spreading Flame*, 157–58.

Now, however, many questions loomed. How would the church define itself? Organize its worship? Find secure authority? Evangelize? Ward off dangerous teaching? In other words, once the "given" framework of Judaism passed away, what would take its place? The three centuries after the fall of Jerusalem provided answers to these questions. We turn now to the means that the church employed to find stability and to sustain its growth in the period after the apostles (that is, the "subapostolic" period). But as we do, it is well to be reminded of how symbolically important was the Roman destruction of Jerusalem. By making it impossible for Judaism to continue in a normal course of development, the Romans also forced great changes upon the Christian church. The turning point of Christian history at Jerusalem in A.D. 70 was the church's emergence on its own.

Links to the Past

Christianity has maintained a special relationship with Judaism. That relationship would later lead to tragic consequences, especially in circumstances where Christians dominated a local culture or nation and where Jews were regarded as second-class citizens. In those circumstances the near kinship of the two religions raised Christian ire, which all too often flamed into violence when Jewish communities went about the practice of their ancestral faith.

Viewed from another perspective, however, the links between Judaism and Christianity can be seen in a more positive light. Although the church would go on to break from Judaism, it is a remarkable fact that the main problems of the church's early centuries were problems shaped by Judaism. First, Christians asked, What is truth? If the church went beyond Judaism in finding ultimate truth in a personal revelation from God—that is, in the life and work of Jesus Christ—still, the church drew upon its Jewish heritage in believing that divine revelation held the key to life's most important realities.

Second, Christians asked, How do we know the truth? Again, if in answering this question the church went beyond Judaism to rely on the writings of the New Testament and the testimony of the apostles to Christ, still that trust in a written revelation from God and reliance upon leaders who provided authoritative interpretations of that written revelation followed the Jewish pattern of honoring sacred books and studying them diligently.

Third, Christians asked, How do we put the truth into action? If the church went beyond the organization of life around the ritual year of the temple and the activities of local synagogues, still the church's own development of bishops and the planting of new churches under the leadership of local elders, priests, or ministers expanded upon what had been a Jewish way of nurturing the faithful and organizing to face the world.

The early church benefited from its ties to Judaism in one other important way. For several decades after A.D. 70, the church continued to enjoy the legal status that the Jews had won through hard and difficult trial. Normally in the Mediterranean world of that time, nations conquered by Rome were forced to adapt local religions to Roman religion; they had to recognize Rome's gods along with their own. The fierce monotheism of the Jews had therefore been a source of ceaseless conflict from the first century B.C., when Rome reached out to enfold Judea. Eventually Rome came to recognize Judaism as a legal religion, despite Jewish refusal to acknowledge the Roman gods. This status as a *religio licita* protected the Christian church through its association with Judaism, even after the destruction of Jerusalem had in fact driven the two religions apart.

As the Christian church moved out into the Roman world, its Judaic roots would be obscured, but even beneath the surface, those roots remained a critical part of what Christianity had been and what it would become.

Outward from Jerusalem

The stabilization of the church on its own is an involved story. Movement from self-definition dictated by a Jewish agenda to self-definition appropriate for a missionary religion expanding throughout the Mediterranean world and beyond was certainly influenced by the general conditions of the time. The Roman peace *(pax Romana)* that had been established by Caesar Augustus, who ruled from 27 B.C. to A.D. 14, provided political and social stability, making possible the easy movement of ideas and people. The pervasive Hellenistic culture that accompanied the expansion of Roman political power made a common *(koinē)* form of the Greek language available to all relatively learned people who lived under Roman rule. The dispersion of Jews from Judea, which had been going on for several centuries before the time of Christ, meant that communities of God-fearers who studied the Hebrew Scriptures were sprinkled widely throughout the Roman world. By the first century A.D. there was also a widespread dissatisfaction with the inherited religions of the Mediterranean, which were sinking all too rapidly into either stale philosophical argument or nominal political observance. The Christianity that spread outward with increasing speed from Judea after the year 70 was able to take advantage of each of these existing conditions.

Yet in order to expand in this Roman world, the new religion of Christianity needed much more than generally favorable political, social, and religious conditions. The dispersion of Jewish synagogues throughout the Mediterranean might provide a base of operations for Christian missionaries, as the Book of Acts describes for Paul and his colleagues. Yet Christian claims about a "crucified Messiah" or about the existence of non-Jews who became "children of Abraham" by faith (Gal. 3:7) offended Jews deeply and drew determined opposition down upon the church. In a similar fashion, Rome might provide peaceful conditions for travel and the spread of new ideas, but the empire was also jealous and would not stand by patiently when upstarts insisted that, not Caesar, but only Jesus the Christ, should be called Lord. Roman persecution, which flared under the emperors Nero (from A.D. 64), Domitian (from 90), and Marcus Aurelius (in 177) before being exerted systematically by the emperors Decius and Valerian (mid-third century) and Diocletian (start of the fourth century), took deadly aim at the new faith.

Even more serious than religious opposition from Judaism and persecution from Rome, the early church faced a welter of internal uncertainties. Could clear lines be drawn between true worship of Jesus Christ and the era's multitude of Greek, Roman, and Middle Eastern religions that also featured revelations from a high God and appeals for dedicated moral life on earth? Could the intense spiritual life of Christianity be distinguished from the colorful spirituality of groups that modern historians call Gnostic for their reliance on various forms of secret wisdom *(gnōsis)?* Toward the end of the second century the Christian apologist Irenaeus listed 217 forms of such religions, some of which borrowed liberally from Christian doctrines or practices. Could the church, moreover, succeed in promoting the kind of moral purity that Jesus and the apostles described as appropriate for servants of God? The moral world into which the church was moving was one in which leaders, especially Roman emperors, often indulged in the most degenerate practices, and ordinary people were often more than eager to follow the leader.

So it was that beset by external foes and menaced by ideas and practices threatening its internal character, the church moved out into the wider world. Once stripped of a Jewish framework by the events involved in the destruction of Jerusalem, how would the church make its way? Answers to these life-threatening challenges could be perceived, at least in outline, within one or two generations after the deaths of the apostles Peter and Paul, which probably occurred under Nero in the years 64–67. By the year 112, Ignatius, leader of the Christian church in Antioch of Syria, could urge fellow believers to "follow the bishop as Jesus Christ followed the father."[6] His injunction revealed the emergence of a system of church organization constructed around locally powerful bishops who were assuming the tasks of guiding the faithful in their localities while deliberating with fellow bishops in other places about the general direction of the church.

At least by the time that Ignatius made this reference to bishops, there were also circulating among the expanding Christian congregations two collections of Christian documents—one, the fourfold gospel account of the life of Christ recorded by Matthew, Mark, Luke, and John, the other collection containing copies of ten to thirteen letters from the apostle Paul. It was not long until these two collections would be permanently joined by the Acts of the Apostles to constitute a "new testament" of sacred writings to set alongside the "old testament" of the Hebrew Scriptures and so provide authoritative written guidance for the church.

In roughly the same period that witnessed the evolution of an episcopal system of church organization and a scriptural record of Christ and the meaning of his life, there also began to appear short, concise summaries of what it meant to be a Christian or to join a local congregation. These creeds (from Latin *credo*, "I believe," or *credimus*, "we believe") would prove immensely useful both as a way of marking out the boundaries of Christian faith and as introductions to its character for inquirers or the children of believers.

Along with the episcopate and the canon of Scripture, the early creeds became the anchors that stabilized the church in its earliest subapostolic history. The means by which the church came into its own—after the climactic events in Jerusalem of A.D. 70 and in the face of external and internal pressure—can thus be summarized simply as creed, canon, and episcopacy. But in each case a simple word conceals historical development that was as complex as it was important.

Alternative Perspectives on Earliest Christian History

Two large difficulties stand in the way of interpreting the nature of this early history. First is the fact that hard evidence for a half-century or so from the end of the New Testament era is scarce. Historians and theologians are thus required to fill in with imagination, speculation, or informed hunches what went on between the era illuminated by the New Testament and the period from about 110, when the flow of evidence, though at first only a trickle, begins again.

6. Bettenson, *Documents of the Christian Church*, 63.

The second difficulty is that the hard evidence that does exist for early subapostolic history is simply not definite or full enough to answer many of the legitimate questions we are eager to ask about this early Christian era. The result is that historical accounts of this period are even more dependent upon the framework of meaning—the stance of the interpreter—brought to bear on these questions than is usually the case for historical inquiry. The most obvious difficulties created by alternative frameworks of meaning divide Christian from non-Christian accounts. The most interesting differences divide the various branches of Christianity from each other.

Responsible historians, Christian or not, try to base their accounts of the early church as securely as possible on the best available evidence. Yet precisely because that evidence is so sparse, the standpoint of the historians—that is, the systems of belief and assumption that historians bring to their tasks—becomes a most important factor for interpretations of early Christian history. Take as an example the relatively scant information that exists for how the various writings that now make up the New Testament were pulled together into one authoritative collection. Christians who believe that God was using those documents to draw men and women to faith in his Son are likely to interpret the evidence that does exist at least in part as human responses to the authentic power of God. Non-Christian historians, who may be secularists or followers of another religion, might have great respect for the integrity of the early Christians but will probably regard the construction of the New Testament as a process guided entirely by actions, attitudes, beliefs, practices, and decisions arising from human circumstances. Historians of whatever sort should be able to cooperate in research on issues related to individual questions of fact—for example, it is now generally agreed that Ignatius wrote most of the letters ascribed to him around the year 110 and that some of the writings that Ignatius actually wrote quote the Gospel of Matthew as if it were a sacred Scripture from God. But historians are likely to diverge when it comes to broader interpretations of what was going on—in this instance, a Christian conclusion that Ignatius was responding to the work of the Holy Spirit in promoting the revelation of Christ in the Gospel of Matthew, as opposed to a non-Christian conclusion that factors limited to the character of the written Gospel and to Ignatius's situation provide all the explanation necessary for his use of the Book of Matthew.

Differences among Christians are more interesting (at least to Christians) because they occur among people who agree that early church practices, writings, and activities have a divine as well as a human source. Such differences grow out of alternative understandings of the

Christian faith. In turn, these differences of broad theological perspective shape the understanding of the evidence available from the early church.

To oversimplify, it is possible to describe a Roman Catholic, an Orthodox, and a Protestant interpretation of early Christian history, each of which depends on basic assumptions concerning the way in which God guides the church. Catholic belief in the apostolic origin of church tradition and of the apostolic character of the bishop's office means that Catholic interpretations of the early church are likely to see a more central, more positive role for the actions of the early bishops in constructing the institutions, organizing the sacred writings, and guiding the worship of believers. By contrast, Orthodox belief in God's guidance of the church through organic processes of worship, liturgy, and corporate action means that Orthodox interpretations of the early church are likely to see common patterns of prayer, gradually evolving habits in using the New Testament, and consensus growing up around credal statements as the crucial shapers of early Christian history. Again by contrast, Protestant belief in the normative power of Scripture along with Protestant suspicion of human institutions means that Protestant interpretations of the early church are likely to stress the foundational role of the New Testament writings and to be more willing than either Catholics or the Orthodox to find flaws in early church practices or decisions.

It is important to remember that these alternative perspectives represent shades of difference. Christians are almost universally united in believing that the early church was built upon an *apostolic* foundation, that is, on the work that God began in the apostles through the presence of Christ and then carried on through the testimony of those apostles to Christ as recorded in the New Testament and as worked out in the institutions of the early church. For Roman Catholics, apostolicity continues as a living authority in Scripture and among the bishops, and so guides the creation and use of creeds. For the Orthodox, apostolicity marks the organic development of the whole church in Scripture, episcopacy, and creeds. For Protestants, apostolicity is visible most directly in the New Testament and then as a reflection from the New Testament in the work of the bishops and the creeds of the church.

The practical difference among these views lies in attitudes toward the three stabilizing elements of creed, canon, and episcopacy. Each tradition honors all three, but Protestants lay greatest stress on the apostolicity of the New Testament, Roman Catholics on the outworking of apostolicity through the agency of the bishops, and the Orthodox on the general apostolic guidance of the church that became most visible in the promulgation of the ecumenical creeds of the fourth and later centuries.

These differences in perspective may seem abstruse, but especially given the relative scarcity of hard evidence for the history of the church in the period roughly 70/80 through 130/140, they mean a great deal for interpreting the story of the church during the subapostolic period.

Canon

The word "canon" is derived from a Greek term, perhaps borrowed from the Phoenicians; it probably originally meant a rod or ruler for measuring objects. Its application to the books of the Bible can thus be traced to the series of gradations found on measuring rods (hence multiple individual items gathered for one purpose) and, even more important, to the function of such measures as rules or norms (hence the sense of "canon" as a standard). The first recorded use of the word for the authoritative list of books in the Bible came in the year 367 from Athanasius, bishop of Alexandria in North Africa. Well before that time, however, the church had been using writings concerning the life and work of Christ. It had also been moving toward consensus as to which of those writings should be regarded as the authoritative norm for Christian beliefs and practices. As the church did so, it both reaffirmed its connection to Judaism (by imitating the Jews in holding to a select list of sacred books) and broke decisively with the Jewish past (by claiming that the Hebrew Scriptures were incomplete in themselves without the addition of the New Testament).

The practical circumstances that led to the definition of a New Testament canon grew out of the lived realities of the church's life. The church required standards for worship and models for prayers, liturgies, and sermons. The church needed reading material for public and private devotion. The church needed a theological standard for responding to non-Christian critics and for adjudicating doctrinal disputes within its own ranks, and it needed a set text to translate as the gospel message moved out of the Hellenistic Mediterranean into the Latin west and then farther east toward Asia and north into Europe. For all these purposes, an established list of authoritative writings about Christ and the meaning of his work rapidly became a pressing necessity.

The beginnings of the process by which a select list of writings was treated as an authoritative New Testament can be glimpsed in the New Testament itself, where the Second Epistle of Peter speaks of Paul's writings as subject to the same distortions that "ignorant and unstable people" visit upon "the other scriptures" (2 Peter 3:16). Very early in the subapostolic period, collections of Paul's writings were circulating among the churches, soon to be joined (certainly not much later than A.D. 100) by the four Gospels, which were also circulating as a unit. Toward the end of the second century, Irenaeus of Lyons offered an interesting and, to believers of his day, plausible account of why four gospels existed to tell of the life of Christ: "For, since there are four zones of the world in which we live, and four principal winds, while the church is scattered throughout all the world, and the 'pillar and ground' of the church is the gospel and the spirit of life; it is fitting that she should have four pillars, breathing out immortality on every side, and [kindling human life anew]. From which fact, it is evident that the Word, . . . He who was manifested to men, has given us the gospel under four aspects, but bound together by one Spirit."[7]

As comfortable as it would make Protestants to think that the New Testament always existed with firm, crisp boundaries marking it off from all other kinds of literature, the existing historical evidence shows that, though the Pauline collection and the fourfold gospel collection were used as authoritative documents from a very early period, it took a process of more than two centuries to define the precise shape of the New Testament.

In that process, as so often in Christian history, the challenge of heresy played a decisive role. The first known assertion of a definite canon of Christian writings appeared in Rome about the year 144. The author was Marcion, who had traveled to Rome from Asia Minor with a message about the God of love. Marcion's teaching appeared to be Christian because he held that Jesus Christ revealed divine love to its fullest extent. But when leaders of the church in Rome found out the details of Marcion's message, they were appalled, for it turned out that Marcion's God of love was a violent opponent of the evil deity of law who dominated the Old Testament. As part of his message, Marcion claimed to define the limits of an authoritative Scripture concerning Christ. For Marcion, that Scripture contained an edited version of the Gospel of Luke (which cut out all of Jesus' references to the Old Testament) and ten letters of Paul (who supposedly showed that grace triumphs over law). Later commentors have noted that Marcion was the first biblical critic, though sadly not the last, to do his most important work with a penknife.

7. "Irenaeus against Heresies," 3.11.8, in *The Writings of Irenaeus*, vol. 1, ed. and trans. Alexander Roberts and James Donaldson, vol. 5 of *Ante-Nicene Christian Library* (Edinburgh: T. & T. Clark, 1868), 293.

Marcion's attack on the Gospels and some of the epistles that the church, through an intuitive process, had already been treating as divine Scripture spurred several efforts to define the sacred writings more carefully. Within a generation of Marcion's death in about 160, several notable developments occurred. Irenaeus was joined by the apologists Justin and Justin's pupil Tatian in defending the fourfold Gospel of Matthew, Mark, John, and a full text of Luke. Other Christian leaders paid Marcion the sincerest form of flattery by imitating his publication of lists setting out the contents of a New Testament. The earliest of these lists that has yet been discovered dates from Rome toward the end of the second century. It was published in 1740 by Lodovico Antonio Muratori, an Italian priest and archaeologist, and is therefore known as the Muratorian Canon.

This list is a particularly instructive document for showing that by the year 200 there existed a set of authoritative Christian writings substantially, but not exactly, like what we now recognize as the New Testament. Although the language of the Muratorian Canon is not always entirely clear, the standard interpretations of it highlight a series of categories revealing continuity and discontinuities with the later New Testament:

Books in the Muratorian Canon also in the later New Testament—the four Gospels; Acts; letters of Paul to seven churches (in this order: Corinthians [two], Ephesians, Philippians, Colossians, Galatians, Thessalonians [two], and Romans); letters of Paul to Philemon, Titus, and Timothy [two]; Jude; 1, 2, and 3 John; and the Apocalypse of John.

Books in the Muratorian Canon not in the later New Testament—the Wisdom of Solomon, the Apocalypse of Peter, and two letters "forged in the name of Paul" to Laodicea and Alexandria against "the heresy of Marcion."

Books in the fixed New Testament not mentioned in the Muratorian Canon—1 and 2 Peter, James, Hebrews.

Writings otherwise discussed in the Muratorian Canon—The canon says that the Shepherd of Hermas "ought to be read" but does not deserve to be listed with the writings of the "prophets" and "apostles." The document is cut off as it begins to list writings that are rejected, such as a new book of psalms written by followers of Marcion.[8]

From the end of the second century, movement to what became the fixed New Testament canon was rapid. Origen (ca. 185–ca. 254), the learned theologian from Alexandria, used all twenty-seven of the canonical New Testament books but noted lingering disputes over Hebrews,

---

8. Bettenson, *Documents of the Christian Church*, 28–29.

Athanasius on the Canon (A.D. 367)

I fear lest . . . some few of the simple should be beguiled from their simplicity and purity, by the subtilty of certain men, and should henceforth read other books—those called apocryphal—led astray by the similarity of their names with the true books. . . . Forasmuch as some have taken in hand, to reduce into order for themselves the books termed apocryphal, and to mix them up with the divinely inspired Scripture . . . it seemed good to me also . . . to set before you the books included in the Canon, and handed down, and accredited as Divine.

There are, then, of the Old Testament, twenty-two books in number. . . . Again it is not tedious to speak of the [books] of the New Testament. These are, the four Gospels, according to Matthew, Mark, Luke, and John. Afterwards, the Acts of the Apostles and Epistles (called Catholic), seven, viz. of James, one; of Peter, two; of John, three; after these, one of Jude. In addition, there are fourteen Epistles of Paul. . . . And besides, the Revelation of John.

These are fountains of salvation, that they who thirst may be satisfied with the living words they contain. In these alone is proclaimed the doctrine of godliness. Let no man add to these, neither let him take aught from these. . . .

But for greater exactness I add this also, writing of necessity; that there are other books besides these not indeed included in the Canon, but appointed by the Fathers to be read by those who newly join us, and who wish for instruction in the word of godliness. The Wisdom of Solomon, and the Wisdom of Sirach, and Esther, and Judith, and Tobit, and that which is called the Teaching of the Apostles [the *Didache*], and the Shepherd. But the former, my brethren, *are* included in the Canon, the latter being [merely] read.[1]

James, 2 Peter, 2 and 3 John, and Revelation, as well as over books that never secured a full canonical status, like the Shepherd of Hermas, the Epistle of Barnabas, the Teaching of the Twelve Apostles, and the Gospel to the Hebrews. In the early fourth century, the pioneering church historian Eusebius commented specifically on the Book of Revelation. He noted that, since its authorship was sometimes questioned (was it really written by John, the beloved disciple?), it remained with James, 2 Peter, 2 and 3 John, and Jude as books widely used in the church, but still not fully classed with the Gospels, Acts, Paul's writings, 1 Peter, and 1 John as universally accepted. By the end of that same century, lists of New Testament writings with the final twenty-seven books had become standard, as in an Easter letter from Bishop Athanasius in 367 and a document from a synod held in 397 at Carthage in North Africa.

What the lengthy process of fine-tuning the New Testament canon shows is that the main writings about Christ and the early life of the church under the apostles were being used everywhere as Scripture, but also that definitive decisions about every last book were not nearly as important to those who actually lived through these centuries as they would become to later historians and theologians. The key throughout was apostolicity. Where a writing was held to come directly from a disciple of Christ, to arise from the circle or direct influence of one chosen personally by Jesus (for example, the Gospel of Mark was widely held to derive from Peter's eyewitness reports), or to express in a pure form the message of the apostles about Christ, that writing was accepted as canonical. For those Christian writings where the apostolicity of either author or content was in doubt, recognition as a canonical book could take much longer. Thus, the fact that the Book of Hebrews does not begin by announcing the name of its author retarded its full acceptance as Scripture, though the apostolic content of the book and the growing conviction that Paul was the author eventually won the day. (Most modern scholars do not think that Paul was the author.) Where the church concluded that a writing was not apostolic, that work could continue to be recommended for private use, but not as a writing included in the canonical standard.

The fixing of a New Testament canon was an extraordinarily important step in stabilizing the early church. Even a brief examination of that process, however, shows that the foundation provided by writings testifying authentically to the power at work in Christ and communicated by Christ to the church through the testimony of the apostles was critically important to the early Christians as they moved out into the Mediterranean world.

Episcopacy

Something of the same reasoning, though with different results, also surrounded the rise of the bishops as the key agents for organizing the subapostolic church. The interpretive difficulty with respect to the early history of the episcopate is that the forms of church order in the New Testament are quite flexible, while only a half-century later, when evidence once again becomes available, a fairly well-defined rule of the church by bishops is firmly in place. Again, in the absence of a detailed consecutive chain of fact, broader frameworks of belief must be relied upon to fill in the gaps.

The New Testament reveals a relatively fluid situation with respect to church order. Especially in Acts and the Pastoral Epistles (1–2 Timothy and Titus), which probably reflect a situation from the mid–60s or

Irenaeus on the Apostolic Succession (ca. 185)

Those that wish to discern the truth may observe the apostolic tradition made manifest in every church throughout the world. We can enumerate those who were appointed bishops in the churches by the Apostles and their successors [or successions] down to our own day, who never taught, and never knew, absurdities such as these men produce. For if the Apostles had known hidden mysteries which they taught the perfect in private and in secret, they would rather have committed them to those to whom they entrusted the churches. . . . [W]e confound all those who in any way, whether for self-pleasing, or vainglory, or blindness, or evilmindedness, hold unauthorized meetings. This we do by pointing to the apostolic tradition and the faith that is preached to men, which has come down to us through the successions of bishops; the tradition and creed of the greatest, the most ancient church, the church known to all men, which was founded and set up at Rome by the two most glorious apostles, Peter and Paul. For with this church, because of its position of leadership and authority, must needs agree every church . . . for in her the apostolic tradition has always been preserved by the faithful from all parts.

The blessed Apostles, after founding and building up the church, handed over to Linus the office of bishop. . . . He was succeeded by Anacletus, after whom, in the third place after the Apostles, Clement was appointed to the bishopric. He not only saw the blessed Apostles but also conferred with them, and had their preaching ringing in his ears and their tradition before his eyes. . . .

Euarestus succeeded this Clement, Alexander followed Euarestus; then Sixtus was appointed, the sixth after the Apostles. After him came Telesphorus, who had a glorious martyrdom. Then Hyginus, Pius, Anicetus and Soter; and now, in the twelfth place from the Apostles, Eleutherus occupies the see. In the same order and succession the apostolic tradition in the Church and the preaching of the truth has come down to our time.[2]

slightly later, we see the church organized under bishops (*episkopoi*), deacons (*diakonoi*), presiding officers (*hēgoumenoi*), and elders (*presbyteroi*). The apostle Paul commissions elders in some of his visits to local churches and provides guidelines for how "bishops" or "elders" and "deacons" are to do their work of guiding worship and caring for the poor. But the clear assignment of duties that is found by the end of the second century—especially of bishops presiding over a church or churches of a given region—is unknown as such in the New Testament.

The emergence of a hierarchical administration centered on the bishops can be observed in the words of three prominent early church fathers. We have already seen that Ignatius, as early as 112, could urge believers to "follow the bishop as Jesus Christ followed the Father." In the same letter, Ignatius intentionally differentiated among church offices when he went on to say, "Follow the presbytery [or the elders, some of whom were soon to be called "priests"] as the Apostles; and respect the deacons as the commandment of God." The definition of what Catholic and Orthodox traditions would later call sacramental functions is further revealed in Ignatius's description of what the bishop is to do: "Wherever the bishop appears, there let the people be, just as, wheresoever Christ Jesus is, there is the Catholic Church. It is not permitted either to baptize or hold a love-feast apart from the bishop. But whatever he may approve, that is well-pleasing to God, that everything which you do may be sound and valid."[9]

Less than a single lifetime after Ignatius wrote these words, Bishop Irenaeus of Lyons wrote even more concretely about questions of church order. In the great work aimed against the heresies of his day that has been noted already (completed around 185), he said that the bishops guarded the handing on of Christian traditions from the apostles and argued that an unbroken succession of presiding bishops in the various churches guaranteed the continuation of apostolic authority in the church. Furthermore, Irenaeus took special pains to trace the handing-on of authority from bishop to bishop in the church of Rome.

One more lifetime later, Bishop Cyprian of Carthage (d. 259) referred to the full establishment of an episcopal system in the church. His sharpest contention was that "the bishop is in the Church and the Church in the bishop, and that if any one be not with the bishop he is not in the Church." His reasons for making such a claim rooted the exercise of episcopal authority in the original commands of Christ: "Our Lord, whose precepts and admonitions we are bound to observe, ordered the high office of bishop and the system of his Church when he speaks in the Gospel and says to Peter, 'Thou art Peter, etc.' [Matt. 16:18ff.]. . . . Thence age has followed age and bishop has followed bishop in succession, and the office of the episcopate and the system of the Church has been handed down, so that the Church is founded on the bishops and every act of the Church is directed by these same presiding officers."[10]

9. Ibid., 63–64.
10. Ibid., 74, 73.

The interpretation of the process witnessed in the writings of Ignatius, Irenaeus, and Cyprian hinges more on conceptions of the church than on an assessment of evidence. Historians agree that order in the early church grew from Jewish roots, where, for example, synagogues had functioned under elders or presidents. All are also agreed that the episcopal organization of the church represented a striking move beyond Judaism. To Roman Catholics and in some sense for the Orthodox, the bishops needed to rise, since they were the designated successors of the apostles charged with carrying on the apostolic work of testifying to Christ and organizing lives of service to him. The Catholic phrase "the episcopate slept in the apostolate" reflects this belief. Protestants, by contrast, tend to look upon the episcopacy that emerged by the mid-second century as a natural response to circumstances. A Protestant interpretation might begin by suggesting that the James who presided over the activities of the Jerusalem church in the Book of Acts was selected out of a pragmatic necessity, but that he did not confuse his own role with the more basic reality of the apostolic message of Christ and his work. Similarly, the bishops should be regarded as no more than elders with added functional responsibilities. Bishops, like all believers, could be regarded as "apostolic" when and if they upheld the message of the apostles about the salvation found in Christ, but they should not otherwise be considered uniquely apostolic in their ordination or in the exercises of their office.

This basic difference of interpretation once again returns to the question of apostolicity. Protestants ground apostolicity in the message of the New Testament; Catholics expand apostolicity to include the coordination between New Testament writings and the activity of bishops. In both cases, the bishops are regarded as key figures for dealing with heresy, providing teaching, overseeing the baptism of new converts, and providing standards for worship. With their respective views of the church, Catholics have more confidence that the early bishops got it exactly right, while Protestants note errors or the potential for errors, that would one day need to be corrected by a Reformation.

Precise assessment of what the rise of the episcopacy meant for the church thus remains in dispute. What is not disputed is that the system of bishops that arose in the early church became the means for moderating its internal life and organizing its response to the world. As such, the episcopacy was one of the vehicles through which the patterns of the synagogue were exchanged for the church's own method of organization.

This ancient mosaic shows an early ceremony of Christian baptism. Such ceremonies were often occasions for reciting the Apostles' Creed or one of its early variations.

Christian History Archives

Creeds

The third decisive means that stabilized the church was the development of short statements of belief summarizing Christian teaching and introducing inquirers to the faith. Our next two chapters look in greater depth at the great *conciliar* creeds promulgated by councils of the church. Here it is important to note that, before the church was in a position to hold a general council, a different kind of credal statement had already become common in the church.

These other creeds were *baptismal*. They were formulated first as a way to organize teaching for catechumens (converts undergoing instruction). But soon they came to serve other purposes as well, especially for marking out boundaries between genuine belief and its heretical imitations.

As with the fixing of the New Testament canon and the rise of the bishops, apostolicity was critical in making the creeds such important tools in the church. Already in the New Testament itself, references had begun to appear to "the tradition" or to "the traditions" (NRSV: 2 Thess. 3:6; 1 Cor. 11:2) handed on from the apostles to the church. In the subapostolic church, the baptismal creeds were held in high regard as standing for apostolic teaching and so preserving the message of Christ.

The statement of faith known as the Apostles' Creed and used widely in the Western churches illustrates the creed-making process at work. The definitive version of the Apostles' Creed in its final form was not

Early Credal Statements

Ignatius of Antioch (ca. 110)

Turn a deaf ear to any speaker who avoids mention of Jesus Christ who was of David's line, born of Mary, who was truly born, ate and drank; was truly persecuted under Pontius Pilate, truly crucified and died while those in heaven, on earth, and under the earth beheld it; who also was truly raised from the dead, the Father having raised him, who in like manner will raise us also who believe in him—his Father, I say, will raise us in Christ Jesus, apart from whom we have not true life.[3]

The Old Roman Creed (ca. 340)

I believe in God almighty [the Father almighty]
And in Christ Jesus, his only son, our Lord
Who was born of the Holy Spirit and the Virgin Mary
Who was crucified under Pontius Pilate and was buried
And the third day rose from the dead
Who ascended into heaven
And sitteth on the right hand of the Father
Whence he cometh to judge the living and the dead
And in the Holy Ghost
The holy church
The remission of sins
The resurrection of the flesh
The life everlasting.[4]

The Apostles' Creed (final text, ca. 700)

I believe in God the Father almighty, creator of heaven and earth;

And in Jesus Christ, His only Son, our Lord, Who was conceived by the Holy Spirit, born of the Virgin Mary, suffered under Pontius Pilate, was crucified, dead and buried. He descended to hell, on the third day rose again from the dead, ascended to heaven, sits at the right hand of God the Father almighty, thence He will come to judge the living and the dead;

I believe in the Holy Spirit, the holy catholic Church, the communion of saints, the forgiveness of sins, the resurrection of the body, and the life everlasting. Amen.[5]

recorded until the seventh century. But early versions of what is often called the Old Roman Creed, which closely resemble the Apostles' Creed, have been traced back to the second century.

The early versions of the Apostles' Creed and similar statements were used to prepare converts for baptism. By the third century it was a widespread custom in the church for those who were about to be baptized (usually taking place at Easter) to first answer a series of questions that took the form "Do you believe in God the Father almighty . . . ? Do you believe in Jesus Christ . . . ? Do you believe in the Holy Spirit . . . ?" These creeds were thus first a way to teach about the Trinitarian faith and, then, for those joining the church, a way to express this faith as their own.

The apostolicity of these statements, however, gave them broader importance. Teaching aids prepared for the church's educational purposes came to be important also for ordinary worship and for fending off heresy. Repetition of the creed became habitual in liturgies precisely because it reminded believers of the bedrock realities that had first been experienced by the apostles and then passed along.

The use of creeds to guard the church's teaching soon became almost as important as their use for new and old believers in the church. Looking at the form of words in the Apostles' Creed as an example, almost every phrase can be seen to protect the church against heretical teaching. To mention only a few of many possible examples, the creed's affirmation that God was both "father" and "maker of heaven and earth" rebutted the persistent Gnostic teaching that the God revealed in Christ was a deity of pure spirit who looked upon the material world as an encumbrance to be overcome or a weight to be set aside. In similar fashion, the creed's affirmations that Christ was born and that he suffered on the cross and died took direct aim at a wide range of Docetic heresies that claimed that Christ only seemed to take on flesh and to interact physically with the world. The creed's confession that Jesus was "Christ" harkened back to disputes with Jews over whether Old Testament teachings found their culmination in Jesus of Nazareth. The proclamation of belief in "the holy catholic Church" (in the third, or Holy Spirit, section of the creed) affirmed the universality of Christianity; it struck at various Christian groups such as the followers of Marcion, who set themselves up as select, limited bodies claiming to be the only ones who truly understood God's ways with the world. Although these creeds did not originally arise as fences against heretical teaching, they soon came to fill that important function.

The early baptismal creeds, along with the conciliar creeds that followed, functioned as apostolic summaries of the Christian faith. They were distilled from the broader teachings of Scripture and they guided the outward practices of the church. Along with the foundational message of the New Testament and the work of the bishops, they allowed the church to know its own mind.

Several standards can be used to divide the history of Christianity into distinct periods. Such divisions are cause for endless debate, with one exception. The exception is the divide that almost all commentators have seen between the church as described in the New Testament and the church that developed in the age after the apostles had passed from the scene. In that division the great historical event was the Roman destruction of Jerusalem in A.D. 70. Before that time, Christianity was emerging in a definitely Jewish context. After that time, Christianity rapidly became a distinct religion. Although much else was involved as the church moved out on its own, the most momentous aspects of that move were the establishment of a fixed set of authoritative Christian writings added to the Hebrew Scriptures, the emergence of an episcopal system to order the church's life, and the development of succinct statements of faith to express its grasp of the truth. Canon, episcopate, and creed were, in this sense, the vehicles upon which the Christian church traveled as it began its journey outward from Jerusalem to the uttermost parts of the earth.

***

Prayer infuses Christian life, in both its private and corporate expressions. When the first Christians wanted to learn how to pray, they turned to the Lord's Prayer for guidance. The Lord's Prayer provided an authoritative—and uniquely Christian—model of prayer, given by Jesus to his disciples, which showed how to address the Christian God and what could properly be asked of "our Father in heaven."[11] This one prayer not only shaped the practice of prayer but also laid the foundation for Christian thought and writing about prayer from well before the end of the second century and Tertullian's treatise *On Prayer,* to the present day.

One of the first nonscriptural references to the Lord's Prayer can be found in the *Didache* (also called Teaching of the Twelve Apostles), which many scholars date at the end of the first century. The *Didache* was used for teaching converts the basics of Christian faith and practice as the church moved out into the Mediterranean world. From it we see that the Lord's Prayer formed a central part of Christian devotional practice from the

---

11. Agnes Cunningham, *Prayer: Personal and Liturgical* (Wilmington, Del.: Michael Glazier, 1985), 21–22.

earliest days of the church. In addition to the Lord's Prayer, the *Didache* also includes thanksgiving prayers that were used in the celebration of the Eucharist, closing with the Christian hope for Christ's return expressed in the Aramaic prayer *Marana tha!* (Lord, come!).

> *Do not pray as the hypocrites do but pray as the Lord has*
> *commanded in the Gospel:*
>> *Our Father, who art in heaven, hallowed be Thy name;*
>> *Thy kingdom come; Thy will be done on earth as it is*
>> *in heaven; give us this day our daily bread,*
>> *and forgive us our debts as we also forgive our*
>> *debtors; and lead us not into temptation, but deliver*
>> *us from evil; for Thine is the power and the glory*
>> *for evermore.*
> *Say this prayer three times a day.*[12]

Further Reading

Aune, David E. *The New Testament in Its Literary Environment*. Philadelphia: West-minster, 1987.

Bruce, F. F. *The Spreading Flame: The Rise and Progress of Christianity from Its First Beginnings to the Conversion of the English*. Grand Rapids: Eerdmans, 1958.

Ferguson, Everett. *Backgrounds of Early Christianity*, 2nd ed. Grand Rapids: Eerd-mans, 1993.

Frend, W. H. C. *The Rise of Christianity*. Philadelphia: Fortress, 1984.

Hamman, Adalbert. *How to Read the Church Fathers*. New York: Crossroad, 1993.

How We Got Our Bible [*Christian History*, no. 43]. 1994.

Lightfoot, J. B., and J. R. Harmer, eds. *The Apostolic Fathers* (texts of Clement, Igna-tius, Polycarp, the *Didache,* and others). Grand Rapids: Baker, 1984 (orig. 1891). Many of these works are available in several other editions as well, like Maxwell Staniforth, trans., *Early Christian Writings*. (New York: Penguin, 1968); or Henry Bettenson, ed., *The Early Christian Fathers* (New York: Oxford University Press, 1956).

MacMullen, Ramsay. *Christianizing the Roman Empire (A.D. 100–400)*. New Haven: Yale University Press, 1984.

Smith, M. A. *From Christ to Constantine*. Downers Grove, Ill.: InterVarsity, 1971.

Turner, H. E. W. *The Pattern of Christian Truth: A Study in the Relations between Or-thodoxy and Heresy in the Early Church*. London: A. R. Mowbray, 1954.

Wilken, Robert L. *The Christians as the Romans Saw Them*. New Haven: Yale Uni-versity Press, 1984.

12. "The Didache," 8:2–3, trans. James A. Kleist, in *Ancient Christian Writers: The Works of the Fathers in Translation*, no. 6 (Westminster, Md.: Newman, 1961), 8.

2

Realities of Empire:
The Council of Nicaea (325)

Some of the freshest expressions of joy and desire in the early Christian community come from papyri and potsherds that were preserved in the deserts of Egypt. The following hymn may date from as early as the third century and was inscribed on an ostracon—a fragment of pottery that the less affluent commonly used as writing material—discovered in the 1920s at Oxyrhynchus, an ancient ruin ten miles west of the Nile. This hymn is noteworthy for its relationship to the psalms of praise, its allusions to the New Testament, and above all for its joy in calling on all creation, in heaven and on earth, to worship the Trinity.

> *May none of God's wonderful works*
> *keep silence, night or morning.*
> *Bright stars, high mountains, the depths of the seas,*
> *sources of rushing rivers:*
> *may all these break into song as we sing*
> *to Father, Son and Holy Spirit.*
> *May all the angels in the heavens reply:*
> *Amen! Amen! Amen!*
> *Power, praise, honour, eternal glory*
> *to God, the only Giver of grace.*
> *Amen! Amen! Amen!*[1]

1. A. Hamman, ed., *Early Christian Prayers* (Chicago: Henry Regnery, 1961), 69.

On May 20, 325, the Christian church entered a new era. On that day about 230 bishops gathered at Nicaea, then a major city in Bithynia (now small-town İznik in Turkey). The occasion marked the first "ecumenical," or worldwide, council of the church. Its business—to adjudicate the meaning of Jesus' divinity—dealt with the very heart of the Christian faith. What made the council such an extraordinarily important turning point was not just the doctrinal question at stake but the way in which political and social forces combined with the critical theological issue. The idea for the council did not come from the bishops. Rather, they had been summoned by the great Roman emperor himself, Constantine (ca. 288–337). After such a summons and after dealing with such an issue, the church would never be the same.

Parallel developments led to the council at Nicaea. On the one side was the church's ongoing effort to define the nature of Christ and the character of his work. On the other was the rise to power of an emperor friendly to the church. It was a potent combination.

The specific theological issue before the council at Nicaea concerned the teachings of Arius (ca. 250–ca. 336), a presbyter from Alexandria in Egypt on the North African coast. The broader issues at stake involved questions that had been asked for at least 150 years. The central question was how to define Jesus' special status as, in the phrases of the New Testament, "the Son of God," the "Word" or "Logos" of God, and the Savior who was "one with the Father." Any number of solutions had been proposed to this question. Yet many of the best-known efforts to define precisely the nature of Christ's divine character had clearly been unsatisfactory.

One set of answers stressed the unity of the Godhead. Its proponents were sometimes called Monarchianists because they held so firmly to the unity (or "monarchy," from Greek words meaning "one source") of God. Some Monarchianists, like Sabellius, a Roman teacher of the early third century, taught that the one God had appeared in different modes throughout history; that is, "Father," "Son," and "Spirit" were three names for one reality appearing in three different guises. (They came to be known as modalists.) Other Monarchianists were called adoptionists because they believed that Jesus had been specially adopted by God and so imbued with the fullness of the divine presence.

Neither of these views satisfied the church, since they either undercut the conviction that Jesus was a distinct person or shortchanged the fullness of his deity.

Another set of answers stressed the distinctions between the Father and the Son. In this effort the great Alexandrian theologian Origen (ca. 185–ca. 254) was the leader. Origen was extraordinarily creative and highly educated, but also highly speculative. He had held that Jesus was "generated" from the Father, but also that this generation was "eternal." By this formula Origen hoped to preserve both the unity of the Trinity (a word first coined toward the end of the second century by Tertullian, a brilliant North African lawyer from Carthage) and the distinction between the Father and the Son.

Some who followed in Origen's train of thought, however, did not share his concern for balance. Arius of Alexandria was such a one. When in 318 he communicated his views to his bishop, Alexander, he so stressed the unified, eternal character of God the Father that the Son was reduced to a lower status. Arius, who called Alexander a Sabellian for stressing the unity of the Father and the Son, for his part thoroughly subordinated the Son to the Father. In response, many in the church wondered how such a subordinated Christ—who was more than human, yet less than fully God—could impart salvation to humanity. To Arius, however, the transcendence of the Father and the need to pursue logically the meaning of divine unity mattered more than anything else.

From the time Arius began to air his views in 318 to the time the council met at Nicaea seven years later, a tangled series of meetings, letters, arguments, and debates took place. During that same period, political developments in the Roman Empire also began to exert an impact on theology.

The last major persecution of Christians had taken place under the emperor Diocletian in the years following 303. Diocletian, one of the most capable and efficient emperors of the later Roman Empire, attacked the church because he saw it as a divisive force in the Mediterranean world. Dedicated as he was to unifying the empire and providing for its stability, Diocletian hoped that the elimination of Christianity would reduce disruption from religious conflict. He also took many other steps to make the empire run more efficiently. One of these had unexpected consequences.

In order to provide for the better administration of an empire that stretched from the Middle East to the British Isles, Diocletian divided his realm into four administrative districts. Over the westernmost district he installed Constantius Chlorus, the father of Constantine, who would eventually emerge as the successor to Diocletian as chief emperor. Before Constantine became emperor, however, he had to overcome a lengthy series of military and diplomatic hurdles. Diocletian abdicated the imperial throne in 305, which left three rivals to fight each other for the right to become his successor. From the West, Constantine emerged as a strong challenger. When in 312 Constantine defeated one of his main rivals, Maxentius, at the battle of Milvian Bridge, north of Rome, he emerged as co-emperor with Licinius.

In the long view, Constantine's victory at Milvian Bridge was much more important for the history of Christianity than for the history of Rome. Just before the battle with Maxentius, Constantine apparently saw a vision that changed the course of his life as well as the course of the Christian church. In the words of Eusebius of Caesarea, the most important early church historian and later a confidant of Constantine, Constantine was praying to the god of his father when "he saw with his own eyes the trophy of a cross of light in the heavens, above the sun, and an inscription, CONQUER BY THIS attached to it. . . . Then in his sleep the Christ of God appeared to him with the sign which he had seen in the heavens, and commanded him to make a likeness of that sign which he had seen in the heavens, and to use it as a safeguard in all engagements with his enemies."[2] Thereafter, Constantine took as his personal emblem the labarum, or the intertwined first two letters of Christ's name in Greek, ☧. Even more momentously, he immediately arranged with his fellow emperor, Licinius, to issue a decree legalizing the Christian faith and making toleration of all peaceful religions the rule throughout the empire.*

From that point, Constantine's course was set. As the years advanced, he gained power in the empire and also grew more resolute in promoting the Christian faith. As early as 314 Constantine asked several synods of bishops to adjudicate an intramural church quarrel over questions remaining from the persecution by Diocletian. Two years later he himself heard appeals from these cases. In affairs of state, meanwhile, he slowly increased in strength until at last, in 324, Constantine overcame Licinius to rule as the sole Roman emperor.

Constantine was every bit as concerned as Diocletian had been about the stability of the empire and about the difficulties created by religious

---

2. J. Stevenson, ed., *The New Eusebius: Documents Illustrative of the History of the Church to A.D. 337* (London: SPCK, 1960), 299–300.

*Traditionally, this act of legalization is called the Edict of Milan, but since it was not officially an edict and did not come from Milan, there is some difficulty with the traditional label. Christianity was not established as the only legal religion of the empire until the end of the fourth century during the reign of Theodosius (379–95).

strife. To Constantine, however, the best course was not to suppress Christianity but to exploit its potential for unity. Thus, once he had gained sole control, Constantine immediately set out to heal the strife that was bedeviling the church. By the year 324, that strife centered on the teaching of Arius, but also included many other practical questions such as debates on how to set the date for Easter and how to resolve disputes between the largest episcopal cities. By overcoming the church's internal strife, Constantine hoped both to settle a religious problem and to find a powerful, much needed cultural glue for the Roman world.

To Constantine, who would eventually be baptized in 337 as he approached the end of his life, Christianity became both a way to God and a way to unite the empire. He inserted himself into the doctrinal debates swirling around Arius for two quite distinct purposes, which he spelled out in a letter explaining why he called for a council at Nicaea: "My design then was, first, to bring the diverse judgments found by all nations respecting the Deity to a condition, as it were, of settled uniformity [that is, to clarify doctrine for the sake of the church]; and, second, to restore a healthy tone to the system of the world, then suffering under the power of grievous disease [that is, to end religious strife for the sake of the empire]."[3]

And so he called for a council. At first it was to meet in Ancyra (modern-day Ankara), the major center of Roman power in the East. But then Constantine had the meeting moved to Nicaea, which was nearer to his military headquarters. To the council came bishops mostly from the East, including a young assistant to Bishop Alexander of Alexandria by the name of Athanasius, who would devote his life to defending the teaching hammered out at Nicaea. Also in attendance were two presbyters dispatched from Sylvester, bishop of Rome, as well as the bishop of Carthage, a bishop from Gaul, and (as a reminder of Christianity's beginnings) four bishops with Jewish names from Persia. (Traditionally it is also held that the personage eventually known as Santa Claus, St. Nicholas of Myra in Lycia, modern southwestern Turkey, was also present.)

The results of the council's deliberations were decisive in every way. Its definition of Christ's divine nature set a course for Christian orthodoxy that has been maintained to the present. The council's "canons," or rulings, on administrative and procedural matters established precedents for the exercise of power in the church. The way in which the

---

3. Quoted in W. H. C. Frend, *The Rise of Christianity* (Philadelphia: Fortress, 1984), 497.

council defined the relationship of the Father and the Son also had immediate relevance for church–state relationships in Constantine's "new" Roman Empire. And because it was the emperor himself who called the council, chaired its deliberations, and undertook to implement its directives, the church's history was decisively turned from its course as an alien, pilgrim, and even persecuted body to the potential benefits, but also perils, of establishment (the state support of religion). For each of these reasons, the Council of Nicaea was a great turning point in the history of the Christian church.

Nicaea and Doctrine

The doctrinal issue at Nicaea was absolutely critical because it centered not only on who Jesus was in his person but also on who Jesus was in his work as Savior. Arius's teaching, which survives only in fragments and in quotations from the works of his opponents, communicates great respect for Jesus, patient attention to the Scriptures, and overwhelming awe at the being of God. For those reasons its subversion of Christian teaching was all the more serious.

Arius grounded his faith in the absolute transcendence and absolute unity of God. In his words: "We acknowledge one God, Who is alone ingenerate (*agenneton,* i.e., self-existent), alone eternal, alone without beginning *(anarchon),* alone true, alone possessing immortality, alone wise, alone good, alone sovereign, alone judge of all, etc."[4] With such a view of God, it seemed only logical to Arius that, however much the church should honor Jesus, it should not consider him in terms reserved for the Father. Thus, since only the Father has not been created, the Son must be a creation "begotten" from God like all other forms of existence. Christ may have shared more of the Father than any other human being, but as a creature he would not have known the innermost recesses of the divine mind. Moreover, as a creature made by God, Jesus was liable to change and, in potential though not in fact, to sin. Arius's heavy reliance on logical reasoning is illustrated by a syllogism that opponents later quoted him as defending in several debates: "If the Father begat the Son, he that was begotten had a beginning of existence; hence it is clear that there was when the Son was not. It follows then of necessity that he had his existence from the non-existent."[5] English translation of this syllogism is difficult, for Arius was careful not

4. Quoted in J. N. D. Kelly, *Early Christian Doctrines* (New York: Harper & Row, 1978), 227.

5. Henry Bettenson, ed., *Documents of the Christian Church,* 2nd ed. (New York: Oxford University Press, 1963), 40.

Arius on the Status of the Son

Arian doctrine was set to music, and the popularity of its hymns and chants contributed to the spread of Arianism. While presenting his case at the Council of Nicaea to Emperor Constantine, Arius burst into song:

The uncreated God has made the Son
A beginning of things created,
And by adoption has God made the Son
Into an advancement of himself.
Yet the Son's substance is
Removed from the substance of the Father:
The Son is not equal to the Father,
Nor does he share the same substance.
God is the all-wise Father,
And the Son is the teacher of his mysteries.
The members of the Holy Trinity
Share unequal glories.[1]

to say "there was *a time* when the Son was not," since Arius conceded that the Son had been begotten before time began. Yet the key assertion remained, that Jesus was subordinate to the Father, not only in the functional sense that he came to earth to do the Father's will, but in the metaphysical sense of being a creature subordinate in his essence to the Father.

Arius enhanced his argument by quoting from the Bible in a way that revealed deep study of Scripture, but also that caused great uneasiness among his opponents. For example, he apparently referred often to the monologue by Wisdom in Proverbs, chapter 8. With many others in the early church Arius understood Wisdom as a personification of Christ, but against the main current of orthodoxy he maintained that the statement in verse 22, about Wisdom being created at the beginning of God's work, indicated that Jesus did not share the Father's divine essence. Similarly, Arius fastened on passages in the Gospels where Jesus spoke of the Father as "greater than I" (John 14:28) or where Jesus was said to grow (Luke 2:52) or to suffer human privations (thirst in John 4:7 and 19:28, fatigue in John 4:6). He likewise made much of passages elsewhere in the New Testament that called Jesus the firstborn (for example, Rom. 8:29; Col. 1:15). In studying the Bible, Arius maximized

Noteworthy in this early
depiction of the Council of
Nicaea of 325 is the trampling
underfoot of Arius (and his
heresies).

Stoumaras, Athens

whatever he could find that suggested differences between the Father
and the Son.

Arius's appeal to what he considered the logic of monotheism illustrates a recurring tendency throughout Christian history to subject the
facts of divine revelation to current conceptions of "the reasonable." If,
Arius argued, God was absolutely perfect, absolutely transcendent, and
absolutely changeless, and if he was the originator of all things—without himself being derived from anything else—then surely it was obvious that everything and anyone else in the universe was set apart from
God. And if everything and anyone was set apart from God, then Jesus
too must be set apart from God. Yes, Jesus may have played a special
role in the creation and redemption of the world, but he could not himself be God in the sense that the one God was uniquely divine. There
could be only one God, therefore Christ must have been created, Christ
(like all creation) must be subject to change and even to sin, and Christ
(again, like all created beings) could not have full knowledge of the
mind of God.

These arguments, which rested so comfortably on logical intuitions
and which could be supported by a dextrous use of the Bible, nonetheless came under immediate attack. Consternation at what came to be
called Arianism arose from several sources.

In the first instance, Arius's use of the Bible seemed selective or so-
phistic. He was accused of reading meanings into innocent passages
that distorted the rightful sense of the text. For their part, the opponents of Arius could also drag passages out of their proper context, but
the range of biblical material deployed against Arius was vast. Texts
like John 1:1, where the Logos is said to be "with God" in the beginning
and, in fact, to *be* God grounded the orthodox use of the Bible. Anti-
Arian texts also included statements about Jesus being in the form of
God (Phil. 2:6), bearing the stamp of God's nature (Heb. 1:3), sharing

the divine glory (1 Cor. 2:8), or remaining always the same (Heb. 13:8). Even Arius's use of Proverbs 8 received a sharp rebuke when the orthodox pointed to verse 30 and its assertion that Wisdom was "always" with God in the work of creation.

Opponents on both sides were well versed in Scripture. If both sides practiced a more fanciful exegesis than is now standard in the church, still it was important for the orthodox to show that Arius's views were clever innovations that could not withstand careful scrutiny. Important as such debates over biblical passages were, however, the rebuttal of Arianism depended even more heavily on two other strategies.

What might be called the logic of salvation, to match Arius's logic of monotheism, was the main theme in the decades-long effort of Athanasius (ca. 296–373) to define and defend the orthodox position. Athanasius, who eventually became bishop of Alexandria, but who would also be exiled five times for his defense of Jesus' divinity, did not consider Arius's arguments as philosophical curiosities. Rather, he viewed them as daggers aimed at the very heart of the Christian message. His memorable treatise *De Incarnatione* (Of the incarnation) was written early in the dispute with Arius. It summarized as follows the case he would continue to make for the rest of his life: If Christ were not truly God, then he could not bestow life upon the repentant and free them from sin and death. Yet this work of salvation is at the heart of the biblical picture of Christ, and it has anchored the church's life since the beginning. What Athanasius saw clearly was that, unless Christ was truly God, humanity would lose the hope that Paul expressed in 2 Corinthians 5:21, "that in [Christ] we might become the righteousness of God." C. S. Lewis is only one of many later commentators to hail Athanasius for the fidelity of his convictions. "He stood for the Trinitarian doctrine, 'whole and undefiled,' when it looked as if all the civilised world was slipping back from Christianity into the religion of Arius—into one of those 'sensible' synthetic religions . . . which, then as now, included among their devotees many highly cultivated clergymen."[6]

Very much in keeping with Athanasius's rejection of Arianism, but based more on lived experience than a direct theological argument, was intuitive opposition from multitudes of ordinary believers. Prayer in the church had always ascended to God in the name of Christ, so much so that to separate the Son from the Father seemed to sever the chance for humans to communicate with the divine. Bap-

---

6. C. S. Lewis, introduction to *St. Athanasius on the Incarnation: The Treatise "De Incarnatione Verbi Dei,"* trans. and ed. A Religious of C.S.M.V. (Crestwood, N.Y.: St. Vladimir's Seminary Press, 1953 [orig. 1944]), 9.

Athanasius on the Incarnation

What—or rather *Who*—was it that was needed for such grace and such recall as we required? Who, save the Word of God Himself, Who also in the beginning had made all things out of nothing? . . . For He alone, being Word of the Father and above all, was in consequence both able to recreate all, and worthy to suffer on behalf of all and to be an ambassador for all with the Father.

For this purpose, then, the incorporeal and incorruptible and immaterial Word of God entered our world. In one sense, indeed, He was not far from it before, for no part of creation had ever been without Him Who, while ever abiding in union with the Father, yet fills all things that are. But now He entered the world in a new way, stooping to our level in His love and Self-revealing to us. . . . [Pitying] our race, moved with compassion for our limitation, unable to endure that death should have the mastery . . . He took to Himself a body, a human body even as our own. Nor did He will merely to become embodied or merely to appear; had that been so, He could have revealed His divine majesty in some other and better way. No, He took *our* body. . . . He, the Mighty One, the Artificer [Creator] of all, Himself prepared this body in the virgin as a temple for Himself, and took it for His very own, as the instrument through which He was known and in which He dwelt. Thus, taking a body like our own, because all our bodies were liable to the corruption of death, He surrendered His body to death in place of all, and offered it to the Father. This He did out of sheer love for us.[2]

tism in the church had always used the Trinitarian formula "in the name of the Father and of the Son and of the Holy Spirit" (Matt. 28:19). Hymns in the church regularly praised Jesus as the Savior, who, as from God and of God, restored fallen humanity to God. In short, the day-to-day life of the church—the "common sense" of ordinary believers—rebelled against Arius's proposals. Ordinary believers did not usually possess the technical skill to counter Arius's arguments. As worshiping beings, however, they knew that to take divinity from Christ was to take hope from their souls. As so often in the church's history, the saying *lex orandi lex credendi* (the principles, or "law," of prayer determine the principles of formal belief) held true in the crisis of the early fourth century.

The bishops who met at Nicaea were not all of one mind, either on the seriousness of the Arian threat or on the best means of meeting it. But their declaration of first principles eventually, after a struggle lasting for

[handwritten note in top margin: NOTICE PROGRESSION + CORRECTION of CREED — p43 — separates of Central — Nicene — Constantinople]

The Nicene Creed

From the First Council of Nicaea (325)

We believe in one God, the Father Almighty, Maker of all things visible and invisible.

And in one Lord Jesus Christ, the Son of God, begotten of the Father, Light of Light, very God of very God, begotten, not made, being of one substance with the Father; by whom all things were made; who for us men, and for our salvation, came down and was incarnate and was made man; he suffered, and the third day he rose again, ascended into heaven; from thence he shall come to judge the quick and the dead.

And in the Holy Ghost.

As Expanded at the First Council of Constantinople (381)

We believe in one God, the Father Almighty, Maker of heaven and earth, and of all things visible and invisible.

And in one Lord Jesus Christ, the only-begotten Son of God, begotten of the Father before all worlds, Light of Light, very God of very God, begotten, not made, being of one substance with the Father; by whom all things were made; who for us men, and for our salvation, came down from heaven, and was incarnate by the Holy Ghost of the Virgin Mary, and was made man; he was crucified for us under Pontius Pilate, and suffered, and was buried, and the third day he rose again, according to the Scriptures, and ascended into heaven, and sitteth on the right hand of the Father; from thence he shall come again with glory, to judge the quick and the dead; whose kingdom shall have no end.

And in the Holy Ghost, the Lord and Giver of life, who proceedeth from the Father, who with the Father and the Son together is worshiped and glorified, who spake by the prophets. In one holy catholic and apostolic Church; we acknowledge one baptism for the remission of sins; we look for the resurrection of the dead, and the life of the world to come. Amen.[3]

most of the rest of the fourth century, became a bedrock for Christian life and theology. The council's key assertions were as follows:

1. Christ was *very God of very God*. Jesus himself was God in the same sense in which the Father was God. Differentiation between Father and Son may refer to the respective tasks each took on or to the relationship in which each stands to the other. But the key matter is that Father, Son, and Holy Spirit are all truly God.

2. Christ was *of one substance with the Father.* The Greek word used in this phrase (*homoousios,* from *homo-,* "same," and *ousia,* "substance") led to great controversy, both because this technical philosophical term is not found in the Bible and because a large faction in the church preferred the assertion that Jesus was "of a similar substance with the Father" (using the key word *homoiousios,* from *homoi,* "similar," plus *ousia;* later writers referred dramatically to the importance of the distinguishing *i,* or iota, the smallest Greek letter). In the end *homoousios* won out because it reinforced as unequivocally as possible the fact that Christ was truly "very God of very God." The term was held to be a just summary of Jesus' own teaching, that "I and the Father are one" (John 10:30).

3. Christ was *begotten, not made.* That is, Jesus was never formed as all other things and persons had been created but was from eternity the Son of God.

4. Christ became human *for us men, and for our salvation.* This phrase succinctly summarized the burden of Athanasius's concern, that Christ could not have brought salvation to his people if Christ were only a creature. Humanity could not pull itself up to God. Salvation was of God.

The Nicene formula of 325 did not immediately win the consent of the church. Arius's logic continued to exert an appeal. The use of words like *homoousios* that were not found in Scripture troubled many. Since key terms like "substance" had a lengthy history in Hellenistic thought, ambiguity often attended the importation of these terms into Christian theology. And because even the most ardent Christ-centered theologians could engage in controversy in order to vindicate themselves, as well as to bring glory to God, the debate over the divinity of Christ was marked with much, often bitter, political maneuvering. Yet when Athanasius and other anti-Arians made it clear that "one substance" did not deny the separate person and work of Father, Son, and Holy Spirit, the Nicene statement eventually began to win acceptance.

Finally, at a council called in 381 at Constantinople by the emperor Theodosius, the assembled bishops reaffirmed the main propositions of the Nicene formula and produced the slightly modified statement that is now known as the Nicene Creed. This final version expanded the section on Christ's birth and his suffering under Pilate, included minor modifications in some of the wording from 325, and produced a fuller statement on the Holy Spirit. The formula at Nicaea had affirmed only that "we believe in the Holy Spirit." Yet after 325 a group of heretical theologians, who came to be known as Pneumatomachians, or Fighters against the Spirit, had begun to deny a separate existence for the Holy

Spirit. The expanded formula of 381 clarified that, even as Jesus was a fully divine person, so also was the Spirit.[†]

The Nicene Creed has remained for nearly seventeen centuries a secure foundation for the church's theology, worship, and prayer. Not only does it succinctly summarize the facts of biblical revelation, but it also stands as a bulwark against the persistent human tendency to prefer logical deductions concerning what God must be like and how he must act to the lived realities of God's self-disclosure. And it powerfully restates the realities of Christ's divine nature, his incarnation as a human being, and the work of salvation he accomplishes for his people. The turning point in Christian history represented by the Nicene Creed was the church's critical choice for the wisdom of God in preference to human wisdom. Theologically considered, no decision could ever be more important.

Nicaea and Politics

Yet Nicaea represented more than just a watershed in Christian doctrine. Because it was Emperor Constantine who called for a council in 325 (as also Emperor Theodosius did in 381) and because imperial politics played a central role in the entire debate over Arianism, the church's decision about the divinity of Christ turned out to have great importance for the political sphere as well.

The political meaning of Nicaea is suggested by brief reference to events in the mid-fourth century. At various times in his career as bishop of Alexandria, Athanasius was banished by the emperors Constantius II and Julian. For his part, Constantius II (emperor 337–61) exerted his considerable abilities both to shore up the fabric of the empire and to promote the Arian views he personally espoused.

The larger question posed by imperial-ecclesiastical connections was new because of the dramatic conversion of Constantine and the empire's turn to toleration, and then support, of Christianity.[7] The basic question was this: given the fact that the emperors would now, in some fashion or other, support the church, where did the emperors fit in relationship to the church? Although this question was not quite as

---

[†] The Latin word *filioque*, which means "and from the Son," was a seemingly small, but highly divisive later addition to the Nicene-Constantinopolitan Creed. In A.D. 589 the Third Council of Toledo inserted *filioque* after the affirmation of faith in "the Holy Spirit . . . who proceeds from the Father." Gradually adopted by the Western church, this doctrine of the Holy Spirit proceeding from both the Father and the Son ("double procession")—as opposed to from the Father only ("single procession")—was a major factor in the later split between the Eastern and the Western churches (see chapter 6).

7. The general picture in this section, as well as specific quotations, are from George Huntston Williams, "Christology and Church–State Relations in the Fourth Century," *Church History* 20 (September 1951): 3–33 and (December 1951): 3–26.

momentous as the issue of Christ's divinity, it was a question of great contemporary significance and also one that would continue to be of central importance in Christian history for more than a thousand years thereafter. (In some sense, it is a question that continues to be important wherever, in the modern world, rulers of the state are also professing Christians.)

In the fourth century, Arians—both emperors and their supporters—tended to favor direct imperial control of the church. As he set about solidifying his own power and also working his will in the church, Emperor Constantius is reputed to have said, "Let whatsoever I will, be that esteemed a canon." That is, Constantius wanted his wishes for the church to be treated with the same religious seriousness as accorded the canons promulgated by the councils (these "canons" were official statements of the councils, usually dealing with disputed questions). He wanted, in other words, to have the church recognize the word of the emperor as, in some sense, the word of God.

By contrast, the orthodox or catholic party thought it was essential for the church to preserve a certain degree of autonomy over its own affairs. This stance is illustrated by words spoken by Bishop Ambrose of Milan to Emperor Theodosius about the year 390. After a dispute between the emperor and the bishop involving Theodosius's conduct toward a subject colony, Ambrose refused to allow Theodosius to take part in Communion until the emperor made a public confession of his sinful action. When Theodosius resisted, Ambrose is said to have replied, "The emperor is in the church, not above it." Ambrose, in other words, wanted to treat even the emperor as an ordinary Christian when it came to the church's most sacred rites.

In the contest concerning ecclesiastical and imperial power, both Arians and catholics shared several convictions. Both agreed that Christ was the head of the church, that God had ordained the emperor to rule over terrestrial affairs, and that kingship involved the traditional idea of a lord and a satrap (that is, a relationship where the lord exercises a fairly complete rule over the satrap, or vassal). The specific teachings of Arius became critically important in this dispute at the place where subordination was defined. Arians, who believed that the Son was subordinate to the Father, applied the Lord–satrap relationship to God (the lord) and Christ (the satrap). Since the Son was subordinate to the Father, so too the kingdom of the Son (the church) must be subordinate to the kingdom of the Father (the empire). Therefore, the authority of the bishops must be subordinate to the authority of the emperor. It was even proper to call the emperor a bishop of the bish-

Something of the imperial grandeur of Emperor Constantine, who was so important in so many ways for Christianity during the fourth century, comes through in this bust, despite the toll of the years.

Christian History Archives

ops, since the bishops (as servants of the Son) received their authority derivatively from the emperor (as the servant of God).

The orthodox rejected this reasoning at every point. They believed that the Son was consubstantial (equal in being) to the Father, and they applied the lord–satrap relationship to the Trinity and the bishops of the church. Since the Son was consubstantial with the Father, so too the kingdom of the Son (the church) was of equal dignity to the kingdom of the Father (the empire). Therefore the authority of the bishops must be coequal to the authority of the empire, with the implication that the bishops were properly the chief authorities in matters concerning the life of faith, while the emperor was supreme in affairs of the world. As a consequence, when the emperor was in the church as a Christian, the emperor was under the authority of the bishops, since in the church the bishops spoke for Christ, who was God.

The logic of these connections was not always as apparent at the time as it now appears in retrospect. But several important conclusions followed for the relationship of church and state, once the Nicene position came to prevail. Most important, to affirm the consubstantiality of the Son was to affirm a degree of independence of the church from the state and the state from the church. The ancient world did not practice divided sovereignties, and especially the Eastern church would continue to vest great authority over both church and state in the empire. But in the West, and to some extent also in the East, acceptance of the Nicene Creed preserved a certain degree of autonomy for the church. In the course of the fourth century, Nicene Christology affirmed the principle that prayer, worship, preaching, the use of Scripture, and the sacraments all deserved a sphere of liberty. Because the work of the Son was *homoousios* with the work of the Father, the life of the church had an independence that no instrument of state could transgress. This foundation established the basis for later relationships between institutions of state and of church, particularly in the West. It made this result of Christological debate an extraordinarily important turning point in the political history of Christianity as well.

Nicaea and Christendom

Notwithstanding the way that the Nicene Creed represented a charter of liberty for the church over against the empire, the more obvious reality after 325 (or even 312) was that a decisive corner had been turned in church history. Once Constantine began to act on behalf of the church, and once his successors began simply to assume that imperial rule had *something* to do with the church, the church had left behind the conditions of its first three centuries. Those conditions had underscored the church's existence as a pilgrim community, not at home in any part of the world, since the power of the state could be turned at any moment to uproot believers, propel them into exile, or disrupt the regular order of worship and Christian service. Even if active Roman persecution was rare and even if local Christian communities often developed considerable stability in the pre-Constantinian era, the ever-present truth was that believing communities could hope for no permanent security in this life.

With the conversion of Constantine, the reality of the church as a pilgrim community gradually gave way. Especially over the course of the fourth through seventh centuries, as the Christian faith spread into northern and western Europe, the actions of rulers in initiating, promoting, supporting, and (often) dictating to the church gradually accustomed leaders in both church and state to notions of establishment. When rulers publicly acknowledged the centrality of the church to all of life, it was difficult for the church not to respond by assuming that it had a vitally important role to play in this life, as well as for the life to come. Much good came of this adjustment, especially as the church's evangelistic mission benefited from the help of rulers and when the church contributed its resources to the work of civilizing Europe's barbarian hordes. But the cost was also high. A world where an emperor could make the critical decision to resolve a great doctrinal crisis was a world in which the emperor's legitimate concerns for worldly order, success, wealth, and stability almost had to become concerns as well in the church.

In these terms, Nicaea was a turning point that set Christianity on a course that it has only begun to relinquish, and that only reluctantly, over the past two or three centuries. That course was the addition of concerns for worldly power to its birthright concern for the worship of God. The complexity of the Nicene situation makes it very difficult to pronounce snap judgments on this great turning point. At the initiation of the emperor, the church reaffirmed the doctrine of the divinity of Christ, which has proved to be an immensely significant foundation for virtually all Christian life, work, and worship in the centuries that followed. Yet because of the emperor's actions, the sphere of worldly concerns for which he stood gradually assumed greater and greater importance in the church. The distinction between church and world that Nicene Christology preserved was, in fact, compromised by the very events that led up to the declaration of Nicaea.

In this sense, Nicaea bequeathed a dual legacy—of sharpened fidelity to the great and saving truths of revelation, and also of increasing intermingling of church and world. The monks, examined in chapter 4, who in the fourth century began to trickle out of "Christendom" into the desert or on to lonely mountain peaks, were one response to what had happened at Nicaea. They were, in effect, saying that it was necessary to create some distance from Christendom (that is, the union of church and state) in order to find Christ. Yet what the monks often studied as they left the establishment faith that came to birth with the emperor's actions at Nicaea was the biblical reasoning that led up to the Nicene Creed, and the creed itself.

This combination—of momentous doctrinal declaration and critical alteration in the church's relationship to the world—is what together make the Council of Nicaea one of the most decisive events in church history outside of the New Testament.

Although persecution mostly ceased in the Roman Empire with the Edict of Milan in 313, that was not the case for the relatively substantial Christian community in Persia, whose king, Shapur II, unleashed a wave of persecution between 339 and 344. The prayer below is from one of the martyrs of that period—Gustazad, a high official in the king's court. Gustazad had renounced and then returned to the Christian faith. The "shepherd" he refers to is Simeon bar Sabba'e, a Persian bishop who was martyred the day after his protégé. The prayers of the martyrs are significant for their resolute confidence in Jesus and for their trust in the power of martyrdom to build up the faith in others.

Praise to you, Lord Jesus: I was a lost sheep, and you brought me back; I had strayed from your holy fold, and by the exertions of that most capable of your shepherds, Simeon, you found out where I was.

He went out to look for me, and he put me with those of your sheep that had been fattened for the slaughter. I was to be a son to the apostles, a brother to the martyrs who had received the garland in the west, a good example to your people in the east.

Let them not fall away, let them not lose the true faith— faith in Father, Son and Holy Spirit, the truly Existing, the glorious King, whom all that worship the Holy Trinity, in heaven and on earth, confess and ever will confess, age after age. Amen.[8]

Further Reading

Barnes, Timothy D. *Constantine and Eusebius.* Cambridge: Harvard University Press, 1981.

Bray, Gerald. *Creeds, Councils, and Christ.* Downers Grove, Ill.: InterVarsity, 1984.

Brown, Harold O. J. *Heresies: The Image of Christ in the Mirror of Heresy and Orthodoxy from the Apostles to the Present.* Garden City, N.Y.: Doubleday, 1984.

Brown, Peter. *The Rise of Western Christendom: Triumph and Diversity, A.D. 200–1000.* Cambridge, Mass.: Blackwell, 1996.

Grant, Michael. *Constantine the Great: The Man and His Times.* New York: Scribner's, 1994.

Haas, Christopher. *Alexandria in Late Antiquity: Topography and Social Conflict.* Baltimore: Johns Hopkins University Press, 1996.

Heresy in the Early Church [*Christian History*, no. 51]. 1996.

Kelly, J. N. D. *Early Christian Doctrines.* 5th ed. San Francisco: Harper & Row, 1978.

Pelikan, Jaroslav. *The Christian Tradition.* Vol. 1, *The Emergence of the Catholic Tradition (100–600).* Chicago: University of Chicago Press, 1971.

Rusch, William G., ed. *The Trinitarian Controversy.* Philadelphia: Fortress, 1980.

Smith, M. A. *The Church under Siege.* Downers Grove, Ill.: InterVarsity, 1976.

Stevenson, J., ed. *A New Eusebius: Documents Illustrative of the History of the Church to A.D. 377.* London: SPCK, 1960. Eusebius's indispensable history is available in many other editions, like Eusebius, *The History of the Church from Christ to Constantine,* trans. G. A. Williamson (New York: Penguin, 1965).

Worship in the Early Church [*Christian History*, no. 37]. 1993.

8. Hamman, *Early Christian Prayers,* 59.

3

Doctrine, Politics, and Life in the Word: The Council of Chalcedon (451)

One of the most highly regarded Latin poets of Christian antiquity, Aurelius Clemens Prudentius, left prominent government office at age fifty-seven to retire to a monastery and dedicate the rest of his life to serving God by writing hymns and poems. Although Prudentius died in about 413—several decades before the Council of Chalcedon—his Christmas hymn "Corde natus ex Parentis" (Of the Father's love begotten) expresses in lyric form what the ecclesiastical councils hammered out in doctrinal propositions: Jesus is fully divine, coequal with the Father (harking back to the Nicene Creed), and fully human, being born as a baby (anticipating the Chalcedonian Definition).

> *Of the Father's love begotten*
> *Ere the worlds began to be,*
> *He is Alpha and Omega,*
> *He the source, the ending he,*
> *Of the things that are, that have been,*
> *And that future years shall see.*
> *Evermore and evermore.*
>
> *O that birth for ever blessèd!*
> *When the Virgin, full of grace,*
> *By the Holy Ghost conceiving,*
> *Bore the Saviour of our race;*

And the Babe, the world's Redeemer,
First revealed his sacred face,
Evermore and evermore.

O ye heights of heaven, adore him;
Angel hosts, his praises sing;
Powers, dominions bow before him,
And extol our God and King;
Let no tongue on earth be silent,
Every voice in concert ring,
Evermore and evermore.[1]

On May 23, 451, the Eastern Roman emperor, Marcian, summoned an ecumenical council of bishops that he hoped would "end disputations and settle the true faith more clearly and for all time."[2] The council met at Chalcedon, just across the Bosporus from Marcian's capital, Constantinople. About 520 bishops attended, all but four from the Eastern section of the Roman Empire (two were from North Africa and two, who exerted an influence far out of proportion to their number, were legates from the bishop of Rome, Leo I). After fifteen arduous sessions from October 8 to November 10, the council succeeded in finding a formula that satisfactorily answered the momentous question for which it had been called. That question was itself a legacy of the church's great fourth-century councils (especially at Nicaea in 325 and Constantinople in 381), which had forthrightly affirmed the divinity of Jesus by specifying that he was "God of very God" and "of the same substance" as the Father. But on the basis of that declaration, fresh problems arose. If Jesus was fully divine, how was he human? And if Jesus was both human and divine, how did that humanity and that divinity coexist?

Chalcedon's answer to these questions has stood the test of time— Jesus was "one person" consisting of "two natures." But despite Em-

---

1. Maurice Frost, ed., *Historical Companion to Hymns Ancient and Modern* (London: Clowes, 1962), 161–62.
2. Quoted in W. H. C. Frend, *The Rise of Christianity* (Philadelphia: Fortress, 1984), 770.

peror Marcian's hope, it did not define the church's doctrinal life "for all time"; nor did it bring an end to the acrimonious disputes that had led to the council. Nevertheless its deliberations were immensely significant. The Council of Chalcedon was an important event—and a critical turning point—in the history of Christianity both because it clarified orthodox Christian teaching and also because of the way in which it accomplished that clarification.

As it had at the Councils of Nicaea and Constantinople, so at Chalcedon the church took up questions of ultimate importance concerning the person and work of Christ. In the broader sweep of church history, Chalcedon showed that it was possible, through judicious use of one era's dominant forms of thought, to define critical aspects of Christianity as handed down in the Scriptures. Moreover, Chalcedon showed that such necessary theological work can succeed despite an environment of brutal ecclesiastical strife and despite the reality of cultural division within the church itself. In these terms Chalcedon was a threefold triumph: a triumph of sound doctrine over error in the church, a triumph of Christian catholicity over cultural fragmentation, and a triumph of discriminating theological reasoning over the anti-intellectual dismissal of philosophy, on the one hand, and over a theological capitulation to philosophy, on the other.

These three triumphs and their encouragement for later believers, however, all depended upon the successful formulation of Christological doctrine. And that was a success hardly imaginable in the ebb and flow of theological, ecclesiastical, personal, and dynastic controversy that eventually converged at Chalcedon. Only by sketching the course of that controversy is it possible to realize the importance of Chalcedon's Definition. Only by grasping the importance of that definition can we realize how momentous Chalcedon has been for the entire life and thought of the Christian church. And only by glimpsing that momentous significance can we be encouraged by the three historical triumphs that made Chalcedon another of the great turning points in the history of Christianity.

The Course of Controversy

Tracing the course of controversies that led to the Chalcedonian statement is a complicated task. A full array of learned theologians and ambitious ecclesiastical officials debated passionately and exhaustively the finest details, as well as the most major assertions, having to do with the divinity and humanity of Jesus. The account that follows, though it mentions many names and touches on several points in dispute, provides only a much-simplified picture of the tangled road that

The association of Mary with Jesus, as in this sixth-century Egyptian tapestry, became increasingly important in the history of the church after discussion began on the role of Mary as *theotokos*.

Icon of Virgin. Egypt, Byzantine period, 6th century. Tapestry weave, wool, 178 X 100 cm. © The Cleveland Museum of Art, 1997, Leonard C. Hanna, Jr., Bequest, 1967.144.

led to Chalcedon. Likewise, the "scorecard" that is provided to chart members of the opposing "teams" fails to indicate the many nuances that were brought to the fray from almost all who opened their mouths on the subject. Yet even simplified accounts are helpful, for they provide a flavor of the intense exchanges that led to the council. In addition, by indicating some of the passion brought to the debate, even a simplified history can show how vitally important that struggle was for those who were engaged in it.

Although speculation over the exact character of Christ's person had surfaced regularly from the time of Justin Martyr in the mid-second century, probing discussion on the issue moved squarely into the forefront as a result of the Arian controversy. Athanasius's ultimately convincing response to Arius had stressed Christ's full divinity. Athanasius argued—and the church as a whole came to acknowledge the eternal significance of his conclusion—that without full divinity, Christ could not impart the salvation to which the Bible and the church's worship testified. But once this redemptive truth was established, the church began to ask what it should think about the *person* of Christ. How did Jesus' full divinity (which was often described in terms of the divine Logos, or "Word" of God, from John 1) relate to the humanity of his earthly existence? Athanasius's own writings described the divine Logos taking on a human body, but he seemed to imply (without stating it in so many words) that the Logos took the place of the human soul in the Incarnate Jesus.

A "Scorecard" for Chalcedon

Word-Flesh Christology	Word-Man Christology
Alexandria (North Africa)	Antioch (Syria)
Christ is a fully integrated person; problems are the incompleteness of the humanity or the changeableness of the deity	Christ has a full divine and a full human nature; problem is division of the person
Athanasius	
Apollinaris of Laodicea	vs. Theodore of Mopsuestia
Cyril, bishop of Alexandria	vs. Nestorius, archbishop of Constantinople
Eutyches, monk in Constantinople	vs. Flavian, archbishop of Constantinople
Dioscorus, bishop of Alexandria	vs. Flavian, archbishop of Constantinople
Theodosius II (emperor 408–50)	vs. Pulcheria and Marcian (emperor 450–57)
	Proterius, in Egypt
Monophysitism of the Copts	

The theologian who made this "Logos-flesh" or "Word-flesh" concept explicit was Apollinaris of Laodicea (ca. 310–ca. 390). In an effort to conquer Arianism fully, he defended the divinity of Jesus to the hilt, but he did so by picturing Jesus as a combination of divine soul (or Logos) and human body. For Apollinaris, the life of Jesus showed "one nature" made up of flesh and the divine intelligence. When commenting on the relation of Apollinaris's views with Athanasius's, the historian Richard Norris has concluded that Apollinaris "does not forget or ignore a human center of life and consciousness in Jesus [as Athanasius did]. He denies it."[3] (Because theologians and bishops as-

---

3. Richard A. Norris, trans. and ed., *The Christological Controversy* (Philadelphia: Fortress, 1980), 23. This book is an excellent collection of the documents most important in the controversy.

sociated with the great see of Alexandria in North Africa held views
that tended in the same direction as Apollinaris's, although usually expressed with greater caution, this "Word-flesh" Christology is also
known as Alexandrian.)

Apollinaris's effort to define the person of Christ drew an immediate
response. Much of the opposition came from the see of Antioch, on the
Syrian coast, whose bishops had long contended with the bishops of Alexandria and Constantinople for primacy in the Eastern Roman Empire. The leading proponent of Antiochene theology was Theodore of
Mopsuestia (ca. 350–428). As would be characteristic of Christology
propounded from Antioch, Theodore taught that Christ always was
completely human as well as completely God; Christ possessed two full
"natures"—one human and the other divine. From the viewpoint of
Theodore and like-minded Antiochenes, the Alexandrian Word-flesh
construct was riddled with errors. It seemed, first, to downplay the reality of Christ's humanity. But second, and looming larger in that period, the Alexandrian position seemed to suggest that the divine Logos
was subject to weakness, change, and alteration.

The dispute between Apollinaris and Theodore initiated a great
eruption of controversy that spread over the whole first half of the fifth
century. Nestorius (d. ca. 451), a monk from Antioch who upheld Theodore's position, was named bishop of Constantinople in 428. Early in
his bishopric, Nestorius preached a controversial sermon denying that
Mary was *theotokos* (the bearer of God). He asserted that Mary did not
give birth to "God." Rather, she gave birth to the human Jesus, whose
humanity—though united with the divine Logos—must be understood
as separate and distinct from his divine nature.

As an aside, it is worth noting that Nestorius's reference to Mary indicates the growing significance of the mother of Jesus in Christian
thought by the end of the fourth century. In the second century, theologians like Justin Martyr and Irenaeus had begun to contrast Mary's
obedient service to God with Eve's earlier disobedience. As part of Irenaeus's notion of "recapitulation," in which God repeated (perfectly)
what humanity had early done (sinfully), Mary's faithful service was
viewed as recapitulating Eve's unfaithfulness. By the mid-fourth century, it was becoming customary to call Mary "ever-virgin," as Athanasius did, and so to affirm her perpetual virginity. Spurred by arguments
like Nestorius's on the *theotokos*, debate about the humanity of Christ
heightened also the importance of Mary in the church's general consciousness. These internal reasons for greater attention to the person
of Mary and her work in giving birth to Jesus were also strengthened
by the new cultures into which Christianity was expanding. In both the

Cyril of Alexandria versus Nestorius of Constantinople

Cyril's Second Letter to Nestorius

I shall even now remind you, as my brother in Christ, to make the balance of your teaching and your thinking about the faith as safe as possible for the laity, and also to keep in mind that to cause even one of these little ones who believe in Christ to stumble wins implacable wrath. . . .

[The] one Lord Jesus Christ must not be divided into two Sons. . . . [For] Scripture says not that the Logos united to himself the person of a human being but that he became flesh. And for the Logos to become flesh is nothing other than for him to "share in flesh and blood as we do" [Heb. 2:14]. . . . He did not depart from his divine status or cease to be born of the Father; he continued to be what he was, even in taking on flesh. . . . And this is how we shall find the holy fathers conceived things. Accordingly, they boldly called the holy Virgin "God's mother" [*theotokos*], not because the nature of the Logos . . . took the start of its existence in the holy Virgin but because the holy body which was born of her, possessed as it was of a rational soul, and to which the Logos was hypostatically united, is said to have had a fleshly birth.[1]

Nestorius's Second Letter to Cyril

The rebukes which your astonishing letter brings against us I forgive. . . . [Standing] against your prolixity, . . . I will attempt to make my exposition brief and maintain my distaste for obscure and indigestible haranguing. . . .

Everywhere in Holy Scripture, whenever mention is made of the saving dispensation of the Lord, what is conveyed to us is the birth and suffering not of the deity but of the humanity of Christ, so that by a more exact manner of speech the holy Virgin is called Mother of Christ, not Mother of God. Listen to these words of the Gospels: "The book of the birth of Jesus Christ, son of David, son of Abraham" [Matt. 1:1]. It is obvious that the son of David was not the divine Logos.[2]

Mediterranean world and in northern Europe, goddesses had always played a prominent role in the pagan religions. Those who were accustomed to worshiping female deities found in Mary, not exactly a substitute god, but a female figure to whom it seemed only natural to pay religious attention. By the time that Nestorius introduced debate on Mary as *theotokos*, forces inside the believing community as well as outside, from pagan religious habits, were combining to push Mary into the forefront of the church's life.

In response to Nestorius's proposals, including his refutation of Mary as "God-bearer," came an immediate and thunderous counterattack from Alexandria. The bishop of that city, Cyril (d. 444), immediately rebuked Nestorius for denying that Jesus was "one incarnate nature of the divine Logos."[4] To Cyril and the other Alexandrians, it seemed as if Nestorius and his kind were presenting a nearly schizophrenic Jesus, with two "persons," hardly relating to each other at all. As part of his polemic, Cyril also appealed to the bishop of Rome, Celestine, to support his attack on Nestorius.

Sadly, the battle that followed soon became personal and episcopal as well as theological. The sees of Alexandria and Antioch had long been arrayed against each other as countervailing centers of influence in the early church. Sometimes inadvertently, at other times with malice aforethought, Alexandria and Antioch competed to exert controlling influence over Constantinople, which was a vitally important see because of the presence of the Roman emperor. The various archbishops of Constantinople were often in a position, because of their own standing or because of influence with the emperor, to tip decisively the balance of power toward Alexandria or toward Antioch. Heightening an already contentious situation, all three major Eastern sees competed against each other to enlist support from the bishop of Rome, who was traditionally recognized as the key church leader in the West. The power of the popes (as the bishops of Rome were already being called) grew after the Roman emperors moved the imperial capital to the East in Constantinople and strengthened even further after the barbarian invasions beginning in the early fifth century undercut imperial rule in Rome. As a result, although Rome was never as fully engaged in detailed Christological argument as Antioch, Alexandria, or Constantinople, the judgments of Rome were always of great importance, either for supporting one or the other of the Eastern antagonists or for offering its own independent opinion on controversial theological issues. These intra-Eastern and East–West circumstances explain why intense debate over the nature of Christ's person spilled over into intense ecclesiastical competition.

After Nestorius promulgated his Antiochene views from Constantinople and Cyril of Alexandria went on the attack against them, the next step was to try to get the warring sides together. This was attempted at a meeting at Ephesus in 431, where, as it turned out, both groups were

4. Ibid., 27.

well represented. Yet the outcome, had not the issues been so serious, would have been comic. Feelings between supporters of the Antiochene and Alexandrian positions ran so high that the two groups could not meet in the same place, and so the bishops representing the two opinions met separately in different conclaves. The result: each excommunicated the other. This stalemate prompted the emperor to get involved. In an effort to pacify an expanding dispute, Emperor Theodosius II took the side of Cyril and banished Nestorius.

Controversy, along with tempers, soon flared up again. A leading monk at Constantinople, Eutyches (ca. 378–454), defended the basic Alexandrian position by publishing his opinion that Christ possessed only "one nature after the union."[5] That is, he reiterated the conviction that Jesus had an integrated personality and that this personality should always be described with only one set of (largely divine) attributes. In response, Flavian (d. 449), the archbishop of Constantinople, accused Eutyches of committing heresy by confounding Christ's two natures. Fitting action to the word, Flavian banished Eutyches from Constantinople. Undaunted, Eutyches appealed his case to both Alexandria and Rome. Responding positively to an opportunity to defend the Alexandrian Christology, Dioscorus (d. 454), who was both Cyril's nephew and Cyril's successor as bishop of Alexandria, organized a council in Ephesus to support Eutyches. At this meeting, Dioscorus also arranged to depose Flavian from the bishopric of Constantinople. Flavian, in his turn, appealed for support to the bishop of Rome, Leo I.

Much was at stake when Leo entered the fray. In general terms, Leo's position as Roman bishop was accompanied by what had become a characteristic Roman or Western approach to Christian teaching. We return to these characteristic differences in chapter 6, but it is helpful to highlight a few important contrasts here. Where the Roman, Western mind-set was concrete, practical, and legal, the Eastern mind-set gravitated toward abstraction, passion, and speculation. The Roman world used Latin, the East used Greek. Tertullian, in the West, had not thought it worthwhile to consider what Jerusalem (the Christian faith) had to do with Athens (the traditions of speculative philosophy). By contrast, his Eastern contemporary Clement of Alexandria had promoted the Christian study of Greek speculative thought as a useful exercise for the church. These differences were more tendencies of intellectual disposition than out-and-out conflicts of doctrine, but they had continued to develop from the time of Tertullian and Clement. By the fifth century it was clear that the West respected doctrinal formulas,

5. Ibid., 28.

like the Nicene-Constantipolitan Creed, for the way they ended debates
and settled questions. In the East, by contrast, such doctrinal formulations had come to be regarded as incitements to broader, deeper, and
more profound theological speculation. So for Leo to enter the largely
Eastern debates over the nature of Christ's person was to bring, not just
another opinion, but a notably different cast of mind to bear on the
critical issue.

Furthermore, the fact that it was this particular pope who brought
Western thinking to bear on Christological questions was of great consequence. Serving as pope in Rome from 440 to 461, Leo I is often
called "the Great" because of his talent, seriousness, and dedication,
and because of his lasting significance in the history of Christian
thought. Besides his role in the Christological debates, he also advanced arguments about the bishop of Rome as the successor of Peter,
which continue to be respected in the Roman Catholic Church to this
day. Leo's mettle as a leader had been severely tested when waves of
barbarians swept out of the North to attack Rome. In the absence of effective secular authority, Leo took the lead in negotiating with Attila
the Hun in 451 and in easing the destruction when the Vandals overran
Rome in 452. Leo's driving goal in doctrine as well as for church order
was to secure stability in an age of fragmentation. The message he sent
in response to Flavian's request was thus doubly significant, for it not
only came out of the West but also came from one of the very few great
men of his age.

Leo's response to Flavian, which is always referred to as his *Tome*,
took a forthright position on the Christological question—Jesus was a
single "person" with two "natures." Roots of this wording went back to
Tertullian, but Leo here amplified them with careful grounding in
Scripture and careful application to the present quarrels. As had Athanasius in the debate over Christ's divinity, Leo showed how the question of the humanity and divinity of Christ bore directly on the hope of
salvation. Thus, the birth of Christ "came about so that death might be
conquered and that the devil, who once exercised death's sovereignty,
might by its power be destroyed, for we would not be able to overcome
the author of sin and of death unless he whom sin could not stain nor
death hold took on our nature and made it his own."[6] In addition, Leo
added careful statements about the ways in which it was appropriate,
and the ways in which it was not appropriate, to say that human and
divine attributes were exchanged in Christ's single earthly person. Here
he was addressing the complex question of *communicatio idioma-*

6. Ibid., 146.

tum—the interchange of attributes, or qualities. Is it proper, for example, to say that "God died" on the cross or that "the man Jesus knew all things"? In his *Tome* Leo walked a tightrope that many before and since have fallen off. "Each 'form'" of Christ as God and human "carries on its proper activities in communion with the other."[7] With these words Leo kept together distinctiveness of natures along with unity of person.

Although Dioscorus refused to recognize Leo's *Tome* when it first arrived in 449, it later became a keystone of the definition at Chalcedon. The fact that some in the East took so little notice of Leo's advice, however, reminds us that the Christological disputes concerned ecclesiastical power as well as theological orthodoxy. Leo, in fact, was not at all pleased with noises from Constantinople that questioned Rome's primacy in the church. Yet throughout the East at this time, respect rather than deference marked the general attitude toward the bishop of Rome. Responding specifically to Dioscorus's refusal to consider Leo's *Tome* at the Council of Ephesus in 449, Leo called that gathering a robber synod and appealed for another council to rectify the situation.

Enter the emperor Marcian, along with more complications. Marcian, as it happens, had only just become emperor. On July 28, 450, the previous ruler, Theodosius II, who had been a strong supporter of Alexandrian Christology (and therefore of Dioscorus), was thrown from his horse and killed. Theodosius's sister, Pulcheria, however, was an ally of Leo and also supported a Christology that emphasized Christ's two natures (closer to the Antiochene position). When she became the power behind the throne and chose Marcian to be her consort—and hence the new emperor—her opinions tipped the balance against Dioscorus. All of this imperial maneuvering became intensely relevant to the history of Christianity when Marcian called for a council to settle the question once and for all.

After the intense deliberations at Chalcedon, Marcian himself read out the critical formulation on October 25, 451:

> Following the holy fathers, we confess with one voice that the one and only Son, our Lord Jesus Christ, is perfect in Godhead and perfect in manhood, truly God and truly man, and that he has a rational soul and a body. He is of one substance [*homoousios*] with the Father as God, he is also of one substance [*homoousios*] with us as man. He is like us in all things except sin. He was begotten of his Father before the ages as God, but in these last days and for our salvation he was born of Mary the virgin, the *theotokos*, as man. This one and the same Christ, Son, Lord, Only-begotten is made known in two natures [which exist] without con-

7. Ibid., 150.

fusion, without change, without division, without separation. The distinction of the natures is in no way taken away by their union, but rather the distinctive properties of each nature are preserved. [Both natures] unite into one person and one hypostasis [that is, substance]. They are not separated or divided into two persons but [they form] one and the same Son, Only-begotten, God, Word, Lord Jesus Christ, just as the prophets of old [have spoken] concerning him and as the Lord Jesus Christ himself has taught us and as the creed of the fathers has delivered to us.[8]

This Chalcedonian Definition represented a delicate balancing act. Its assertions about "one and the same Christ," as well as the series of negations ("without confusion, without change, without division, without separation"), leaned toward Alexandria. The definition acknowledged that Alexandria's insistence on the unity of Christ's person was entirely correct. Yet at the same time, the strong emphasis on the two natures of Christ, reflecting the direct influence of Leo's *Tome*, leaned more toward Antioch. Even while insisting on the integrity of Christ's person, it was necessary to maintain his full humanity as well as his full divinity.

It took longer for the East to accept the Definition of Chalcedon than the West. In Egypt particularly, determined opposition arose to the formula. An Egyptian bishop, Proterius, said at Chalcedon that if he signed the statement he would be signing his death warrant. Six years later he was indeed killed by a mob because of that very act. So strong was Alexandrian, Word-flesh Christology in Egypt that, in opposition to almost the whole rest of the church, the Nestorian "Monophysite" position (that Jesus had only one [Greek *monos*] nature [*physis*]) became official dogma in the Egyptian church. (To this day the Coptic Church of Egypt retains a Monophysite Christology.) Rancorous intramural theological quarreling that continued with great intensity after Chalcedon in North Africa constituted one of the factors that weakened Christianity in that region and so prepared the way for the triumph of Islam, sweeping out of Arabia in the mid-seventh century.

In the West, by contrast, there was almost immediate satisfaction with Chalcedon. Soon, in fact, even most of the East came to agree that this was a good statement of the delicate mystery lying at the heart of Christianity itself.

The dense interconnections at Chalcedon between doctrine and authority, however, meant that not all was settled by this council, even for

8. Tony Lane, ed., *Harper's Concise Book of Christian Faith* (San Francisco: Harper & Row, 1984), 50.

the West. Grateful as he was that Chalcedon followed his *Tome*, Leo was not pleased with other conclusions of the council, especially its Canon 28, which supported the dignity of the archbishop of Constantinople in terms that he felt should be reserved for himself. As a result, although Chalcedon largely settled the doctrinal issue, it did not bridge the growing divide between East and West. Historians commonly see the differences in mind-set and views of ecclesiastical authority that Chalcedon highlighted as strong portents of the eventual split between the Eastern and Western churches. W. H. C. Frend, for example, claims that "the positions taken by Rome and Constantinople . . . at Chalcedon [on the relative power of the two sees] . . . were not to be reversed. Politics rather than religion postponed the final schism until 1054."[9] That schism of 1054 is the subject of chapter 6, but here it is important to note both the success of East and West in reaching agreement on the person of Christ and also the continuing disengagement of style and authority that pointed toward the Great Schism.

The Theological Importance of Chalcedon

Despite the inability of the decision in 451 to draw Eastern and Western churches together, Chalcedon was still a critical point in clarifying Christian teaching. Of first importance was the way the balanced statement of Chalcedon articulated fundamental Christian doctrine. The key affirmations of the definition reflected the main themes of the New Testament—that Christ was a united and integrated person, that he was both God and man, that his human and divine natures were not confused, and that these natures were harmoniously joined in a single individual. Chalcedon reflected that teaching, moreover, with commendable caution. It did not try to force the Bible to say more than it did in order to satisfy the intellectual curiosity of the fifth century. As many later commentors have noted, Chalcedon had the effect of constructing a fence within which further reflection on the person of Christ could continue. Yet whatever else might be said, it was always necessary to affirm both one person and two natures. In this sense, Chalcedon did not so much solve the technical Christological problem as confine it.

But the reason such delicate confining was necessary concerned much more than technical issues of philosophical and theological speculation. Getting questions right about the person of Christ was important because Christ and what he did were of immeasurable importance. No one at the time captured this more succinctly than Leo I,

9. Frend, *The Rise of Christianity*, 790.

as illustrated by the way in which his *Tome* moved effortlessly back and forth between the narrow question of how to relate divinity and humanity in Christ and the broader question of how human beings can be redeemed:

> Since . . . the characteristic properties of both natures and substances are kept intact and come together in one person, lowliness is taken on by majesty, weakness by power, mortality by eternity, and the nature which cannot be harmed is united to the nature which suffers, in order that the debt which our condition involves may be discharged. In this way, as our salvation requires, one and the same mediator between God and human beings, the human being who is Jesus Christ, can at one and the same time die in virtue of the one nature and, in virtue of the other, be incapable of death. That is why true God was born in the integral and complete nature of a true human being, entire in what belongs to him and entire in what belongs to us.[10]

By putting insights like this in a formula, Chalcedon preserved space for further thought on the person of Christ while it offered reassurance for the great work of salvation that this "one and only Son" performed.

There is, however, a second way in which Chalcedon marked an especially critical turning point in the history of Christian teaching. Although it telescopes much history to put it this way, Chalcedon may be said to have marked the successful translation of the Christian faith out of its Semitic milieu (where words and concepts were shaped primarily by the revelation of the Old Testament) into the Hellenistic milieu (where words and concepts were shaped primarily by traditions of Greek thought and Roman might). Part of the great series of convulsions that stretched from before Arius's heresy through the time of Chalcedon was a problem of translation in the narrow sense. How could the church find ways of translating words from the Bible (written in Hebrew, Aramaic, and a simplified Koine Greek heavily under Semitic influence) into Latin and more formal Greek? Immense confusion, for instance, reigned for nearly a century over the question of whether the Greek terms *ousia* and *hypostasis* should be used for the essential "God-ness" shared by the Father and the Son, or whether they should refer to the particular "God-ness" embodied in Father, Son, and Spirit more distinctly. Added consternation came as Latin-speaking Westerners tried to find equivalent expressions in their language both for these Greek terms (which were mainstays in the history of Greek philosophy) and the terms of Scripture. A standard grid of translation

---

10. Norris, *The Christological Controversy*, 148.

Already well established by the fourth century, as illustrated in this Egyptian copy of the Book of Acts, was the mixture of text and illustration that has continued in Bibles through the centuries.

The Pierpont Morgan Library, New York.
G.67,f.107v,f.110r.

was finally agreed upon in 362 at a council in Alexandria, so that the Greek *ousia* would equal the Latin *substantia* (the generic God-ness), and the Greek *hypostasis* would equal the Latin *persona* (the specific manifestation of God-ness). Only with that clarification having been made could the Nicene formula be finalized. And that finalization set the stage for the road to Chalcedon.

Chalcedon testified to the success of translation at an even more profound level than these technical issues, complicated and important as they were. Again to simplify, Chalcedon marks a final, triumphant stage in a process whose beginnings can be glimpsed in the New Testament. In Acts 11:20, a passage helpfully highlighted by the work of the Scottish missiologist Andrew Walls, we read that "some . . . men from Cyprus and Cyrene . . . went to Antioch and began to speak to Greeks also, telling them the good news about the Lord Jesus."[11] It is not Jesus the *Christ* (or Messiah) whom these unnamed Jewish Christians proclaim to the Greeks in Antioch, for that would have been to ask non-Jews to become experts in the history of Hebrew religion before they could understand what it meant to acknowledge Jesus as the promised Messiah. Rather, to Greeks who did not know the Hebrew Scriptures, the proclamation is of Jesus as *Lord*, the one from God who will rule over all nations and all other rulers. In the broader sense of translation, Chalcedon represents the completion of the work begun by those unnamed "men from Cyprus and Cyrene" who carried the gospel across the border from a Jewish conceptual world to a Hellenistic conceptual world.

11. Andrew F. Walls, *The Missionary Movement in Christian History: Studies in the Transmission of Faith* (Maryknoll, N.Y.: Orbis, 1996), 52.

For the later history of Christianity—which would one day spread into myriads of cultures far removed from Middle Eastern Judaism and Mediterranean Hellenism—what happened at Chalcedon could not have been more important. Chalcedon proved that the heart of the gospel message could be preserved, even when that message was put into a new conceptual language. The words *ousia, hypostasis, substantia,* and *persona* do not appear in Scripture as technical terms, and the Bible has very little direct connection to the conceptual worlds in which these terms arose and acquired their own intellectual history. Yet Chalcedon showed that the message of God becoming incarnate to effect the salvation of his people was a message that could be heard distinctly, adequately, and powerfully in precisely these extrascriptural terms and within that non-Judaic intellectual milieu.

For the history of Christian doctrine, Chalcedon was thus vitally important in two ways. It represented a wise, careful, and balanced restatement of scriptural revelation. And it also represented successfully the translation of biblical revelation into another conceptual language. Chalcedon was not Pentecost, but because its work faithfully synthesized scriptural history, the Hellenistic world could now hear "the wonders of God" in its own tongue. Because the work of Chalcedon faithfully *translated* scriptural teaching, the Hellenistic world could now *express* the wonders of God in its own conceptual language. Both synthesis and translation would need to happen again and again and again.

The Intellectual and Cultural Importance of Chalcedon

Chalcedon marked a critical turning point for one more reason. The counterbalancing mistakes that led to Chalcedon represented more than just narrow doctrinal errors. When taken to an extreme, Alexandrian, Word-flesh Christology greatly undercut confidence in the full humanity of Christ. This kind of error has reappeared continually in the church's history as a tendency to devalue all that the full humanity of Christ entails: that is, the realms of the body, flesh, nature, the natural, ordinary day-to-day life, regular human activity, even suffering and pain. Extreme Alexandrian theology was so dominated by the divine Logos as to question the value of anything in the world. The great significance of Chalcedon for later church history was to condemn this extreme, to pull back from superspiritual neglect of the world.

By contrast, Antiochene, Word-man Christology, when taken to an extreme, greatly subverted the organic connection between the divine and the human. This kind of error has also reappeared constantly in the church's history as a tendency to divide life into sacred bits and secular

natural vs spiritual

bits, to keep the things of God and the things of the world hermetically sealed off from one another. Extreme forms of Antiochene Christology have thus had a secularizing effect by failing to recognize the organic connections between life in this world (which Jesus honored by becoming a part of it) and life in God (which Jesus integrated with life in this world). The great significance of Chalcedon for later history was to restrain such a division, to pull back from a fragmented approach to earthly life.

Chalcedon's insistence on both the integrity of Christ's person and the duality of his natures established a tremendously important guide for Christian life in the world. By extension, the definition demands both serious attention to worldly existence (the Antiochene stress on the full humanity of Christ) as well as a full spirituality as believers enter the world (the Alexandrian stress on the integrity of Christ's person). The genius of Chalcedon was to draw these perspectives together and to insist that neither tendency outweigh the other.

In the end, however, the Definition of Chalcedon retains its momentous significance not simply because it is such a skillful, well-balanced statement. Rather, it remains one of the great turning-point documents of church history because the statement faithfully represents the reality about which it speaks. Christians can live in the world and also for the glory of God—the fact of one "person" can coexist with the fact of two "natures"—because it really happened, as the apostle John wrote, that "the Word became flesh and made his dwelling among us" (John 1:14).

Amid the swirl of doctrinal controversy, ordinary Christians continued to work through issues of daily existence in the context of worship and prayer. The ancient Christians inscribed their prayers not only on papyrus and pottery but also in stone. Increasing in number after the fourth century, prayers cut in stone can be found on houses, churches, and tombs, especially in Egypt. In contrast to pagan inscriptions of the same era, the Christian prayers reflect a hope that overcomes sorrow. The following prayer comes from a fifth-century Egyptian stone epitaph that characteristically draws on Scripture and church liturgy. Its depiction of paradise as a luxuriant garden with refreshing waters would have been particularly inviting in the hot, desert regions of the Near East:

> O God, give him rest with the devout and the just
> in the place where green things grow

and refreshment is and water,
the delightful garden
where pain and grief and sighing
are unknown.
Holy, holy, holy Lord God, Sabaoth;
heaven and earth are full of your holy glory.[12]

Further Reading

Cullmann, Oscar. *The Christology of the New Testament.* Philadelphia: West-minster, 1959.

Jalland, Trevor. *The Life and Times of St. Leo the Great.* New York: Macmillan, 1941.

Kelly, J. N. D. *Early Christian Doctrines.* 5th ed. San Francisco: Harper & Row, 1978.

Norris, Richard A., Jr., trans. and ed. *The Christological Controversy.* Philadelphia: Fortress, 1980.

Pelikan, Jaroslav. *Mary through the Centuries.* New Haven: Yale University Press, 1996.

Schaff, Philip, ed. *The Creeds of Christendom.* 6th ed. 3 vols. New York: Harper, 1919. Reprint, Grand Rapids: Baker, 1990.

Sellers, R. V. *The Council of Chalcedon: A Historical and Doctrinal Survey.* London: SPCK, 1953.

Women in the Early Church [*Christian History,* no. 17]. 1988.

12. A. Hamman, ed., *Early Christian Prayers* (Chicago: Henry Regnery, 1961), 84.

4

The Monastic Rescue of the Church: Benedict's Rule (530)

*S*t. Benedict wrote his Rule in the first part of the sixth century in order to guide monks to holiness and correct the monastic abuses of his day. Five centuries later, Bernard of Clairvaux (1090–1153) was called to reform the Benedictine monasteries that had lapsed into worldliness. Contemporary issues propelled Bernard, a mystic passionately devoted to God, into playing a major role in politics and ecclesiastical renewal. A renowned preacher and writer, Bernard was so popular that many of the best medieval Latin hymns were ascribed to him, even though actual authorship is uncertain.

One of these hymns, "O Sacred Head, Now Wounded," exemplifies some of the finest aspects of continuity in the tradition of Christian devotion. The original Latin version dates from the twelfth century. The Lutheran hymnist Paul Gerhardt translated it into German in the seventeenth century, and in the next century Johann Sebastian Bach arranged it for his *Passion Chorale.* Then in the nineteenth century the Presbyterian scholar and pastor James W. Alexander translated it into English. The lyrics present a stirring contemplation of God's love displayed on the cross and the loving response that Christ's suffering calls forth, themes that were always prominent when monasticism was at its best.

> *O sacred Head, now wounded,*
> *With grief and shame weighed down;*
> *Now scornfully surrounded*
> *With thorns Thine only crown:*
> *How pale Thou art with anguish,*

With sore abuse and scorn!
How does that visage languish
Which once was bright as morn!

What Thou, my Lord, has suffered
Was all for sinners' gain;
Mine, mine was the transgression,
But Thine the deadly pain.
Lo, here I fall, my Savior!
'Tis I deserve Thy place;
Look on me with Thy favor,
Vouchsafe to me Thy grace.

What language shall I borrow
To thank Thee, dearest Friend,
For this Thy dying sorrow,
Thy pity without end?
O make me Thine forever;
And should I fainting be,
Lord, let me never, never
Outlive my love to Thee.[1]

The rise of monasticism was, after Christ's commission to his disciples, the most important—and in many ways the most beneficial—institutional event in the history of Christianity. For over a millennium, in the centuries between the reign of Constantine and the Protestant Reformation, almost everything in the church that approached the highest, noblest, and truest ideals of the gospel was done either by those who had chosen the monastic way or by those who had been inspired in their Christian life by the monks. If we remember that "the monastic way" included all who "separated" from the world and followed a "rule" of discipline—women as well as men—we can say much the same for the more recent centuries of the church's history. The monastic contribution to that which is "true, noble, right, pure, lovely, and admirable" (Phil. 4:8) may have shrunk in visibility over the past few

1. Robert K. Brown and Mark R. Norton, eds., *The One Year Book of Hymns* (Wheaton, Ill.: Tyndale, 1995), entry for March 28.

centuries, but it still remains high. At the end of the twentieth century, it is only necessary to mention Mother Teresa of Calcutta, founder of the Order of the Missionaries of Charity, to make the point.

Even a Protestant who thinks monasticism is flawed in ways that will be suggested at the end of this chapter can make such claims on its behalf with a clear conscience. Protestantism itself, we may well remember, began with the monastic experiences of Martin Luther. Once Luther, John Calvin, Thomas Cranmer, Menno Simons, and other leaders of the Reformation concluded it was necessary to break from the Roman Catholic Church, they drew support for their theology first from Scripture, but then immediately from the writings of monks. Luther and Calvin, especially, returned repeatedly to the work of Augustine (354–430), who had been not only a learned theologian, busy bishop, and energetic polemicist but also the founder of a monastic order. In fact, Luther began his biblical study and theological reflections as an *Augustinian* monk.

The breadth and depth of monastic influence in the church can be sketched quickly by observing the lineage of attitudes and actions that have been approved by almost all Christians everywhere. If we read the Scripture in our native languages, we benefit from a tradition of biblical translation inspired by the monk Jerome (ca. 342–420). If we sing together the praises of Father, Son, and Holy Spirit, we follow where the hymn-writing monks Gregory (ca. 540–604) and Bernard of Clairvaux led the way. If we pursue theology, we inevitably find ourselves indebted to the monks Augustine and Thomas Aquinas (ca. 1225–74). If we pray for the success of Christian missions, we ask for blessing upon enterprises pioneered by the monks Patrick (ca. 390–ca. 460), Boniface (680–754), Cyril (826–69) and his brother Methodius (ca. 815–85), and Raymond Lull (ca. 1233–ca. 1315). If we are interested in the past record of Christianity in English-speaking areas of the world, we cultivate a historical concern begun by a monk, the Venerable Bede (ca. 673–735). If we glory in the goodness that God imparted to the created world, we follow where the friar Francis of Assisi (1181/82–1226) blazed the trail. Monasticism was never a perfect answer to the question of how to live the Christian life. Its impact, nonetheless, cannot be underestimated. And that impact has been largely for the good.

It is difficult to specify a single turning point at which monasticism began to influence the church decisively.[2] For the most important turn-

---

2. For the account that follows, I draw especially on W. H. C. Frend, *The Rise of Christianity* (Philadelphia: Fortress, 1984); F. F. Bruce, *The Spreading Flame: The Rise and Progress of Christianity from Its First Beginnings to the Conversion of the English* (Grand Rapids: Eerdmans, 1958); and Christopher Dawson, *The Foundation of Christendom* (New York: Sheed & Ward, 1967).

ing point in the development of monasticism, there are in fact a number
of prime candidates. It could be the first recorded monk, Antony, who
left his family's farm in Egypt sometime around 270 to go out by himself
to the edge of the desert in order to find God. It might be his fellow Egyptian Pachomius, who around 320 established the first cenobitic (or communal) monastery under the guidance of a "rule" (or set of regulations)
for a life of prayer. It could be Basil of Caesarea, one of the Cappadocian
Fathers, who did so much to define the Holy Spirit as a full member of
the Trinity. About 370 Basil wrote a rule for the monasteries under his
care in Cappadocia (modern eastern-central Turkey) that serves to this
day as the basic guide for monastic life in the Orthodox Church. Athanasius, the great fourth-century defender of Christ's divinity, could be singled out as a key figure in the rise of monasticism, since his biography of
Antony both identified monasticism solidly with doctrinal orthodoxy
and greatly expanded knowledge of monastic ways in both East and
West. It could also be Martin of Tours, who in 360 founded the first monastery in what is now France, and so began the momentous career of monasticism as the primary bearer of Christianity into northern Europe. Or
it could be John Cassian, who, living in the south of France early in the
fifth century, wrote an influential book that distilled much of the monastic wisdom of the East for dissemination in the West.

But as important as all these and many other early influences were
for the emergence of monasticism, it is almost certainly Benedict of
Nursia (in Italy) who gave the most decisive, and most beneficial, shape
to monasticism. It is to Benedict and his famous Rule that the Christian
church owes a series of invaluable gifts—for regulating a zealous spirit
that had often bordered on fanaticism; for curbing a practice of asceticism that easily slid over into Gnosticism, Docetism, or worse;* for
preserving the centrality of Scripture in a movement that made much
of inner spiritual illumination; for recalling prayer to the heart of the
Christian life; for linking exalted religious experience with the basic realities of work, study, eating, and sleeping; and, not least, for providing
an ideal of monastic life in which reformers have found inspiration and
encouragement for fifteen hundred years.

---

*Gnosticism and Docetism are related heresies that regard the physical world as in-
ferior to the purely spiritual. The word "docetism" comes from the Greek *dokeō*,
"seem"; Docetists believed that Jesus was a spiritual being who only *seemed* to be human. This devaluing of the human body sometimes led to ascetic extremes, which
Benedict sought to curb. For example, hearing that a certain hermit had chained himself in his cave, the saint sent him this message: "If you are indeed a servant of God, do
not chain yourself with chains of iron. But rather, let Christ be the chain that binds
you." Quoted in Esther de Waal, *Seeking God: The Way of St. Benedict* (Collegeville,
Minn.: Liturgical, 1984), 22–23.

One of the many memorials
of Benedict and his work is
this commemorative stamp
from France.

Tony Lane

The magnitude of Benedict's significance in the history of Christianity is not, however, matched by knowledge of his life. About forty years after his death (and the precise year of death is not even known), Pope Gregory I wrote a series of dialogues on noteworthy believers of previous eras; his account of Benedict contains almost all the solid biographical information we have about him.

Benedict (ca. 480–ca. 550) was educated at Rome, where he found the prevailing standards so degenerate that he abandoned the city for a life of solitary religious devotion at Subiaco. Because of his growing reputation for spiritual insight, a number of others gathered around him. Eventually Benedict is said to have founded twelve separate monasteries with twelve monks each, but it is also reported that in these early years he was the object of jealous attacks by some who had originally come out to seek the life of prayer with him. Sometime around 525 Benedict moved south of Rome to Monte Cassino, where he established a monastery that exists to this day.[†] It was probably after arriving at Monte Cassino and as part of an effort to reform the general practice of monasticism that Benedict composed his *regula*. This Rule soon won nearly universal approval as providing the shape for monas-

---

[†]Monte Cassino, the "cradle of the Benedictine Order," has been destroyed and rebuilt several times, the most recent destruction coming in World War II when Allied commanders bombed the monastery in the mistaken belief that it was held by the Germans.

ticism in the West. Its only serious rival was the Celtic monasticism inspired by St. Patrick in the fifth century and spread by St. Columba (ca. 521–97) from a famous monastery on the Isle of Iona off the coast of Scotland. Benedict's Rule was read also with appreciation in the East; it became the norm for tens of thousands of new monastic communities in Europe, and it served as an inspiration for the slightly altered ideals that created the Mendicant Orders (or "friars") in the twelfth and thirteenth centuries. Never in the recorded history of Christianity has a person whose own life remains so obscure done a deed with greater public consequences.

In order to gain a better sense of how important Benedict's Rule was in shaping the course of monasticism, and also how pivotal monasticism became in shaping the course of Christianity, it is necessary to probe a little more deeply into the motives that led to the rise of monasticism as an institution. That exercise will, in turn, make it possible to see why Benedict and his Rule were so critical to the spread of monasticism throughout the Middle Ages, and it also will put us in a position to make an evaluation of the gifts (and problems) that monasticism bequeathed to the church.

Motives and Circumstances

Conditions in the fourth and fifth centuries provided powerful motivations for the spread of monasticism. The persecutions under Decius in the mid-third century and under Diocletian in the early fourth century took place at the same time that economic difficulties disoriented traditional patterns of life throughout many parts of the Roman Empire, especially Egypt. The first monks, like Antony, who left Egyptian cities for the desert, were thus departing from a world where both spiritual and secular conditions lay in disarray.

Much more important for the spread of monasticism, however, was reaction to the church's greatest success. With the rise of the Constantinian church–state establishment, the life of a Christian "professional" offered considerable potential for worldly preferment. Although intraecclesiastical strife and strenuous differences of opinions with the emperors could make life precarious for bishops and priests, service in the church after Constantine could also offer stability, access to power, and a reasonable opportunity for wealth. Monasticism was a response, often inarticulate, that reflected spiritual concern about the church's success. The self-denial and privations of the monks, although a result now of self-imposed decisions, were a way of recovering the ideals of martyrdom. To be sure, the monastic effort to seek out an existence of living martyrdom threatened to create a two-tiered picture of Christianity. Soon monks, or the "athletes of God," seemed to be pursuing the true Christian faith, while ordinary people in ordinary human circumstances were consigned to a subordinate spiritual status. Yet even with the dangers posed by such a division (monks thinking of their spirituality more highly than they ought, ordinary people thinking too little of the spirituality within their daily life), the monastic response to the Constantinian situation proved effective. In order to save critical Christian ideals such as self-sacrifice and humility, as well as to promote Christian disciplines like prayer and study of the Scriptures, the monks became the conscience of Christendom.

Ironically, however, the monastic willingness to forsake all to follow only Christ eventually bequeathed its own form of worldly reward. Monks gave up the prospect of economic gain and the practices of married life, but they received in return considerable respect and at least some anchorage in turbulent times. It is probably not a coincidence that Antony began monastic practice shortly after the disruptive reign of Decius, or that Benedict's Rule became so popular immediately after the final collapse of the Roman Empire in the West (the last Roman emperor was expelled from Italy in 476, less than a decade before Benedict's birth). Monasticism did not hold out prospects of wealth or sensual enjoyment, but it did offer the western Mediterranean world a hope of stable Christian community at times of severe social disorder.

If the growth of monasticism depended upon general conditions in the Roman-Christian world, it also drew on several important strands of spiritual, theological, and biblical tradition. What could be called the inner motivations of monasticism already enjoyed a vigorous heritage by the fourth and fifth centuries.

The most important, and most enduring, of these inner motives was commitment to the Scriptures. Antony, the first of the monks, had gone into the desert after hearing Matthew 19:21 read during a Sunday service ("If you want to be perfect, go, sell your possessions and give to the poor, and you will have treasure in heaven. Then come, follow me"). Antony had only recently received a substantial inheritance of land from his parents. In these circumstances, the text so captured his attention that he went out and did exactly as the Gospel enjoined.

In addition, the monks returned repeatedly to injunctions and models of living especially drawn from the New Testament. Paul's discussion of marriage from 1 Corinthians 7, for example, exerted a direct impact ("Now to the unmarried and the widows I say: It is good for them to stay unmarried, as I am"). John the Baptist's life in the desert as an unmarried seeker for God loomed just as large, but not as large as the example of Jesus, who forsook family and wealth to do his Father's bidding and who often went into the wilderness to pray. The ideal was to seek God single-mindedly—to pray without ceasing (1 Thess. 5:17). Monks believed this effort would be aided by removing worldly distractions. The life of prayer, in turn, would transform them into a charitable and hospitable people.

Immersion in Scripture remained a permanent characteristic. Even if there came periods in monastic history when the use of Scripture grew perfunctory, preoccupation with the Bible was constant. Most early records of cenobitic monasticism in Egypt contain the stipulation that would-be novices memorize twenty psalms, two epistles, or a biblical passage of comparable length as a requirement to enter the monastery. Similarly, Benedict's Rule is thickly studded with biblical quotations, and injunctions to constant reading (in Scripture and other Christian literature) make up a major part of his concern. Even in periods of modern church history when Protestants and Catholics had nothing good to say about each other, it is striking that Protestants continued to remember that they owed a great debt to the monastic houses that had preserved, copied, and studied the Scriptures throughout the Middle Ages. Monasticism, in brief, was built upon a foundation of Scripture.

At the same time, the ascetic drift of early Christian spirituality strongly influenced the way in which Scripture was applied in the formation of monasticism. In the West, where practical solutions were more important than theological speculation, the standard view of reconciliation with God exerted considerable influence on how the Bible was read. That view was being systematized by Tertullian at the end of the second century in a way that favored what would later emerge as monastic spirituality. Tertullian held that the one who sought reconciliation needed to pass through distinct stages: penitence (or active sorrow for sin), mortification (deadening of the flesh through ascetic practices), merit (securing of the right to be rewarded by God), and satisfaction (reparation by alms, fasting, or other good works for the damage done to God's holiness). These stages were all dependent upon God's grace displayed by Christ on the cross, but they had the effect of making conscientious human effort quite important. In terms growing from Tertullian's formulations, monasticism represented serious, systematic, and full-time attention to the divine requirements for reconciliation.

Eastern asceticism had other sources. During the third century, Clement and Origen had put Neoplatonic forms of thought to use in the church. Their foundational Christian convictions made such Greek thought relatively safe for use by believers, but the Neoplatonic tendency to treat the created realm as only a shadow of ultimate realities—

which were located beyond the material realm—nonetheless remained
to influence Christianity. Such teachings promoted a spirituality that
tended to devalue ordinary physical existence and stress the purely
spiritual.

This Neoplatonic influence was strongest in the East, but it occurred
in the West as well. Augustine's path-breaking autobiography, the *Confessions* (written 397–401), described in detail his passage through various philosophical and religious stages on the journey to Christian
faith. Among those stages were a period of fascination with Platonism
(with its hierarchy of forms) and another with Manichaeanism (with its
conception of a universe sharply divided between forces of good and
evil). Augustine's conversion to Christianity meant his liberation from
the toils of these religious systems, but it did not mean that their influence was entirely effaced. One of his characteristic metaphors for serious Christian living remained a journey upward out of the materiality
of day-to-day life into realms of pure spirituality. Thus, in the *Confessions*, Augustine's Christian evaluation of his own struggle with sin was
couched in language drawn from Neoplatonic thought: for example,
"But I did not stay in the enjoyment of my God; I was swept away to
you by your own beauty, and then I was torn away from you by my own
weight and fell back groaning toward these lower things. Carnal habit
was this weight."[3]

These varied influences in the world of early Christianity—whether
Neoplatonic, Platonic, or Manichaean—all moved in the same direction. They tended to view the ideal Christian life as passing from the ordinary, the material, and the terrestrial into the extraordinary, the spiritual, and the celestial. When combined with the Scriptures' repeated
injunctions to, for example, "set your hearts on things above" (Col. 3:1)
or to avoid worry "about your body, what you will wear" (Matt. 6:25
and Luke 12:22), these influences exerted a powerful motive for monasticism. By definition, the monastic way was designed precisely to allow
creatures of the earth to rise toward a purer spirituality.

The particular monastic renunciation of sexual practice flowed from
this more general tendency. Paul's injunction to remain unmarried, if
possible, was the spark, but much of the shape for the monastic ideal
of chastity was provided by the dualism—especially the dualism between spirit and matter—so prevalent in Greek thought. The physical
world, as perceived by many early theologians, was the realm in which
Satan exerted his greatest influence. Regulating that world as carefully

---

3. *The Confessions of St. Augustine,* trans. Rex Warner (New York: New American Library, 1963), 153.

as possible was a way of forsaking the ruler of this present darkness for the Lord of Light.

This perception of the world as an active, ever-tumultuous scene of spiritual combat also fueled the monastic surge. Especially in the Egypt of early monasticism, but also throughout most of the early church, believers were deeply fascinated by demons, angels, and conflict between spiritual forces in high places. The way in which monasticism deployed this largely biblical picture of the world was that monks, as full-time ascetics, were widely considered to be the only ones spiritually fit enough to contribute directly in that struggle. Early accounts of Antony featured his wrestling with demons and the ungodly passions they incited. Such emphases remained a potent spur to monasticism throughout its earliest centuries.

The story of Simeon Stylites (ca. 390–459) shows clearly how different the thought processes of early Christians could be from our own. Simeon, who lived out his life in the general vicinity of Antioch in Syria, became an anchorite (or solitary monk) in early adulthood. At some later stage he departed into a desert region where he began building a pillar as his place of abode. For the last decades of his life, he remained perpetually on this pillar, which he continued to construct until it reached a great height. Simeon obviously felt that this act of self-isolation allowed him to concentrate solely on spiritual realities and to prepare him for taking an active part in the supernatural warfare that enveloped the earth. Although moderns might consider Simeon more of an eccentric than a saint, it is important to realize why a relatively full account of Simeon has come down in history. His life was well recorded for the simple fact that Simeon's contemporaries found him an immensely attractive figure. A steady stream of visitors presented itself to the pillar. Simeon's direct influence led to conversions and to breakthroughs where warring church factions were reconciled. It is even reported that Simeon's commendation of the Chalcedon Definition greatly assisted its acceptance in his region. Only when we realize how the account of a sunburned ascetic passing messages (and life's meager necessities) up-and-down in a bucket from a lofty pillar could have struck such a responsive chord will we begin to understand why monasticism proved so satisfying to so many earnest Christians and exerted such a powerful force throughout the whole Christian world.

One of the difficulties in presenting early monasticism is that the record is so varied. For every extreme ascetic like Simeon, many revered figures existed who were known for gentleness, moderation, wisdom, and extraordinary hospitality displayed toward the outcast and fallen. A danger in studying monasticism is that this equally significant strain can be overshadowed by the more bizarre, even if many desert fathers discouraged extreme practices. In general, what made the early monks so compelling was their reputation as great people of prayer.

Monasticism grew, therefore, not only because it was a form of Christian organization and a collection of Christian ideals attractive during the time of transition to the public establishment of the church. Even more important for the growth of monasticism was its connection to some of the most basic theological tendencies and spiritual instincts of early Christian history. That combination of general conditions and inner spiritual propulsion, especially when it produced a remarkable array of spiritual and practical services, helps explain how monasticism emerged as such a potent force and why it remained so central for such a long stretch of the church's history.

Benedict and His Rule

The Rule of Benedict played a decisive role in the history of monasticism, and therefore in the history of Christianity, because it combined the zeal of earlier monastic pioneers with a carefully balanced concern for stability. Benedict's Rule is famous for codifying vows of obedience, stability, and *conversatio morum* (continual conversion) which led on to the more general vows of poverty, chastity, and obedience. But it was equally noteworthy for its far-sighted concern for what it would take to keep individual monks and entire monastic communities on an even keel. The Rule, though a relatively long document of some eighty large-print pages in Timothy Fry's English edition, was also intentionally flexible. It suggested how its own guidelines could be adapted to local conditions defined by different stages of the ecclesiastical year, different climates, different quantities of available food and drink depending on the monks' health, age, and even degree of spiritual maturity.

Benedict's Rule was not a manual for slackers. It enshrined, for example, the wisdom of the first Christian centuries about higher spirituality in sternly forbidding personal possessions: "Above all, this evil practice [of private ownership] must be uprooted and removed from the monastery. We mean that without an order from the abbot [the leader], no one may presume to give, receive or retain anything as his own, nothing at all."[4] The Rule also made it clear that even younger members were to join the search for perfection. It made provisions for older monks to sleep in the same rooms with the younger so that, when the bell was rung for prayers at midnight, all might "rise without delay

4. *The Rule of St. Benedict in English*, ed. Timothy Fry, O.S.B. (Collegeville, Minn.: Liturgical, 1981), 56. Subsequent page references in the text are to this edition.

Almost as early as monasticism for men came separate religious communities for women; this illustration from fifteenth-century France features passages from Scripture, including Psalm 51:15, "O Lord, open thou my lips, and my mouth will show forth thy praise."

The Walters Art Gallery, Baltimore

when the signal is given; each will hasten to arrive at the Work of God before the others, yet with all dignity and decorum" (49). The reason for mixing old and young together was so that "on arising for the Work of God," they might "quietly encourage each other, for the sleepy like to make excuses" (49).

If the Rule was stern, however, it was stern for clear theological reasons. Many of the Rule's most important provisions spelled out the theological justifications for important monastic practices, for example, the critical mandate to work: "Idleness is enemy of the soul. Therefore, the brothers should have specified periods for manual labor as well as for prayerful reading" (69). Benedict himself probably had more the "manual labor" in mind as a standard for work than the "prayerful reading," but his grouping of physical and mental labor together opened the way to the monks' great contribution to learning that would be sustained almost from the first.

The Rule is marked throughout by a concentration on the spiritual realities that monasteries existed to embody. At the foundation was commitment to the practice of prayer: "Whenever we want to ask some favor of a powerful man, we do it humbly and respectfully, for fear of presumption. How much more important, then, to lay our petitions before the Lord God of all things with the utmost humility and sincere devotion. We must know that God regards our purity of heart and tears of compunction, not our many words. Prayer should therefore be short

St. Benedict on Choosing an Abbot

Benedict's care in setting out conditions for selecting the head of a monastery reflect many of the characteristics of his entire Rule:

In choosing an abbot, the guiding principle should always be that the man placed in office be the one selected either by the whole community acting unanimously in the fear of God, or by some part of the community, no matter how small, which possesses sounder judgment. Goodness of life and wisdom in teaching must be the criteria for choosing the one to be made abbot, even if he is the last in community rank. . . .

Once in office, the abbot must keep constantly in mind the nature of the burden he has received, and remember to whom he will have to give an account of his stewardship [Luke 16:2]. Let him recognize that his goal must be profit for the monks, not preeminence for himself. He ought, therefore, to be learned in divine law, so that he has a treasury of knowledge from which he can bring out what is new and what is old [Matt. 13:52]. He must be chaste, temperate and merciful. He should always let mercy triumph over judgment [James 2:13] so that he too may win mercy. He must hate faults but love the brothers. When he must punish them, he should use prudence and avoid extremes; otherwise, by rubbing too hard to remove the rust, he may break the vessel. He is to distrust his own frailty and remember not to crush the bruised reed [Isa. 42:3]. . . . Let him strive to be loved rather than feared.

Excitable, anxious, extreme, obstinate, jealous or oversuspicious he must not be. . . . Instead, he must show forethought and consideration in his orders, and whether the task he assigns concerns God or the world, he should be discerning and moderate. . . . Therefore . . . he must so arrange everything that the strong have something to yearn for and the weak nothing to run from.

He must, above all, keep this Rule in every particular.[1]

and pure" (48). The practice of prayer, moreover, was to mold a life of prayerfulness: "The life of a monk ought to be a continuous Lent. . . . This we can do in a fitting manner by refusing to indulge evil habits and by devoting ourselves to prayer with tears, to reading, to compunction of heart and self-denial" (71).

A life of prayer, however, was not to be artificially divorced from a life of service. It is doubtful that Benedict could have foreseen the myriad activities of practical godliness that later monks pursued who followed his Rule, but aspects of the Rule provided a basis for those later developments. Injunctions, for example, to care for strangers and for the sick contained the seeds for significant future charitable work: "All guests . . . are to be welcomed as Christ, for he himself will say: 'I was a stranger and you welcomed me' [Matt. 25:35]" (73); and "Care of the sick must rank above and before all else, so that they may truly be served as Christ, for he said: 'I was sick and you visited me' [Matt. 25:36]" (59). From such beginnings would grow vast monastic enterprises attending to the body as well as to the soul.

The concluding words of the Rule speak for its entire character; they are calm, judicious, and God-centered, yet also filled with hope for progress, by the grace of God, in the disciplined Christian life: "Are you hastening toward your heavenly home? Then with Christ's help, keep this little rule that we have written for beginners. After that, you can set out for the loftier summits of the teaching and virtues we mentioned above, and under God's protection you will reach them" (95–96).

The ordinary daily round shaped by Benedict's rule varied by place, era, personality of the abbot, and many other factors. Especially the relationship of a monastery's abbot to the neighboring bishop (or bishops) became a major issue through much of the Middle Ages. When some monastic foundations grew large, and even prosperous, the reality of the abbot's power, who might preside over a whole chain of daughter monasteries, was often much greater than that of the local bishops. When such abbots fulfilled the ideals set out for their position in Benedict's Rule, it could be a boon to the church. But when they fell prey to avarice or power-mongering, such abbots could be a disaster for general church affairs and a snare for the ordinary monks.

For their part, the ordinary monks were usually not directly affected by the high politics involving abbots, bishops, and secular rulers. As a typical example, the Benedictine monastery of Durham in England was founded in 1083 through the cooperation of the archbishop of Canterbury, the king of England, the pope, and local church officials. A few centuries later, the daily round in summer of the monks at the Durham monastery looked like this: Up at six for prayers in the church, then a light breakfast, then work or reading. After nine o'clock a series of Masses and meetings were held in the monastic church. The afternoon saw an alternation of work and prayer, with supper at 6:00 P.M., followed by prayers and then an early bedtime. At midnight the monks arose for prayer again.[5] And so it went—*orare et laborare*—praying and

5. See Anne Boyd, *The Monks of Durham* (Cambridge: Cambridge University Press, 1975), 16–18.

Summer Timetable for the Benedictine Monks at Durham, England (14th Century)

The monk's daily life is organized around the *opus Dei,* or "work of God," gathering for communal worship seven times a day based on Psalm 119:164, "Seven times a day I praise you." The services include Psalms, hymns, and readings from Scripture.

Midnight	*Matins* in the church (about one hour)
	Then back to bed
6 A.M.	*Prime* in the church (about 1/2 hour)
	Breakfast
	Work or reading
9 A.M.	Chapter Mass in the church
10 A.M.	Chapter meeting in the chapter house
11 A.M.	High Mass in the church
12 noon	Dinner
	Then siesta
2 P.M.	*Nones* in the church (about 1/2 hour)
	Work
4 P.M.	Vespers in the church (about 1/2 hour)
	Work
6 P.M.	Supper
7 P.M.	*Compline,* the evening prayer, in the church (about 1/2 hour)
	Then to bed, later in summer than in winter

In winter, Matins was a few hours later, and other adjustments were made throughout the day.[2]

working, praying and working, throughout the passing of the seasons and the rolling of the years.

Well before the Benedictine monastery was established in Durham, monastic establishments for women had become commonplace throughout Europe. Early praise for virginity played a part in the growth of female monastic orders. Cyprian in the third century had called virgins the flower of the church; especially after the Virgin Mary became more prominent in the church's liturgy and theology after the fourth and fifth centuries, cenobitic life for celibate women became important as well. Throughout the Middle Ages, the monastic life provided one of the few venues in which women were allowed (and some-

Three Women Writers

From Hildegard of Bingen's vision of the Son of Man

[Your Creator] loves you exceedingly, for you are His creature; and He gives you the best of treasures, a vivid intelligence. He commands you in the words of His Law to profit from your intellect in good works, and grow rich in virtue, that He, the Good Giver, may thereby be clearly known. Hence you must think every hour about how to make so great a gift as useful to others as to yourself by works of justice, so that it will reflect the splendor of sanctity from you, and people will be inspired by your good example to praise and honor God.[3]

Hadewijch, from her poem "To Learn Mary's Humility"

The Father in the beginning
Kept his Son, Love,
Hidden in his bosom,
   Until Mary,
   With deep humility indeed,
In a mysterious way disclosed him to us.
Then the mountain flowed down into the deep valley,
And that valley flowed aloft to the height of the palace.
Then was the castle conquered
Over which long combat had taken place.[4]

Catherine of Siena, from a letter to Pope Gregory XI urging him to return the papacy from Avignon to Rome

Answer the summons of God! who is calling you to come, hold, and possess the place of the glorious shepherd St. Peter, whose vicar you are. Lift up the banner of the holy Cross. Come, that you may reform the Church with good shepherds, giving back to her the col–our of most ardent charity that she has lost; for so much blood has been sucked from her by wicked devourers that she is pale. But take heart, and come, Father! Do not make the servants of God wait, who are afflicted in longing.[5]

times even encouraged) to express publicly their grasp of the Christian faith. Thus, Hildegard of Bingen (1098–1179), founder and first abbess of the Benedictine community at Rupertsberg on the Rhine, was renowned for her mystical visions, but also for a remarkable set of writings on scientific, theological, and musical subjects as well as for discerning correspondence with kings, bishops, and leaders of other monastic institutions. The historian Caroline Walker Bynum has recently published a dramatic account of the way in which exceptional religious women in the thirteenth and fourteenth centuries won unusual hearing for their writings, dialogues, and prayers.[6] This recognition came about through widespread respect for their rigors in fasting and their experience of mystical union with Christ in the Eucharist. That respect was the vehicle for women like Hadewijch (writings from 1220–40), the first great poet in Flemish, and Catherine of Siena (ca. 1347–80), whose ministry included ecclesiastical and papal reform, to have the sort of impact in their day that the life of self-denial had won for Simeon Stylites in his day.

The pattern established by Benedict's Rule came to be applied widely and with great effect. For men and women, in all parts of Europe and beyond, through times of monastic flourishing and periods of monastic decay, it remained a beacon pointing back to the disciplined stability of a spiritual ideal and forward toward growth into eternal blessedness.

A Brief Outline of Important Monastic Developments in the Middle Ages

A sketch is not the best way to treat the complex history of monasticism during the European Middle Ages, but it may be enough to suggest the great importance of monasticism as sustaining and expanding the church in that era.

In the first instance, the missionary expansion of Christianity was unthinkable apart from the activity of monks. A fine survey of world missions by Stephen Neill, who himself served as a missionary in India, divided the missionary history of the Middle Ages into a five-hundred-year period (500–1000) in which the main task was to draw the barbarians into the Christian orbit and a succeeding five hundred years (1000–1500) in which the great task was to turn nominally Christian Europeans into genuine believers.[7] The key element in both of these gigantic efforts was monasticism.

In Neill's first phase, monks of several kinds did the pioneering work that was necessary to spread news of Christianity beyond the settled boundaries of the old Roman Empire northward, westward, and eastward into barbarian Europe. Celtic missionaries were pioneers, with Patrick's preaching in Ireland during the fifth century as the vanguard.

6. Caroline Walker Bynum, *Holy Feast and Holy Fast: The Religious Significance of Food to Medieval Women* (Berkeley: University of California Press, 1987).

7. Stephen Neill, *A History of Christian Missions* (New York: Penguin, 1964), 61–139.

Later missionaries from England and Scotland combined Celtic forti-
tude with Benedictine order in using monastic foundations as a way of
anchoring missionary outreach. Thus, Boniface (680–754), who is
often called the apostle of Germany, lived until age forty as a monk in
England but then traveled widely in what is now modern France, Germany, and the Low Countries in a series of pathbreaking mission tours.
One of the most enduring of his many legacies to northern European
Christianity was the founding of a Benedictine monastery at Fulda
(northeast of Frankfurt, Germany), which long remained a center for
further missionary outreach. Of the monk Boniface, the modern historian Christopher Dawson once wrote that he "had a deeper influence
on the history of Europe than any Englishman who has ever lived."[8]

Similarly, the missionary expansion of Christianity in eastern Europe came about in the ninth century through the monks Cyril and
Methodius, brothers by blood as well as in their vows. Their willingness
to translate the Bible and liturgical materials into Slavonic, the common language of the region around Great Moravia and Bohemia, now
part of the Czech Republic, was an innovation. It also sealed a bond between eastern Europe and the Orthodox Church that remains to this
day.

The missionary effectiveness of the monks usually depended as
much upon their plain virtues as upon more highly visible exertions in
preaching or teaching. For a monastery to be established in a pagan
area allowed the local population to see the application of Christianity
to daily existence, as monks tilled the soil, welcomed visitors, and carried out the offices of study and daily prayer. So arose the saying that
the monks civilized Europe *cruce, libro, et atro*—with cross, book, and
plow.

In the second half of the Middle Ages, much of the itinerant preaching that won nominally Christian Europeans to firmer Christian conviction came from the new orders of mendicant friars (monks on the
road, so to speak). The skillful preaching promoted by the Dominicans
and the practical godliness of the Franciscans both had a great impact.
As they ministered to those in immediate surroundings, the friars also
maintained earlier monastic concerns for mission beyond European
Christendom. Some of the writings of the Dominicans' greatest theologian, Thomas Aquinas (ca. 1225–74), for example, were designed for
use as apologetics to Muslims. For their part, Franciscans from the
time of St. Francis engaged actively in cross-cultural evangelism. A lay

8. Christopher Dawson, *The Making of Europe* (New York: Meridian, 1974 [orig.
1932]), 185.

Franciscan, Raymond Lull, was the first Westerner to devise and carry out a full-fledged mission strategy among Muslims. Lull followed his own advice that Europeans learn Arabic in order to communicate the gospel in Islamic regions. His life ended during a fourth mission trip to Muslims, when again his actions matched his words. "Missionaries will convert the world by preaching, but also through the shedding of tears and blood and with great labour, and through a bitter death."[9]

If virtually all cross-cultural proclamation of the gospel in the Middle Ages was done by monks and friars, so learning was virtually a monastic monopoly. Even in the time of Benedict, other monastic leaders had grasped the importance of preserving the critical documents of the Christian past. Cassiodorus of Rome (ca. 485–ca.

Christian History Archives

This stylized depiction from Asia Minor (now Turkey) gathers together many of the activities for which the monks were renowned.

580) retired from public life in 540 in order to found a monastery, the *Vivarium,* along Benedictine lines where secular as well as Christian writings could be saved. The Vivarium became a widely imitated model. In the seventh century, a revival of Benedictine monasticism in England at Lindisfarne, and then Jarrow, on the eastern coast, lay behind the immense contribution to biblical, theological, and historical learning from the Venerable Bede, who wrote the first history of the English church. Thomas Aquinas, it is worth remembering, not only authored the most important theological writings of the thirteenth century but also directed the critically important exercise of reintroducing Aristotle back into Europe. The way in which Aquinas carried out that exercise—with care to discriminate those aspects of Aristotle illuminat-

9. Neill, *History of Christian Missions,* 137.

ing Christian thinking from those needing to be rebutted or modified
in order to preserve Christian realities—left an example that has guided
Christian interaction with worldly wisdom to the present.

Service in Christ's name to the world, no less than concern for missions and learning, characterized monasticism. Benedict's admonition
to shelter the traveler and care for the sick blossomed into a wide variety of more general assistance. As one of many possible examples, in
1098 Robert of Molesme founded a monastery in Citeaux in eastern
France on the basis of the purified Rule of Benedict. The Cistercians (or
White Monks, because of their dress) that spread from Citeaux were
notable for their strict internal discipline and also for locating new
monasteries in wild, difficult locations. Cistercian efforts at surviving
in such places eventually led to considerable skill at draining swamps,
clearing forests, breeding cattle and sheep, and raising grains appropriate to their new locales. These skills, in turn, were eventually passed on
to surrounding communities, with beneficial results for all. Not much
more than a century after the founding of the Cistercians, St. Francis's
dedication to the poor, the sick, and the disabled propelled the Franciscan order into the forefront of humane service offered to the Europeans least able to help themselves.

Finally, the cycles of monastic renewal, decay, and renewal again
came more or less to define cycles of general revival and decline in the
church. Most notably, a period of striking ecclesiastical degeneration
in the ninth and tenth centuries was challenged, and then reversed,
through a series of administrative and spiritual reforms associated
with the founding of a monastery at Cluny in southern France in the
year 909. Then, as the effects of this monastic renewal began to be felt
over the next century and a half, even to the highest reaches of the Vatican, another set of monastic foundations sparked another surge of renewal. In the late eleventh century, just about the same time that Robert of Molesme established the monastery in Citeaux, Bruno of Cologne
founded a monastery at La Grande Chartreuse only a short distance to
the east, from which eventually came the Carthusian order. The
Carthusians combined the eremetic (individual cells) and the cenobitic
(common meals) in encouraging fresh devotion, contemplation, and
ascetic practices. The extraordinarily important work of Bernard of
Clairvaux in the twelfth century—as promoter of spirituality, author of
hymns, defender of orthodoxy, and assistant to popes—flowed out of
the spirit represented by the foundations at Citeaux and La Grande
Chartreuse. Again, the emergence of the Dominicans and Franciscans
in the thirteenth centuries sparked another cycle of renewal in the life,
thought, and service of the church.

This brief sketch of medieval monastic history should not be taken to mean that Christianity existed only within monastic circles, nor that monastic life always avoided decay and corruption. In fact, nonmonastic support, whether by donations from rich nobles or the willingness of poor families to send sons or daughters into the monastic life, played an important part in fueling the dynamism of monasticism. But when all necessary qualifications have been made, it remains true that the immense range, depth, and spiritual vigor of monasticism was the driving force of the Christian faith for a very long time indeed. In that sense, Benedict's pivotal role in the history of monasticism is more than enough to qualify the promulgation of his Rule as one of the great turning points in the history of Christianity.

A Few Words of Evaluation

Assessment of monasticism by a Protestant will naturally reflect more general Protestant principles. Thus, Protestant convictions about the centrality of justification by faith are bound to raise questions about whether monasticism encouraged harmful notions concerning the possibility of salvation by works. Clearly, moments of monastic renewal were inspired as thoroughly by trust in divine grace and dedication to God's unique holiness as any moments in the later history of Protestantism. But whether in ordinary monastic times the stress on what the monks had vowed to *do* did not obscure the foundational reality of God's grace is a question that any Christian might legitimately raise. To be sure, a Protestant cannot raise such a question with an entirely clear conscience, since the history of Protestantism reveals a bent toward legalism, in which various things that Protestants are or are not supposed to do or believe have become as much substitutes for the gospel of grace as any wayward monasticism. But questions regarding the centrality of grace are questions that monasticism will always hear especially from the Protestant family of Western Christians.

The most serious theological questions about monasticism are not, however, restricted to a Protestant provenance. They concern, rather, basic realities fundamental to all sorts of Christians. First, does ascetic privation of the body affect the true seat of sinfulness? Granting the Christian mandate to do all things "in a fitting and orderly way" (1 Cor. 14:40) and the reality of the bond between flesh and spirit underscored by the incarnation, it is possible to suggest that the bent of the heart, rather than the mere disposal of the body, is the key matter in godliness.

If so, a second question surfaces. Does the incarnation of Christ, with the full humanity affirmed by Chalcedon, justify withdrawal from the world in the way that monks practiced this withdrawal? The argument that it does not grows out of the New Testament observations that, unlike the disciples of John, Jesus' disciples came mingling with sinners as well as eating and drinking. It remains one of the most striking passages of the Gospels to read in John 2:11 that Jesus revealed "his glory" through his first miracle, at Cana of Galilee, by turning water into wine and thereby enabling a wedding feast to go on. If the Son of God did such a thing to promote joyful celebration with the body (though, of course, within limits of moderation) and joyful celebration of marriage (though, of course, it is not recorded that Jesus ever married), we have at least a hint that celibate, ascetic life is not intrinsically more godly than wedded, celebratory life.

A historian, however, even a Protestant historian of Reformed leanings who thinks that life in ordinary society and married sexuality are gifts of God to be highly prized, will raise questions about the theological justification of monasticism only with diffidence. What a historian will see in looking back is that, almost by themselves, monks for more than a thousand years sustained what was most noble and most Christ-centered in the church. A historian must also recognize that the holiness of monastic life—though never perfect, always in need of reform, and occasionally sunk in corruption—remains today, more than seventeen hundred years after Antony went into the desert, a guide and inspiration to large sections of the Christian church. That recognition will temper, though not eliminate entirely, theological questions about the implications of the incarnation and ideals of the Christian life. That recognition, whatever lingering qualms it may carry for a Protestant, is enough to certify the emergence of the monasticism represented by Benedict's Rule as not only a critical turning point in the history of Christianity but even, by God's grace, the very rescue of the church itself.

Although Benedict was recognized and revered early on as a major spiritual figure in the church, it was his Rule, and not his personal life, that was paramount. Gregory the Great wrote of Benedict that "if anyone would like to get the true picture of this man of God let him go to the Rule he has written, for the holy man could not have taught anything but what he had first lived."[10] The following twentieth-century collect (or short, concise prayer) ex-

10. Quoted in de Waal, *Seeking God,* 25.

presses Benedict's enduring influence on many, both lay and monastic, who look to the Rule as a guide to the disciplined Christian life.

> *Almighty God,*
> *by whose grace St. Benedict,*
> *kindled with the fire of your love,*
> *became a burning and a shining light in the church:*
> *inflame us with the same spirit*
> *of discipline and love,*
> *that we may walk before you*
> *as children of light;*
> *through Jesus Christ our Lord.*[11]

Further Reading

Athanasius. *The Life of St. Anthony the Great.* Willits, Calif.: Eastern Orthodox Books, 1987.

Cahill, Thomas. *How the Irish Saved Civilization.* New York: Anchor, 1995. Contains much on the activities of Celtic monks.

Dawson, Christopher. *The Formation of Christendom.* New York: Sheed & Ward, 1967.

de Waal, Esther. *Seeking God: The Way of St. Benedict.* Collegeville, Minn.: Liturgical, 1984.

Knowles, David. *The Benedictines.* New York: Macmillan, 1930.

———. *Saints and Scholars: Twenty-Five Medieval Portraits.* Cambridge: Cambridge University Press, 1962.

Leitzman, Hans. *A History of the Early Church.* Vol. 4; *The Era of the Church Fathers.* Trans. B. L. Woolf. New York: Charles Scribner's Sons, 1952.

The Rule of St. Benedict in English. Ed. Timothy Fry, O.S.B. Collegeville, Minn.: Liturgical, 1981.

The Sayings of the Desert Fathers: The Alphabetical Collection. Rev. ed. Trans. Benedicta Ward, S.L.G. Kalamazoo, Mich.: Cistercian Publications, 1984.

11. From the *Alternative Service Book,* quoted in ibid.

5

The Culmination of Christendom: The Coronation of Charlemagne (800)

Theodulf of Orléans knew about the pomp and honor accorded to kings. Exiled from his homeland of Spain possibly because of invasion by the Islamic Moors, he became a favored member of Charlemagne's court and in 800 was appointed archbishop of Orléans by the future Holy Roman emperor. Theodulf also knew how fortune and favor can suddenly turn, how one can plummet abruptly from public acclamation to rejection and condemnation. In 817 he was accused of conspiring in a rebellion against Louis the Pious (Charlemagne's son and successor), divested of his office, and thrown into prison, where he wrote this hymn. A familiar Palm Sunday processional, it honors another who was by turns praised and vilified and who, by his resurrection and ascension, was ultimately vindicated as the one true King.

All glory, laud, and honor
To thee, Redeemer, King,
To whom the lips of children
Made sweet hosannas ring.
Thou art the King of Israel,
Thou David's royal Son,
Who in the Lord's name comest,
The King and blessed One!

The people of the Hebrews
With palms before thee went;

Our praise and prayer and anthems
Before thee we present:
To thee, before thy passion,
They sang their hymns of praise;
To thee, now high exalted,
Our melody we raise.

Thou didst accept their praises;
Accept the prayers we bring,
Who in all good delightest,
Thou good and gracious King!
All glory, laud, and honor
To thee, Redeemer, King,
To whom the lips of children
Made sweet hosannas ring![1]

———————— ❧ ————————

By the year 800, celebration of December 25 as the birth of Christ was a well established practice. Also well-established by that time was the mixture of Christian content and pagan festivity that has characterized Christmas Day in the West from at least the fifth century through the present. Although Christian rites like three services in church or pagan practices like jolly feasting were nothing new at Christmas by the year 800, something of much broader historical importance happened on that day, leaving a permanent mark on the history of Christianity.

The turning point took place at Rome in the church dedicated to St. Peter. At the end of the day's principal service, Charles, king of the Franks (in modern France and much of Germany), rose from praying before the tomb of the apostle. As he did so, Pope Leo III advanced, and in the words of an eyewitness, "the venerable holy pontiff with his own hands crowned Charles with a most precious crown."[2] Then the people—in fact, "all the Roman people," according to the annals of the Franks—arose as one. They had been told what to say; three times a

1. "All Glory, Laud, and Honor," trans. John Mason Neale, in *Trinity Hymnal*, rev. ed. (Atlanta: Great Commission Publications, 1990), 235.

2. Four contemporary accounts of the coronation—the *Annals of Lorsch*, the *Frankish Royal Annals*, the *Life of Pope Leo III*, and Einhard's *Life of Charlemagne*—are provided in Brian Tierney, ed., *The Middle Ages*, vol. 1, *Sources of Medieval History*, 5th ed. (New York: McGraw-Hill, 1992).

great shout rang out: "Carolo Augusto a Deo coronato, magno et pacifico imperatori, vita et victoria" (To Charles Augustus, crowned by God, great and peace-giving emperor of the Romans, life and victory).

The turning point that Charlemagne's coronation represents in the history of Christianity is not on the same order as the Council of Nicaea or the founding of the monasteries. If the events on Christmas Day in the year 800 had not happened, much the same results would probably have marked the development of Christianity in the Middle Ages. At the same time, however, the event was a dramatic symbol of relationships undergoing permanent change. It stood for a new form of Christian existence that was replacing the Christianity passed on from the time of Constantine, or even of Benedict. This event also an-

This statue of Charlemagne from Zurich communicates some of the imperial self-assurance that made him a terror to his foes and such a strong supporter of the church.

ticipated the future, for the way that the great king Charles and the pope, as supreme head of the Western church, conducted their business on that fateful Christmas Day outlined the shape of Christian life in the West for at least the next seven or eight centuries.

Charlemagne had come to Rome in the summer of 800 as the climax of fifty years of cooperation between the Frankish rulers and the bishops of Rome. His immediate purpose was to vindicate Pope Leo III from charges of corruption leveled by the Roman nobility. This task had been accomplished well before Christmas. Charlemagne was lingering in Rome to await better weather and more favorable general circumstances for returning to his court, across the Alps, in Aachen (Aix-la-Chapelle). His mind was probably already on preparations for yet another summer of warfare against the Saxons, his twenty-first or twenty-second annual campaign. According to the biography of Charlemagne written by one of his most faithful diplomats, Einhard, Charlemagne did not even want the titles "emperor" and "Augustus." As Einhard put it, "He would not have set foot in the Church the day that they were conferred, although it was a great feast-day, if he could have foreseen the design of the Pope."

But he did attend, the pope did give him the imperial crown, and Charlemagne did continue to use the titles that hitherto had been reserved for the long line of Roman emperors extending from Julius Caesar to Irene, who was then reigning in Constantinople as empress of Byzantium, even as Leo placed a crown on Charlemagne's brow. The turning point in church history that this event symbolizes will be clear when three questions are answered: (1) How did the pope come to have power enough to crown a Roman emperor? (2) How had the king of the Franks risen to a position to be so crowned? (3) And how did this new relationship between the pope and the greatest ruler of northern Europe shape the centuries-long period of Western history usually referred to simply as Christendom?

The Rise of the Papacy

A subject like the rise of the papacy cannot be treated with complete objectivity. Roman Catholics, who view the bishop of Rome as the vicar of Christ bearing unique apostolic responsibilities, will obviously regard that history differently from the Orthodox, who regard the pope as only one of several key patriarchs. Perspective differs even more with Protestants, who, despite almost every other imaginable difference among themselves, agree that the pope is not the divinely designated successor of the apostles. Still, it is possible to chart the sequence of developments by which the concept of the pope as the bearer of apostolic authority emerged. Whether that emergence came about through the work of the Holy Spirit, the conniving of men, or an unfathomable combination of divine and human actions is a question to be answered more by theological conviction than historical research.[3]

The term "pope" itself has a long history. The Greek word *papas* was originally applied to high ecclesiastical officials of all kinds; for example, the bishop of Alexandria was called *papas* around the middle of the third century. In the West, the Latin *papa* was likewise a term of respect for a variety of church authorities. The *Oxford English Dictionary* records that as late as 640 the term was applied to Desiderius, bishop of Cahors (in southern France). Centuries before then, however, the use of the term *papa* had begun to be reserved for the bishop of Rome. That

---

3. *The New Catholic Encyclopedia* and *The Oxford Dictionary of the Christian Church* were indispensable in preparing this section.

stricter usage prevailed at least from the pontificate of Leo the Great (440–61). After the eleventh century, the title *papa* was used exclusively for the bishop of Rome.

The history of the papacy should be of interest to all Christians, even those who reject the Catholic interpretation of the pope's importance. Most of the major doctrinal and institutional developments in the history of Christianity significantly involved the bishops of Rome in some way. Since debate about the role of the papacy itself was always connected with first-order discussions of theology, church order, and the church's place in the world, to study that subject is, inevitably, to study the others as well. An additional benefit from a historical examination of the papacy is to see once again how gradual, slow, and incremental can be developments that eventually exert a tremendous influence in the church. It was out of a crucible of experiences that the papacy emerged. Attending to those experiences makes for clearer understanding of the history, whatever one thinks of the doctrine of the papacy itself.

Actions from Rome that exerted broad influence appear early in the church's history. According to the Catholic Church's official list of popes, Peter was succeeded by Linus (perhaps the figure in 2 Tim. 4:21), then Anacletus (or Cletus), then Clement. From this Clement, who may have belonged to an aristocratic household (but is probably not the Clement of Phil. 4:3), a letter survives that admonished and encouraged the Christians in Corinth. Written about A.D. 96, it attempts to deal with problems related to the deposing of several presbyters in the Corinthian church. For the future, Clement's epistle was important for the pattern of influence it anticipated, with authoritative counsel reaching out from a Roman center to the boundaries of the church.

Over the next several centuries, a number of events, personalities, and circumstances contributed to the growing authority of the Roman bishop. During the second century, various bishops of Rome were called upon to coordinate rebuttals to different heresies, and usually they performed that task competently. Toward the end of the second century, Victor (pope 189–98) exerted considerable influence in fixing a common date for Easter. Given the centrality of liturgy in the church's life, the person who could coordinate celebrations of a great feast like Easter was bound to reap a reward of respect. Consultation between outlying bishops and Rome also dates from an early period, but the first official decretal (or authoritative letter) from a pope in formal response to the query of another bishop did not come until 385 under Pope Siricius.

In this mosaic from the Lateran in Rome, St. Peter is handing the symbols of office to Pope Leo III and to the Emperor Charlemagne. In symbolism that would have pleased Charlemagne, the two are pictured on a level with each other, and he is receiving his office directly from Peter rather than from the pope.

Well before that action, however, different popes had begun to reflect directly on the nature of their office. Around the year 255 Bishop Stephen used a passage from Matthew—"and I tell you that you are Peter, and on this rock I will build my church" (16:18)—to defend his own views in a dispute with Cyprian of Carthage. After the Constantinian legalization of the church, a council in Sardica (343) ruled formally that the decisions of local councils may be appealed to the bishop of Rome. And Damasus I, who occupied the papal chair from 366 to 384, attempted to provide a formal definition of the Roman bishop's superiority over all other bishops. In an action that would have tremendously far-reaching consequences, Damasus also commissioned his secretary, Jerome, to produce a standard edition of the Bible in Latin. The resulting *Vulgate* became *the* Scriptures of the Latin Middle Ages and the key biblical version in the Catholic Church until well into our own century.

Already by the fourth century it had become apparent that the ecclesiastical centrality of the Roman bishop had much to do with the political centrality of Rome. As the empire's First City, and a site of great symbolic and practical importance, even after Constantine moved the imperial capital to Constantinople in the East, Rome naturally attracted ecclesiastical influence as well as economic activity and political power. After Constantine's move to the East, the increasingly obvious failure of imperial representatives to maintain the city's dignity magnified the prestige of her bishops, who succeeded where the empire failed.

The internal development of the church also underscored Rome's importance. Parts of the New Testament, although mostly written before a substantial Christian community existed in Rome, nonetheless reflect the early significance of the city for church history. The Book of Acts ends with the apostle Paul arriving in Rome; the Epistle to the Romans is the fullest expression of Paul's mature theology; the Pastoral Epistles probably reflect a somewhat later view of Christian developments in Rome; and the Book of Revelation that closes the New Testament contains many veiled references to Rome (perhaps as the ten-horned, seven-headed beast out of the sea in 13:1). The early church's special attention to martyrs and the places where they died made the well-established stories that both Peter and Paul were martyred in Rome under Emperor Nero (during the period A.D. 64–67) doubly significant. Partly for these specifically Christian reasons and partly for its strategic location as the hub of the empire, the Roman church soon became respected, wealthy, and influential.

These roots of Roman ecclesiastical supremacy were nurtured by the capable activities of many popes. To be sure, some Roman bishops were nonentities or political selections who never rose above the debased conditions of their appointment. A few strayed dangerously, if not fatally, in their doctrinal opinions. But most were at least competent, and some were giants.

The pontificate of Leo I, whose critical contribution to the Council of Chalcedon we have already noted, witnessed a considerable expansion of papal authority, both because of Leo's actions and because of his specific attention to this issue. In addition to his strategic role in defending Rome against invading barbarians, the doctrinal weight of his *Tome* on the person of Christ, and his studied assertion of papal primacy in dialogue with the patriarch of Constantinople, Leo took several steps that clarified the nature of papal authority. Extending the earlier efforts of Pope Stephen, Leo further articulated Matthew 16:18 as a foundation undergirding the authority of the Roman bishops as successors of St. Peter. In addition, early in his pontificate Leo obtained from the emperor, Valentinian III, an edict that defined the superiority of the pope over all other Western bishops in matters related to civil law. In other words, Leo increased the power of the papacy both by capably exercising and by explicitly defending papal authority.

Leo's actions set the stage for further expansion of papal authority by his successors. Gelasius I, who was pope from 492 to 496, followed Leo by participating in debates concerning Christ's person that continued to boil in the East. Like Leo, Gelasius held firmly to the combination of Christ's two natures in one person against a variety of Monophysite views. Again like Leo, he also took pains to define the nature of ecclesiastical authority. In a widely cited letter he expounded the theory that, of the two legitimate powers God had created to rule in the world, the spiritual power—which the pope represented—held primacy over the secular whenever the two conflicted. Such theories were always harder to enact than to publish, but Gelasius's words contributed significantly to theories about church–state relationships that would mold the character of later European society.

The summit of the early papacy, however, was reached in the pontificate of Gregory I (590–604), who, along with Leo, is often styled "the Great." Gregory was born a noble Roman but, after founding several monasteries, eventually joined one himself, where he became renowned for his sanctity and sagacity. This reputation led the pope to call Gregory into diplomatic service on behalf of the church and eventually brought him to the papal chair itself. The list of Gregory's energetic accomplishments as pope is breathtaking. Not only did he oversee Roman defenses against the attacks of the Lombards, carry out complicated negotiations with the Roman emperor in Constantinople, reform the finances of the church, and reorganize the boundaries and responsibilities of Western dioceses. He also was a passionate student of Scripture and formidable reformer of worship. Gregory's own biblical expositions, especially a commentary on the Book of Job, became staples of study throughout the entire Middle Ages and beyond. Their threefold method of exegesis (literal, mystical, moral) likewise established an enduring standard. His *Life of Benedict* gave monastic ideals a major boost in the West. His writings on the duties of bishops highlighted the care of souls as the key activity for all pastors. He reformed liturgical uses and regularized the celebrations of the Christian year. His efforts in promoting music in church lent his name to the plainsong "Gregorian chants" that still influence sacred music. And he was highly regarded as a preacher, especially for his ability to apply the balm of the gospel to the many tumults and disasters of his time.

As if this were not enough, Gregory also oversaw extraordinarily important adjustments in the church's missionary strategy. Through his own experience as a church diplomat, he had become disillusioned with prospects for relationships with the East, but at the same time he took advantage of other opportunities to send missionaries north and west into several strategic European centers. These missionary endeavors led, for example, to the conversion of Arian Visigoths in Spain to orthodoxy. Most famously, they sent Augustine (to be distinguished from the great North African theologian) on a missionary journey to England, which led to the conversion of the Angles and Saxons and also hastened the process whereby Rome absorbed Celtic forms of Christian faith. (The story from the Venerable Bede in the eighth century—that,

Gregory the Great on Pastoral Care

Gregory wrote *Liber regulae pastoralis* (A Book of Pastoral Care) in 590, the first year of his papacy. For nearly a thousand years, it was the Western church's principal guide to pastoral counseling. Charlemagne's adviser Alcuin recommended it to the archbishop of York in 796 with these words: "Wherever you go, let the pastoral book of St. Gregory be your companion. Read and re-read it often, that in it you may learn to know yourself and your work, that you may have before your eyes how you ought to live and teach."[1] "Rulers" in *Pastoral Care* refers to those in spiritual authority, namely bishops and priests who are responsible for the care of souls.

We have said in the *Books on Morals* that either discipline or compassion is greatly wanting, if one is exercised independently of the other. But rulers in their relations with subjects should be animated by compassion duly considerate and by discipline affectionately severe. This is what the Truth teaches concerning the man who was half-dead and was taken to an inn by the care of a Samaritan, wine and oil being applied to his wounds, the wine to cauterize them, and the oil to soothe them. Thus it is necessary that he who sees to the healing of wounds should apply in wine biting pain and in oil soothing tenderness for wine cleanses suppuration and oil promotes the course of healing. In other words, gentleness is to be mingled with severity; a compound is to be made of both, so that subjects may not be exasperated by too great harshness, nor enervated by excessive tenderness.

This, as St. Paul says, is well symbolised by that Ark of the Tabernacle, in which, together with the Tables, were the rod and the manna; because if with the knowledge of the Sacred Scriptures in the breast of the good ruler there is the restraining rod, there should also be the manna of sweetness. Wherefore, David says: "Thy rod and Thy staff, they have comforted me." It is with a rod that we are smitten, but we are supported by a staff. If, then, there is the correction of the rod in striking, let there be the comfort of the staff in supporting.

There should, then, be love that does not enervate, vigour that does not exasperate, zeal not too immoderate and uncontrolled, loving-kindness that spares, yet not more than is befitting. Thus, while justice and clemency are blended in supreme rule, the ruler will soothe the hearts of his subjects even when he inspires fear, and yet in soothing them, hold them to reverential awe for him.[2]

upon seeing fair-haired slaves in Rome and finding out they were Angles, the future pope declared, "Non Angli, sed angeli" [not Angles, but angels] and thereupon resolved to send missionaries to England—may in fact be authentic.)

The crowning glory of Gregory's pontificate was that somehow, despite the immense responsibility that poured from every direction into his hands, he seems to have remained a humble, pious Christian. When in the midst of a controversy, Patriarch John of Constantinople insisted that Gregory address him as the "universal patriarch," Gregory's response was not only a telling diplomatic rejoinder but also almost certainly a genuine indication of his own spiritual concern. Gregory replied that he cared to be known only as "servus servorum Dei" (a servant of the servants of God), a title that Roman bishops have continued to use to this day.

Gregory's pontificate established the norm for the Middle Ages, but it is little wonder that his successors fell far short of his high standard. Popes in his train might share his interest in ecclesiastical diplomacy or further the church's outreach into Europe or even occasionally duplicate some of his sensitive spiritual concern. For the most part in the two or three centuries after Gregory, however, the papacy struggled to overcome the final decay of the Western Roman Empire and a series of debilitating economic, political, and social reversals.

Significant ecclesiastical events also marked important developments for the papacy. When the Synod of Whitby (664) in England secured the agreement of Celtic Christians to follow the Roman liturgical year, it meant an expansion of Rome's jurisdiction and led to a dynamic Celtic contribution to Roman missionary efforts. The papacy's sponsorship of Boniface's missionary journeys during the first half of the eighth century also drew the papacy more and more into the concerns of northern Europe.

The events that led directly to the papal coronation of Charlemagne in 800 feature the popes more as subtle diplomats than inspiring spiritual leaders. In 751 Pope Zacharias sanctioned the election of Pepin the Short as king of the Franks, in replacement of the decrepit Merovingian line. Three years later Pope Stephen II personally crowned Pepin as king, the first time such an action had taken place. In exchange, Pepin extracted Rome from its last lingering tie to Constantinople. Shortly thereafter in 756 Pepin also bestowed on the pope a special "Donation," which gave the pope control of Italian territories won by Pepin from the Lombards and also committed his successors to act as protectors of the papacy. The papal coronation of Pepin's son as emperor on Christmas Day in 800, in other words, had clear antecedents.

To trace the rise of the papacy from New Testament times to the age of Charlemagne is to pose a puzzle. No one act or single line of thematic development shaped the papacy. Yet by 800 an elaborate mixing of elements had created a situation in which the Roman bishop was regarded unquestionably as the prime ecclesiastical figure in the West and as the personal representative of Western Christianity to the East. To be sure, the authority exerted by popes to the time of Charlemagne did not yet approach what would come in the following centuries. A whole series of momentous events had yet to occur before the height of papal authority was reached in the pontificate of Innocent III (1198–1216). In the mid-ninth century Nicholas I would exert papal authority against the East (again) but also against the secular rulers who succeeded Charlemagne. The reform of church life spurred by the foundation of the monastery in Cluny in 909 would eventually see Leo IX assert Western supremacy over the East in "the Great Schism" (1054), Gregory VII secure penance from the German emperor Henry IV during a fierce contest of wills (1077), and Urban II proclaim the first Crusade (1095).

What made the papal coronation of 800 so important was not that it represented the height of papal power. Rather, it represented a *strategic alliance* between the papacy's gradually expanding influence and a political power that, like the pope, was also expanding in influence. To understand why 800 represented such a strategic moment, it is necessary to step back from explicitly ecclesiastical affairs and look at the broader geopolitical picture.

The Rise of Northern Europe

The event at Rome in 800 was linked through an elaborate skein of connections to widely scattered events all throughout the Mediterranean world.[4] It is no exaggeration to say that the course leading to the papal coronation of Charlemagne in 800 was influenced nearly as much by a non-Christian contemporary of Gregory the Great, who never set foot in Europe, as it was by Gregory and his papal successors. That contemporary was the prophet of Islam, Mohammed, who was born about 570. After he received what are recorded in the Koran as revelations from the angel Gabriel, Mohammed gathered a small following in and around Mecca, in the Arabian Peninsula. In 622 he and his band were driven out of Mecca by rivals. Their retreat to Medinah (the *Hegira*) was turned, however, into victory as more and more Arabs

---

4. The account that follows modifies Henri Pirenne, *Mohammed and Charlemagne* (London: Allen & Unwin, 1939).

Expansion of Islam, ca. 800

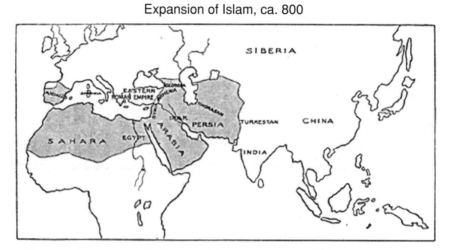

rallied to the cause of Allah and his prophet. In 630 Mohammed returned in triumph to Mecca. Two years later, when Mohammed died,
Arabia was one-third Muslim. Two years after that, under Abu Bakr, all
Arabia had turned to Islam. Within another decade, Arab armies inspired by Islamic teaching had taken Syria, Palestine, and Persia (modern Iran) and had conducted raids as far east as the borders of India.
In 642 Islam entered Egypt.

This westward move of Islam played a critical role in the history of
Christianity. As we have seen, the East–West axis around which Christianity had grown was already strained. Yet the Christian world was
still anchored by Rome in the West and Constantinople in the East. As
a consequence, the geographical heart of Christianity remained the
Mediterranean. Greek was still the language of choice for refined theological discussion. Missionary beachheads, like the one Gregory's Augustine established in Kent, England, seemed nearly irrelevant to the
main centers of Christian thought, organization, and power.

When, however, Islam moved west, everything changed. Despite internal disputes in the mid-seventh century that slowed the pace of expansion for nearly a century after Mohammed's death, the westward
tide of Islam seemed irresistible. Attacks began on Constantinople, still
a vigorous imperial capital, in 674. By 698 Carthage, the home of Tertullian and Cyprian, was in Islamic hands. With Carthage under control, Islamic navies fanned out to subdue the eastern Mediterranean. In
711 Islamic troops of the powerful Umayyad dynasty crossed over the
narrow band of water at the mouth of the Mediterranean into Gibraltar
(or *gib-al-Tarik,* the "rock *[gib]* of Tarik," who commanded the Islamic

forces). Within a decade Muslim armies had crossed the Pyrenees into what is now France.

The precise impact of Muslim expansion on Christian history has been a matter of contentious debate for a long time. Yet a fairly general consensus exists on at least several aspects of the big picture.

1. The spread of Islam eastward over Egypt and North Africa was made easier by the weakness of Christianity in those regions. Heavy taxes imposed by Constantinople, as well as plundering armies from Persia, made North Africans ready for new rulers. The centuries of Christian infighting, which combined strife over doctrine with wearisome contests for power, further undermined the internal strength of the Christian community. Some historians have even speculated that the Egyptian preference for forms of Christian theology stressing the unity of God (especially Monophysitism) predisposed North Africans toward the radical monotheism of Islam. The fact that, within the norms of the ancient world, Muslim conquerors were relatively tolerant also eased the transition from Christian to Islamic rule.

2. The spread of Islam accelerated the division between Eastern and Western forms of Christianity, especially by making communications between the eastern and western Mediterranean much more difficult. As we will see in the next chapter, formal division between the Western Catholics and the Eastern Orthodox depended upon developments in the church as well as in the broader world. Yet in that wider context, the vigorous presence of Islam in the Mediterranean was a most important factor in sundering the church. Even if the will had existed to bridge East–West, Greek–Latin, patriarchal–papal differences within Christianity, the strain in politics, military affairs, trade, and communications that an expanding Islam exerted on both parts of the church would probably have been too great.

3. Most important for Charlemagne's coronation as emperor in 800, the expansion of Islam turned the attention of the papacy from the East to the North. This geographic refocusing signaled papal willingness to give up on the ideals of a Mediterranean Roman Empire in exchange for a new Roman Empire of the North. (To underscore the power of the imperial ideal associated with Rome, it is striking to note that about two hundred years later in what is now Russia, Vladimir accepted the Christian faith and soon his successors were proclaiming Moscow as "a new Rome.") When the crowds addressed Charlemagne as Augustus, they were deliberately evoking the majesty of Rome. The popes leading up to Leo III had come to realize that the old connection between Rome and Constantinople was now bankrupt. The emperor in the East could not secure Europe against Islam; besides, it was also clear that

increasingly obvious cultural differences were making East–West co-operation difficult, even if Islam were not in the picture. So it was that the papacy exchanged an eastern for a northern partner.

4. Finally, after the seventh century, it becomes impossible to understand the internal course of Christian history without bringing Islam fully into the equation. In the East, Islamic scruples against images played a role in how the Byzantine church defended its use of icons. A few centuries later, the spectacle of Islamic rulers in Jerusalem, combined with anguished appeals for help from the Eastern Roman emperor, provoked the call for crusades. Within the sphere of learning, Islam exerted a more pacific influence. When Europeans in the eleventh and twelfth centuries became curious about the philosophy and science of the ancient world, they found it more convenient to translate Arabic editions of Greek texts than to use copies of the originals locked away in Byzantium. The Western resurgence of learning in the twelfth and thirteenth centuries, which was very much a distinctly Christian enterprise, also benefited from Islamic models in mathematics, history, and other areas of thought.

Thus, the spread of Islam had the most important impact imaginable in the transition of Western Christianity from a Mediterranean, eastern-oriented faith to an expressly European, northward-looking form of religion. This Islamic context, moreover, enables us to understand the dynamics that led to Charlemagne's appearance at Rome in the year 800.

Charlemagne's grandfather was Charles Martel (ca. 690–741) who, as mayor of the palace to the Merovingian kings, was the effective ruler of the Franks. Charles Martel's memorable successes as a military and political leader provided the indispensable foundation for what would later take place under Charlemagne. On the geopolitical side, Charles Martel was the commander who successfully led the Franks in 732 against the Islamic Saracens at Poitiers, the high-water mark of western Islamic expansion. It would take more than seven centuries for the Muslims to be driven completely out of Europe from the Iberian Peninsula, but the tide had begun to turn. While it is possible to exaggerate the decisive influence of this one battle, it is also true that Charles Martel, along with his successors, came to be seen as the saviors of Europe.

On the ecclesiastical side, Charles Martel also took steps with far-ranging consequences. Early in his career, he initiated friendly approaches to the popes as if he were leader of the Franks in fact as well as in power (approaches his son Pepin would continue after he assumed the kingship). Charles Martel also directly assisted Boniface and other Anglo-Saxon missionaries who were busy among the Germanic tribes of northern Europe. Since Boniface was acting in his missionary work as the direct agent of the pope, Charles Martel's support for this activity also enhanced the status of Frankish power in the eyes of Rome.

Charlemagne eventually succeeded to the alliances that his grandfather had initiated and his father Pepin had developed. From the beginning of his rule as king of the Franks in 768, Charlemagne acted in concert to expand his own power and to strengthen connections with the pope. By the time he came to Rome in 800, Charlemagne's success against the Saxons to his north and east, the Spanish to his west, and the Lombards to his south had made him lord over more of Europe than anyone since Theodosius at the end of the fourth century.

Thus it was that, when Pope Leo III crowned Charlemagne the "new" emperor, it only solidified a connection that had been developing for more than half a century. The popes had turned to the north, where a strong imperial household was emerging. In the terms of medieval society, Charlemagne never considered himself a vassal of the pope. Rather, he held himself to be responsible to God alone for the welfare of his people. But whatever Charlemagne thought of his own role, the link with Rome was now secure. For the next 800 years and more, the politics, learning, social organization, art, music, economics, and law of Europe would be "Christian"—not necessarily in the sense of fully incorporating norms of the gospel, but because the fate of the Western church centered in Rome had been so decisively linked with the new "Roman" emperor over the Alps.

Charlemagne took the notion of church–state cooperation, which was a legacy from the days of Constantine, and by fixing it to Europe bequeathed "Christendom" to succeeding generations. Christendom would endure its dark days, like the political and moral chaos from around 850 to approximately 1000, or the plague decades of the fourteenth century. It would also experience periods of renewal, like the Carolingian renaissance of faith and learning in the early ninth century, the reform brought about by the friars in the twelfth and thirteen centuries, or the Renaissance and Reformation in the fifteenth and sixteenth centuries. Throughout, Christendom endured as the shape of Christian existence in the West. Even when battered by the emergence of Protestantism and the rise of the modern nation-state, even when attacked by secular trends in the seventeenth and eighteenth centuries, even when the title "Holy Roman emperor" that dated from Charlemagne was permanently abolished by Napoleon in 1806, aspects of Christendom survived. The fact that, to this day, church establishments of one kind or another exist in most northern and western European countries, long after the majority of European people have stopped practicing the Christian faith, represents a remnant of the Christendom established by Charlemagne's coronation.

The Christianity of Christendom

The Christendom of the European Middle Ages affected the practice of the Christian faith in every way. The "medieval synthesis," as it is sometimes called, harmonized (at least in theory) what we today regard as separate sacred and secular spheres of life. The ideal symbolized by the cooperation between Charlemagne and Pope Leo III was an integrated view of life in which everything—politics, social order, religious practice, economic relationships, and more—was based on the Christian faith as communicated by the Roman Catholic Church and protected by the actions of secular rulers.

The spiritual ideal that developed under the umbrella of Christendom bore strong resemblance to other major expressions of Christianity. But it also had distinct features that, not surprisingly, continue to play a tremendous role in the Roman Catholic Church as well as a significant role in all forms of the faith that descend, however tangentially, from Western Christendom.

The central religious convictions of Christendom were that human beings, because they are corrupted by sin, need to be saved, and that this salvation is wrought by the merit of Christ communicated through God's grace. The distinctive medieval shape of these convictions was the belief that saving grace comes to people through the sacraments in a social setting defined by the cooperation of church and state.

Sacramental theology evolved throughout the Middle Ages, but by the time of Thomas Aquinas in the thirteenth century, earlier anticipations had assumed a formal definition. In Aquinas's terms, a sacrament was "the sign of a holy thing insofar as it makes men holy."[5] That is, sacraments stood for spiritual realities and worked toward the salvation of those who participated in them.

The theological rationale for a comprehensive sacramental system involved some elements shared by all times and places in Christian history and some that were distinct to Christendom in the Middle Ages. In the first place, the sacraments were thought to exhibit the principles of the incarnation, whereby the most important spiritual realities were embodied in a material form. Next, sacraments were thought to express the objective character of God's action on behalf of humanity. Re-

5. Thomas Aquinas, *Summa of Theology,* III, q. 60, a. 2, c, from *An Aquinas Reader,* ed. Mary T. Clark (Garden City, N.Y.: Doubleday, 1972), 481.

Aquinas on the Sacraments

The sacraments are used as signs for man's sanctification. Therefore, they can be considered in three ways and in each way it is suitable for words to be added to the sensible signs. First of all, they can be considered in reference to the cause of sanctification, which is the Word incarnate, to whom the sacraments are somewhat conformed insofar as the word is united to the sensible sign, just as the Word of God in the mystery of the incarnation is united to sensible flesh.

Second, sacraments may be considered with reference to the man who is sanctified and who is made up of soul and body, to whom the sacramental remedy is suited insofar as through the sensible element it touches the body, and through faith in the words it reaches the soul. . . .

Third, a sacrament may be considered with reference to the sacramental signification. Now, Augustine says [*On Christian Doctrine* 2], "words are the chief signs used by men" for words can be formed variously to signify diverse mental ideas, so that we can through words express our thoughts with greater precision. And so to make the sacramental signification perfect, it was required to determine the signification of sensible things through definite words. For water may signify both a cleansing on account of its humidity, and refreshment by its coolness; but when we say, "I baptize thee," it is clear that we use water in baptism to signify a spiritual cleansing.[3]

ceiving God's grace depended upon actually receiving the vehicle of that grace, and not so much on how one felt about the transaction. Finally, the sacraments were held to reinforce the essentially social structure of grace, the fact that Christ worked for his people together. This belief especially heightened the significance of the institutional church, through which the sacraments were given.

As the church formalized the sacramental practice into a system embracing seven sacraments, it became clear that the ideal of geographic comprehensiveness that inspired Christendom was matched by the ideal of a comprehensive life course. The seven sacraments of the medieval Catholic Church offered the specific touch of God's grace to all of the critical stages in a normal life. Baptism was the sacrament for birth. Confirmation was the sacrament for coming of age. Penance was the sacrament for the confession of sin. The Eucharist was the sacrament for spiritual nourishment. Marriage was the sacrament for creating a family. Extreme unction was the sacrament for death. And Ordi-

The Walters Art Gallery, Baltimore

In the Middle Ages, celebration of the Eucharist was central not only to church life but also, as depicted here, to religious observance in private homes.

nation was the sacrament making possible a spiritual organization—that is, the church and the priesthood—to provide all the other sacraments for the critical transitions of life. In the emergence of the sacraments and of a broader sacramental theology, the witness of Scripture was not irrelevant. Yet more important was the application of general theological principles and worship practices to the varied conditions of earthly existence. By the time learned theologians got around to providing rationales for the various sacraments and their uses, the system was already pretty much in place.

The sacramental system as it developed in Christendom required that the organized church play an indispensable role as the agent through which the sacraments brought God's grace to every stage of life. As the sacraments mediated God's grace in Christ to needy sinners, so the church was the sole mediator of the sacraments. The theology of the Middle Ages expanded upon earlier hints to show how Christ had commissioned the church to fulfill its role in distributing the sacraments and designated the ordained leaders of the church, especially the pope, to act as successors to the apostles in fulfilling the mandate of Christ to guide his people.

With its central sacramental role in the salvation of sinners, the church also assumed immense significance for every other aspect of culture. Since the salvation of sinners is the most important imaginable task in life, leaders of the political sphere must cooperate with the church as it fulfills its spiritual tasks; those who exercise the mind must direct learning in ways that are compatible with church teaching; economic relationships should be structured to support the church in its mission; and ideals of social order will naturally imitate patterns that God has set for the church. In other words, with the widespread agreement that salvation was the most important reality, and the further agreement that salvation was communicated through and by the sacraments, it had to follow that the church, as the administrator of the sacraments, should offer a foundation for everything else in life.

In practice, the comprehensive unities of Christendom's medieval synthesis rarely functioned with the harmony or the efficiency that the ideal suggested. For one thing, many of the rulers who succeeded Charlemagne and who were supposed to support the church loyally were, like Charlemagne, not keen on assuming the subordinate status to which they had been assigned. Many of them, in fact, either exercised or attempted to exercise the dominion that, in theory, belonged to the pope. For another, some of the institutional arms of the church, especially the vigorous orders of monks and friars that were essential for putting the church's spiritual goals into practice, were often nearly as difficult to regulate as secular rulers. In addition, the effects of both human nature and divine grace kept the system from functioning as it came to be outlined. Dignitaries exalted to high ecclesiastical position sometimes acted like devils, common ordinary believers with no special standing in the church often reflected the work of Christ as effectively as their ecclesiastical superiors.

Yet for all its failures, medieval Christendom remained a powerful ideal. At the heart of the ideal was the comprehensive presence of divine grace in all of life. And at the heart of the ideal in practice was the harmonious cooperation of the rulers of church and state.

Of course, not every characteristic of Christendom that developed in the Western Middle Ages, that remains in the modern Roman Catholic Church, or that still can be found in many forms of Western Protestantism was present with Charlemagne and Leo III. Yet the symbolic import of their action—with the pope providing a crown to the most powerful ruler in Europe while invoking the memory of imperial Rome—is, in the light of history, incredibly potent. There was now a new comprehensive empire to replace the one destroyed by the drift of East–West disengagement and the armies of Islam. In this new empire, the institutional church with the pope at its head would exert immense theoretical importance. Christian reality would in fact often come close to mirroring the theoretical unities embodied in the ideal of Christendom. Eventually, after many centuries, Christendom would be fatally wounded—by the Renaissance, by Protestantism, by the modern nation-state, by Western atheism, and, most recently, by the vigorous spread of Christianity far beyond the boundaries of Europe. But as a symbol for the inauguration of a new, long-lasting, and far-reaching phase of Christian history, it is hard to top the coronation at St. Peter's in Rome on Christmas Day in the year 800.

Like the hymn-writer Theodulf, Alcuin (ca. 735–804) was a prominent foreigner in Charlemagne's court. He was educated at the cathedral school in the northern English city of York, where he became a teacher and librarian. Alcuin so impressed Charlemagne upon their meeting at Parma in 781 that he was invited to become the king's theological and political adviser. Alcuin supported a strong role for the emperor in protecting and governing the church. He may even have played a part in engineering Charlemagne's coronation as Holy Roman emperor. In addition to initiating liturgical reform, Alcuin became an architect of the Carolingian renaissance, establishing schools and libraries that both aided the spread of literacy among the Franks and preserved important historic and literary documents. The following prayer reflects this Christian scholar's devotion to God and desire for wisdom:

> *Eternal Light, shine into our hearts,*
> *Eternal Goodness, deliver us from evil,*
> *Eternal Power, be our support,*
> *Eternal Wisdom, scatter the darkness of our ignorance,*
> *Eternal Pity, have mercy upon us;*
> *that with all our heart and mind and soul and strength*
> *we may seek thy face and be brought by thine infinite mercy*
> *to thy holy presence; through Jesus Christ our Lord.*[6]

Further Reading

Bede, The Venerable. *The Ecclesiastical History of the English People.* Many editions.

Davis, Raymond, ed. *The Book of Pontiffs (Liber Pontificalis): The Ancient Biographies of the First Ninety Roman Bishops to A.D. 715.* Liverpool: Liverpool University Press, 1989. English selections.

6. George Appleton, ed., *The Oxford Book of Prayer* (Oxford: Oxford University Press, 1985), 70.

Dawson, Christopher. *The Formation of Christendom*. New York: Sheed & Ward, 1967.

Everyday Faith in the Middle Ages [*Christian History*, no. 49]. 1996.

Hoyt, Robert S., and Stanley Chodorow. *Europe in the Middle Ages*. 3rd ed. New York: Harcourt Brace Jovanovich, 1976.

Oden, Thomas C. *Care of Souls in the Classic Tradition*. Philadelphia: Fortress, 1984. On Gregory the Great.

Richards, Jeffrey. *Consul of God: The Life and Times of Gregory the Great*. London: Routledge & Kegan Paul, 1980.

Thorpe, Lewis G. M., trans. *Two Lives of Charlemagne: Einhard and Notker the Stammerer*. New York: Penguin, 1969.

Van Engen, John. "The Christian Middle Ages as an Historiographical Problem." *American Historical Review* 91 (June 1986): 519–52.

Women in the Medieval Church [*Christian History*, no. 30]. 1991.

6

Division between East and West:
The Great Schism (1054)

Gregory of Nazianzus (329–89) was one of the three Cappadocian Fathers (with the brothers Basil of Caesarea and Gregory of Nyssa) who championed Trinitarian orthodoxy in the second half of the fourth century. The three Fathers are known for their defense of the full divinity of the Holy Spirit, while Gregory of Nazianzus also entered more broadly into the ecclesiastical politics of his day by serving as patriarch of Constantinople and even presiding briefly over the Constantinopolitan Council of 381, which confirmed (and expanded) the Nicene Creed. Several aspects of Gregory's teaching became very important in later Orthodox theology, especially his stress on the incomprehensibility of God and the necessity of purification for the theologian who would write on holy matters. His hymns, like the one below, also strike a characteristically Eastern note by stressing Christ as the Light who illuminates all things in heaven and earth and to whom the faithful are drawn.

> O Light that knew no dawn,
> That shines to endless day,
> All things in earth and heav'n
> Are lustred by thy ray;
> No eye can to thy throne ascend,
> Nor mind thy brightness comprehend.
>
> Thy grace, O Father, give,
> That I may serve in fear;

Above all boons, I pray,
Grant me thy voice to hear;
From sin thy child in mercy free,
And let me dwell in light with thee.[1]

For the Latin, Western church, the early eleventh century was a period of accelerating reform. While the papacy was languishing in degradation throughout most of the tenth century, renewal was already at work in the church through the restoration of monastic ideals and the sincerity of important rulers. The foundation of a new monastery based on Benedict's Rule in 909 at Cluny in France led to a multiplication of monastic houses and a new zeal for upholding Benedict's ideals. The height of reforming interest among the Holy Roman emperors, successors of Charlemagne, was reached with Henry III (emperor 1039–56), who was both personally pious and eager for reform. When Henry came to Rome in 1046 in order to be formally crowned as emperor, he found the papacy enmeshed in the local political quarrels that had beset the office for more than a century. The papacy, it seems, was the last element in the church to resist the tide of reform. Henry took immediate steps to initiate change by removing three rival claimants for the papal chair and securing the election of a German bishop as the new pope. Henry's plans seemed to be frustrated, however, when this new pope soon died and a second German appointment likewise passed away after only a brief tenure. But Henry persevered, and his third German selection, Bishop Bruno of Toul, would as Pope Leo IX (1048–54) cooperate fully with Henry in working to focus the church's attention more directly on spiritual and ecclesiastical matters. The reforms that Leo and Henry pursued most vigorously concerned simony (the sale of church offices) and enforcing the ideal of celibacy among the European priesthood. An underlying reform, however, had much greater repercussions for all of church history, namely, the restitution of dignity to the papacy itself. To equip the pope to do what all reformers wanted him to do, the papacy itself would have to be extracted from local political strife and

---

1. "O Light That Knew No Dawn," trans. John Brownlie, *Trinity Hymnal*, rev. ed. (Atlanta: Great Commission Publications, 1990), 25.

would have to exert an independent authority in governing the church.[2]

As helpful as such measures proved for strengthening the church in the West, immediate difficulties arose when Leo raised his sights to the East. Relations between the Eastern and Western churches had for centuries been in decline. A sharp dispute during the second half of the ninth century between two capable leaders, Pope Nicholas I (858–67) and Photius, the patriarch of Constantinople (intermittently 858–86), had strained connections between the churches. For reasons probably having to do with the Western acceptance of the *filioque* addition to the Nicene Creed, patriarchs of Constantinople from the year 1009 no longer included the name of the Roman bishop in the diptychs, or the formal lists maintained at Constantinople of the other patriarchs living and dead whom Constantinople recognized as doctrinally sound. The rupture between Eastern and Western churches that occurred during the pontificate of Leo IX should not, therefore, be disconnected from a very long history of disengagement and estrangement. Yet events at the middle of the eleventh century remain important in their own right.

Tangled political-ecclesiastical strife precipitated the crisis. Emperor Henry III, Pope Leo IX, and the Eastern (or Byzantine) emperor, Constantine IX (1042–55), had entered negotiations in order to make common cause against Norman knights who were invading southern Italy and threatening property and authority belonging to all three. Part of the agreement they reached to resist the Normans was the stipulation that the pope regain authority over the few Greek churches in Italy and that the Byzantine emperor persuade the Eastern patriarch, Michael Cerularius (1043–59), to forward Leo a "synodical letter" of the sort that had traditionally been sent to Rome after the election of a new patriarch, but which Cerularius had not done. The patriarch was in no mood to comply. Rather, he reciprocated against Western takeover of the Greek churches in Italy by demanding that Latin churches in Constantinople conform to Greek rites (these churches had kept a Saturday fast, used unleavened bread in the Eucharist, and maintained other liturgical practices that differed from Eastern usages). When these Latin churches refused Cerularius's demands, he shut them down. To add further complications, Cerularius in 1053 persuaded the Eastern metropolitan of Bulgaria, Leo of Ochrida, to write a letter to the West com-

2. The narrative for this turning point relies especially on Williston Walker, with Richard A. Norris, David W. Lotz, and Robert T. Handy, *A History of the Christian Church*, 4th ed. (New York: Charles Scribner's Sons, 1985); Timothy Ware, *The Orthodox Church*, new ed. (New York: Penguin, 1993); and John Meyendorff, *The Orthodox Church*, 3rd ed. (Crestwood, N.Y.: St. Vladimir's Seminary Press, 1981).

This photograph from the early twentieth century shows the great Hagia Sophia with the Islamic minarets that were added after the fall of Constantinople.

plaining about the heavy-handed incursion of "Frankish" (or Western) practices into Bulgaria. In response to this letter, Pope Leo enlisted one of his most trusted advisers, Cardinal Humbert, to pen a reply. In 1050 Leo had called Humbert to Rome from a monastery in Lorraine, and Humbert immediately became the pope's right-hand man in attacking simony. Zealous Humbert undoubtedly was, but not diplomatic. His response to Leo of Bulgaria was a stinging reassertion of Roman claims to primacy in the church.

The event that propelled degenerating ill will into schism was Pope Leo's capture by Norman troops later in 1053. Recognizing how greatly imperiled all Byzantine property now was in Italy, the Eastern emperor Constantine persuaded Patriarch Cerularius to join him in dispatching more conciliatory missives to the pope. In response, Leo appointed a three-man legation to visit Constantinople and negotiate a more satisfactory relationship with the East. Unfortunately, neither the legation, which was headed by Cardinal Humbert, nor Patriarch Cerularius, was in the mood for compromise.

No sooner did the Roman legation arrive in Constantinople than word also came that Leo IX had unexpectedly died. Nothing daunted,

Humbert thrust a stiff papal letter (which he had written himself) onto Cerularius. That letter reminded the patriarch in no uncertain terms that "as a hinge, remaining unmoved opens and shuts a door, so Peter and his successors [at Rome] have an unfettered jurisdiction over the whole Church, since no one ought to interfere with their position, because the highest See is judged by none."[3] Cerularius responded in kind by rejecting the letter and by questioning whether now, since the pope was dead, Humbert was even a properly credentialed legate. Humbert was offended and resolved to leave Constantinople at once. But before he did so, he entered the great church of Hagia Sophia (Holy Wisdom), placed on the altar a bull excommunicating Cerularius, shook the dust off his feet, and left. It is reported that an Eastern deacon hastened after Humbert, trying to return the bull, but the overture was rebuffed, whereupon the paper was dropped in the street. Soon thereafter Cerularius excommunicated the papal legation.

Traditionally, these events from 1054 have been called the Great Schism between the Orthodox and Catholic churches, but there were in fact at least two serious efforts in succeeding centuries to repair the breach. In 1274 a reunion council met in Lyons, France, and came to an agreement on church practice and the creed. But that agreement was rejected by the Orthodox in the East, once their delegates returned home. A century and a half later, the Eastern emperor and the Eastern patriarch both journeyed to another reunion council, this one in Florence, Italy. After intense debate for several months in 1438–39, all but one member of the large Eastern delegation agreed to a formula designed to heal the schism. But once again, overwhelming resistance in the Eastern churches rose against the terms of agreement. Nonetheless, in what proved a losing battle, the Eastern emperor John VIII and his successor, Constantine XI, both continued to defend the agreement.

Constantine XI, in fact, supported East–West reconciliation literally unto death. When the Turks attacked Constantinople in April 1453, this crisis brought all Christians in the city together. Early in the morning on May 29, Constantine attended a united service for Orthodox and Catholics in the Hagia Sophia. Then he went out to battle, where he met his death. The same day the Turks captured the city and transformed Hagia Sophia into a mosque. With Emperor Constantine XI died not only the Byzantine Empire but also the last serious effort to repair the Orthodox–Catholic schism (until, that is, the 1960s).

3. Henry Bettenson, ed., *Documents of the Christian Church,* 2nd ed. (New York: Oxford University Press, 1963), 97.

The Great Schism of 1054 was a major turning point in Christian history because it brought to a head centuries of East–West cultural disengagement, theological differences, and ecclesiastical suspicion. It also symbolized the isolation that would attend the Eastern churches for most of the millennium to follow. The various Eastern Orthodox churches have passed through cycles of decay and renewal since the eleventh century. During the same period the Orthodox Church continued to be the principal Christian expression for a large part of the inhabited globe. Yet even at the end of the twentieth century, Orthodoxy remains mostly separated from currents affecting other Christians, whether Catholic, Protestant, or indigenous non-Western.

To put the events of 1054 in perspective, it will help to note the circumstances and events that led to that divide. Fuller attention to the meaning of the Great Schism must, however, also include at least brief treatment of the Crusades, for these ventures from the West sealed the schism. It should also note the entrance of Orthodoxy into Russia, for with the Islamic conquest of Constantinople, Russia became the leading center of the Orthodox faith. A final brief outline of Orthodoxy in the modern world is also appropriate in a chapter focusing on the division between East and West, which only in the twentieth century has begun to be healed.*

East–West Division

Historical anticipations of the events that transpired at Constantinople in 1054 stretched back to the early history of the church. As early as the end of the first century, it was possible to perceive pointed differences between major representatives of what would one day be called West and East. Thus, historian Henry Bettenson thinks that the Epistle of Clement sent from Rome to Corinth about the year 96 displays "the emergence of the characteristic Roman Christianity. Here we find no ecstasies, no miraculous 'gifts of the Spirit,' no demonology, no preoccupation with an imminent 'Second Coming.' The Church has settled down in the world, and is going about its task 'soberly, discreetly and advisedly.'"[4] By the end of the second century, such "Roman" characteristics were thoroughly matched by "Greek" tendencies arising from the other end of the Mediterranean.

---

* The term "Orthodox," when used for the Eastern (or "Greek" or "Greco-Russian") churches, refers to the conviction in these bodies that they possess the "right teaching," "right worship," or even "true glory" (all possible translations of the Greek words underlying "orthodoxy").

4. Henry Bettenson, introduction to *The Early Christian Fathers* (New York: Oxford University Press, 1956), 2–3.

In chapter 3 we noted briefly the differences in temperament and intellectual disposition between the contemporary theologians Tertullian of Carthage (ca. 160–ca. 225) and Clement of Alexandria (ca. 150–ca. 215). These differences are worth another look, since the divergent mentalities of the two notable leaders, although separated by only a few hundred miles on the North African coast, would loom larger and larger as the centuries passed. Again, Tertullian's first language was Latin, Clement's was Greek. Tertullian boldly challenged the pagan cultures of his day with the realities of the Christian faith, while Clement sympathetically sought aid for Christianity from the best that paganism offered. Tertullian coined new words (like "Trinity") and was eager to construct formulas of faith *(regula fidei)*, which he then expected to end theological debate. Clement meditated at great length on the truths of the faith and used formulas to stimulate discussion about the ultimate realities of Christianity. Tertullian was a lawyer, Clement a philosopher. Tertullian reasoned toward action, Clement reasoned toward truth.

The traits that set Tertullian and Clement apart from each other pointed to what would later become distinct religious cultures. The range and nature of the differences that resulted have been sensitively summarized by the Orthodox historian and bishop Timothy Ware:

> From the start Greeks and Latins had each approached the Christian Mystery in their own way. At the risk of some oversimplification, it can be said that the Latin approach was more practical, the Greek more speculative; Latin thought was influenced by juridical ideas, by the concepts of Roman law, while the Greeks understood theology in the context of worship and in the light of the Holy Liturgy. When thinking about the Trinity, Latins started with the unity of the Godhead, Greeks with the threeness of the persons; when reflecting on the Crucifixion, Latins thought primarily of Christ the Victim, Greeks of Christ the Victor; Latins talked more of redemption, Greeks of deification. . . . These two distinctive approaches were not in themselves contradictory; each served to supplement the other, and each had its place in the fullness of Catholic tradition. But now that the two sides were becoming strangers to one another—with no political and little cultural unity, with no common language—there was a danger that each side would follow its own approach in isolation and push it to extremes, forgetting the value in the other point of view.[5]

In the centuries that followed, these early tendencies received powerful reinforcement from momentous historical events. Constantine's

---

5. Ware, *The Orthodox Church*, 48–49.

fourth-century decision to move the seat of empire from Rome to the East meant that the new Roman power in Constantinople would evolve in a climate influenced by the Greek language, by Greek preferences in intellect, and by Greek temperamental dispositions. Later in the seventh century when the forces of Islam moved out from the Arabian world across North Africa and took control of communications on the Mediterranean Sea, the east–west division of the Roman Empire meant even more. Now, despite heroic but increasingly sporadic efforts, even elementary contact between East and West had to surmount an alien imperial power as well as ingrained cultural tendencies. As the papacy looked northward for support to the barbarian tribes that, under Charlemagne, were seeking to revive the Roman Empire on their own terms, even stronger forces were tugging East and West apart. When a new Islamic power, the Turks, began to encroach upon the Byzantine Empire from the east, the Western response was often indifference, except for the Crusades, which ultimately did their own part to divide the two great Christian regions.

Over the course of time, concrete theological differences also separated the West from the East. To this day, the Eastern church remains astounded at the casualness with which the West added the word *filioque* to the Nicene Creed. (See explanatory note in chapter 2 above.) From the sixth century, when Western churches began to insert "and the Son" in the section of the creed that speaks of the Spirit's procession from the Father, the Orthodox complained that the West was violating the spirit as well as the letter of what had transpired at Nicaea— the spirit by acting unilaterally in making the change, and the letter by violating an explicit canon of the council that the wording of its formula was not to be changed. Moreover, the Eastern churches argued that the Western addition was a grievous theological error. In this view, the Western urge to equalize relationships among the members of the Trinity short-circuited the full personality of the Spirit and so crippled understanding of what the Spirit was to do. That task, in the words of Orthodox theologian John Meyendorff, is "to bring about the unity of the human race in the Body of Christ," but to do so by imparting "to this unity a personal, and hence diversified, character."[6]

The other theological difficulty that eventually crystallized was Eastern resentment at claims for papal supremacy. From the start, there was considerable willingness to grant preference ("first among equals") to the bishop of Rome by the four original Eastern patriarchates (Alexandria, Antioch, Constantinople, and Jerusalem, with Constantinople

6. Meyendorff, *The Orthodox Church*, 197.

The Second Council of Nicaea on Icons

One of the convictions that distinguishes the Orthodox Church is adherence to the decisions of seven ecumenical councils from the early Christian centuries. The seven are the First Council of Nicaea (325), the First Council of Constantinople (381), the Council of Ephesus (431), the Council of Chalcedon (451), the Second Council of Constantinople (553), the Third Council of Constantinople (680), and the Second Council of Nicaea (787). This last of the "ecumenical" councils defines the Orthodox use of icons with the following words:

> To make our confession short, we keep unchanged all the ecclesiastical traditions handed down to us, whether in writing or verbally, one of which is the making of pictorial representations, agreeable to the history of the preaching of the Gospel, a tradition useful in many respects, but especially in this, that so the incarnation of the Word of God is shewn forth as real and not merely phantastic, for these have mutual indications and without doubt have also mutual significations.
>
> We, therefore, following the royal pathway and the divinely inspired authority of our Holy Fathers and the traditions of the Catholic Church (for, as we all know, the Holy Spirit indwells her), define with all certitude and accuracy that just as the figure of the precious and life-giving Cross, so also the venerable and holy images, as well in painting and mosaic as of other fit materials, should be set forth in the holy churches of God, and on the sacred vessels and on the vestments and on hangings and in pictures both in houses and by the wayside, to wit, the figure of our Lord God and Saviour Jesus Christ, of our spotless Lady, the Mother of God, of the honourable Angels, of all Saints and of all pious people. For by so much more frequently as they are seen in artistic representation, by so much more readily are men lifted up to the memory of their prototypes, and to a longing after them; and to these should be given due salutation and honourable reverence, not indeed that true worship of faith which pertains alone to the divine nature; but to these, as to the figure of the precious and life-giving Cross and to the Book of the Gospels and to the other holy objects, incense and lights may be offered according to ancient pious custom. For the honour which is paid to the image passes on to that which the image represents, and he who reveres the image reveres in it the subject represented.[1]

emerging as the "Ecumenical Patriarchate" after the movement of the
Roman capital to that city). Most of the Orthodox churches that were
later organized in other regions were willing to make the same conces-
sion to Rome (these are the autocephalic, or "self-headed," churches
like those of Bulgaria, Romania, Serbia, or Russia, which carry on a
substantially autonomous life). Problems arose and were compounded
by distance and obstacles to communication, when Rome acted by itself to settle questions of doctrine or practice as if it did not need counsel from anyone else. In the words of Nicetas, the Eastern archbishop
of Nicomedia, who wrote in the twelfth century after differences had
hardened,

> We do not deny to the Roman Church the primacy amongst the five sister
> Patriarchates. . . . But she has separated herself from us by her own
> deeds, when through pride she assumed a monarchy which does not be-
> long to her office. . . . How shall we accept decrees from her that have
> been issued without consulting us and even without our knowledge? If
> the Roman Pontiff, seated on the lofty throne of his glory, wishes to thun-
> der at us . . . and if he wishes to judge us and even to rule us and our
> Churches, not by taking counsel with us but at his own arbitrary plea-
> sure, what kind of brotherhood, or even what kind of parenthood can this
> be? We should be the slaves, not the sons, of such a Church, and the
> Roman See would not be the pious mother of sons but a hard and impe-
> rious mistress of slaves.[7]

The expression of such Eastern misgivings led, predictably, to further antagonism. In addition, it is a sad reality that differences over this
question of authority were often expressed from both East and West in
anything but a charitable spirit.

In the process of drifting apart, the East and West had suffered moments of sharp, focused antagonism that anticipated the break of 1054.
In the mid-seventh century, debate in the East about the ramifications
of Chalcedon spilled over into a temporary division. When an Eastern
patriarch averred that Christ had only one will (thus, a "Monothelite"
position, from *mono*, "one," and *thelos*, "will") and the pope blithely
agreed, consternation among Eastern and Western theologians esca-
lated rapidly, people were called names, and a division resulted that
took about thirty years to restore. In this conflict, as in conflicts to
come, a key issue was the exercise of authority, with the East dealing
collegially with a strong emperor and with the laity making significant
theological contributions, as opposed to the West approaching issues

7. Quoted in Ware, *The Orthodox Church*, 50.

much more hierarchically in a context of fragmented political leadership and with theology dominated by clerics. Then in the ninth century the so-called Photian schism, to which reference has already been made, again divided the church briefly. In this case, the patriarch Photius was caught in a power play involving the Eastern emperor and the Western pope. Bad feeling, recrimination, and finally excommunications were the result, with lingering damage to efforts at keeping East and West together. The story of these earlier schisms only underscores the fact that long before the critical events of 1054, disengagement had advanced very far indeed.

Other events in the centuries surrounding 1054 also greatly affected the future course of the Orthodox Church. From the outside, no event had greater impact on Eastern Christianity before the Muslim capture of Constantinople in 1453 than the Crusades. In the internal history of Orthodoxy, no event was more important than the coming of Orthodoxy to Russia.

The Crusades Seal the Schism

The crusading movement began in 1095 when Pope Urban II (1088–99) proclaimed to a sort of revival meeting in Clermont, France, that "God wills" the rescue of the Holy Land from Islam. As an indication that the breach of 1054 was not at the time considered permanent on either side, Alexius I Comnenus, who became the Eastern emperor in 1081, appealed to the pope for help in holding back the spread of Muslim Turks. Pope Urban, who was carrying on the reform efforts that Leo IX and his successors had promoted, recognized the validity of Alexius's appeal and was trying to respond. In addition, Urban believed that an armed expedition from Europe to the Holy Land would also relieve escalating pressures in his homeland. The tendency to violence that was built into the feudal system of competing lords and aggressive knights had become a mounting concern for the church. Its efforts to curtail the widespread violence had led to what were called the Truce of God and the Peace of God, church-enforced periods when fighting was supposed to stop. To these efforts Urban now added the ideal of a crusade. If it would be possible to drain violence from Europe by enlisting nobles, with their warring knights, squires, and peasant foot soldiers, to rescue for Christianity the sacred sites taken by Muslims in the Holy Land while at the same time providing assistance to the Byzantine Empire and the Orthodox Church, that would be a triumph indeed.

Unfortunately, Urban's pious hopes and the truly noble ideals that at least some of the crusaders brought to their task led to mostly ironic and tragic results. As they unfolded, the Crusades never accomplished

The destruction and bloodshed that came upon Constantinople in 1204 as a result of the Fourth Crusade are sanitized considerably in this Victorian print.

Christian History Archives

as much good as supporters hoped, while evil consequences, unintended and unforeseen by proponents like Urban, proliferated.

The First Crusade did succeed in capturing Jerusalem in 1099. But it accomplished this with such crass military bluntness—slaughtering Jews and Arab Christians as well as Muslims—that already the underside of the crusading ideal was becoming altogether too apparent. Moreover, the hope that Western knights and their retainers might help Byzantium and the Eastern church proved illusory. Even with the first wave of armed soldiers from the West, who stopped off at Constantinople on their way to Jerusalem, there was so much trouble that Alexius did all in his power simply to get rid of his troublesome Western visitors.

Later Crusades only made matters worse. The Fourth Crusade of 1202–4 was a special disaster that so deeply poisoned relations between East and West that it would be justified to see it, rather than the events of 1054, as the final break between the two great traditions in the church.

This sordid tale can be told quite simply. As in earlier crusades, high-minded idealists were joined by others who took part entirely for material gain. This time the latter faction totally dominated the former. Under the influence of Venetian merchants, who were mostly concerned about plunder and power, the crusade turned aside from its supposed objective (to do battle with Islam) and came to Constantinople seeking what it could devour. In April 1204 an army made up of Venetian, French, and Flemish soldiers took the city. The description of

Steven Runciman, the twentieth century's leading historian of the Crusades, is sobering:

> [When] the leading Crusaders were established in the Great Palace, . . . their soldiers were told that they might spend the next three days in pillage. The sack of Constantinople is unparalleled in history. For nine centuries the great city had been the capital of Christian civilization. It was filled with works of art that had survived from ancient Greece and with the masterpieces of its own exquisite craftsmen. . . . But the Frenchmen and Flemings were filled with a lust for destruction. They rushed in a howling mob down the streets and through the houses, snatching up everything that glittered and destroying whatever they could not carry, pausing only to murder or to rape, or to break open the wine-cellars for their refreshment. . . . Palaces and hovels alike were entered and wrecked. Wounded women and children lay dying in the streets. For three days the ghastly scenes of pillage and bloodshed continued, till the huge and beautiful city was a shambles.[8]

After this orgy of destruction, the Latins attempted to set up a replacement for the Byzantine emperor. They failed miserably. Within a few decades the city was regained by Eastern Orthodox Byzantines. Even before the end of 1204, Pope Innocent III had condemned the murderous conquest of the city.

But the damage had been done. Again the extreme but well-considered words of Steven Runciman are worth quoting at length:

> There was never a greater crime against humanity than the Fourth Crusade. Not only did it cause the destruction or dispersal of all the treasures of the past that Byzantium had devotedly stored, and the mortal wounding of a civilization that was still active and great; but it was also an act of gigantic political folly. It brought no help to the Christians in Palestine. . . . In the wide sweep of world history the effects were wholly disastrous. . . . When a new, more vigorous Turkish tribe appeared, under the leadership of the brilliant house of Osman, the East Christian world was too deeply divided to make an effective stand. . . . Meanwhile hatred had been sown between Eastern and Western Christendom. . . . It was perhaps inevitable that the Church of Rome and the great Eastern Churches should drift apart; but the whole Crusading movement had embittered their relations, and henceforward, whatever a few princes might try to achieve, in the hearts of the East Christians the schism was complete, irremediable and final.[9]

8. Steven Runciman, *A History of the Crusades,* 3 vols. (New York: Cambridge University Press, 1954), 3:123.
9. Ibid., 130–31.

For the Eastern Church, as also for the Islamic world, which received many more violent attacks (though few more bloody) from the West, the Crusades were a mark of sheer barbarism. Not only did they cement the schism of 1054, but they also remained a festering memory that poisoned communications between parts of the Christian church for many centuries to come, perhaps even to this day.

Russia

If the Crusades were the great nemesis for Orthodoxy in the centuries surrounding 1054, its great advance was extension into Russia.[10] As earlier with Constantine and Charlemagne in the West, so in the tenth century a powerful ruler played a central role in the expansion of the East. An unstable political situation faced Prince Vladimir when about the year 980 he succeeded to the crown of Kyivan Rus.[†] Vladimir's grandmother Olga had converted to Christianity, but Vladimir's predecessor maintained loyalty to his ancestral faith. Russian religion at the time was a combination of unofficial animism, with considerable reverence for material objects, along with acknowledgment by political leaders of a plurality of gods. Upon becoming monarch, Vladimir first attempted to stabilize his rule by promoting pagan worship. Then after military triumphs brought him into contact with the Byzantine Empire and after he was offered the sister of the Byzantine emperor as a bride, if only he would convert to the Eastern Orthodox faith, Vladimir became a Christian. While his own acceptance of the faith seems to have been sincere, Vladimir also clearly regarded the new religion as a means of unifying his people. Hard on the heels of his own conversion, Vladimir brought the citizens of Kyiv to the Dnieper River for baptism; he imported icons, priests, and liturgical vessels from Byzantium; and he granted an official tithe to the church while also assigning it public duties.

Thus established, Orthodoxy took several centuries to move out from urban centers of power until it became deeply rooted in the countryside. But when, amid great changes like the transfer of political supremacy from Kyiv to Moscow, Orthodoxy did win the adherence of ordinary Russians, that alliance was solidly fixed.

---

10. For this section, I am grateful for the perspective provided by Professors Daniel Kaiser and Thomas Hopko in lectures held in 1988 to commemorate the first thousand years of Christianity in Russia; to Nicholas Zernov, *The Russians and Their Church* (London: SPCK, 1954); and to much advice from my friend, Professor Mark Elliott.

[†] This follows the modern Ukrainian spelling; the common English spelling "Kiev" follows the Russian.

The form of Russian Christianity that emerged shared much with other centers of Eastern Orthodoxy. Connections between church and state were always close. The center of active faith remained liturgical practice, prayer, and monastic devotion rather than doctrine or even church order. The use of icons was important from the start as an aid to worship, with these stylized portraits of saints and biblical figures considered a visible reminder of the materiality of Christ's incarnation. Soon saintly figures from Russia also became subjects of iconography. Ascetic spirituality, stressing the *kenōsis* (or emptying) of the self for and to God, became every bit as important in the Russian church as in the earlier churches of the Greek East.

This Russian icon from the fifteenth century depicts "Christ in glory."

By Andrei Rublyov (ca. 1411), Tretyakov Gallery, Moscow

Important contributions to the later development of Orthodoxy in Russia took place in the first century after Vladimir's conversion. Upon his death, the throne descended to his son Svyatopolk, who immediately conspired against his brothers, Boris and Gleb, as a way of securing power. When Svyatopolk's henchmen went after the two brothers, they resolved not to resist. Inspired by their Christian convictions, Boris and Gleb met death gladly in order to avoid a bloody civil war. For their piety and for suffering voluntarily, Boris and Gleb were designated Passion Bearers and became honored saints of the church.

Not long after their demise, the most important Russian monastery, the Petchersky Lavra (Monastery of the Caves), was established in Kyiv. Under St. Theodosius (d. 1074), this monastery became known for its identification with the poor. In a manner similar to St. Francis, Theodosius sought poverty and aspired to a literal following of Christ. It was his custom, as he visited his fellow monks in their cells, to cast extra food or garments that he found into the fire. As recorded by an early hagiographer, Theodosius would then say, "It is wrong for us, who are monks and have renounced the world, to collect property in our cells. How can a monk offer God a pure prayer if he has hidden possessions? Are you deaf to the words of Our Lord: 'For where thy treasure is, there is thy heart also' . . . ? Therefore, brothers, let us be satisfied with such clothes and food as we receive from the cellarer according to the rule; let us keep nothing in our cell, so that we may pray to God with our whole heart and mind."[11] Anticipating much that followed, this student of humility also came to exercise considerable influence among the Russian nobility.

The lives of notable believers like Boris, Gleb, and Theodosius were not typical of early Russian Orthodoxy, but the ideals they embodied became extraordinarily important for Russian Christian history. Later periods of monastic revival inspired widespread renewal in Russia. Tensions with rulers were an ever-present reality, but so also were the periodic appearances of saintly monarchs or nobles whose attention to the church actually did more good than harm. Schisms over how best to pursue the Christian life characterized Orthodoxy in Russia as in other forms of Christianity elsewhere. One of the most famous of those divisions came in the wake of St. Sergius's fifteenth-century renewal of monasticism, when his successors divided into Possessors (who held that careful use of economic and political resources was acceptable) and Non-Possessors (who pursued poverty relentlessly). Ideals of ascetic humility and of suffering would also remain to inspire generations of ordinary believers and occasional intellectual luminaries, like Fyodor Dostoyevsky in the nineteenth century and Aleksandr Solzhenitsyn in the twentieth.

When the schism of 1054 divided the Eastern and Western churches, the unquestioned center of Orthodoxy was the Byzantine Empire, with Constantinople as it splendid capital. Yet the resilience of Orthodoxy over the eons that followed, along with the possibility of its reemerging significance almost one thousand years later at the end of the twentieth century, would depend even more on what was happening in the vast northerly reaches of Russia than in the splendid churches of Byzantium.

Orthodoxy in the Twentieth Century

As Christianity moves rapidly toward the thousand-year anniversary of the events at Constantinople in 1054, it is appropriate to ask, What of the schism? What of the churches that resulted? The rest of this book

---

11. Nestor, "A Life of St. Theodosius," in *A Treasury of Russian Spirituality,* ed. G. P. Fedotov (New York: Sheed & Ward, 1948), 40.

is concerned largely with the Western church, its own division into Protestants and Catholics during the sixteenth century, its cycles of decline and renewal, its varied engagements with culture and society, and its missionary efforts outside the West. A few paragraphs, however inadequate in themselves, may still give some sense of the historic Eastern tradition as it exists in the late twentieth century.

As of the early 1990s, the Orthodox family of churches, as enumerated by Bishop Kallistos (Timothy) Ware, himself an English convert to Orthodoxy, numbered about 140 million adherents worldwide.[12] About half of these adherents are part of the Russian and Ukrainian Orthodox churches; less than 10 million remain in the four ancient patriarchates of Constantinople, Alexandria, Antioch, and Jerusalem; large numbers are found in the Romanian, Greek, Serbian, Bulgarian, and Georgian (former Soviet Union) churches; many millions are part of the Orthodox "diaspora" created by immigration from Eastern Europe to Australia, the Americas, and Western Europe; and smaller groups are found in East Africa, Japan, Finland, and predominantly Roman Catholic countries of central Europe like Poland, the Czech Republic, and Slovakia.

Although these Orthodox churches are themselves often divided by political, religious, and ethnic antagonisms, certain features of Orthodoxy remain strikingly similar to the church that Cardinal Humbert visited in 1054. The liturgy remains the heart of Orthodox life and theology. Monasteries, often linked to the extensive monastic network on Mount Athos in Greece, continue to supply most of the church's theologians, bishops, and active leaders. Theologians continue to be preoccupied with questions (like the difference between God's "essence" and his "energy") and concepts (like the "apophatic" theology of negation that experiences God by escaping finite categories of ordinary human discourse) that remain too abstruse for most Westerners to fathom. The veneration (not worship) of icons remains a prime way for the Orthodox to honor the reality of the incarnation (believing that since Christ took flesh, Christian attention to physical objects like icons is good). And the Orthodox continue to regard themselves as *the* "one holy catholic and apostolic Church" of which the Nicene Creed speaks. Moreover, the location of Orthodoxy in the East means that this whole family of Christians largely escaped the influence of the great cultural events—Renaissance, Reformation, Scientific Revolution, Enlighten-

---

12. Ware, *The Orthodox Church*, 6–7. David Barrett in 1997 put affiliation with the worldwide Orthodox communion at 215 million ("Annual Statistical Table on Global Mission: 1997," *International Bulletin of Missionary Research* 21 [January 1997]: 25).

An Orthodox procession on the Feast of Theophany (January 6) at St. Vladimir's Theological Seminary in Crestwood, New York.

St. Vladimir's Seminary

ment, Commercialism—that have proved so prominent in the Western history of Christianity over the last several centuries.

If much in Orthodoxy is the same, however, so too have some things changed. Especially the Communist epoch—stretching from the Russian Revolution of 1917 to the collapse of Communist regimes in 1989 and following—deeply affected Orthodox life and practice. As closely as Orthodoxy had been tied to the ruling houses of imperial Russia, so violently was it persecuted by Lenin, Stalin, their successors, and their puppets in Eastern Europe. As faithfully as some Orthodox attempted to live under Communism, so disconcerting has it been to awaken into the new political, economic, and cultural pluralism of the post-Communist era. Almost anything in the wild swirl of reports that have come out of central and eastern Europe concerning Orthodoxy since 1989 may be true. There has been a regression to heavy-handed use of state power to attack enemies. There has been a fresh surge of spiritual discipline and vitality. Interest in the Scriptures has grown. Xenophobic attacks on Western missionaries have increased. Orthodox monasteries are harvesting a full crop of new recruits. Orthodox churches now seek primarily political power. And more. How Orthodoxy will survive its Communist and post-Communist traumas remains to be seen. Probably more than anything that has happened in its history since 1054, with the exception of the Muslim conquest of Constantinople in 1453, the Communist era has forced Orthodoxy to confront the reality of change.

Other developments of the twentieth century also offer hints about significant innovation. Within the United States, where the largest Orthodox diaspora exists, the formation of the Orthodox Church in America (OCA) in 1970 represented an especially important development. Originally one of several competing Russian jurisdictions in the West, the OCA was established in part as an effort to move beyond ethnic Orthodoxy, to promote the use of English, and deliberately to seek adherents of non-Russian as well as Russian background. The fate of the OCA will tell much to interested non-Orthodox Christians, for it is perhaps the largest experiment in recent history to see if Orthodoxy can exist outside the ethnically confined boundaries that have traditionally structured Orthodox life. Another American jurisdiction, the Antiochean Orthodox Church, is conducting a similar experiment, though under different circumstances. Its reception in 1986 of the Evangelical Orthodox Church, a body of former evangelical Protestants seeking fuller contact with historical faith, also gives this Orthodox communion a less ethnic, more generically Christian character than most other churches in the diaspora.

Of all changes affecting the Orthodox church in recent years, however, the one that is both most visible and most directly related to the events of 1054 is renewed contact with the Roman Catholic Church. At the start of the twentieth century, preliminary movement between Rome and Constantinople was initiated by Greek, or Eastern Rite, Catholics in Ukraine. (Eastern Rite Catholics follow the Orthodox liturgy but are in communion with the pope.) Such efforts, however, were largely isolated until the Catholics' Second Vatican Council (1962–65) ignited a burst of ecumenical activity. As a consequence of the council's initiation, Pope Paul VI and Athenagoras, the ecumenical patriarch of Constantinople, met in Jerusalem in January 1964, the first time such a meeting had taken place since the Council of Florence in 1439. In 1965 the anathemas of 1054 delivered by Humbert and Cerularius were revoked. In 1980 formal theological dialogue began between the Catholics and the Orthodox, although the course of these discussions was compromised by violence in Ukraine (where Eastern Rite Catholics and Orthodox fought over church property returned after the fall of the Communist regime) and the former Yugoslavia (where Orthodox Serbs and Catholic Croatians renewed bloody conflict that had flared during World War II and many times before). During the pontificate of John Paul II (1978–), Catholic–Orthodox communication has grown, in part because the current pope's Polish background included direct contact with Orthodox churches, the first pope to enjoy such connections for a very long time. In 1987 the pope and Patriarch Demetrios I met in Rome, where they together recited the Nicene Creed (without the *filioque*). Eight years later, in June 1995, John Paul II again met the ecumenical patriarch, now Bartholomew I, who was the main speaker at a Mass celebrated by the pope.

It is therefore only in recent years that the momentum toward East–West division, of which 1054 is the most visible symbol, has begun to

Joint Statement on Orthodox–Catholic Relations

Top-level communication between the Orthodox and Roman Catholic churches resumed only after the Second Vatican Council of the early 1960s. The first formal acknowledgment that the scars of 1054 were finally beginning to heal came in a joint statement from Pope Paul VI and Patriarch Athenagoras I, dated December 7, 1965. After referring to a meeting earlier that year in Jerusalem, the two leaders concentrated on overcoming the effects of the past:

> Among the obstacles along the road of the development of these fraternal relations of confidence and esteem, there is the memory of the decisions, actions, and painful incidents which in 1054 resulted in the sentence of excommunication leveled against the Patriarch Michael Cerularius and two other persons by the legate of the Roman See under the leadership of Cardinal Humbertus, legates who then became the object of a similar sentence pronounced by the Patriarch and the Synod of Constantinople.
>
> One cannot pretend that these events were not what they were during this very troubled period of history. Today, however, they have been judged more fairly and serenely. . . . Pope Paul VI and Patriarch Athenagoras I with his Synod, in common agreement, declare that:
>
> a) They regret the offensive words, the reproaches without foundation, and the reprehensible gestures which, on both sides, have marked or accompanied the sad events of this period.
>
> b) They likewise regret and remove both from memory and from the midst of the Church the sentences of excommunication which followed these events, the memory of which has influenced actions up to our day and has hindered closer relations in charity; and they commit these excommunications to oblivion.
>
> c) Finally, they deplore the preceding and later vexing events which, under the influence of various factors—among which, lack of understanding and mutual trust—eventually led to the effective rupture of ecclesiastical communion.[2]

be reversed. To employ a distinction that has not always been observed in these pages, few events in modern *church history* are as important as renewed Orthodox–Catholic contacts. But the potential significance of these contacts for the *history of Christianity* depends more on the spiritual vitality to be found in these two ancient churches than on their ability to repair what was broken nearly one thousand years ago in one of the great turning points of both church history and the history of Christianity.

The Orthodox have a rich tradition of teaching on prayer, rooted in the practice of hesychasm, from the Greek *hésychia,* which means stillness, quietness, or rest. Hesychastic prayer is also called the prayer of the heart, prayer that goes beyond the intellect to involve all aspects of a person's being—body, soul, and spirit. The Jesus Prayer (cited below), which dates from as early as the fifth century with St. Diadochus of Photice, particularly exemplifies this tradition. It is a short, simple prayer invoking the name of Jesus derived from the appeals for mercy made to Jesus by the blind men in Matthew 9:27, 20:30, and Luke 18:38, and blind Bartimaeus in Mark 10:47. Hesychists attempt to repeat, or "breathe," the prayer continually.

The practice of hesychasm was cultivated for many years in the Greek Orthodox tradition and experienced a renewal in Russia in the nineteenth century among both the laity and monks. The anonymous author of the late nineteenth-century spiritual classic *The Way of a Pilgrim* is a layperson who finds in the Jesus Prayer a way of obeying Paul's injunction in 1 Thessalonians 5:17, "Pray without ceasing," and of focusing the mind and heart on God. After serving for seven years as a Russian bishop, Theophan the Recluse (1815–94) retired to a monastery in order to pursue the life of prayer in seclusion. He corresponded with many people, particularly women, throughout Russia, answering their questions about prayer.

> The practice of the Jesus Prayer is simple. Stand before the Lord with the attention in the heart, and call to Him: "Lord Jesus Christ, Son of God, have mercy on me!" The essential part of this is not in the words, but in faith, contrition, and self-surrender to the Lord. With these feelings one can stand before the Lord even without any words, and it will still be prayer.[13]

Further Reading

Clendenin, Daniel B. *Eastern Orthodox Christianity: A Western Perspective.* Grand Rapids: Baker, 1994.

13. Igumen Chariton of Valamo, comp., *The Art of Prayer: An Orthodox Anthology,* trans. E. Kadloubovsky and E. M. Palmer (London: Faber & Faber, 1966), 89.

————, ed. *Eastern Orthodox Theology: A Contemporary Reader*. Grand Rapids, Baker, 1994.

The Crusades [*Christian History*, no. 40]. 1993.

Fedotov, G. P., ed. *A Treasury of Russian Spirituality*. New York: Sheed & Ward, 1948.

Hussey, J. M. *The Orthodox Church in the Byzantine Empire*. Oxford: Clarendon, 1986.

Meyendorff, John. *Byzantine Theology: Historical Trends and Doctrinal Themes*. 2nd ed. New York: Fordham University Press, 1983.

————. *The Orthodox Church*. 3rd ed. Crestwood, N.Y.: St. Vladimir's Seminary Press, 1981.

The Millennium of "Russian Christianity" [*Christian History*, no. 18]. 1988.

Palmer, G. E. H., Philip Sherrard, and Kallistos Ware, trans. and ed. *The Philokalia: Compiled by St. Nikodimos of the Holy Mountain and St. Makarios of Corinth*. 4 vols. London: Faber & Faber, 1979–95.

Ware, Timothy. *The Orthodox Church*. New ed. New York: Penguin, 1993.

Wybrew, Hugh. *The Orthodox Liturgy: The Development of the Eucharistic Liturgy in the Byzantine Rite*. Crestwood, N.Y.: St. Vladimir's Seminary Press, 1990.

Zernov, Nicholas. *The Russians and Their Church*. London: SPCK, 1954.

7

The Beginnings of Protestantism:
The Diet of Worms (1521)

Martin Luther wrote, translated, paraphrased, or adapted at least thirty-seven hymns for a wide variety of uses in church and home. Some of his first efforts from the early 1520s, with their versified renditions of the Ten Commandments and the Apostles' Creed, were anticipations of the questions and answers of his Small Catechism and the sermons of his Large Catechism, which provided simple, straightforward explanations of the faith. As a hymn-writer he is of course best known for "Ein' feste Burg ist unser Gott" (variously translated as "A Mighty Fortress Is Our God," "Our God He Is a Castle Strong," and still other ways), which was written some years after the beginning of the Reformation as Luther came out of a season of internal doubt. Some of the hymns he wrote in the heat of intense polemical debate made the basic points of his theology sing. One of these hymns from 1523 was an expressive, if loose, rendition of Psalm 130:

> *From trouble deep I cry to thee,*
> *Lord God, hear thou my crying;*
> *Thy gracious ear, oh, turn to me,*
> *Open it to my sighing.*
> *For if thou mean'st to look upon*
> *The wrong and evil that is done,*
> *Who, Lord, can stand before thee?*
>
> *With thee counts nothing but thy grace*
> *To cover all our failing.*

The best life cannot win the race,
Good works are unavailing.
Before thee no one glory can,
And so must tremble every man,
And live by thy grace only. . . .

Although our sin be great, God's grace
Is greater to relieve us;
His hand in helping nothing stays,
The hurt however grievous.
The Shepherd good alone is he,
Who will at last set Israel free,
From all and every trespass.[1]

At six o'clock in the early evening of April 18, 1521, the hour had arrived for Martin Luther. The scene was an improvised imperial hall in
Worms, a modest city of roughly seven thousand inhabitants located
down the Rhine River from Strasbourg and just a little south of Mainz.
Luther, at thirty-seven years of age, had been a monk for over fifteen
years. He was appearing before Charles V, a young man of only twenty-
one who, besides serving as king of Spain, had been elected Germany's
Holy Roman emperor (and therefore a successor to Charlemagne) less
than two years before. The imperial diet (or formal assembly) that convened at Worms in January of that year marked Charles's first visit to
his German lands. The emperor understood Latin, but his own education (and language of choice) was French. Everything spoken in German had to be translated into Latin for him, and also for the large ret-
inue of Italian church officials who were in attendance.

If Charles lacked experience as emperor and if his linguistic skills
were not as advanced as many of the others who were assembled at
Worms (including some of the princes), there was no doubt about the
extent of his power. Not all his titles were secure, but Charles nonetheless presided over more of Europe than any single individual since
Charlemagne some seven centuries before. He was, in a partial listing,
"by God's Grace, Augmentor of the Realm of Germany; of Spain, the

---

1. Luther, "The Hymns," in *Luther's Works*, 55 vols. (St. Louis: Concordia; Philadelphia: Fortress, 1955–76), 53:223–24. This set is referred to hereafter as *LW*.

Two Sicilies, Jerusalem, Hungary, Dalmatia, Croatia, etc., King; Arch-
duke of Austria, and Duke of Burgundy, etc. etc."[2]

The day before, on April 17, Luther had appeared in the emperor's
presence for the first time. Spread out on a table in the imperial chamber were Luther's writings. (There was such a pile of them that Charles
and his aides, when first they came into the chamber, expressed doubt
that any single person could have written so much.) Luther had been
summoned to Worms to recant. He was being asked to confess publicly
to his mistakes in what he had written about the gospel, the nature of
the church, and the current state of Christendom. When asked on the
previous day if he would recant, Luther responded that the works were
of several different kinds. And then he requested one more day to pon-
der his reply. The imperial secretary was not pleased, for as he reminded Luther and the assembled onlookers, everyone knew why
Luther had been given an imperial safe-conduct to Worms. He had had
plenty of time to prepare. Nonetheless, because of the emperor's "in-
nate clemency,"[3] Luther was granted his request.

But now he could delay no longer, and the charge came once again:
"Come then; answer the question of his majesty, whose kindness you
have experienced in seeking a time for thought. Do you wish to defend
all your acknowledged books, or to retract some?"

Luther, who obviously had considered his reply carefully, responded
that his books were of three kinds. Some were works of simple piety
that no Christian ruler or church official could possibly want to be
withdrawn. A second category were works directed against "the papacy
and the affairs of the papists as those who both by their doctrines and
very wicked examples have laid waste the Christian world with evil that
affects the spirit and the body." Luther did not think anyone would
want to defend the evils that those books attacked. But the third kind
of writing, Luther conceded, did contain some things that were overly
harsh, which he was willing to consider retracting, but only on one very
important condition. At this point, Luther laid down his gauntlet:
"Therefore, I ask by the mercy of God, may your most serene majesty,
most illustrious lordships, or anyone at all who is able, either high or
low, bear witness, expose my errors, overthrowing them by the writings

---

2. Quoted in Gordon Rupp, *Luther's Progress to the Diet of Worms* (New York: Harper
Torchbook, 1964 [orig. 1951]), 96. Rupp provides excellent coverage of the circumstances leading to the Diet, as do also Martin Brecht, *Martin Luther*, vol. 1, *His Road to Reformation* (Philadelphia: Fortress, 1985); and Roland Bainton, *Here I Stand: A Life of Martin
Luther* (Nashville: Abingdon, 1950)

3. All quotations in this section are from "Luther at the Diet of Worms," *LW* 32:103–
31.

North Wind Picture Archives

Luther's actual appearance before Charles V took place in a much smaller room, but it may in fact have been just as dramatic as shown here.

of the prophets and the evangelists. Once I have been taught I shall be quite ready to renounce every error, and I shall be the first to cast my books into the fire." And so Luther ended his defense.

But he had not been explicit enough for the imperial court. The emperor's spokesman pressed him again. Luther had not really answered the question. Would he recant or not? Deal plainly, not with a "horned," or ambiguous, reply. Then Luther spoke words that augured one of the most momentous changes in the history of Europe, and one of the most significant in the history of the church: "Since then your serene majesty and your lordships seek a simple answer, I will give it in this manner, neither horned nor toothed: Unless I am convinced by the testimony of the Scriptures or by clear reason (for I do not trust either in the pope or in councils alone, since it is well known that they have often erred and contradicted themselves), I am bound by the Scriptures I have quoted and my conscience is captive to the Word of God. I cannot and I will not retract anything, since it is neither safe nor right to go against conscience."

With these words, Protestantism was born. Luther's conscience was captive to "the Word of God," to the living, active voice of Scripture. Moreover, what he felt Scripture taught clearly were truths about human nature, the way of salvation, and the Christian life—truths that he was certain had been badly obscured, even obliterated, by the very church officials who should have been their most faithful defenders. With this dramatic statement in the most exalted company a sixteenth-century European could imagine, the foundations of Protestantism were set out for all to see: Protestants would obey the Bible before all other authorities. And what many Protestants would find in the Bible was a message of salvation by grace at least substantially similar to the one that Luther had discovered for himself in the pages of the Scriptures.

Protestant historians have tended to treat the Diet of Worms as if it were significant only for Luther's dramatic speech. Everything that followed is sometimes seen as simply natural consequences. After Worms, Luther was protected by his prince, Frederick the Wise of Saxony, as an illustration of the bond that immediately grew up between Protestantism and defenders of local and national authority. Luther went directly from Worms to a retreat at the Castle Wartburg, where, in a great burst of activity, he produced a magnificent German translation of the New Testament, testimony to Protestant reliance on Scripture. Luther soon would leave the monastery and take a wife, setting the Protestant course for family and vocation. From Worms, at least in Protestant eyes, there was no turning back.

In fact, however, Luther's address to the emperor did not close the Diet of Worms. Words that the emperor's secretary spoke in reply to Luther on that April day also deserve to be heard, perhaps most of all by Protestants. After Luther had finished speaking, this official rebuked him sternly for setting himself up as superior to the great councils of the Catholic Church that had already ruled on many of the issues Luther was also addressing. "In this," the imperial secretary told Luther, "you are completely mad. For what purpose does it serve to raise a new dispute about matters condemned through so many centuries by church and council? Unless perhaps a reason must be given to just anyone about anything whatsoever. But if it were granted that whoever contradicts the councils and the common understanding of the church must be overcome by Scripture passages, we will have nothing in Christianity that is certain or decided."* Luther's conscience was captive to the Word of God. But the imperial court was quick to ask a disturbing and discerning question—what if everyone simply followed

---

*The official was Johann Eck, but not the famous Eck with whom Luther had earlier carried on a momentous theological debate.

his or her own conscience? The end result was obvious—"we will have nothing certain."

The next day, April 19, while Luther engaged in private dispute with representatives of the pope and emperor, Charles V caused to be read a document he had written with his own hand. Charles reminded his German nobles that he was descended from the "most Christian" monarchs of Germany, Spain, Austria, and Burgundy, who, "to the honor of God, the strengthening of the faith, and the salvation of souls," had each and every one "remained up to death faithful sons of the church." Charles, to say the least, was not impressed with what he had heard the day before. "It is certain," he concluded, "that a single friar errs in his opinion which is against all of Christendom and according to which all of Christianity will be and will always have been in error both in the past thousand years and even more in the present." Charles felt he had been called as emperor to defend the true faith, and he also felt it would be "a great shame" to himself and all the nobles of Germany if, during their age, "not only heresy but suspicion of heresy or decrease of the Christian religion should through our negligence dwell after us in the heart of men and our successors to our perpetual dishonor."

When we consider these responses to Luther along with his own words before the emperor, we can see more clearly what was at stake at the Diet of Worms. Not only was there now a great division in the West concerning how best to define the Christian faith—Protestants and Catholics would go separate ways that, more than five centuries later, are still distinct. But also the relation between civil and ecclesiastical power would change as some rulers, both great and petty, broke with the pope in their move toward Protestantism, while others, who remained Roman Catholic, discovered how much the pope now needed to rely upon them. In addition, Luther also intimated a whole new sense of the self against what Charles and his allies regarded as the settled wisdom of the ages. The authority of the individual conscience had been proclaimed over against the authority of church councils, in contradiction to the weight of tradition, and in the very face of the emperor himself. Even though Luther spoke of his conscience as bound by Scripture, he had introduced, with moving power, a new principle of authority. In a word, Europe—and the church—would never be the same.

At this point in the book, the author's own convictions play an even larger role than usual in defining key turning points in Christian history. Viewed with strict impartiality, the events associated with the Reformation in the sixteenth century were not as important as the movement of the church out of Judaism or the stabilizing of its basic teachings about Christ at Nicaea and Chalcedon. It is even a question worthy of serious thought whether the Protestant Reformation and its Catholic counterpart should be regarded as more significant in Christian history than the earlier division between Western and Eastern churches, or the explosion of the Christian faith outside the West that has taken place in the twentieth century.

Nonetheless, because I am a Protestant who thinks that Martin Luther understood the heart of the Christian gospel as well as anyone in the history of Christianity since the age of the apostles, I naturally regard his life and work as a vital turning point in church history. At the same time, however, as a student more generally of Western history since the sixteenth century, it is clear to me that Protestantism—in conjunction with the emergence of modern nation-states, the beginnings of the modern economy, and the explosion of learning in Europe from the time of the Renaissance—eventually brought radical changes to European Christendom, and that some of those changes have been anything but healthy for Christian life and thought. Yet again, as someone who remains by conviction outside of the Roman Catholic Church and yet who has come to conclude that Roman traditions are sometimes admirably strong where Protestant traditions are notoriously weak, I am predisposed to regard the resurgence of Roman Catholicism from the middle of the sixteenth century (in the Catholic Reformation, or Counter-Reformation) as another decisive turning point in the world history of Christianity.

With such convictions, the sixteenth century seems simply to overflow with critical turning points. First is the theological contribution of Luther, which (in my view) reasserted an enduring and essential element in Christian theology. Second is the reconfiguration of Europe (and, by later extension, the European colonies that became the United States and Canada) away from Christendom to the modern secular world. For this key change, the English Act of Supremacy from 1534 is a dramatic symbol. Third is the reenergizing of the Catholic Church, especially in its missionary outreach beyond the boundaries of Europe, which is most notably marked by the founding of the Society of Jesus under Ignatius Loyola in 1534 (with papal approval soon thereafter). These turning points are the subjects of this and the next two chapters. They made the age of Luther and Loyola—which is also the era of John Calvin, Charles V, Christopher Columbus, Nicolas Copernicus, Albrecht Dürer, Elizabeth I, Erasmus of Rotterdam, Henry VIII, Margaret of Navarre, Menno Simons, Michelangelo, Thomas More, Philip II, William Tyndale, Francis Xavier, and many more—such an important century in the history of Christianity.

The Life of the "Wild Boar"

In *Exsurge Domine*, the papal bull (or written mandate, from Latin *bulla*, "seal") of June 1520, which sought to bring Martin Luther to heel, Pope Leo X called Luther "the wild boar from the forest" whose tongue was a "fire." More than he knew, the pope was correct. But whether he was correct in the sense that he intended—that Luther was "seek[ing] to destroy" the church—or, conversely, that Luther wreaked havoc on structures that separated people from God, depends upon what you think of Luther.[4]

He was born in Eisleben, a Saxon mining town, in 1483. Within a decade Columbus would set sail to the West, the last of the Islamic Moors would be pushed out of Spain, and his somewhat older contemporary, Erasmus of Rotterdam, would begin a lifelong study of the Greek texts of the New Testament. Europe was changing fast. Luther's parents gave him the best education they could afford, in the hopes that he would become a lawyer and then perhaps a prosperous town councilor. But by the time his university career came to an end, realities of the unseen world pressed harder upon Luther than material ambition. In 1505, to the consternation especially of his father, he entered the Augustinian Cloister (monastery) in Erfurt. Twenty years later Luther would repudiate his monastic vows, but it is a remarkable bridge to the preceding millennium of Christendom that the first Protestant came to his foundational convictions as a monk. Of special importance for Luther's personal and theological development was the wise counsel of Johann von Staupitz (ca. 1468–1524), the supervisor of the German Augustinians. When Luther besieged Staupitz with recitals of his own inadequacy before God, Staupitz (who died peacefully in the Roman church) urged him to study the Scriptures. Staupitz also arranged for Luther to take an advanced degree in theology so that, as a practical antidote to his spiritual depression, he could become a university teacher and put his great energies to profitable use. Thus, shortly before he turned thirty, Luther began his lifelong job as an instructor in Sacred Scripture at the new University of Wittenberg.

The demands of the monastery and his teaching gave Luther more than enough to do, but they were not enough to satisfy his personal quest for holiness. Luther eventually left the monastery, not because he neglected monastic discipline, but because he took that discipline as seriously as humanly possible. His sense of sin was great and caused him much distress. Even more distress was caused by the fearsome image

4. Pope Leo X, "Exsurge Domine," in *Readings in Church History*, ed. Colman J. Barry (Westminster, Md.: Newman, 1967), 2:29.

Luther on His Own Spiritual Breakthrough

When in 1545 Luther prepared an introduction to his collected Latin writings, he looked back to the momentous change that had taken place nearly thirty years before:

Through I lived as a monk without reproach, I felt that I was a sinner before God with an extremely disturbed conscience. I could not believe that he was placated by my satisfaction. I did not love, yes, I hated the righteous God who punishes sinners, and secretly, if not blasphemously, certainly murmuring greatly, I was angry with God, and said, "As if, indeed, it is not enough, that miserable sinners, eternally lost through original sin, are crushed by every kind of calamity by the law of the decalogue, without having God add pain to pain by the gospel and also by the gospel threatening us with his righteousness and wrath!" And thus I raged with a fierce and troubled conscience. Nevertheless, I beat importunately upon Paul at that place, most ardently desiring to know what St. Paul wanted.

At last, by the mercy of God, meditating day and night, I gave heed to the context of the words, namely, "In it the righteousness of God is revealed, as it is written, 'He who through faith is righteous shall live.'" There I began to understand that the righteousness of God is that by which the righteous lives by a gift of God, namely by faith. And this is the meaning: the righteousness of God is revealed by the gospel, namely, the passive righteousness with which merciful God justifies us by faith, as it is written, "He who through faith is righteous shall live." Here I felt that I was altogether born again and had entered paradise itself through open gates. There a totally other face of the entire Scripture showed itself to me. Thereupon I ran through the Scriptures from memory. I also found in other terms an analogy, as, the work of God, that is, what God does in us, the power of God, with which he makes us strong, the wisdom of God, with which he makes us wise, the strength of God, the salvation of God, the glory of God.

And I extolled my sweetest word with a love as great as the hatred with which I had before hated the word "righteousness of God." Thus that place in Paul was for me truly the gate to paradise.[1]

of God that predominated in his thought, especially of God as the perfectly righteous Judge who sent his Son to show humanity the full and terrible reality of divine righteousness. Concerning this righteousness, Luther pondered, labored, studied, strove, and pondered some more. He was especially perplexed with a range of pertinent scriptural texts. On these, as he put it, he "beat importunately."

Most perplexing of all were these words from the first chapter of Romans—"For in the gospel a righteousness from God is revealed." How could the revelation of God's righteousness, which forces humans to see how unworthy they are when set against the perfections of divine holiness, ever constitute a gospel message of good news? How could reconciliation with God possibly come from a display of God's righteousness? Finally, after several years of intense struggle over such questions, he found a clue in a single clause from Psalm 31—"deliver me in your righteousness." With that insight Luther could make sense of his discovery in Romans 1 concerning "a righteousness that is *by faith* from first to last" and hear with relief that "the righteous will live by faith." The key, as Luther would put it many years later, was that in Christ the sinner could receive the righteousness of God as a gift.

None of Luther's inner theological turmoil or his hard-won breakthroughs in understanding Scripture caused even a ripple on the ecclesiastical seas. In fact, Luther later concluded that his own journey resembled the paths taken by many others in the church's earlier history, like Augustine in the fourth century, the Bohemian reformer John Hus in the early fifteenth century, or the Dutch preacher John Wessel of Gansfort (d. 1489). It was only when Luther began to protest against current church practices, which he thought obscured the free gift of grace to be found through faith in Christ, that his private discoveries led to public antagonism. As a prime example, the protest of his Ninety-Five Theses against the selling of indulgences in 1517 made him a figure of instant controversy, not so much because of the theology underlying the theses, but because important church officials, including the pope, received a share of monies raised by indulgence sales.

Soon, however, ecclesiastical resistance to Luther's increasingly public appeals for reform moved beyond debate over abuses to serious wrestling with basic theological issues. Growing public controversy revealed a Luther who was as prolific in published polemics as he was earnest in private theological reflection. The theological disputes that flourished in the wake of the Ninety-Five Theses represented the first full-scale exploitation of the printing press in European history. The torrent of words that flowed from Luther's pen represented a marvel in his age and became a treasure for study thereafter, especially in the twentieth century as more complete editions of Luther's works have become more readily available.

The remarkable nature of Luther's literary productivity is shown especially by what he published in 1520. Apart from the distinct value of each work, together they provided much of the bulk that was laid on the table at Worms during the confrontation with Charles V. In 1520 alone Luther published, besides a flurry of less substantial writings, five major books. His *Treatise on Good Works* claimed to show how faith in Christ was, strictly speaking, the only good work that God expected from repentant sinners; moreover, the "work" of faith was something humans could perform only by grace because faith itself was a gift from God. Luther's aggressive *The Papacy of Rome* intimated that the pope should be called Antichrist because, although he was supposed to be the vicar of Christ, he actually kept people from understanding and heeding the message of the gospel. His *Address to the Christian Nobility of the German Nation* was a rousing appeal to leaders north of the Alps to throw off the tyranny—economic and political

Luther's Wife, Catharina von Bora. Portrait by Lucas Cranach, jun.

Catharina von Bora.

Courtesy of the Billy Graham Center Museum

When in 1525 Luther married the former nun Katherine von Bora, he gave the same sort of impetus to the Protestant clerical family as he had earlier provided for Protestant theology.

as well as spiritual—that bound them to Rome. His *Babylonian Captivity of the Church* presented a searching examination of the church's sevenfold system of sacraments. By claiming to find only baptism and the Lord's Supper, and perhaps confession, as sacraments authorized by Christ in the New Testament—and by arguing that the Catholic Church's domination of sacramental practice had turned them into works of self-righteousness—Luther threatened the very foundations of Christendom as it had grown up around the sacramental system. In contrast to the sharp polemics of these other works, Luther's last major book from 1520, *The Freedom of a Christian*, was a much more irenic effort to explain how a believer, redeemed entirely by the exercise of divine grace, would nevertheless naturally be active in doing good works. Luther, with his gift for paradox, put it like this: "A Christian is a perfectly free lord of all, subject to none. A Christian is a perfectly dutiful servant of all, subject to all."[5]

5. Luther, "The Freedom of a Christian," *LW* 31:344.

These works from 1520 raised the challenge to which the Diet of Worms of the next year was the response. When Luther's interpretation of the gospel, and of the church framework necessary to support that understanding of the gospel, was rejected by both pope and emperor, the move toward Protestantism accelerated. Soon after his appearance at Worms, Luther prepared a revised church order for worship in addition to translating the New Testament into German. In 1525 further decisive actions clarified what Luther felt was a proper response to the gospel. In rapid succession he married Katherine von Bora, herself a former nun; he chastised rebellious peasants for thinking that his interpretation of gospel freedom legitimated political rebellion; and he published a lengthy defense of "the bound will" against the humanist and biblical scholar Erasmus. These moves showed clearly what Luther felt a reformed church should look like. It no longer needed a special priestly caste to do the real work of God; it certainly should not be taken as an excuse to disrupt the social order; and it should fully embrace Augustine's understanding of human nature as willfully captive to its own selfishness until God changed the will to honor himself.

The last twenty years of Luther's life were not as dramatic as the years between 1517 and 1525, which had made him both the most revered and the most hated man in Europe. Books, especially sermons and lectures on various parts of the Bible, continued to pour from his pen. Amid all his weighty tomes, Luther's own favorite was the Small Catechism from 1529, which in simple questions and answers explained the Ten Commandments, the Apostles' Creed, and the Lord's Prayer, along with a few principles of daily Christian living in light of his understanding of the gospel.

In that same year, Luther engaged in a momentous debate at Marburg, in southwest Germany, with Ulrich Zwingli, the reformer of Zurich in Switzerland and a near-exact contemporary of Luther. At that debate, the two Protestant leaders found that they could agree on most points of doctrine and practice, but not on the meaning of the Lord's Supper. Luther held that Christ was truly present in the Supper, Zwingli that he was present only symbolically. Inability to resolve that troubling issue indicated more clearly than any previous event that the reform in which both Luther and Zwingli played such prominent roles would lead to Protestant *churches* rather than to a reform of the one Western church. In 1530 Luther's closest colleague, Philipp Melanchthon, presented a digest of his and Luther's theological convictions to an imperial diet at Augsburg. When that document was signed by several of the important princes in atten-

Luther on the Apostles' Creed

Luther's exposition of the Apostles' Creed was the heart of his Small Catechism.

The First Article: Creation

"I believe in God, the Father almighty, Maker of heaven and earth."
What does this mean?

Answer: I believe that God has created me and all that exists; that he has given me and still sustains my body and soul, all my limbs and senses, my reason and all the faculties of my mind, together with food and clothing, house and home, family and property; that he provides me daily and abundantly with all the necessities of life, protects me from all danger, and preserves me from all evil. All this he does out of his pure, fatherly, and divine goodness and mercy, without any merit or worthiness on my part. For all of this I am bound to thank, praise, serve, and obey him. This is most certainly true.

The Second Article: Redemption

"And in Jesus Christ, his only son, our Lord: who was conceived by the Holy Spirit, born of the virgin Mary, suffered under Pontius Pilate, was crucified, dead, and buried: he descended into hell, the third day he rose from the dead, he ascended into heaven, and is seated on the right hand of God, the Father almighty, whence he shall come to judge the living and the dead."
What does this mean?

Answer: I believe that Jesus Christ, true God, begotten of the Father from eternity, and also true man, born of the virgin Mary, is my Lord, who has redeemed me, a lost and condemned creature, delivered me and freed me from all sins, from death, and from the power of the devil, not with silver and gold but with his holy and precious blood and with his innocent sufferings and death, in order that I may be his, live under him in his kingdom, and serve him in everlasting righteousness, innocence, and blessedness, even as he is risen from the dead and lives and reigns to all eternity. This is most certainly true.[2]

dance, the resulting Augsburg Confession became the doctrinal standard for the Lutheran churches that were emerging in German, Scandinavian, and eastern European regions. In 1534 Luther finished his translation of the entire Bible, on which he had been working with the help of many colleagues for more than a decade. His health was precarious and his moods often stormy in his last years; he died in February 1546.

Luther's Theology of the Cross as Turning Point

There are many worthy reasons for studying the life of Martin Luther. Students of the German language celebrate him for his linguistic genius and for making the speech of the Saxons (enshrined in a Bible translation with more impact in Germany than the King James Bible had in England) the standard of the modern German language. Those who study the family find Luther's marriage a landmark in the development of modern forms of social interaction. Historians of the church find Luther an incredible dynamo in reconstituting the ecclesiastical structures of the sixteenth century. Roland Bainton, author of one of the best lives of Luther, once said that in Germany, Luther did all by himself what in England it took Bible-translator William Tyndale, liturgist Thomas Cranmer, preacher Hugh Latimer, hymn-writer Isaac Watts, and several generations of theologians to do.[6] For the student of genius (or psychological compulsion), the Luther who published some kind of treatise, sermon, lecture, or biblical exposition on the average of once every three weeks during his adult life is a natural object of interest.

But why regard Luther and what he wrote as a turning point in the history of Christianity? Efforts to answer that question lead at first to relatively troubling conclusions, that is, if we take the historical shape of Luther's life at all seriously.

First, Luther could never be considered a model of Christian decorum. Rather, he was a blunt and sometimes crude writer who was almost as likely to embarrass his supporters and protectors as to edify them. Listen to Luther, for example, on the subject of education. After some of the first Protestant reforms were instituted, a great falling away took place in the schools and universities of Germany as parents concluded that weaknesses in the Catholic Church automatically spilled over into the educational institutions historically linked to the church. However plausible this failure to promote education might first seem in light of Luther's own arguments against Rome, Luther himself would have none of it. Parents who did not see to their children's education were "shameful, despicable, damnable parents who are no parents at all but despicable hogs and venomous beasts, devouring their own young."[7] The Luther of these frank opinions was also the one who, on more than one occa-

6. Bainton, *Here I Stand*, 301.
7. Luther, "A Sermon on Keeping Children in School," *LW* 46:211.

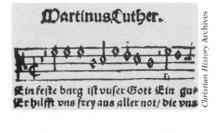

This print shows how Martin Luther's most famous hymn, "A Mighty Fortress," appeared very soon after it was first published.

sion, counseled a monarch experiencing marital difficulties to imitate the polygamous rulers of ancient Israel and take a second wife. Or what should we say about the Luther who could make this boast in the early years of reform: "While I slept or drank Wittenberg beer with my friends Philipp [Melanchthon] and [Nicholas] Amsdorf, the Word so greatly weakened the papacy that no prince or emperor ever inflicted such losses upon it."[8] In sum, it is not for propriety or diffidence that Luther is remembered in the history of Christianity.

Neither, at a more serious level, is it possible to remember Luther as a well-balanced, healthy-minded personality. Luther never enjoyed the serenity, the holy demeanor, or the victorious Christian life that many other worthies in the history of the church exemplified. He was, by contrast, constantly beset by internal struggles, doubts, and depressions. In his rapid shifts of mood he could be nearly manic. Martyn Lloyd-Jones, the great preacher from Wales, had these aspects of Luther's person in view in 1967, on the 450th anniversary of the Ninety-Five Theses, when he noted laconically, "Genius, brilliant brain that he was, [Luther] was subject to attacks of depression. . . . He was very human. Not only did he suffer from attacks of depression, he was a great hypochondriac, particularly with respect to his bowels. He talked a lot about that. That is why I mention it."[9]

Most seriously, Luther was also manifestly a sinner, especially by the standards he himself had proclaimed from the Scriptures. With his open personality, moreover, Luther's marks of spiritual disobedience were all too obviously on display. Of special damage in the history of the West were Luther's harsh denunciations of the Jews in 1543, just three years before his death. In extreme language Luther called upon the rulers of Germany to drive the Jews out of their lands, take most of their wealth, and forbid their rabbis to teach. It can be said in his defense that he was acting for theological reasons and because he had heard that Jewish teachers were trying to

8. Luther, "Eight Sermons at Wittenberg," *LW* 51:77.

9. D. Martyn Lloyd-Jones, *Luther and His Message for Today* (London: Evangelical Press, 1968), 18.

entice Protestants and Catholics away from Christian faith. Yet the sinfully violent way in which he published his arguments cast one of the seeds into the ground that has been bearing much bitter fruit ever since.

In short, what made Luther's teaching an important turning point were not his impeccable spiritual credentials. To be sure, he could be genuinely compassionate, deeply loving, and unexpectedly humble, and he had many extraordinary gifts. But it was much more the vision of God that gripped Luther, and which he then communicated through sermons, tracts, and treatises, that made a mark on the history of Christianity. That vision of God, which shattered many of the religious conventions of Luther's day, first broke through to the depths of his own being and then forced the West as a whole to pay attention.

Luther was not interested in abstract pictures of God. Not for him Christian equivalents of Aristotle's Unmoved Mover or Plato's perfection of eternal form. Even conceptions of God that had inspired other notables in the Christian church were not his primary concern. He appreciated the God of love who had meant so much to German mystics of previous generations. He did use some of the things that Thomas Aquinas had said about God's rule over the physical and rational worlds (though he could never bring himself to say anything good about Aquinas, whom he considered, without troubling to read him thoroughly, a promoter of salvation by mental good works). And he certainly learned something from Augustine's picture of God as pure moral light and Augustine's depiction of the Trinity as constant divine interaction. But these and other reputable Christian images of God were for Luther secondary.

We can sense the heart of Luther's concern about God if we begin with his public efforts at reform—with the Ninety-Five Theses that he displayed in Wittenberg on October 31, 1517. The first of the Ninety-Five says simply: "When our Lord and Master Jesus Christ said, 'Repent,' he willed the entire life of believers to be one of repentance." The last four theses carry us even closer to his main concern:

92. Away then with all those prophets who say to the people of Christ, "Peace, peace," and there is no peace!
93. Blessed be all those prophets who say to the people of Christ, "Cross, cross," and there is no cross!
94. Christians should be exhorted to be diligent in following Christ, their head, through penalties, death, and hell;
95. And thus be confident of entering into heaven through many tribulations rather than through the false security of peace.[10]

10. Luther, "Ninety-Five Theses," *LW* 31:33.

Luther's hard-won understanding of God that had come through arduous meditation upon the first chapter of Romans is here beginning to emerge. Religion as personal reassurance gives way before religion defined by a crucified savior. But still Luther is quite enigmatic.

Only a few months later Luther expressed matters more clearly when he proposed some other theses for a debate at Heidelberg: "The person who believes that he can obtain grace by doing what is in him adds sins to sin so that he becomes doubly guilty." Luther thus attacked the notion that the exertion of mere human energy could secure reconciliation with God. But this chastening message was not the knell of doom. Rather, such realities can increase the desire to humble oneself and "seek the grace of Christ." Then Luther put it as plainly as he could. "He deserves to be called a theologian . . . who comprehends the visible and manifest things of God seen through suffering and the cross. . . . A theologian of glory calls evil good and good evil. A theologian of the cross calls the thing what it actually is."[11]

The crucial element in Luther's idea of God was again a paradox: to understand the power that made heaven and earth, it was necessary to know the powerlessness that hung on a Roman gibbet. To conceive the moral perfection of deity, it was necessary to understand the scandal, the shame, the pain, and the sordidness of a criminal's execution. For Luther, in short, to find God was to find the cross.

Luther often drew upon the first chapter of 1 Corinthians to explicate his theology of God as revealed in and by the cross:

> For the message of the cross is foolishness to those who are perishing, but to us who are being saved it is the power of God. For it is written: "I will destroy the wisdom of the wise; the intelligence of the intelligent I will frustrate." Where is the wise man? Where is the scholar? Where is the philosopher of this age? Has not God made foolish the wisdom of the world? For since in the wisdom of God the world through its wisdom did not know him, God was pleased through the foolishness of what was preached to save those who believe. Jews demand miraculous signs and Greeks look for wisdom, but we preach Christ crucified: a stumbling block to Jews and foolishness to Gentiles, but to those whom God has called, both Jews and Greeks, Christ the power of God and the wisdom of God. For the foolishness of God is wiser than man's wisdom, and the weakness of God is stronger than man's strength. (Vv. 18–25)

11. Luther, "Heidelberg Disputation," *LW* 31:50–53.

Such biblical passages defined the essence of God for Luther, and so he spoke much about the cross. To him, Christianity begins with Christ dying for sinners; Christianity becomes a reality in human lives when women and men enter into Christ's death by suffering the destruction of their own pretensions as they stand *coram Deo* (in the very presence of God).

As an instinctive polemicist, Luther also spoke against the mind-set opposed to a theology of the cross, or what he called a theology of glory. To Luther, a theology of glory meant two things. First, it urges humans to trust themselves, to make their own efforts the basis of security in this life and the life to come. A theology of glory asks people to do what lies within their own power, to be up and doing, in order to gain acceptance from themselves, from fellow humans, and, most important, from God. A theology of glory guides humans to think that if we could only discipline ourselves properly, we would finally and ultimately please God. With insidious effect, a theology of glory urges humans to think that what *we* do for God matters most in creating a spiritual life, rather than what *God* has done for us.

Second, Luther also argued that a theology of glory does even further damage by encouraging humans to trust in their own wisdom. It encourages men and women to rely upon their own understanding of God and their own understanding of the world as a sufficient guide for life. It urges humans to think that what the mind discovers about self, others, the world, and God can open a path to righteousness.

It was this kind of talk that gave many early readers of Luther's works the idea that he was a revolutionary who wanted to overthrow all inherited institutions, whether civil, educational, or ecclesiastical. Luther's harsh response to such notions, as in his remarks to parents who neglected the education of their children, shows that this reading was a misinterpretation. Luther actually had much respect for traditional civil authority; he thought that the seven liberal arts developed in the Middle Ages and even newer modes of inquiry (like historical study) could be better pursued by those who had been saved by grace; and he held that no one could be redeemed who did not participate in the life of the visible church. What Luther denounced as a theology of glory was not human activity as such or the inestimably valuable contribution of human traditions and structures. It was rather the idea that these activities, traditions, and structures were in themselves life-giving. Capacities given by God they certainly were, but capacities that should be exercised in grateful thanksgiving for the gift of grace that was bestowed purely through God's good pleasure in the person of Jesus Christ.

Luther eventually came to think that his earnest efforts as a monk were rooted in a theology of glory. He had believed that systematic, conscientious, ardent, self-denying religious service would win acceptance with God, peace of soul, respect from his fellow spiritual pilgrims, and, in the end, an easeful death. But all such notions were banished when he found the cross.

What Luther found at the cross of Jesus utterly confounded him: disdain and derision, insecurity unto death, desertion by friends, the collapse of hope for the future, a death with hated malefactors, the wrath of the whole world—and God.

What did Luther mean when he talked about finding God through suffering and the cross? He meant, first, that the one who wished to find God would have to look toward Calvary, where God had made himself most fully known. But to realize that the cross was where God had most completely revealed himself was then to realize that any hope for the self would involve a secondary crucifixion of the sinful self. It would involve an existential awareness of how infinitely impure the sinner was before the holiness and purity of the living God. It meant, also, that the way to the one true God who revealed himself at Calvary would lead to intellectual humility and a confession of the gross ignorance of all humanity before the mystery of God's wisdom displayed at the cross.

Why did these realizations lead to the cross? They led to the cross, Luther held, because the cross reveals the Creator, the majestic, all-powerful God suffering—and suffering *for us*. Luther could even say that the cross shows us the dreadful mystery of God tasting death for us. Where could we find a clearer exposé of the depths of human sinfulness than to know that we could be made right only through the death of God Incarnate. Believers, therefore, can embrace the cross, but only if they despair of themselves, only if they forsake a theology of glory.

For Luther it was also a pivotal axiom that the cross reveals the all-loving God as also the all-mysterious God. At the cross the creation itself took hold of the Creator; the creation entombed the Creator. At the cross the loftiest heights came down to the deepest depths; at the cross the hands of men pierced the hands that made humankind. There could be no greater mystery.

Thus, as Luther constantly repeated, the cross must always remain utterly scandalous. It was a scandal for Jews, and all who sought God through moral exertion; it was a scandal for Greeks, and all who sought God through the exercise of the mind. The cross, for Luther, revealed the judgment of God that no amount of human work could make humanity successful; no amount of diligent study could make humanity truly wise; no amount of human exertion could provide enduring joy. The cross, in sum, was God's everlasting "no" to the most fundamental human idolatry of regarding the self as a god. It was God's final word of condemnation for all efforts to enshrine humanity at the center of existence.

Luther's "evangelical breakthrough" was an excruciatingly long time in coming for himself, but it also had a remarkable effect once announced, because these denunciations of a theology of glory seemed so fanatical, so excessive, or what we might today call so counterintuitive. But for those who could follow Luther's chain of reasoning or, as was more often the case, who recognized the pilgrimage of their own hearts in what he wrote, there was great reward. A theology of the cross did not only destroy, it also opened up. And what it opened up was God's everlasting "yes" to those who had come to the end of themselves. Here is how Luther put it:

> For where man's strength ends, God's strength begins, provided faith is present and waits on him. And when the oppression comes to an end, it becomes manifest what great strength was hidden under the weakness. Even so, Christ was powerless on the cross; and yet there he performed his mightiest work and conquered sin, death, world, hell, devil, and all evil. Thus all the martyrs were strong and overcame. Thus, too, all who suffer and are oppressed overcome.[12]

With these words, Luther echoed what the apostle Paul had said to the Corinthians. If humans embrace the cross, they may be scorned as spineless and foolish. But that is not the last word, for to embrace the cross is also to embrace the world as it actually is in its most essential reality. We also come to know "the mystery of God . . . Christ, in whom are hid all the treasures of wisdom and knowledge" (Col. 2:2–3). To embrace the scandalous cross is to be embraced in turn by Jesus. The blood-streaked figure enfolds those who come to him and ushers them into the kingdom of God. The theology of the cross shows how to become a child of God.

For Luther, and for those whom his message illuminated with a force like lightning, the cross became the pathway to life. To be sure, it was a life that continued to bear the marks of crucifixion. Luther did not forget the words that Barnabas and Paul had spoken to the Christians in Antioch: "We must go through many hardships to enter the kingdom of God" (Acts 14:22). And so he often repeated the reminder,

---

12. Luther, "The Magnificat," *LW* 21:340.

"We are Christians and have the gospel, which neither the devil nor men can abide, in order that we may come into poverty and lowliness and God may thereby have his work in us."[13] Or as Luther affirmed in the words of his best-known hymn, "A Mighty Fortress Is Our God": "And though this world, with devils filled, should threaten to undo us; / We will not fear, for God hath willed his truth to triumph through us."

The very last words that Luther wrote summed up the essence of his vision of God. At the end of a brief essay he lapsed from Latin into German: "Wir sind Bettler. Das ist wahr."[14] We are beggars. That's the truth. But for Luther such acknowledgment was not despairing, for he had come to see that, because of the cross, God now heard the beggar's cry.

Perhaps the most effective representative of Martin Luther's theology in the twentieth century was the German pastor Dietrich Bonhoeffer, who was put to death by the Nazis only weeks before the Allied liberation of Germany in 1945.

Christian History Archives

In some ways, Martin Luther's Christian faith marks a strange beginning for Protestantism. He spent nearly as many years as a monk as he did in laboring to reconstruct the church outside of Roman Catholicism. His profound engagement with Scripture was encouraged by his monastic superior. He believed much more firmly in predestination than have many later Protestants. His high view of the sacraments (that is, that God genuinely regenerated infants in baptism and that Christ was truly present in the bread and wine of the Lord's Supper) has been shared by very few Protestants outside the Lutheran churches. While he exalted the Scriptures as the final authority for all of life, he scorned the notion that all people alike enjoyed equal authority in interpreting Scripture. His criticisms of Catholic church practice were as sharp as he could make them, but he also held that no one would be redeemed who did not share in the preaching, fellowship, and sacraments of the

13. Ibid., 348.
14. Luther, "Table Talk," *LW* 54:476.

visible church. He thought the pope had become the Antichrist, not primarily as an interpretation of biblical prophecy, but as a result of a chain of theological reasoning (the pope bears Christ's name, but the pope keeps people from finding Christ; therefore, the pope must be Antichrist). And he believed that the word "reformation" should be reserved for God's promise to create a new heaven and a new earth at the end of time. In these convictions and more, Luther opened a door through which most later Protestants did *not* pass.

Yet for many notable believers in succeeding centuries, Luther's vision of God was an elixir. Without his profound rooting in Luther's depiction of the misery of human sinfulness, the mysterious passion of Christ, and the pure joy of the resurrection, the church music of Johann Sebastian Bach (1685–1750) is simply not imaginable. Just as surely, the leaders of German Pietism like Philipp Jakob Spener (1635–1705) drew on Luther's convictions about the inwardness of faith to inspire their movement. Luther's gift for paradox directly inspired the paradoxes of Søren Kierkegaard (1813–55), the melancholy Dane who punctured religious pretense in his own day as thoroughly as Luther had in his. Luther's words defined the cross that Dietrich Bonhoeffer (1906–45) bore in passive, and then active, resistance to Hitler and the Nazis, resulting in his martyrdom. In a striking display of cross-cultural influence, specific writings of Luther were influential in the "evangelical breakthroughs" experienced by a series of notable English Protestants, including John Bunyan (while reading Luther's commentary on Galatians), John Wesley (responding to Luther's preface to the Book of Romans), and Charles Wesley (reading from the Galatians commentary). Since the Second Vatican Council of the early 1960s, it has even been possible to hear Roman Catholic commendation of Luther's key insights. Thus, one among the flurry of books published in 1983 to commemorate the 500th anniversary of Luther's birth was by the Jesuit Jared Wicks, who was at that time a professor at the Gregorian University in Rome. Wicks retained several substantial disagreements with Luther but also commended him at length for being, among other things, "a forceful teacher of lived religion." As such, Wicks went on, Luther "can be a resource for the enrichment of personal spirituality for members of all Christian confessions. In many of Luther's works, one does not have to read far before touching on the subject of conversion from proud self-reliance to trusting acceptance of God's grace."[15]

---

15. Jared Wicks, S.J., *Luther and His Spiritual Legacy* (Wilmington, Del.: Michael Glazier, 1983), 26.

The turning point in the inner history of Christianity marked by Martin Luther relates very much to the gift that his works passed on to individuals like Bach, Spener, Kierkegaard, Bonhoeffer, Bunyan, and the Wesleys. What they found in him was a powerful reassertion of grace, specifically of grace communicated through the self-giving life and the sacrificial death of Jesus Christ. Luther's significance, therefore, is not in providing something new to the church, though his modes of expression were often striking in their originality. Rather, Luther's significance was in providing a timely, effective reminder that the hope of the Christian, now and forever, rises from the transaction that occurred at the cross and the empty tomb that his weeping disciples encountered on the third day.

Luther's importance for the outer history of Christianity, however, lies in the timing of his theological contribution. His powerful effort to strip encumbrances from the church's message of grace took place at a time of great strain for Europe's inherited patterns of national, economic, intellectual, and ecclesiastical life. Because of its timing, Luther's message of divine grace in Christ soon joined other tremors that were also overturning European traditions in church and society. Aspects of that outer history, and the turning points that accompanied Luther's evangelical breakthrough, are the subject of the next two chapters. The claim that Luther's work represented a significant turning point in the history of Christianity hinges in part on his participation in the broader social and cultural changes at work in sixteenth-century Europe. Even more, however, that claim is an assertion that Luther's vision of God was timely, necessary, and—despite all the bluster and excess with which it was expressed—correct.

———————— ❦ ————————

Martin Luther tried to encourage a faithful attentiveness to the message of grace by reforming the weekly service of Christian worship. Luther retained more of medieval liturgy than all of his fellow Protestants, except the Anglican Church under the leadership of Thomas Cranmer. One of his earliest efforts to provide such a reformed liturgy he called simply the *Deutsche Messe*, the "German Mass." For most of his life as a reformer, he continued to make liturgical suggestions and to write prayers, responses, and hymns. One of his collects that was often used at Easter and at funerals follows (modernized slightly):

> *Almighty God, who by the death of your Son has brought to*
> *nothing sin and death and by his resurrection has brought*

again innocence and everlasting life so that, delivered from the devil's power, we may live in your kingdom: Grant us that we may believe this with all our heart and, steadfast in this faith, praise and thank you always; through the same your son Jesus Christ our Lord. Amen.[16]

Further Reading

Bagchi, David V. N. *Luther's Earliest Opponents: Catholic Controversialists, 1518–1525*. Minneapolis: Fortress, 1991.

Bainton, Roland H. *Here I Stand: A Life of Martin Luther*. Nashville: Abingdon, 1950.

Brecht, Martin. *Martin Luther*. 2 vols. Philadelphia: Fortress, 1985–94.

Haile, H. G. *Luther: An Experiment in Biography*. Garden City, N.Y.: Doubleday, 1980.

Lull, Timothy F., ed. *Martin Luther's Basic Theological Writings*. Minneapolis: Fortress, 1989. A well-edited selection from the 55-volume American Edition of Luther's Works.

Martin Luther. [*Christian History*, no. 34]. 1990 and [no. 39] 1993.

McGrath, Alister E. *Luther's Theology of the Cross*. Oxford: Basil Blackwell, 1985.

Oberman, Heiko A. *Luther: Man between God and Devil*. New Haven: Yale University Press, 1990.

Pelikan, Jaroslav. *The Christian Tradition*. Vol. 4, *Reformation of Church and Dogma (1300–1700)*. Chicago: University of Chicago Press, 1984.

———, ed. *Interpreters of Luther*. Philadelphia: Fortress, 1968.

Steinmetz, David C. *Luther in Context*. Bloomington: Indiana University Press, 1986.

Watson, Philip S. *Let God Be God: An Interpretation of the Theology of Martin Luther*. Rev. ed. Philadelphia: Fortress, 1970.

16. Luther, "The Collects," *LW* 53:134.

8

A New Europe: The English Act of Supremacy (1534)

One of the great debates of the Reformation era concerned the use of music in church. As noted in the Introduction, various answers came from Protestants and from the Catholic Church to the question of how best to use music in church. The answers were instructive for what they revealed of basic theological positions. Lutherans, for example, made full use of organs and trained choirs, along with much congregational song, because of Luther's insistence that traditions that helped drive home the meaning of the gospel should be retained. By contrast, most Reformed and Anabaptist branches of Protestantism were more suspicious of traditions in general and so tried to ground their singing directly in the Bible. Taken altogether, the church as a whole was the great beneficiary from this ferment over music in church, since it led to a great deal of new hymn-writing. One of the most widely known hymns of the era was William Kethe's paraphrase of Psalm 100 from 1561. Since Kethe published this paraphrase as an English Protestant exile in Geneva, it is fitting that the tune to which it is often sung (Louis Bourgeois's "Old Hundredth") was itself first published only ten years before in the *Genevan Psalter,* or hymnbook of the church in Calvin's Geneva.

> All people that on earth do dwell, sing to the Lord with cheerful voice;
> Him serve with fear, his praise forthtell, come ye before him and
> rejoice.

175

The Lord ye know is God indeed; without our aid he did us make;
We are his folk, he doth us feed, and for his sheep he doth us take.

O enter then his gates with praise, approach with joy his courts unto;
Praise, laud, and bless his name always, for it is seemly so to do.

For why? The Lord our God is good, his mercy is for ever sure;
His truth at all times firmly stood, and shall from age to age endure.

The pace of negotiations between King Henry VIII of England and Pope Clement VII accelerated dramatically toward the end of 1532. Anne Boleyn, whom Henry wanted as a new wife to replace Catherine of Aragon, was pregnant. If the child, whom Henry desperately hoped would be a boy, was to be legitimate and a recognized heir to his throne, Henry had to marry Anne and do so in a hurry. But still the pope had not consented to an annulment of Henry's marriage with Catherine, the widow of Henry's late brother, Arthur. Henry had wed Catherine in 1509. But now a combination of politics (especially the desire for a male heir to the throne) and religion (particularly the fear of violating Levitical marriage regulations) had convinced Henry that his marriage to Catherine was invalid. Henry had not, however, succeeded in convincing Pope Clement. Or even if the pope may have been convinced, he could not act on Henry's request for a divorce because of his own reliance—caught up in the midst of Italian political strife—on the Holy Roman emperor, Charles V. So long as the pope owed his security to Charles, he could not permit Henry to divorce Catherine. She, after all, was the emperor's aunt, and Charles was determined that his aunt's honor should not be violated.[1]

At this impasse, Henry VIII took what seemed to be the only course open to him. If the pope would not give him a divorce, he would find someone who would. If finding someone else to ratify the divorce meant that England's church must break from the "universal" Roman Catholic Church, then break away it would.

1. This account of English events is indebted especially to A. G. Dickens, *The English Reformation,* 2nd ed. (University Park: Pennsylvania State University Press, 1989); as supplemented by G. R. Elton, *Reform and Reformation: England, 1509–1558* (Cambridge: Harvard University Press, 1977); and Christopher Haigh, ed., *The English Reformation Revised* (New York: Cambridge University Press, 1987).

For Henry's urgent purposes, it was fortunate that the means for taking this revolutionary step of separating the English church from Rome were at hand. Henry's new archbishop of Canterbury, Thomas Cranmer, was willing to ratify the divorce and marry Henry to Anne Boleyn without waiting for the pope's permission. Even more important, Henry's Parliament, which had been in session intermittently since 1529, was willing to enact the legal measures required to back up the archbishop's actions.

At Henry's insistence, this "Reformation Parliament" had already taken preliminary steps toward a full declaration of ecclesiastical independence. It had made it much more difficult for cases in ecclesiastical courts to be appealed outside the country, and it had made it almost equally difficult for English money to be sent to Rome.

Courtesy of the Billy Graham Center Museum

As in this picture, so in real life, Henry VIII towered over his clergy, whether Protestants (on the left) or Catholics (on the right).

Shortly after Henry's marriage to Anne Boleyn in January 1533, Parliament took the next step of flatly prohibiting appeals of English church decisions to Rome. As one historian describes the situation, "Archbishop Cranmer then held court and decided that the king was not living in bigamy. In English law, as just remodeled, there was no appeal from his sentence."[2]

In 1534 Parliament took the final steps in what had become an inevitability. It first decreed that church taxes formerly paid to Rome should go to the monarch. It then passed an Act of Supremacy, which forever altered the situation of the church in England. The rolling cadences of Parliament's official action are very different from the snappy phrases of modern political speech, but their intent was entirely clear:

2. Charles M. Gray, *The Harbrace History of England*, vol. 2, *Renaissance and Reformation England* (New York: Harcourt Brace Jovanovich, 1973), 39.

Albeit the King's Majesty justly and rightfully is and oweth to be the Supreme Head of the Church of England, and so is recognized by the clergy of this realm in their Convocations, yet nevertheless for corroboration and confirmation thereof, and for increase of virtue in Christ's religion within this realm of England, and to repress and extirp all errors, heresies, and other enormities and abuses heretofore used in the same; be it enacted by authority of this present Parliament, that the King our Sovereign Lord, his heirs and successors, kings of this realm, shall be taken, accepted, and reputed the only Supreme Head on earth of the Church of England, called *Anglicana Ecclesia;* and shall have and enjoy, annexed and united to the imperial crown of this realm, as well the style and title thereof, as all honours, dignities, pre-eminences, jurisdictions, privileges, authorities, immunities, profits, and commodities, to the said dignity of Supreme Head of the same Church belonging and appertaining; and that our said Sovereign Lord, his heirs and successors, kings of this realm, shall have full power and authority from time to time to visit, repress, redress, reform, order, correct, restrain, and amend all such errors, heresies, abuses, offences, contempts, and enormities, whatsoever they be, which by any manner spiritual authority or jurisdiction ought or may lawfully be reformed, repressed, ordered, redressed, corrected, restrained, or amended, most to the pleasure of Almighty God, the increase of virtue in Christ's religion, and for the conservation of the peace, unity, and tranquillity of this realm; any usage, custom, foreign laws, foreign authority, prescription, or any other thing or things to the contrary hereof notwithstanding.[3]

Involved as the prose was, no one, then or now, mistook the consequences: England's church no longer was in fellowship with Rome; England's church had broken from the "catholic" church; England's church belonged to the English (or at least to the English king). For opposing this and similar moves, dedicated Catholics like Bishop John Fisher and Sir Thomas More would go to the block. For urging Henry on toward a more complete Reformation, dedicated Protestants like Robert Barnes and John Frith would join them.

The break from Rome that Henry carried out with the assistance of his archbishop of Canterbury and the English Parliament symbolizes a most important turning point in Christian history, but not because it carries the theological weight of a Council of Nicaea or, closer in time, a Diet of Worms. Henry's decision had a general effect on Christendom only because it had a particular effect on England. But the nature of that particular effect illustrates a powerful new trend in European

---

3. Gerald Bray, ed., *Documents of the English Reformation* (Minneapolis: Fortress, 1994), 113–14.

Christianity that, taken in its many instances, constituted a vitally important turning point in the history of the church.

That turning point was the rise in Europe during the second phase of the Protestant Reformation of self-consciously local, particular, and national forms of Christianity. Before the Reformation there had been many local varieties of the faith, and the division between the Eastern and Western churches had created a long-standing schism within the church. But even the first Protestants like Martin Luther hoped they could encourage comprehensive changes in the existing universal church. They did not set out to break up Western Catholicism or to establish local "churches." By the time of England's Act of Supremacy in 1534, however, more and more European regions were setting up their own distinct forms of the Christian faith. They were not promoting toleration or religious pluralism in a modern sense, but they were definitely establishing small-scale alternatives to the universal Catholic Church. This development forever changed the face of Christianity in the West.

Centrifugal Forces in Christendom

The centrifugal forces that, when viewed in retrospect, can be seen as anticipating the breakup of the Western church in the sixteenth century were of several kinds. A recent generation of outstanding historians has been stressing continuities between the pre-Reformation and Reformation periods, and with good reason.[4] Regionalism, nationalism, tumultuous new patterns in economic and social life, as well as broad intellectual upheaval were all well advanced before the appearance of Protestantism. By the same token, while the specific Christian activities of Protestant reformers brought considerable innovation in the sixteenth century, the religious questions and church situations they addressed had all been thoroughly explored in the fourteenth and fifteenth centuries. The rise of Protestantism, as well as the rise of a variety of national Protestantisms, in short, represented continuity with the past as well as discontinuity toward the future.

In the larger sphere of European history, Protestantism acted as an accelerator for forces or developments that were already well underway by 1517 and Martin Luther's posting of the Ninety-Five Theses. In the political realm, for example, Protestantism would re-

---

4. For example, Heiko A. Oberman, *The Harvest of Medieval Theology* (Cambridge: Harvard University Press, 1963); Steven Ozment, *The Age of Reform, 1250–1550* (New Haven: Yale University Press, 1980); Eamon Duffy, *The Stripping of the Altars: Traditional Religion in England, 1400–1580* (New Haven: Yale University Press, 1992).

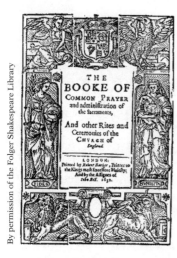

Thomas Cranmer's greatest literary, as well as theological and liturgical, monument was the Book of Common Prayer, here shown in an edition from the seventeenth century.

quire local rulers or urban councils with the ability to act self-confidently and with a fair measure of independence. To use England again as an example, Henry VIII's declaration of ecclesiastical independence in the 1530s was unthinkable apart from the labors of his father, Henry VII, in reuniting a fractured kingdom and asserting the authority of the Tudor household. When Henry VII defeated the much-maligned Richard III at the battle of Bosworth Field in 1485, he brought an end to many decades of destructive dynastic feuding, often called the War of the Roses. When Henry succeeded in extracting England from foreign entanglements, pacifying his main rivals among the nobility, and securing a firm line of succession for the House of Tudor, he gave England a stronger sense of nationhood than it had ever enjoyed. The loyal Roman Catholic Henry VII thus paved the way through the strength of royal rule for his son to break from Rome.

The growth of nationalism—or, put more accurately, increased concentrations of power around a central monarchical house—also took place in lands that would remain substantially Catholic. In Spain, the marriage of Ferdinand of Aragon and Isabella of Castile allied their two Iberian nations and hastened the emergence of a unified Spain. What such protonational unification could mean in terms of wealth and expanded power is suggested by the willingness of the Spanish royal couple to finance Columbus's voyages to the New World. Even more important at the time, the union of royal households also enabled Spain to finish the centuries-long task of subduing the Moors of Muslim Grenada and all but wiping out the Islamic presence in Europe.

Similarly, although patterns of centralized national authority differed radically among the European nations, the general trend in each of these areas was toward greater concentration of political power pointing toward the modern nation-state. Whether the expanding authority of the king of France; or strengthening self-confidence among some of Germany's many duchies, principalities, electorates, and imperial cities; or unexpected assertions of local autonomy in some eastern European regions—the general trend in politics throughout the fif-

teenth century was to heighten identification with localities. For the
Catholic Church, these developments often meant growing tension between local rulers and emissaries from Rome, whether such tension
eventually led to breakaway Protestant churches (as in Germany, Scandinavia, Britain, and eventually the Netherlands) or merely to greater
independence for rulers who remained loyal to the church.

Forces at work in European economic life were also moving toward
greater local vitality and less automatic deference to a central religious
authority. The Black Death, or plague, had wreaked havoc in the middle decades of the fourteenth century. Economic depression followed
the decline of population, abandonment of fertile land, and curtailing
of trade. But by the mid-fifteenth century, economic expansion was
once again the order of the day. Trade, population in rural and urban
areas, and agricultural production were all generally improving, although wars, bad weather, and political entanglements meant that
prosperity in some regions could coincide with depression in others.
Improving economic activity alongside heightened concentrations of
local political power increasingly made money a point of friction between Rome and the Catholic countries of Europe. Virtually no area of
Europe was spared strife over money between the Roman curia and
local authorities. Sometimes this strife created preconditions for Protestantism, as in Henry VIII's restrictions on sending taxes to the pope
and Martin Luther's appeal to the German princes to keep their money
at home. In other situations, like the struggle for economic dominance
among rival Italian city-states, quarreling with Catholic officials was an
accepted part of life within the church. As a last motor for economic
change, the expansion of Europe into the New World eventually led to
the influx of new money and the redistribution of existing resources.
While English and French explorations in the New World usually dis-
appointed investors, Spanish and Portuguese returns became substantial over the course of the sixteenth century.

The main economic point that needs to be stressed is not any simple
equation between an increase of trade and the rise of Protestantism.
Rather, it is that Europe's economic recovery created new centers of
financial power, new situations for potential friction, and new opportunities for fiscal resentment. Those new situations were stirring the
pot of traditional European allegiances, in both church and state, well
before the potent ingredient of Protestant theology was added to the
brew.

The combination of tectonic movement in political and economic
life naturally had repercussions in social relationships. By the start of
the sixteenth century, monarchs had begun to align themselves with

holders of urban wealth in order to counteract the power of the landed nobility. For its part, the hereditary nobility did better in some places than in others at retaining traditional powers, but general trends were working against the nobility's effort to preserve its preeminence by replacing feudal loyalty and land-based income with trade and circulating money. Nothing like the modern middle class yet existed, but especially in the cities the increasing numbers of merchants, lawyers, and master craftsmen—all of which grew in strength as the European economy continued to expand—added to social volatility. Peasants increasingly exchanged feudal obligations for contractual and money connections; in western Europe serfdom soon became a distant memory. In the midst of a shifting social world, the roles of the clergy also experienced considerable strain. Whether lower clergy (who were soon bypassed in wealth and education by urban merchants), powerful lord-bishops and abbots of wealthy monastic houses, or the prelates who carried out the direct bidding of the pope—all levels of ecclesiastical authority were being forced to renegotiate the honored social status that had long been simply part of the fabric of European life.

If change was the order of the day in political, economic, and social relationships, it was certainly the case for intellectual life as well. The printing press, developed by Johann Gutenberg of Strasbourg and Mainz in the mid–1450s, was affecting the pace and intensity of intellectual exchange all throughout Europe by the end of the fifteenth century. More important, the cluster of new intellectual strategies that historians call the Renaissance was significantly shaping the emerging ideas that printed books circulated. Styles of Renaissance intellectual life could differ dramatically, from the pious to the skeptical, the ironic to the affirmative, or the restive to the serene. Southern forms of the Renaissance came first and produced dramatic innovations in literature (for example, the love sonnets of Petrarch [1304–74]) and painting (for example, Giotto, Fra Angelico, Raphael), as well as science and classical learning (with Leonardo da Vinci [1452–1519] excelling in all). But intellectual energies in northern Europe were not far behind and would, as exemplified by Erasmus of Rotterdam (ca. 1469–1536), also produce prodigies of scholarship. Yet the specific accomplishments of individual luminaries were less important than what might be called the spirit of the Renaissance. Above all, promoters of Europe's "new learning" were impatient with authority that rested on settled medieval traditions and exasperated by intellectual conformity to medieval ideals. They sought instead the freshness of ancient intellectual authority, above all in returning to the written sources of European civilization. So it was that earnest searching for authentic ancient texts—Latin and Greek, pagan and Christian—was an ongoing European preoccupation for several generations before Protestants deployed the authority of another ancient text, the Bible, as a justification for rejecting traditional Catholic deference to the papacy.

Grand historical connections that involve widespread populations across a century or two are always immensely complex. Therefore, it is important to note two mistakes that have regularly marred interpretation of the general changes in Europe and also the specific religious convulsions that resulted in Protestantism. The first mistake is to treat the dynamic cultural activity that accelerated throughout fifteenth-century Europe as a mere anticipation of the Reformation. Those dynamics had a life and logic of their own. Some would coincide neatly with later Protestant emphases, some would slide easily into the renewed Catholic Church of the sixteenth century, and some are difficult to square with any of the religious developments that followed. They had their own historical integrity, even if the political, economic, social, and intellectual life of Europe was also everywhere closely tied to religion.

The second mistake is to reduce the religious developments of the sixteenth century to functions of these other dimensions of European cultural change, as if, for example, all the powerful leaders who became Protestants did so merely to take over the lands and influence of the Catholic Church. Certainly interconnections existed, but the motives that drove the early Protestants, as well as their Catholic opponents, are often best explained in precisely the religious terms with which they expressed them—that is, Protestants abandoning the Catholic Church in order to pursue what they held to be the way of salvation, Catholics working to strengthen the church as the only antidote to what they regarded as the spiritual chaos brought about by Protestantism. The key to understanding the importance of the sixteenth century for Western Christian history is to realize that the job of historical analysis has only just begun once connections between religious and other spheres of life are recognized.

Crises in the Church

In order to grasp the character of the Protestant and Catholic Reformations of the sixteenth century, it is even more important to see something of the preceding era's ecclesiastical history than to note connections between religion and other aspects of European history. Practical difficulties of several sorts had beset the Catholic Church for at least two centuries before the appearance of Protestantism. For the first three-quarters of the fourteenth century, the papacy had been headquartered in Avignon, on the border of the French kings' territory, because of persistent turmoil in the Eternal City and French eagerness to curb the independence of the popes. While at Avignon (in what opponents called a Babylonian Captivity), the papacy succeeded in streamlining administrative procedures and improving communications within the church. But the political entanglements besetting the Roman church during its sojourn in Avignon kept papal attention focused on this-worldly concerns and did little to encourage spiritual or religious insight.

What followed was even worse. The drive to return the papacy to Rome led to a complicated, often sordid, intensely competitive period in which two, and sometimes even three, rival popes clamored for political and religious recognition. This period, usually called the Great Schism, witnessed rival colleges of cardinals electing counterpopes in Rome, Avignon, and occasionally elsewhere. Quite apart from delicate questions about who was right and who was wrong in these involved maneuverings, the competition for papal supremacy again had the effect of exalting temporal and marginalizing eternal considerations in the business of the church.

The Great Schism was finally brought to an end by a church reorganization that at first seemed to promise reform in religious practice as well as ecclesiastical structure. The idea that a council made up of bishops and other high church officials could dictate peace to a divided church gradually gained momentum and eventually led to a major church conclave at Constance in the far southern reaches of Germany. The Council of Constance, which met intermittently from 1414 to 1418, was indeed successful at ending the scandal of a divided papacy. It also set the tone for much that followed in the fifteenth century by its insistence on a fuller participation by bishops and other leaders in the church's decision-making process than either of the rival papacies of the immediately preceding period had allowed.[5] At the same time, if the Council of Constance and its most important successor council at Basel in Switzerland (1431–37) succeeded with organizational reforms, the verdict for spiritual reform was less favorable. Later Protestants especially drew attention to the fate of the Czech reformer John Hus (ca. 1372–1415), who, after agitating from his Prague pulpit for spiritual reforms as well as more local church autonomy, was lured to Constance by the offer of safe conduct. After being interviewed by church author-

---

5. On Constance as the great "tone-setting event" of this period in church history, see John Van Engen, "The Church in the Fifteenth Century," in *Handbook of European History, 1400–1600*, ed. Thomas A. Brady, Jr., Heiko A. Oberman, and James D. Tracy, 2 vols. (Grand Rapids: Eerdmans, 1994–95), 1:305–30, esp. 313–15.

ities there, however, Hus's safe conduct was revoked, under the troubling principle that it was not necessary to keep one's word to a heretic. And for his "heretical" views (which included a concentration more on the Bible than on church authority as well as a willingness to question the dicta of church decrees), Hus was burned at the stake.

The conciliar movement, as this appeal to councils was called, did achieve substantial reforms. But its successes were mostly procedural. Conspicuous largely by their absence in the conciliar age were the type of specifically spiritual insights that Bernard of Clairvaux had communicated to several popes in the twelfth century, the inspiration to prayer and self-giving that St. Francis had provided in the early thirteenth century, and the theocentric theology that Thomas Aquinas had offered for the church's use in the second half of that same century.

By no means was it the case that the church was entirely a spiritual wasteland in the fifteenth century. The Brethren of the Common Life, a movement of renewal in the Netherlands and northern Germany, spread twin ideals of godliness and human service through its schools, charities, and writings. The best-known writing was *The Imitation of Christ,* usually attributed to Thomas à Kempis (ca. 1380–1471). This book encouraged spiritual self-discipline as a means toward finding union with God in Christ. Reforming currents were also found in the intellectual preoccupations of Renaissance leaders. The sermons and lectures of John Colet (ça. 1466–1519) in England, for example, recaptured central themes from the Pauline Epistles for audiences in Oxford and London. Other Renaissance intellectuals, like Erasmus or the Spanish churchman Cardinal Ximénez (1436–1517), labored industriously to secure the most exact possible text of the Greek New Testament as an aid for promoting a purer form of Christianity. In addition, many localities witnessed either faithful Christian teaching, earnest lay religion, or both.

Although edifying spiritual currents persisted among some of Europe's learned clergy and some of the populace at large, the formal concerns of the church seemed always to feature politics, contests for power, and ostentatious display rather than solicitude for godly life and thought. When in the second half of the fifteenth century the papacy recovered the authority it had earlier ceded to the councils, the worldly preoccupations of the church's hierarchy seemed only to increase. Examples of those preoccupations dominated the pontificates of the last three great representatives of what is often called the Renaissance papacy.

Alexander VI (1492–1503) was an astute political leader, a skillful diplomat, and a careful shepherd of the church's fiscal resources. Alexander also supported missionary work in North and South America and in the Far East and by so doing anticipated extremely important developments in the later history of Christianity. In addition, his patronage of the arts led to some truly memorable works, including Michelangelo's *Pietà*. Yet a spiritual leader Alexander was not. Earlier in his life he had been reprimanded by Pope Pius II for immoral living, and much of his energy as pope was consumed by efforts to forward the careers of his son Cesare Borgia and several other illegitimate children. Alexander was succeeded—after a monthlong pontificate for Pius III (1503)—by Julius II (1503–13). Julius won the papacy in part through bribery and in part through delicate negotiations with the Borgia family. Like Alexander, Julius was a shrewd diplomat. But even more than his predecessor, he was a man of action who, through vigorous military campaigns, greatly expanded the pope's temporal jurisdiction. Julius was also a great builder as well as a great warrior-diplomat. His foundations included the Vatican Library, many other architectural triumphs, and a series of memorable artistic commissions (including Michelangelo's frescoes on the vault of the Sistine Chapel). To his credit, Julius tried to end the selling of church positions and generally to clean up the administration of the papacy. But the epitaph for which he has ever since been remembered was written by Erasmus, in the witty but savage dialogue "Julius Exclusus." That dialogue pictures Julius arriving at the gates of heaven on a great military charger and being rejected by St. Peter, who cannot be made to understand how the vicar of Christ could have turned from humility, service, and devoted spiritual life to warfare and diplomacy.

Julius's successor, Leo X (1513–21), was more pious than his predecessors but no less convinced that the measure of papal greatness was an increase in papal lands and a sponsorship of the arts. Leo, who had become a cardinal while still in his teens and who rose to power via his family connections as a de' Medici, was a great patron of theater, arts, and music, as well as a great hunter, a great promoter of his many de' Medici relatives, and a great spender of money. In fact, Leo's profligacy as patron and builder, which kept him perpetually strapped for cash, lay behind his authorization of the sale of indulgences in Germany, against which Luther's Ninety-Five Theses was such a forceful protest.

The temporal concerns of the Renaissance popes, like the earlier failure of conciliarism and the scandal of a divided papacy, were not in themselves a complete disaster. The church, in both Western and Eastern divisions, had survived the missteps of leaders before. Later Protestants would also come to learn from their own experience that failures at the top, however discouraging, are never fatal to a church. Nonetheless, the persistent fascination for over two centuries with political

Erasmus versus the Catholic Church

From Erasmus's dialogue "Julius Exclusus," as the deceased Pope Julius approaches heaven.

Julius: What the devil is up? The gates not open? Some one has monkied with the lock.

Spirit: Maybe you have the wrong key. You've got the key of power.

Julius: It's the only I ever had. . . .

Peter: Who are you?

Julius: Can't you see this key, the triple crown, and the pallium sparkling with gems?

Peter: It doesn't look like the key Christ gave me. How should I know the crown which no barbarian tyrant dared to wear? As for the gems and the jewels, I trample them under my feet. . . . Tell me again, what have you done for the Church?

Julius: I found the Church poor. I made her splendid with regal palaces, splendid horses and mules, troops of servants, armies, and officers.

Spirit: And glamorous prostitutes and obsequious pimps.

Peter: But how now? The Church was not like this when founded by Christ. . . . Paul did not speak of the cities he had stormed, the princes he had slaughtered, the kings he had incited to war. He spoke of shipwrecks, chains, dangers, plots. These are the glories of the Christian general. I beseech you, the chief pastor of the Church, have you never thought how the Church began, increased, and was established? Was it by wars, was it by wealth, was it by horses? No indeed. It was by patience, the blood of the martyrs including mine, by prisons and by stripes. You say the Church is increased when the priests have thrown the world into tumult. You consider it flourishing when drunk with debauchery, tranquil when enjoying vices without reproof, and when the grand robberies and furious conflicts are justified by the princes and doctors as the "defense of the Church."[1]

power, wealth, dynastic influence, and temporal advantage eventually began to tell on the entire church. The specific difficulty was persistent inattention to the questions that are most basic to the Christian life: What must I do to be saved? Where can I find secure religious authority? How should the church's spiritual interests be balanced by the need to live in the world? Failure to address these problems meant that at its most basic level, the church was adrift.

Silence in the face of such queries and the absence of leaders who could be respected both for the sheer exercise of authority and for the manifest godliness of their lives allowed the church to spin nearly out of control. The extent of the difficulty would be reflected in the European-wide attention that Protestant reformers received from the late 1510s. But the depth of the crisis is suggested as well by the multitude of reforming voices, societies, and movements that arose *within* the Catholic Church during the same period that Protestants began to move away from the church. Such movements are the concern of our next chapter, but it is important to note them now in order to indicate the magnitude of crisis brought about by the failure of Catholic leadership to expend as much energy in the care of souls as in the pursuit of power. We grasp the reality of the fifteenth-century spiritual crisis, in other words, when we realize that by the end of the next century the Roman Catholic Church had witnessed almost as thorough a renovation from within as was represented from without by the emergence of Protestant churches.

Protestantisms

The rise of Protestantism, therefore, needs to be seen as occurring during an era of general, dynamic change in European society as well as in response to a distinct spiritual crisis in the immediately preceding history of the Catholic Church. When centrifugal forces from European economic expansion and political transformation met centrifugal forces arising from ecclesiastical neglect, the result was a greater degree of fragmentation than almost anyone, including most early Protestants, desired.

The first generation of Protestants spoke with nearly one voice in trying to answer the foundational questions that had been so long neglected by the hierarchy of the church. *What must I do to be saved?* The Protestant answer was to trust by faith in the free grace of God active for the justification of sinners in the work of Jesus Christ. *Where can I find secure religious authority?* The Protestant answer was the Bible as the sole final authority worthy of implicit trust. *How should the church's spiritual interests be balanced by the need to live in the world?* With not quite as much unanimity as on the preceding two questions, Protestant answers nevertheless clustered around the principle that the church was fundamentally a fellowship of priests, with all believers being called to seek God through the mediation of Christ and all believers called to act as Christ's agents in the world. (What the Protestants rejected was a restricted priesthood as well as the conviction that monastic life offered a higher form of spiritual existence than ordinary life in the world. What they offered was a theory of spiritual democracy,

One of the ways in which European regimes tried to get rid of early Anabaptists was to drown them, in a sadistic mockery of Anabaptist defense of adult believer baptism.

though also usually with considerable restrictions of their own as to who could preach and administer the sacraments.)

The earliest Protestant leaders—Luther in Germany, Zwingli in Zurich, Cranmer in England, Martin Bucer in Strasbourg, Philipp Melanchthon as Luther's closest junior colleague, Peter Martyr from eastern Europe, John Knox in Scotland, and many more—expected, or at least hoped, that their diligent attention to the great spiritual questions would lead to a general reformation of the one Western church. When Pope Leo X first took notice of Luther's work and tried to silence him, Luther appealed to a general council, an appeal that he continued to make for several years. Long after Luther gave up hope for a council that would rectify the general situation for the whole church, Protestant stalwarts like Melanchthon and Bucer kept trying to negotiate with Catholic officials in order to promote a general reform that could guide renewal in the entire church. Only in the 1540s did such hopes fade.

When they faded and Protestant leaders looked around, they recognized that a situation had come into existence that almost none of them had anticipated. That new situation was the presence of separate Protestant churches in separate parts of Europe. Their surprise was compounded by the fact that these new churches were separated not only by geography but also by subtle, but important, differences in Christian teaching that almost no one had noticed so long as their attention had been fixed on reforming the whole Western church.

Protestant churches came to be distinguished from each other, in the first place, by the degree of support they received from secular authorities. In several Protestant regions, rulers took the lead in reform and expected, in return, to be accorded a dominant voice in church affairs. So it was in Henry VIII's England, in Zurich, where the city council exercised its authority to the full, and in most of the Scandinavian Protestant churches. The situation in which a monarch or city council controlled the pace of reform came to be known as Erastianism, after Thomas Erastus, a learned physician in Heidelberg who, during a dispute in that city in the late 1550s between various Protestant factions, urged Frederick III of the Palatinate to pacify the situation by taking control of the church into his own hands.

Other Protestants insisted that guidance of the church must remain the primary responsibility of the churches themselves. In the work of John Calvin in Geneva, the reforms that John Knox attempted in Scotland, many other areas in which Reformed (or Calvinistic) teaching predominated, as well as in most of Luther's efforts in Saxony, the principle was implicit that control of church life must remain with properly constituted church officials. This stance was usually accompanied by an expectation that secular authorities would assist the implementation of reform once the proper course had been charted by ministers of the Word. Thus, in Geneva, Calvin approved the cooperation between secular and ecclesiastical authority that led to the execution of Michael Servetus in 1553 after the heretical publications of this Spanish physician had made him a hunted figure in Catholic as well as Protestant Europe. As Calvin viewed the situation, the church had a duty to point out the evil consequences of heresy. Although the state acted properly in protecting the people from the seditious effects of heresy, it did not have the right to tell the church how to preach, administer the sacraments, or carry out church discipline.

The most radical views of church–state relations in sixteenth-century Europe were held by the Anabaptists, who rejected almost all of the links between the sacred and the secular that had been built up in Europe since the age of Constantine. Anabaptists in Switzerland (like Conrad Grebel, Michael Sattler, Felix Manz, and George Blaurock), southern Germany (like Balthasar Hübmeier, Hans Hut, Hans Denck, and Jacob Hutter), and the Netherlands (especially Menno Simons) regarded state regulation of the church as tantamount to corruption of the church. The Anabaptists' rejection of infant baptism and their insistence

Reformed–Anabaptist Debate

In 1578 at Emden in the Netherlands occurred one of the few peaceful disputations of the era between Anabaptists and other Protestants. In an unusual series of discussions—120 sessions lasting from February 27 through May 17—various Reformed leaders of the Netherlands debated spokesmen for the Anabaptists (who were mostly Mennonites) on issues like the Trinity, the nature of human sin, the sacraments, and the resurrection of the body. Here is a short excerpt from the exchange on civil government:

> *Menso* [a Reformed spokesman]: To clarify matters, we should like answers to the following questions.
> First, whether the gentlemen hold that the function of government is a work of the flesh or a work of the Spirit. We hold it to be a work of the Spirit.
> Second, whether or not a Christian may serve in a public office with a good conscience—that is, both determine and execute justice, and protect the good and punish the bad with the sword, and yet remain a Christian and share in salvation while serving in such an office. To this we say yes. . . .
> *Peter of Cologne* [the chief Anabaptist spokesman]: To the first question, we reply by saying that we acknowledge that government exists by divine ordination to rule in worldly affairs. In this sense our answer is yes, and this is the only answer we know how to give.
> In answer to the second question, we say that since we find no record in the New Testament that a Christian in the church served in public office with the sword, we dare not give Menso a yes. If he can furnish us with proof from the New Testament, to which we appeal, we will most gladly give him a yes; otherwise, our answer to the whole question is no. As to whether or not such persons can be saved, we leave that to God. We do not know what more we could say about this.[2]

upon adult baptism after an individual profession of faith grew out of a desire to distinguish Christianity from state citizenship, as well as from a fresh interpretation of teaching about baptism in the New Testament. As much as Anabaptist teachings anticipated later Western convictions about the separation of church and state, at least in the sixteenth century their beliefs were regarded by Catholics and Protestants alike as grave threats to the stability of European Christian society.

The major point here, however, is that once protests against the direction of the Catholic Church led to the appearance of Protestant

Protestants early on tried to enlist historical evidence on their side, as shown in this picture of Martin Luther and John Hus (who had died in 1415) distributing both bread and wine in the Communion.

Christian History Archives

churches, those Protestant churches almost immediately opened up many and various paths to reform. From Erastian conservatives on the Right to Anabaptist radicals on the Left, Protestants brought, not a united voice against Catholic error, but a multiplicity of voices.

That same spectrum soon became apparent in questions of Christian doctrine and practice. Most of the major Protestant leaders agreed, as we have noted, on basic doctrinal affirmations. They believed in justification by faith; often they underscored their opposition to what they regarded as the works-righteousness built into medieval Catholicism by insisting on justification by faith *alone*. Protestants in general affirmed *sola Scriptura*, or the Bible as ultimate authority. And they upheld the priesthood of all believers against the hierarchical Catholic conceptions of the papacy, the monastic life, and the priesthood. On the basis of these shared principles, some of the leaders of the Reformation like Calvin, Melanchthon, and Bucer made at least some efforts to coordinate Protestant reforms in specific cities and territories with Protestant leaders in other regions.

Even before Luther's disagreement with Zwingli at Marburg in 1529 on the question of the Lord's Supper, however, it was clear that Protestant agreement on such general principles did not lead to a unified Protestant expression of Christian faith. Protestant fragmentation was not as complete or as rapid as defenders of the Roman Catholic Church predicted it would become, but fragmentation within Protestantism was, nonetheless, a reality early in the Reformation movement.

In fact, on almost every major issue of Christian doctrine or practical church life, Protestants divided among themselves. Sometimes, as in differences between John Calvin and Philipp Melanchthon concerning predestination, the disagreements were cordial and did not prevent wholehearted cooperation. On other occasions, as in differences over baptism between Anabaptists and many of the magisterial (or state-church) Protestants, the disagreements were vicious and could lead to the weaker party (always the Anabaptists) being exiled, imprisoned, or even executed.

The range of intra-Protestant differences was broad. If Scripture is the final authority, is it strictly speaking the *only* authority? Leaders like Zwingli, most of the Anabaptists, and some of the most rigorous spokesmen of the Reformed tradition said yes. Others like Luther and most leaders of the Anglican Church disagreed; they held that if traditional beliefs and practices did not violate the central teachings of Scripture, then those traditions should be embraced gratefully as useful secondary authorities after Scripture. A practical example shows the difference. Zwingli removed the organ from his church in Zurich because he could not find in Scripture a text mandating the use of the organ in Christian worship, while Luther promoted all kinds of musical instruments in church because he saw no scriptural rule against them; plus, he felt that music offered an effective means for conveying the message of the gospel.

Again, if Scripture is the ultimate authority, how should it be interpreted? Lutherans and the Anglicans tended to say that interpretations should follow the broad themes of the gospel that unite all parts of the Bible (yet long, arduous discussions between Lutheran and Anglican theologians in the 1530s resulted mostly in frustration at the inability to find a common expression of their faith). Most of the Anabaptists held that the key to interpreting Scripture was to follow New Testament commands literally, and especially to imitate the life of Christ, while reading the Old Testament symbolically. Many Reformed Protestants approached the Bible as a unified whole, but with special emphasis on the way that Old Testament revelation, especially God's covenant with Abraham, led to New Testament realities like God's covenanting with individuals, churches, and nations (though some who were not Reformed flatly denied that God any longer covenanted with nations).

Differences of scriptural interpretation, in sum, affected Protestant teaching on almost all major issues: the meaning of the Lord's Supper and baptism, to whom these sacraments were to be administered, what was required in order to have sins forgiven after baptism, what kind of music should be used in church, whether Christians should serve in the military, how local and regional churches should be organized, whether the Roman Catholic Mass should be modified (Luther) or scrapped entirely (Anabaptists and many Reformed), whether Protestant churches should promote learning in the traditional liberal arts, and on and on.

Intra-Protestant differences may have been most intense on the very question of the church itself. Protestants agreed that they were not going to structure relations with the world as those relations had been structured in late medieval Catholicism. Agreement among themselves was much harder to find. Thus, the Church of England retained a chastened notion of apostolic succession. Lutherans, for all practical purposes, adopted a territorial model of ecclesiastical authority. Anabaptists wanted the church to separate entirely from the world. In the next century, serious Protestants like England's Oliver Cromwell tried to combine close state oversight of religion with relative toleration as to how the denominations organized themselves. The proliferation of answers to the question "What is the church?" represented a marked break with the relative unity of the previous millennium and a half. They also point toward the significantly different Protestant strands that continue to affect Christian life around the world to this day.

The host of Protestant differences only rarely erupted into full-scale doctrinal battle, though Protestant violence against Anabaptists was a sad reality throughout the sixteenth century, and intra-Protestant disagreement leading to violence was known in several places throughout Europe. Protestants could keep a relative peace with each other because their common attention was fixed on the errors of Rome, and because most major Protestant groups enjoyed local monopolies in defining and practicing the faith. With rare exceptions, like the city of Strasbourg under the guidance of Martin Bucer and some regions of the Netherlands during the middle third of the sixteenth century, intolerance remained as much a feature of Protestant regions as of Catholic regions. One church for one area was still the norm. The administrative difference now, after the Reformation, was that the Protestant faiths that dominated their respective regions had broken from Rome.

The new situation exemplified by Henry VIII's inauguration of a national English church left much from the medieval past untouched. England, and soon other Protestant regions and churches, would no longer heed the pope. But neither did Henry or other leaders of churches that broke from Roman Catholicism expect anything but legally monopolistic national churches. Yet whatever the desires of such new, post-Catholic leaders, the fact of multiple Protestantisms pointed to a vastly different religious situation in which, one day, different denominations would come to exist within a single territory.

In such terms, the rise of Protestantism also symbolizes the end of the unified Western church, an opening for replacing loyalty to the universal church with loyalty to nations, and a stimulus to forms of thought rejecting the guidance of any church. Evaluation must be subjective for such large-scale developments. As a Protestant myself, it seems to me that the rise of multiple Protestantisms, each tied closely to a local situation, created conditions in which local renewal of the faith could take place more readily and stir hearts more deeply than in the Catholic regions of Europe. The ecclesiastical division of Europe, however, also hastened the secularization of Europe, because the loss of a universal church directly or indirectly encouraged men and women to disregard all traditional authority and to think and act on their own. Protestantism thus may have created a situation anticipating both the secularization that abandoned Christian authority and genuine Christian revival. By contrast, Roman Catholicism, with its renewed commitment to the universality of the church, probably created a situation less propitious for local Christian renewal, but also more propitious for preserving traditional European respect for religious authority, the revelation from God found in Scripture, and Christian tradition itself.

NB

Whether this analysis of long-term effects is correct, the rise of multiple Protestant expressions of Christianity altered not only the landscape of faith but also the shape of Christian Europe. The events that led to an English Protestant church, as also to Protestant churches throughout many areas of Europe, marked a dramatically important turning point in Christian history.

Attention to Henry VIII's Act of Supremacy should be a reminder that during the Reformation, as in all eras, prominent changes in the structures of the church were not the same as enduring spiritual contributions. Dramatic testimony to that reality can be found in the historical influence of Henry's archbishop of Canterbury, Thomas Cranmer (1489–1556). Henry no doubt thought of him primarily as a faithful servant of the Crown. Loyal Catholics considered him a conniving opponent of the One True Church. Fervent Protestants honored him for the courage he displayed in facing execution by fire under Catholic Queen Mary. But for most of the generations since Cranmer's own day, his influence has lived on through the liturgical materials he prepared for the reformed English church, most especially for the Anglican Book of Common Prayer. That great repository of prayers, responses, biblical readings, and settings for baptism and Communion has had a profound impact wherever Anglican or Episcopal churches were established and far beyond. A prayer for unity that Cranmer composed for the annual Anglican service marking the accession of the current monarch is a fitting closing to a chapter focusing mostly on how events in the sixteenth century divided the Western church.

O God, the Father of our Lord Jesus Christ, our only Saviour, the Prince of Peace: Give us grace seriously to lay to heart the great dangers we are in by our unhappy divisions. Take away all hatred and prejudice, and whatsoever else may hinder us from godly Union and Concord: that, as there is but one Body, and one Spirit, and one Hope of our Calling, one Lord, one Faith, one Baptism, one God and Father of us all, so we may henceforth be all of one heart, and of one soul, united in one holy bond of Truth and Peace, of Faith and Charity, and may with one mind and one mouth glorify thee: through Jesus Christ our Lord. Amen.

Further Reading

Bossy, John. *Christianity in the West, 1400–1700.* New York: Oxford University Press, 1985.

Brady, Thomas A., Jr., Heiko A. Oberman, and James D. Tracy, eds. *Handbook of European History, 1400–1600.* 2 vols. Grand Rapids: Eerdmans, 1994–95.

Cameroun, Euan. *The European Reformation.* New York: Oxford University Press, 1991.

Dickens, A. G. *The English Reformation.* 2nd ed. University Park: Pennsylvania State University Press, 1989.

Dickens, A. G., and John M. Tonkin. *The Reformation in Historical Thought.* Cambridge: Harvard University Press, 1985.

Eisenstein, Elizabeth L. *The Printing Revolution in Early Modern Europe.* New York: Cambridge University Press, 1983.

Haigh, Christopher. *English Reformations: Religion, Politics, and Society under the Tudors.* New York: Oxford University Press, 1993.

Jones, R. Tudur. *The Great Reformation.* Downers Grove, Ill.: InterVarsity, 1985.

Lindberg, Carter. *The European Reformations.* Cambridge, Mass.: Blackwell, 1996.

Oberman, Heiko A. *The Impact of the Reformation.* Grand Rapids: Eerdmans, 1994.

———. *The Reformation: Roots and Ramifications.* Grand Rapids: Eerdmans, 1994.

Pelikan, Jaroslav. *The Christian Tradition.* Vol. 4, *Reformation of Church and Dogma (1300–1700).* Chicago: University of Chicago Press, 1984.

Scribner, Bob, Roy Porter, and Mikulás Teich, eds. *The Reformation in National Context.* New York: Cambridge University Press, 1994.

Thomas Cranmer and the English Reformation [*Christian History*, no. 48]. 1995.

9

Catholic Reform and Worldwide Outreach: The Founding of the Jesuits (1540)

The flurry of Protestant hymn-writing that burst into Europe alongside the early crises of the Reformation created unusual difficulties for the Roman Catholic Church. So thoroughly was congregational song associated with Protestantism and so effective were Protestants at putting hymns to use that leading figures in the Catholic Church briefly contemplated a ban on music in their services. Church music was "rescued," however, in 1562 near the end of the last session of the Council of Trent. A committee of cardinals secured appropriate musical settings for traditional church texts from Giovanni Palestrina (ca. 1525–94) and other Catholic composers. Armed with examples that showed how music could support, rather than subvert, the church, the Council of Trent authorized the use of appropriate hymns, even as it warned sternly against all music that promoted worldliness or attacks on the papacy. There followed a steady production of new, relatively cautious, but still fresh hymnody by Catholics. Standard guides to hymn literature ascribe the following Easter hymn to an anonymous Jesuit; it was first published in 1695. The composition by Palestrina that is often used as the musical setting for this hymn links it to the sixteenth-century reform of the Catholic Church.

> The strife is o'er, the battle done;
> The victory of life is won;
> The song of triumph has begun.
> Alleluia!

The pow'rs of death have done their worst,
But Christ their legions hath dispersed;
Let shouts of holy joy outburst.
Alleluia!

The three sad days have quickly sped;
He rises glorious from the dead:
All glory to our risen Head!
Alleluia![1]

In the summer of 1539, a Spaniard who had begun his adult life fighting for the king of Spain enlisted for a different cause. Ignatius Loyola, son of a noble Basque family but for many years a priest and earnest servant of the Catholic Church, was now asking Pope Paul III to let him establish a new religious order. Five years before, Loyola had taken the first steps in formalizing the intense devotion that already characterized his life. With six companions—Nicolás Bobadilla, Pierre Favre, Diego Laynez, Simón Rodríguez, Alfonso Salmerón, and Francis Xavier (one from France, one from Portugal, and four from different regions of Spain)—Loyola had sworn vows of poverty and chastity; together they had pledged themselves to seek the conversion of Turkish Muslims in and around Jerusalem. At that gathering in Paris on August 15, 1534, Loyola and his friends also agreed that, if their original intention could not be fulfilled, they would then place themselves at the disposal of the pope for whatever service he would assign. As it turned out, circumstances prevented their journeying to the East and now indeed they were offering themselves directly to the church.

Loyola's journey from Spanish soldier to papal servant was not an easy one. At about age thirty he had been wounded at the battle of Pamplona, fought between Spain and France in May 1521. During a long convalescence he was given devotional literature on the life of Christ. This literature so affected him that he abandoned his career as a soldier. When fully recuperated, Loyola journeyed to the Holy Land and then began study for the priesthood. But by that time he had also

---

1. "The Strife Is O'er, the Battle Done," trans. Francis Pott, *Trinity Hymnal*, rev. ed. (Atlanta: Great Commission Publications, 1990), 275.

Loyola on Meditation

The following is a sample of the directions for meditation in Loyola's *Spiritual Exercises*. It comes from the third of four "weeks" and is numbered sections 200–203 in modern translations.

Second Contemplation

In the morning. From the last supper through the agony in the garden.

Prayer. The usual preparatory prayer.

First Prelude. This is the history of the mystery. Here it will be as follows. Jesus our Lord came down with the disciples from the supper which had taken place on Mt. Zion. After crossing the city of Jerusalem and the valley outside its walls, they came to the garden of Gethsemane, near the foot of the Mt. of Olives. Taking three of the disciples with him, then going a little further by himself, Jesus began to pray, a prayer so intense that he began to sweat drops of blood. Three times he prayed and three times went to rouse the disciples from sleep. When Judas arrived with the soldiers, betraying the Lord with a kiss, and Peter cut off the ear of Malchus, a servant of the high priest, Jesus was seized like a common criminal and led through the valley up to the house of Annas.

Second Prelude. This is to see the place. Here it will be to consider the way from Mt. Zion to the garden, and also the breadth, length and appearance of the garden.

Third Prelude. This is to ask for what I desire. In the passion it is appropriate to ask for sorrow with Christ in sorrow, to be broken with Christ broken, and for tears and interior suffering because of Christ's great suffering for me.[1]

begun to refine a course of discipleship that would later be called the *Spiritual Exercises*. Although later published as a book, the *Exercises* were designed for face-to-face communication. They asked for an intense period of meditation and prayer structured as week-long contemplations of, first, the individual's own sinfulness; second, the kingship of Christ; third, the passion of Christ; and last, the risen life of Christ. Of these *Exercises* the modern Anglican evangelical J. I. Packer has observed that they "appeal to the will through understanding, imagination and conscience. They remain a potent aid to self-knowl-

This seventeenth-century painting shows Loyola receiving final approval for the Jesuits from Pope Paul III.

Verlag Herder, Freiburg

edge and devotion to the Lord Jesus, even for those outside the Catholicism in which they are so strongly rooted."[2]

Loyola's own use of the exercises transformed him as thoroughly as Martin Luther's contemplation of justification by grace had transformed the German reformer. The difference in transformations was not in degree, but in kind. Where Luther had been drawn *away from* the Catholic Church by his Christian pilgrimage, Loyola was drawn *deeper into* the church.

Loyola studied theology for eleven years, first at the universities of Barcelona, Alcalá, and Salamanca, and then from 1528 to 1535 at the University of Paris. While in Paris, Loyola was so zealous that, for a brief period, he was investigated by the Inquisition as someone likely to disturb the peace and good order of the church. But while some in Paris were uneasy with Loyola's intense spirituality, others were drawn to him as a beacon of truth and purpose. The band that pledged themselves to missionary service was the result.

Loyola's petition for a new religious order did not receive an immediate response. More than a year elapsed from the time of its submission to Paul III's issuance of the papal bull on September 27, 1540, that

2. J. I. Packer, "Ignatius Loyola," in *Eerdmans' Handbook to the History of Christianity* (Grand Rapids: Eerdmans, 1977), 411.

formally established the Society of Jesus. A hint of scandal from his years as a Paris student still hung about Loyola. In addition, the petition for the new order had been sponsored by Cardinal Gasparo Contarini, a major force in the councils of the Catholic Church, but also a cardinal suspect in some Catholic eyes because of his desire to bend as far as possible in seeking reconciliation with the Protestants. Despite possible misgivings, the bull was issued. Its title, *Regimini militantis ecclesiae* (On the government of the church militant), spoke for its fervor. The specifications of the bull outlined clearly what sort of society the Jesuits would be:

> Let all the members of the Company know and bear in mind, not only in the early days of their profession but through all the days of their life, that this entire Company and all who compose it are engaged in a conflict for God under the obedience of the most sacred Lord the Pope, and his successors in the pontificate. And although we have learned from the Gospel, and know by the orthodox faith, and firmly profess that all the faithful in Christ Jesus are subject to the Roman Pontiff, as the Head and the Vicar of Jesus Christ, nevertheless, for the greater humility of our Society, and the perfect mortification of each, and the abnegation of our wills, we have deemed it to be very helpful to take upon ourselves, beyond the bond common to all the faithful, a special vow. It is meant so to bind that whatsoever the present Roman Pontiff and his successors may command us concerning the advancement of souls and the spreading of the faith, we shall be obliged to obey instantly as far as lies in us, without evasion or excuse, going to whatever country into which they may send us, whether among the Turks or other heathen, and even to the Indies, or among whatsoever heretics and schismatics, or among any believers whomsoever.[3]

(marginal annotation: OBEDIENCE TO CHURCH)

Thus was founded what the modern historian John Olin has rightly called "the most powerful instrument of Catholic revival and resurgence in this era of religious crisis."[4]

It is indeed difficult to exaggerate the practical and symbolic significance of the founding of the Jesuits. This founding represented, first, one of the finest expressions of the Catholic Reformation that, shortly after Protestant reform began, thoroughly revitalized the Roman Catholic Church. Although there would be many sources and influences contributing to the Catholic Counter-Reformation, the Jesuits would be the most remarkable in winning Protestant regions back to Rome

---

3. Quoted in John C. Olin, ed., *The Catholic Reformation: Savonarola to Ignatius Loyola, Reform in the Church, 1495–1540* (New York: Harper & Row, 1969), 204–5.

4. Ibid., 198.

and, even more, for solidifying the faith of those in Europe who wavered in their loyalty to the Catholic Church.

But, second, the rise of the Jesuits also symbolized the strength of what would become traditional Roman Catholicism all the way from the mid-sixteenth century to the mid-twentieth century. Although the Jesuits would themselves play a sometimes ambiguous role in later Catholic history (even being banned for a short period in the eighteenth century), their zeal in establishing Catholic doctrine and practice in the sixteenth century played a very large role in shaping Roman Catholicism for nearly half a millennium.

Third, the missionary zeal of the Jesuits also made them an extraordinarily potent force in the history of Christianity. Already in their first days that zeal was present for all to see. Even before the pope acted officially to establish the order, one of Loyola's original companions, Francis Xavier (1506–52), had embarked on the missionary journeys that brought the message of Catholic Christianity to India, Malaysia, Indonesia, and Japan. At his death in 1552, Xavier had arrived at the very coast of China. This was done (Protestant readers take note!) 150 years before anything comparable can be found among Protestants and 250 years before anything comparable among English-speaking Protestants. Moreover, the missionary experience of the Jesuits in the sixteenth and seventeenth centuries is a subject of great relevance at the end of the twentieth century, for their history illustrates the possibilities and problems that arise as a religion long nurtured in Europe now spreads throughout the world.

The Sixteenth-Century Reform of the Catholic Church

Long-standing historical debate on sixteenth-century Catholic history features an effort to determine which Catholic actions were direct responses to the challenge of Protestantism and which were a product of internal Catholic impulses. When responses to Protestantism are in view, historians usually speak of "the Counter-Reformation." When internal currents within the church receive attention, historians are prone to talk of "the Catholic Reformation." This debate is important, but it can also obscure a more significant historical reality—that the sum total of counter-reform, reform, papal initiatives, and the Council of Trent left the Catholic Church at the end of the sixteenth century a systematically different body than it had been a century before.

The clearest instance of reform as an internal movement was the great surge in creating new religious orders that dated from the 1520s. In response to motives that paralleled Protestant concerns, but drew on resources sanctioned by the Catholic Church, the new orders revitalized an old solution to a modern array of problems. Just as Benedictine monasticism had sparked broad church renewal in the sixth century and the founding of the monastery at Cluny had done the same in the tenth century, so in the early sixteenth century concern for the decline of the church moved many of the devout to form new bands for the purpose of prayer and service or to reform already existing religious foundations. Most of these new or reformed orders were centered in Italy, although often with significant contributions from non-Italians and with some of the most important new orders, like the Jesuits, founded outside of the Italian peninsula.

The emphases of the new orders ranged from strict devotion to the contemplative life at one end of a continuum to intentional activism in the world at the other. The first of the new orders, the Theatines (founded 1524), was led by two priests who had belonged to the Oratory of Divine Love in Rome; in the new order they continued the emphasis on personal piety and ecclesiastical reform that the Oratory had stressed. One of the founders, Gian Pietro Carafa (1476–1559), would later in 1555 become Pope Paul IV and pursue a rigorous, unbending course in his efforts to strengthen the church. The Theatines remained a small order, as did many of the other new foundations of the first half of the century, like the Clerks Regular of St. Paul (or Barnabites), an order founded in Milan in 1530 that came eventually to include a group of nuns (the Angelic Sisters of St. Paul) and a parallel organization of lay members (the Married Couples of St. Paul).

Considerably larger and more broadly influential were orders that sought to revive older principles from earlier traditions of the monks and friars. As an important example, the Capuchins spun off in 1528 from the Observant Franciscans, the descendants of St. Francis who insisted upon strictly "observing" their founder's ideals of poverty and service. The Capuchins wanted to carry dedication to those founding ideals even further and so struck off a separate existence for themselves. Capuchins regularly set up small, hermitlike settlements in the vicinity of towns. They preached where they could, celebrated the Eucharist regularly, promoted special devotions in association with the main celebrations of the ecclesiastical calendar, and displayed fearless courage in caring for the sick, especially victims of the plague. The reforming efforts of the Capuchins were almost derailed before they were launched, however, when in 1542 one of their best-known preachers, Bernardino Ochino (1487–1564), converted to Protestantism and sought refuge in Calvin's Geneva. For this defection the order came under severe scrutiny, but it was eventually vindicated and went on to inspire many to works of reform.

The Capuchins were joined by still other groups from the Observant Franciscans. The Discalced Carmelites were a mainly Spanish group that took its name from the practice of not wearing shoes (discalced = unshod). Their reforms were inspired by the dynamic leadership of St. Teresa of Ávila (1515–82), whose fervent piety and sharp common sense guided a religious community given over mostly to prayer and contemplation. Teresa's success in establishing parallel monastic foundations (one for men and one for women) was repeated with several of the new or revived orders in other places throughout Catholic Europe. St. John of the Cross (1542–91), who also promoted prayer and mystical spirituality, became the best known of the male Carmelites. A somewhat parallel order, the Franciscan Recollects, also had roots among the Observant Franciscans. The Recollects were established in the 1570s in France and soon thereafter began sending missionaries to North America as well as several other parts of the world.

The significance of Franciscan religious ideals in many of the new orders is indicated by the considerable numbers who eventually became members of the various orders. After about a century and a half of renewed dedication to Franciscan principles, in 1700 there were nearly 35,000 Observants, over 27,000 Capuchins, nearly 13,000 Reformed Franciscans, over 6,000 Discalced Carmelites, and over 9,000 Recollects.[5] No Protestant missionary society would be as large as even the Discalced Carmelites until the twentieth century.

The interpretive point that needs to be made about these new orders—which included the Jesuits as the largest and most active, and countless smaller foundations like the Somaschi and the Ursulines (a women's order)—was their attachment to older medieval ideals of poverty, chastity, and obedience. While many in these orders, especially the Jesuits, eventually competed with Protestants, for the most part their members worried less about besting Protestantism than about living up to ancient ideals and carrying out reform through practices of prayer, meditation, and service with an ancient lineage in the church.

Once the popes finally embarked on reform, papal policy can be seen as a mixture of responses to Protestant challenges and personal desire to purify and revitalize the church. Into the 1530s the papal throne continued to be occupied by men who were at least as involved in secular and political matters as with spiritual concerns. The nature of papal activity began to change, however, when Alessandro Farnese became Pope Paul III in

---

5. These figures and a very helpful summary are found in John Patrick Donnelly, S.J., "The New Religious Orders, 1517–1648," in *Handbook of European History, 1400–1600,* ed. Thomas A. Brady, Jr., Heiko A. Oberman, and James D. Tracy (Grand Rapids: Eerdmans, 1994–95), 2:294, 296.

Paul III (1534-1549) [handwritten annotation]

1534 (serving in that office until 1549). While Paul III continued to exhibit some of the traits of the Renaissance papacy—for example, by letting care for his wider family play a large role in his practical policies—he also initiated measures in response to the drumbeat of reform.

Soon after he became pope, Paul III organized a select commission of reform-minded cardinals and asked them to prepare an assessment of the church and its needs. The members of this committee included Gian Pietro Carafa, the conservative Theatine, but also three cardinals whose ideals for reform included somewhat more conciliatory attitudes toward Protestants and internal critics of the church. Jacopo Sadoleto (1477–1547) was an Italian-born scholar who came to renown in France for his commentary on Romans (1535) and an epistolary exchange with John Calvin in 1539, which marked the high point of serious Catholic–Protestant debate. Reginald Pole (1500–1558), born to a noble English family and (in effect) banished from his native land for refusing to support the divorce of Henry VIII, would much later return to England as papal advisor to Mary Tudor (1553–58) and key figure in the unsuccessful effort to regain his native land for Catholicism. Gasparo Contarini (1483–1542) was a Venetian diplomat and outstanding figure of the Christian Renaissance who had been called to service in the church. Some of Contarini's theological views, as on the question of justification by faith, came as close to accepting Protestant conclusions as any major figure remaining in the Catholic Church of his day.

In 1537 these reform-minded cardinals produced their report, *Consilium de emendanda ecclesia* (Commission for reforming the church), which criticized the recent papacy for exaggerating its claims to power in the church and in society. It also called upon the papacy to concentrate on its spiritual tasks and to let concerns for rule, wealth, and terrestrial dignity fade into the background. Sale of church offices and the failure of bishops to fulfill their tasks as pastors in their dioceses featured large in the commission's report. Although its recommendations proved both too general and too deep to be implemented, the commission pointed the way toward reform that later popes would follow.

During Paul III's tenure occurred also one of the last serious efforts to heal the breach with Protestants. In 1541 a colloquium was convened at Regensburg (or Ratisbon) in southern Germany that drew together Catholics like Contarini, who hoped to conciliate the Protestants, and Protestant leaders like Martin Bucer and Philipp Melanchthon, who also held out hope for reconciliation.[6] Remarkably,

6. Here I am following Peter Matheson, *Cardinal Contarini at Regensburg* (Oxford: Clarendon, 1972).

the colloquium succeeded in crafting an agreement on justification. Although the wording was far too indefinite for Luther, the theologians at the meeting found it possible to agree on two basic points: God is the sole source of salvation, and human good deeds are a necessary response to God's act of bringing salvation. Yet as soon as discussion moved beyond these two points, agreement collapsed. Especially disruptive was Catholic insistence upon transubstantiation in Communion* and the sole power of the church's teaching magisterium to interpret Scripture. The underlying issue defining both areas of disagreement was the religious authority of the pope. On that rock hopes for constructive dialogue foundered and would not be revived again for almost four hundred years.

The Colloquium of Regensburg also marked a turning point in Catholic efforts at reform. Into the early 1540s, Catholic attitudes were divided between those like Carafa, who urged a course of systematic rigor as a way of reforming and restoring the church, and those like Contarini, who urged at least a measure of conciliation to the Protestants. Increasingly after the failure of Regensburg, and also the defection of Bernardino Ochino to the Calvinists, the Catholic Church chose the path of rigor and exclusion over the path of conciliation. As a result, when the general council—which Paul III had been calling for from early in his pontificate—finally convened at Trent in northern Italy in December 1545, it leaned more toward reaffirming historic Catholic ways threatened by Protestantism than toward accommodation with Protestants.

The Council of Trent, which met in three sessions (1545–47, 1551–52, and 1562–63), began with systematic rebuttals to main Protestant assertions, and thus may be seen as an engine of Counter-Reformation. By its last sessions, however, the council had turned toward the future in drawing up policies and confirming principles that made possible a Catholic expansion more on the foundation of the church's own internal resources than in reaction to Protestantism. A few Protestant observers from Germany were invited to the council's sessions of 1551, but by that time there was virtually nothing to say between the two groups, and the contact was entirely barren. Despite the ensuing rebuff of Protestant involvement, the council avoided the extremes of Catholic conservatism. When Cardinal Carafa was elected as Pope Paul IV in 1555, he refused to call the council back into session as a protest against its independence. Yet both his predecessors and successors realized that, if there was to be effective, long-lasting church reform, it

---

* Transubstantiation is the doctrine that the bread and wine of the Eucharist turn into the actual body and blood of Jesus, with only the "accidents" of bread and wine remaining.

The Creed of Pius IV

Soon after the close of the Council of Trent, Pope Pius IV authorized the preparation of a short "Form for Professing the Orthodox Catholic Faith." This document, which is sometimes called the Creed of Pius IV, or the Profession of Faith of the Council of Trent, begins with an affirmation of the Nicene Creed but then proceeds to doctrines in controversy with the Protestants:

II. I most steadfastly admit and embrace the apostolic and ecclesiastic traditions, and all other observances and constitutions of the same [Catholic] Church.

III. I also admit the holy Scriptures according to that sense which our holy Mother Church has held, and does hold, to which it belongs to judge of the true sense and interpretation of the Scriptures; neither will I ever take and interpret them otherwise than according to the unanimous consent of the Fathers. . . .

X. I acknowledge the holy Catholic Apostolic Roman Church as the mother and mistress of all churches, and I promise and swear true obedience to the Bishop of Rome, as the successor to St. Peter, prince of the Apostles, and as the vicar of Jesus Christ.[2]

would have to take full advantage of a conciliar structure. No pope ever attended any session at Trent, but its canons and decrees reaffirmed a dominant, authoritative voice for the pope in the church, although now directed more at spiritual rule than at temporal political power.

Trent appears most as a Counter-Reformation force in its dogmatic conclusions, for many of these were aimed directly at main assertions of the Protestants. Thus, Trent denied that humans were passive in the process of justification, it affirmed Scripture and tradition as coordinate authorities, it mandated the seven sacraments (mostly as defined by Thomas Aquinas) and defined them as necessary for salvation, it called the Mass a truly propitiatory sacrifice of Christ, and it confirmed the Latin Vulgate and the Latin order of the Mass as official church documents against either Scripture or liturgies in local languages.

Since the Second Vatican Council in the early 1960s, a great deal of serious scholarship has been undertaken jointly by Catholics and Protestants concerning the assertions of Trent. In addition, fresh study has scrutinized the Protestant doctrines that elicited these Counter-Reforming assertions along with Protestant assessments of Trent from the time (for example, John Calvin responded to earlier sessions, and Martin Chemnitz published a definitive, four-volume Lutheran refutation). The modern scholarly consensus—worked out with painstaking detail particularly in several dialogues between Lutherans and Catholics and in more programmatic works with titles like *The Condemnations of the Reformation Era: Do They Still Divide?*[7]—is that a core of sixteenth-century differences, particularly on the exercise of papal authority and on the nature of the sacraments, still stands pretty much where it did four hundred years ago. On other matters, however, such as Protestant charges that Trent affirmed salvation by works or Catholic charges that Protestant notions of justification encouraged licentiousness, modern scholars tend to conclude that Catholic and Protestant disputants in the sixteenth century were often addressing extreme statements of their opponents' positions rather than the most responsible, carefully phrased, and conciliatory positions. In other words, modern Protestant–Catholic theological discussion, at least in circles where careful attention to the sixteenth-century record accompanies serious efforts at listening across confessional boundaries, seems to have picked up about where it was dropped at Regensburg. That dialogue continues to examine doctrines that still truly divide Roman Catholics and Protestants. It also shows that much more room for accommodation and discussion exists than was thought in the four hundred years between the closing of Trent and the beginning of the Second Vatican Council, a period when among both Catholics and Protestants interpretations of Trent prevailed that stressed the absolutely irreconcilable character of Protestant–Catholic differences.

The last session of the council reaffirmed the counter-reforming canons and decrees of the first two sessions, but also began to chart a course for the Catholic Church oriented more toward its needs for the future than its quarrels with the Protestants. As a recent student of the subject, Elisabeth Gleason, evaluates its final sessions, Trent "was no longer primarily directed against doctrines of the Protestants or launched in response to their criticism of Catholic belief and practice. Rather, reform under papal leadership went beyond a 'Counter' Refor-

---

7. Karl Lehmann and Wolfhart Pannenberg, eds., *The Condemnations of the Reformation Era: Do They Still Divide?* trans. Margaret Kohl (Minneapolis: Fortress, 1990). Examples of Roman Catholic–Lutheran dialogue are *The Status of the Nicene Creed as Dogma of the Church* (Minneapolis: Augsburg, 1965); *Justification by Faith* (Minneapolis: Augsburg, 1985); and *The One Mediator, the Saints, and Mary* (Minneapolis: Augsburg, 1992). For a fair-minded, well-documented assessment of contemporary Catholic–Protestant differences from an evangelical Protestant perspective, see Norman L. Geisler and Ralph E. MacKenzie, *Roman Catholics and Evangelicals: Agreements and Differences* (Grand Rapids: Baker, 1995).

mation to positive and constructive efforts at building a more tightly organized, better instructed, and effectively controlled church than the old institution before 1563 had been."[8]

Especially during its last meetings in 1562 and 1563, the council began the work of tightening church structures and refining means for promoting church dogma. That this effort would not lead to the kind of reform promoted by Protestants was indicated by several decisions reasserting the elite status of the ordained clergy. For example, in the Eucharist the cup was withheld from the laity and reserved for the priests.

But if Catholic reform would not imitate Protestant reform, it nevertheless was a thoroughgoing work on its own terms. Trent stipulated that bishops were to make regular visits to the churches in their dioceses; they were to hold an annual meeting for instruction and encouragement with all the ecclesiastical officials under their authority; and they were to see to the establishment of a seminary for the training of priests in each of their respective jurisdictions. This last provision eventually created a vast opportunity for orders like the Jesuits, who specialized in teaching, but its more general importance was to make the bishops responsible for ensuring that priests were at least moderately well trained and moderately conscientious in their duties.

Other steps taken at the last session of the council reaffirmed the value of indulgences but also created stiff controls to prevent the excessive practices in selling indulgences that had sparked the Protestant movement earlier in the century. The council also reaffirmed other traditional aspects of Catholic teaching like the veneration of saints. It took steps to define the boundaries of acceptable reading by issuing an index of prohibited books. It innovated by issuing coordinated directions for preparing new editions of a catechism (for the laity), a missal (for worship), and a breviary (for daily reading by priests and members of orders). When completed, these documents contained a significant amount of biblical material, but they also left no doubt that the use of the Bible was to be strictly regulated by the hierarchy of the church. A final emphasis at the last sessions at Trent was stress upon the missionary mandate. By this time many of the orders had already begun a much-expanded missionary activity, but Trent put a stamp of urgency upon efforts to carry the Catholic faith to Asia, North America, South America, and other areas far beyond the borders of Christendom.

When the council had finished its work, Pope Pius IV gave its canons and decrees his full endorsement. He also stipulated that, though he

8. Elisabeth G. Gleason, "Catholic Reformation, Counterreformation, and Papal Reform in the Sixteenth Century," in *Handbook of European History*, 2:333. This entire essay (pp. 317–45) is a useful summary of its subject.

considered the council itself as a source of divine wisdom, the interpretation of its decrees and the forms of implementing its canons rested exclusively with the papal office. With these steps the papacy tied itself to the council's reforms, even as the pope maintained his central authority in the church. This shrewd move ensured that the tensions between pope and council that dominated Catholic history in the wake of the Council of Constance in the early fifteenth century would not be repeated in the wake of the Council of Trent.

One major issue about which Trent remained largely silent was the question of church–state relationships. Well might it choose discreet silence on such a subject, for Pope Paul III's efforts to convene a general council had been frustrated for many years because of strife between Francis I of France and Charles V, king of Spain and the Holy Roman emperor in Germany. Taken by itself, Trent seemed to affirm the traditional superiority of the sacred to the secular sphere. In the outworking of European history, however, the success of reform from Trent depended crucially on the assistance of Roman Catholic monarchs like Francis I and Charles V, who, though they deeply distrusted each other, shared a desire to reassert Catholic unity in their own lands and throughout Europe.

The active cooperation of zealous Catholic reformers and faithful Catholic monarchs proved to be an extraordinarily effective combination from the middle of the sixteenth century. To be sure, quarrels aplenty remained within the church, especially as orders bickered with each other, with diocesan clergy, and with secular rulers, even as Catholic monarchs continued intermittently to plot against each other. (Intra-Catholic tensions, along with Catholic–Protestant strife, would later fuel the horrific Thirty Years' War, which laid waste to much of central Europe from 1618 to 1648.) Yet despite ongoing struggles within the Catholic Church, the reforms set in motion at Trent, with the cooperation of powerful monarchs, supported a massive renewal of Catholic energy, devotion, and temporal success. By 1600, almost all of southern Europe was once again securely Catholic. France, where strong pockets of Reformed Protestantism remained, had been preserved for Catholicism. Other regions where Protestantism had once seemed on the verge of triumph—like southern Germany, the southern part of the Netherlands, Poland, Hungary, and Bohemia—had been largely reclaimed for Rome. Lutheranism was confined to northern Germany, Scandinavia, and the Baltic. Reformed Protestantism was still on the march in Switzerland, southern Germany, parts of Hungary, England, Scotland, and parts of France. But the threat of nearly total dissolution that earlier had seemed a real possibility was no more.

As a result of countering Protestants as well as putting its own house in order, Rome had renewed its strength.

Tridentine Catholicism

So effective were these efforts at Catholic reform that the norms defined at Trent remained overwhelmingly dominant throughout the Catholic Church for nearly four hundred years. In the first instance, Trent gave new meaning to the *Roman* center of Catholicism. While Trent stressed greatly the bishops' role as the prime medium in guiding the church, the bishops' mission was much more carefully defined as mediating Rome's teaching to the people dispersed in the localities. Roman consolidation was never as systematic as papal pronouncements, or the fears of Protestants, suggested. But it was a reality, as indicated in the very names that many of the critical documents commissioned by Trent bore as they went out into the world—the *Roman Catechism* (1566), the *Roman Breviary* (1568), and the *Roman Missal* (1570). Even as the Catholic Church spread to every continent over the course of the next centuries, a more vigorous, more directive Roman center remained one of the principal legacies of sixteenth-century Catholic renewal.

Just as important was the systematization of doctrine and the codification of practice that the Council of Trent advanced. Roman Catholicism of the late medieval period was anything but a theological or ecclesiastical monolith. It is even fair to say that all but the most radical convictions of the most radical Protestants were held by at least some Catholic figures in the three centuries before Luther and Calvin. Several factors combined to allow a large measure of fluidity within the Western church of the Middle Ages. These included the absence of pressing local competition (Orthodoxy was too far away; Islam, while geographically close, was too alien), the preoccupation of the Renaissance papacy with temporal concerns (which provided space for variations in doctrine and practice as long as they did not become politically bothersome), and the long-term effects of the fifteenth-century conciliar movement (adjudicating questions of jurisdiction loomed larger than defining questions of doctrine or practice). Internal variation within the late medieval Catholic Church was not as extensive as it has become in the modern Catholic Church since the early 1960s, but it was still very widely spread and largely acknowledged as an accepted fact of Roman Catholic existence.

Trent moved the Catholic Church a very long way in the other direction. Again, it is possible to overstate the unity of Catholic doctrine and practice after the council, but comparatively speaking, Trent brought a higher degree of uniformity than had ever existed in the Western church. The council's attention to the tasks of the bishops in overseeing the faithful, to the spiritual responsibilities of the pope, and to the production of uniform guides for liturgy and catechesis all were factors unifying as well as reforming the church. For various individual doctrines, like justification, purgatory, or the sacrifice of the Mass, Trent reduced the spectrum of admissible Catholic positions. Often that work of specification was done by elevating a prominent, but not absolutely conclusive strand of earlier teaching into the official position of the church. Thomas Aquinas's employment of Aristotelian philosophical categories for defining transubstantiation, for example, had become widely accepted in the Catholic Church before the sixteenth century, but it was not until Trent that this doctrine was confirmed as *the* Catholic teaching on the subject. The same process was at work in standardizing many church practices, like the hearing of confession, the reaffirmation of marriage and holy orders as sacraments, and the regulation of confirmation,

To Protestants, Trent's success at standardizing Catholic teaching and practices provided further confirmation of their criticism that Rome laid far too much stress on the forms or structures of the faith at the expense of genuine piety of the heart. If there was truth of some kind in this Protestant criticism, nonetheless in Catholic eyes the actions of Trent—and the standardization of Catholic practice and dogma that followed—provided precisely the order, continuity, and direction to keep the church from flying into a thousand self-defined pieces that seemed to be the fate of Protestantism.

The uniformity achieved at Trent never resulted in an entirely uniform Catholic Church. Contingencies of politics, for example, continued to play a major role in shaping the Catholic faith as it was experienced at the local level. Irish Catholicism, which labored under the imperialistic rule of Protestant England; English Catholicism, which worked out a modus vivendi in exile or by lying low in England; French Catholicism, where the kings always guarded their ecclesiastical prerogatives with great care; Italian Catholicism, which never relinquished the family and political orientation of the late Middle Ages; Spanish Catholicism, which was guided by both powerful ascetic mysticism and strong-minded Catholic monarchs; and Polish Catholicism, which came to be the bearer of Polish nationalism as a consequence of Polish political misfortune—these, along with other national variations, made for significant ongoing differences among Catholics. Yet throughout the vicissitudes of the following centuries, Catholicism continued to bear the stamp of Tridentine reform. Only in the twentieth century, in response to worldwide changes in geopolitics, intellectual life, population, commerce, and warfare, would the Catholic Church take up the task of modifying the course established at Trent.

Beyond Europe

The enduring effects of mid-sixteenth-century reform on the Catholicism of Europe were enough to make it a major turning point in the history of Christianity. The importance of those reforms was heightened even more, however, by their impact on the rest of the world. In fact, in the larger scope of things, the turnaround of the Catholic Church represented by the founding of new orders, the redirection of the papacy, and the Council of Trent may have been even more important for the *world* history of Christianity than it was for the *European* history of Christianity.

Efforts at carrying the Christian message beyond the Mediterranean and European worlds had begun in the first century. Stories of far-flung apostolic evangelization, like the report of the disciple Thomas's missionary journey to India, testify to that earlier world-concern of the church. But especially with the spread of Islam, the confinement of the Eastern church to Byzantium and immediately surrounding territories, and the development of the papal-European axis, the worldwide potential of the church was obscured in the thousand years before 1500. Missiologist David Barrett has estimated that in 1500, something like 95 percent of the world's Christian population was concentrated in Europe. Catholic reform of the mid-sixteenth century marks an extraordinarily important turning point in the history of Christianity because it inspired a wide range of active, practical steps that began to translate the worldwide potential of the Christian faith into reality.

Missionary activity of several kinds had played a major role in the earlier expansion of Christianity. The first five hundred years of the church's history witnessed remarkable efforts at cross-cultural evangelism as the essentially Judaic character of early Christianity was successfully translated into the Hellenistic and Roman cultures of the broader Mediterranean world. The next five hundred years saw a series of breakthroughs when missionaries (often organized in itinerant monastic bands) moved northward into barbarian Europe and began a centuries-long process of restating the Christian message in the cultural idiom of the northern tribes. From the work of Patrick in Ireland during the fifth century, through the work of Boniface in northwest Europe in the eighth century and the Orthodox brothers Cyril and Methodius in their ninth-century mission to the Slavs, to the conversion of Russians in Kyiv (modern Ukraine) in the tenth century, vigorous

To their eternal credit, some
Catholic missionaries in the sixteenth century stood up for
indigenous people when other
Europeans did not. This print
shows Bartolomé de Las Casas
in such an attempt.

North Wind Picture Archives

cross-cultural communication of the gospel advanced on a very broad
front.

To carve up the history of missions into five-hundred-year blocks
oversimplifies historical reality, but still it is possible to say that the period from roughly 1000 to 1500 was marked more by efforts at evange-
lizing the baptized within Christendom than by efforts at spreading
Christianity into new, unchurched cultures. During the later Middle
Ages there were a few significant missionary efforts beyond Christian
Europe. As we have seen, the Franciscan mystic Raymond Lull (ca.
1233–ca. 1315) learned Arabic in order to promote Christianity among
the Arabs of North Africa. But on the whole, most efforts at evangelization in this period were the labors of monks and friars among a European population that was often Christian more in name than in reality.

Currents of sixteenth-century Catholic reform drastically altered this
focus of missionary activity and once again launched Christianity on
an aggressive course extending to the whole world. Again, it was the
new or revived religious orders that led the way. Capuchins, who
trailed other orders in promoting cross-cultural witness, nonetheless
by the middle of the seventeenth century had sent missionary members

to the Middle East, the Congo, and the Americas. By that time as well, representatives of the Brothers Hospitallers were at work in South America, Oratorians (founded by Philip Neri [1515–95]) could be found in the Spanish and Portuguese colonies of Asia and America, the Vincentians (from Vincent de Paul [ca. 1580–1660]) were in Madagascar, and the Ursulines had sent women as missionaries into New France (modern Canada).

As much as missionary activity came to characterize most of the new and renewed Catholic orders, it received even more systematic attention from Augustinians, Dominicans, and Jesuits. For Reformation history the Augustinians are often remembered as the order of Martin Luther, and thus as unintentional contributors to the start of Protestantism. From the perspective of world Christianity, however, the same fervor for strict observance that eventually led Luther out of the Catholic Church was equally important for inspiring a dedicated burst of missionary zeal. By 1600 Augustinian missionaries had brought their version of the gospel to Mexico, Peru, Colombia, and Chile in Latin America; to India, China, Malacca, and the Philippines in Asia; as well as to Kenya in Africa and to Arabia. Within another quarter century Augustinians had spread out farther to Japan, Persia, Iraq, and Ceylon (Sri Lanka).

The Dominicans, with their strong traditions of teaching and theological analysis, played an especially important guiding role for the spread of Christianity to the New World. The Dominican priests Bartolomé de Las Casas (1474–1566) and Francisco de Vitoria (ca. 1485–1546) were among the first Europeans to think specifically as Christians about the implications of European contact with America's indigenous peoples. Las Casas, with firsthand experience of the New World in Hispaniola, tried to formulate a strategy for evangelism among Native Americans that combined fervor for the gospel and respect for the Indians as human beings. Vitoria, a leading theologian at Spain's Salamanca University, drew up moral guidelines for respecting the property, lives, and souls of the Native Americans that helped establish principles of modern international relations. In 1537 protests by two other Dominicans, Bernardio de Minaya and Julian Garces, led Pope Paul III to condemn atrocities perpetrated by Spanish conquistadors on the Indians and to declare that Native Americans were entitled to full respect as human beings.

Of all the new or revived Catholic orders, the Jesuits did the most to reinvigorate the missionary vision of the church. Francis Xavier was the first Jesuit missionary, but even by the end of his life in 1552, other Jesuits had begun to fan out throughout Asia and other parts of the world. Xavier's work in Japan was especially important, not only for initiating a Christian presence in that country, but also for highlighting critical questions about the cross-cultural passage of Christianity itself. Xavier began his work in Japan in August 1549 at a fluid time in relations between Japanese rulers and Portuguese traders. Xavier was thus able to take advantage of Portuguese patronage and Japanese curiosity in order to win a hearing for his message. When he died twenty-seven months later, over 700 Japanese had joined the church; by the 1580s, there were 75 Jesuits at work in Japan and perhaps 150,000 converts. This burst of Catholic expansion was brought to a halt in the second decade of the seventeenth century when new, anti-Western rulers gained power in the region of Japan where the Jesuits had been working. The result was a series of violent persecutions and the nearly complete obliteration of Christianity in Japan. But for almost seventy years, Jesuit missionary energy had demonstrated the potential for Christian expansion beyond the confines of Europe.

The Jesuit experience in Japan led, however, to serious debate within European Christian circles about how to communicate Christianity cross-culturally. Xavier, for example, almost by instinct adopted procedures in Japan that contradicted the Jesuits' European norms. To gain a hearing in a highly stratified culture, Xavier asserted himself like a Japanese lord. To reach leaders in Japanese society, Xavier set aside the plain cotton clothing that in Europe reflected the vow of poverty and adopted the silk clothing of the Japanese upper classes. To provide security for his mission, he sought the patronage and protection of Portuguese traders and so gave up the fierce independence (obedience to the pope alone) that marked Jesuit work in Europe. These steps, when pursued by later Jesuits, sparked intense debate at Rome and in Europe about how much it was permissible to adapt traditional Christian forms to new cultural environments.

That debate was heightened when Jesuits inaugurated widespread missionary work in China. When adaptation to local conditions was pursued with determination and self-consciousness, controversy sprang up. The Jesuit missionary Matteo Ricci (1552–1610) was especially keen to find common ground between China's Confucianism and his own Christianity. In the wake of efforts of Ricci's work, prolonged, sometimes acrimonious discussion occurred over what is often referred to as the Chinese Rites Controversy. That discussion was a pioneering exercise on the cross-cultural translation of Christianity. Vigorous opposition among European Jesuits to Ricci's clothing (like Xavier, he dropped common dress for the more elaborate clothing of the literati) as well as to his cultural theology (he thought certain aspects of Chinese veneration for ancestors could be accommodated to Christianity) initiated a debate that lasted for centuries. In this debate

An Issue in the Chinese Rites Controversy

Instructions from Rome to China guided Catholic missionaries along a tightrope. On one side was the danger of making Christianity irrelevant to the Chinese. On the other was the danger of accommodating too much to local custom. As an example of efforts to find a balance, the following is one part of a long response from the Holy Office from 1704 providing guidance with respect to Confucian rites:

In no way and for no reason should Christians be permitted to preside, to serve, or to be present at the solemn sacrifices or oblations that are regularly offered to Confucius and the deceased ancestors in the spring and autumnal equinox of each year. These sacrifices or oblations are tainted with superstition. . . .

These answers should not be taken as condemning merely material presence or participation. It could happen that Christians sometimes are present this way at superstitious actions, with pagans doing superstitious things, Christians giving no approval, either openly or covertly, to what they are doing, and refraining altogether from active participation. Otherwise, hatred and hostility cannot be avoided. Christians, though, should profess their faith, and take care not to lose their faith.

Likewise, the same answers are not opposed to other things being performed in honor of the dead, if they are in keeping with the culture of those pagans, if they are not really superstitious, and do not look superstitious, but are within the limits of civil and political rites. What are these rites? With what precautions could they be tolerated? This should be left to the judgment both of the Reverend Patriarch of Antioch and the Visitor General in the Chinese Empire, and of the bishops and vicars apostolic of those regions. Meanwhile, however, these should take care, with all the zeal and diligence they can, to do away with pagan ceremonies, so that gradually those rites may become the practice established in this matter by Christians and for Christians, which the Catholic Church has piously prescribed for the dead.[3]

the principle was often sounded that genuine Christianity does not depend upon the specifics of European culture. For example, in 1659 Rome's Sacred Congregation for the Propagation of the Faith dispatched a document to three new French Catholic missionaries in Tonkin and Cochin China that set out broad principles of such cultural adaptation: "Do not try to persuade the Chinese to change their rites, their customs, their ways, as long as these are not openly opposed to religion and good morals. What would be sillier than to import France, Spain, Italy, or any other country of Europe into China? Don't import these, but the faith. The faith does not reject or crush the rites and customs of any race, as long as these are not evil. Rather, it wants to preserve them."[9] Such sentiments were not universal, however, and only with great struggle did the leadership of the Jesuits gradually accept the notion that true Christianity in China might look somewhat different from true Christianity in Europe.

That lesson, though hard-won, stood especially the Jesuits in good stead. By no means were all Jesuit missionaries good missionaries. And from a Protestant point of view, Catholic missionary activity in the sixteenth and later centuries often seems overly superficial, inadequately scriptural, and frequently syncretistic (that is, uncritically blending Catholic elements into the fabric of pagan or non-Christian religions). Still, when possible objections have been raised, the record of the Jesuits displays remarkable faithfulness to Christianity, combined with remarkable flexibility in its presentation. To take one of the most compelling examples, the Jesuit mission to New France provided hints as to what a re-contextualization of the Christian faith could look like outside of Europe. Jesuit work among the Huron Indians near Georgian Bay was spearheaded by Jean de Brébeuf (1593–1649), whose arrival in 1625 coincided with a cultural-political crisis among the Hurons. Hard-pressed by disease, warfare, and general anomie, the Hurons turned eagerly to the faith brought by the Jesuits. For his part, Brébeuf sought to adapt the Christian message to Huron culture. He learned their language, translated scriptural and liturgical materials, and ordered his Jesuit subordinates to adopt the Native Americans' lifestyle without complaint. And he even began the effort to restate the Christian message in a Huron idiom, as in a Christmas carol that began:

> Within a lodge of broken bark
> The tender Babe was found,
> A ragged robe of rabbit skin
> Enwrapp'd His beauty round.

As in Japan, the Jesuits' missionary work was cut short by large-scale disaster, in this case the annihilation of the Hurons by the Five Nations Iroquois. In addition, scholarly debate continues as to whether the Jesu-

---

9. Ray R. Noll, ed., *100 Roman Documents concerning the Chinese Rites Controversy (1645–1941)* (San Francisco: Ricci Institute for Chinese-Western Cultural History, 1992), 6.

its' initial success among the Huron came about because of their sensitivity in adapting Christianity or because of the Hurons' disoriented state.

What remains so significant for the history of Christianity, however, is the pioneering recognition of the Jesuits, and some of the other Catholic orders, that the communication of Christianity to non-Europeans must involve a cultural repositioning of the faith. That insight would eventually win widespread recognition within the Catholic Church as others built on the work of the sixteenth- and seventeenth-century missionary pioneers; it would become a foundational principle for the first effective Protestant missions from Moravians and German Lutheran pietists at the end of the seventeenth and early eighteenth centuries; and it would inspire some of the most important cross-cultural work of the great missionary impulse in the nineteenth century, as with Hudson Taylor and the China Inland Mission. Eventually, by the twentieth century, the realization that it was not necessary to be a product of Western culture in order to be a Christian would literally remake the dimensions of the Christian world. That story, however, is the subject of chapter 12 below. Here it is enough to say that, as Roman Catholics responded both to Protestant challenges and to their own impulses for reform, they put in motion developments that would profoundly affect not only the Christian life of Europe but also the history of Christianity in the whole world.

This short prayer from Ignatius Loyola is a fitting summary of his life and the ideals of the Jesuits:

> Teach us, good Lord, to serve thee as thou deservest; to give and not to count the cost; to fight and not to heed the wounds; to toil and not to ask for rest; to labour and not to ask for any reward save knowing that we do thy will. Through Jesus Christ our Lord.[10]

Further Reading

Brady, Thomas A., Jr., Heiko A. Oberman, and James D. Tracy, eds. *Handbook of European History, 1400–1600*. 2 vols. Grand Rapids: Eerdmans, 1994–95.

10. Quoted in *Eerdmans Handbook to the History of Christianity* (Grand Rapids: Eerdmans, 1977), 411.

Broderick, J. *The Origin of the Jesuits.* Chicago: Loyola University Press, 1986 (orig. 1940).

Delumeau, Jean. *Catholicism between Luther and Voltaire: A New View of the Counter-Reformation.* Philadelphia: Westminster, 1977.

Jedin, Hubert. *A History of the Council of Trent.* St. Louis: B. Herder, 1957.

Jones, Martin D. W., ed. *The Counter Reformation: Religion and Society in Early Modern Europe.* New York: Cambridge University Press, 1995.

Meisner, William W., S.J. *Ignatius of Loyola: The Psychology of a Saint.* New Haven: Yale University Press, 1992.

Neill, Stephen. *A History of Christian Missions.* New York: Penguin, 1964.

Noll, Ray R., ed. *100 Roman Documents concerning the Chinese Rites Controversy (1645–1941).* San Francisco: Ricci Institute for Chinese-Western Cultural History, 1992.

Oakley, Francis. *The Western Church in the Later Middle Ages.* Ithaca, N.Y.: Cornell University Press, 1979.

O'Connell, Marvin. *The Counter Reformation, 1559–1610.* New York: Harper & Row, 1974.

Olin, John C. *Catholic Reform from Cardinal Ximenes to the Council of Trent, 1495–1563.* New York: Fordham University Press, 1990.

O'Malley, John, S.J. *The First Jesuits.* Cambridge: Harvard University Press, 1993.

10

The New Piety: The Conversion of the Wesleys (1738)

The first half of the eighteenth century witnessed a burst of hymn-writing in the Protestant world. At the start of the century, Isaac Watts (1674–1748) pushed English-language hymnody beyond biblical paraphrases toward freer, more doctrinal, and more experiential song. Watts was soon followed by the greatest hymn-writer in the history of the language, Charles Wesley, and then by a host of others who made the hymn into the most powerful engine of Britain's eighteenth-century evangelical awakening. Similar creativity was at work in Europe at the same time, where the unprecedented genius displayed in the church music of Johann Sebastian Bach (1685–1750) was accompanied by a general flourishing of sacred song. One of the clearest evidences of links binding the evangelicalism of Britain and the Pietism of Europe, which is the subject of this chapter, was cooperation in hymn-writing. In 1740 John Wesley translated into English a hymn that Count Nikolaus Ludwig von Zinzendorf (1700–1760), the leader of the Moravians, had published only a year before. Its emphasis on the saving work of Christ, as well as on the liberating experience of that salvation, illustrated central themes in the religious revival of that century.

> Jesu, thy blood and righteousness
> My beauty are, my glorious dress;
> 'Midst flaming worlds, in these arrayed,
> With joy shall I lift up my head. . . .
>
> Lord, I believe thy precious blood,
> Which at the mercy-seat of God

Forever doth for sinners plead,
For me, ev'n for my soul, was shed. . . .

Ah, give to all, almighty Lord,
With power to speak thy gracious word,
That all who to thy wounds will flee
May find eternal life in thee.[1]

It was Monday, April 2, 1739. The city was Bristol, a rapidly growing seaport and rising manufacturing center on the west coast of England. Bristol's laboring population was crammed into dank housing on dark, narrow streets. The city's safety net had collapsed. Its old, elegant churches were utterly failing to keep up with the population or provide for its spiritual needs. Riots protesting squalid living conditions had already broken out in the city, and they would be repeated regularly throughout the eighteenth century.

On that day in that place a strange man did a strange thing. The man was short, slightly under five feet five inches, and wiry. He moved as if driven by relentless energy. What made him strange for Bristol was his pedigree. He was an Anglican minister and the son of an Anglican minister in a place where the national Church of England had all but abandoned spiritual support for the ordinary people. In politics he was a Tory, or conservative, who would later denounce the American Revolution as a sinful attack on the God-given social order. He was also a graduate of Oxford University at a time when less than one percent of the college-aged young people in Britain were privileged to attend university. Many of the Bristol laborers had probably never seen an Oxford graduate up close before.

What this strange man did was even more provocative. In eighteenth-century Britain, conventions for every area of life were strict. They were most strict for the churches. The local Anglican rectors were supposed to be in complete control of all spiritual activity in their parishes. Baptists, Congregationalists, and Presbyterians needed special licenses simply to hold worship services. Catholics suffered harsher con-

---

1. *The Works of John Wesley*, vol. 7, *A Collection of Hymns for the Use of The People Called Methodists*, ed. Franz Hildebrandt and Oliver A. Beckerlegge (Nashville: Abingdon, 1983), 309–11.

straints. No one who was not a member of the Church of England could serve as an alderman in Bristol or anywhere else in England. The Anglican Church and the British state worked hand in glove to guide the population. One of the most absolute religious conventions was that preaching took place on Sundays, and it was done in the churches. Anything else was incendiary and fanatical. To preach out of doors was virtually unheard of. If it did occur, it was considered seditious.

But on that April Monday something new, and something very important for the whole history of Christianity—especially its Protestant expression—was taking place. The minister knew what he was doing. Here is how, with characteristic economy of speech, he put it in his journal.

> At four in the afternoon I submitted to be more vile, and proclaimed in the highways the glad tidings of salvation, speaking from a little eminence in a ground adjoining to the city, to about three thousand people. The scripture on which I spoke was this (is it possible any one should be ignorant that it is fulfilled in every true minister of Christ?), "The Spirit of the Lord is upon Me, because He hath anointed Me to preach the gospel to the poor. He hath sent Me to heal the broken-hearted; to preach deliverance to the captives, and recovery of sight to the blind; to set at liberty them that are bruised, to proclaim the acceptable year of the Lord."[2]

The speaker was John Wesley (1703–91). In order to preach the gospel to the poor, he was willing to break the religious conventions that also defined his own well-disciplined life. In order to bring a message of "deliverance, recovery, and liberty" in Christ to people who had never heard that message, Wesley would preach out of doors, he would "submit to be more vile." As he took this momentous step, John Wesley was not alone, for his brother, the hymn-writer Charles (1707–88), was always a full partner in his enterprises.

In several important ways the Wesleys were the most effective proponents of the Reformation's basic message in the two centuries since Protestantism began with the work of Martin Luther, John Calvin, Menno Simons, and Thomas Cranmer. In other ways, the Wesleys were adapters of the Reformation message. In both preserving and adjusting the message of the early Protestants, the Wesleys' work kept alive the message of God's grace and greatly broadened its outreach. But their adjustments to Protestant traditions were—along with the innovations of the Wesleys' fellow Anglican George Whitefield (1714–70)—probably

2. *The Journal of the Rev. John Wesley*, 8 vols. (London: Epworth, 1938), 2:172–73.

William Hogarth's bitingly satiric *Gin Lane* depicted many of the eighteenth-century evils of urban England that the early Methodists also opposed.

Christian History Archives

the most important single factor in transforming the religion of the Reformation into modern Protestant evangelicalism.

The adjustments that the Wesleys made in Protestantism continue to influence decisively the shape of Christianity in Britain, America, and elsewhere in the world where evangelicals have carried the gospel. John Wesley was not so much an innovator as a gifted organizer who creatively exploited other people's new ideas. Thus, George Whitefield and the Welshman Howell Harris had pioneered field preaching, but it was John Wesley who became the great organizer of itinerant, outdoor evangelism. Again, the Moravians had pioneered the small-group cell meeting. But it was John Wesley who attended diligently to organizing these small-group cells into bands, societies, and circuits, and in so doing founded the Methodist Church. Once more, Wesley was not the first Protestant to organize voluntary agencies for reform in society, but his campaigns against slavery and excessive drinking, and for the education of unschooled children, set precedents that many evangelicals have followed ever since.

Wesley also made doctrinal as well as practical changes in the Protestant heritage. He was an Arminian who, unlike most of his Protestant predecessors, held that God by his grace restored free will to lost humanity. John and Charles Wesley also taught that believers could lose their salvation by deliberate, unrepentant sinning. In addition, they taught that Christians should strive to reach a place of "Christian perfection." This perfection did not mean an absolute sinlessness, but it did mean that Christians could expect to be free from every conscious sin in thought, word, and deed. Finally, the Wesleys also placed great stress on the work of the Holy Spirit. While none of these doctrinal contributions was entirely new, they did represent differences from traditional Protestant teaching. Just as Wesleyan practices have continued to mold Protestant life, so too have their doctrinal emphases—whether in entire denominations like the Methodists, and later the Nazarenes and the Assemblies of God, or in a more general way across the spectrum of Protestant churches.

Important as the Wesleys' adjustments to traditional Protestantism were, they also marked an important turning point in church history because of how much of the Protestant heritage they retained. The Wesleys lived in a world that was changing with unprecedented speed—as much for the reorganization of economic life as for the promotion of new ideas, as much for the renovation of politics as for the reconceptualization of the self. Yet in the cauldron of change that Europe became during the eighteenth century, the Wesleys maintained secure ties to the Protestant Reformation. Most important, as heirs of the earlier Protestant movements, John and Charles Wesley vigorously reaffirmed the central message of Protestantism: *sola gratia, sola fide, sola Scriptura*—salvation was by grace alone through faith alone as communicated with perfect authority in the Scriptures.

These Reformation truths were also the living realities that meant the most to John and Charles Wesley. The details of their own conversions show clearly their ties to the Reformation. On May 17, 1738, Charles Wesley and a friend began reading together Luther's commentary on the Book of Galatians. They found the volume "nobly full of faith." Four days later, Charles Wesley could finally say, "I now found myself at peace with God, and rejoiced in hope of loving Christ."[3]

Even more striking was John Wesley's own evangelical breakthrough and the role of the Reformation in that experience. Wesley had recently returned from a failed missionary venture in America. Although he was already known for the earnestness of his "methodical" approach to doing good, this troubled clergyman still lacked the assurance that God had forgiven his sins in Christ. Then on May 24, 1738, just a week after his brother had begun reading Luther on Galatians, John Wesley was also given a new sense of God's grace. Here are the memorable words from his journal: "In the evening I went very unwillingly to a society [meeting] in Aldersgate Street, where one was reading Luther's preface to the *Epistle of the Romans*. About a quarter before nine, while he was describing the change which God works in the heart through faith in Christ, I felt my heart strangely warmed. I felt I did trust in Christ, Christ alone, for my salvation; and an assurance was

---

3. Quoted in A. Skevington Wood, *The Inextinguishable Blaze: Spiritual Renewal and Advance in the Eighteenth Century* (Grand Rapids: Eerdmans, 1960), 109.

John Wesley on Faith

Everywhere they went, the heart of the Wesleys' message was the same—we are sinners who can be reconciled to God only by faith, through his grace. As a guide to the Methodist movement, John Wesley published and then republished several times a series of his own sermons. Always at the head of those sermons was "Salvation by Faith," one that Wesley had preached for the first time at St. Mary's Church, Oxford, on June 11, 1738, less than three weeks after the momentous experience at Aldersgate.

> What faith is it then through which we are saved? It may be answered, first, in general, it is a faith in Christ: Christ, and God through Christ, are the proper objects of it. Herein, therefore, it is sufficiently, absolutely distinguished from the faith either of ancient or modern Heathens. And from the faith of a devil it is fully distinguished by this: it is not barely a speculative, rational thing, a cold, lifeless assent, a train of ideas in the head; but also a disposition of the heart. . . .
>
> Christian faith is, then, not only an assent to the whole gospel of Christ, but also a full reliance on the blood of Christ; a trust in the merits of His life, death, and resurrection; a recumbency upon Him as our atonement and our life, *as given for us*, and *living in us*.[1]

given me that He had taken away *my* sins, even *mine*, and saved *me* from the law of sin and death."[4]

From the time of that experience, the message of God's grace formed the heart of the Wesleys' ministry. In an era when Britain enjoyed virtually no reliable roads, John Wesley traveled constantly to spread the good news of grace in Christ. After Aldersgate in 1738, his preaching tours took him about a quarter of a million miles (mostly on horseback), and he delivered forty thousand sermons (that is, an average of more than two a day). For many years, until Wesley at last won the reluctant admiration of all Britain, he preached these sermons in unfavorable conditions and often in the face of raucous opposition—sometimes outdoors, usually very early in the morning or at twilight, frequently while being heckled by the mob or harassed by the elite. Only in his seventies did Wesley abandon his horse for a carriage. Only in his mid-eighties did Wesley give up preaching be-

4. *Journal of John Wesley*, 1:475–76.

fore dawn. Here is his own account of an early-morning sermon on Wednesday, September 7, 1785, when he was eighty-two years old. "Just as I began, a wasp, though unprovoked, stung me upon the lip. I was afraid it would swell, so as to hinder my speaking; but it did not. I spoke distinctly, near two hours in all; and was no worse for it."[5] For his part, John's brother Charles, who itinerated almost as actively for many years, wrote nearly ten thousand hymns to spread the good news of God's grace.

Through the ups and downs of their very active lives, and while engaged in a considerable number of traumatic controversies, John and Charles Wesley never relinquished this grand theme: God's free grace saves sinners.

Scholars by the score have charted the influence of the Wesleys. But the extent of their impact can be sensed by anyone who has ever attended a Protestant church for any length of time. For when English-speaking Christians gather to worship, the hymns that most powerfully invoke God's grace in Jesus Christ are hymns written by Charles Wesley:

> He breaks the power of cancelled sin, He sets the prisoner free;
> His blood can make the foulest clean; His blood availed for me. . . .
>
> Jesus, Thou art all compassion,
> Pure, unbounded love Thou art. . . .
>
> Jesus, Lover of my soul,
> Let me to thy bosom fly.
>
> Arise, my soul, arise; shake off thy guilty fears;
> The bleeding Sacrifice in my behalf appears.
>
> Love divine, all loves excelling,
> Joy of heaven to earth come down.
>
> O for a heart to praise my God, A heart from sin set free;
> A heart that always feels thy blood so freely shed for me!

It is the same at Christmastime:

> Come, Thou long-expected Jesus,
> Born to set Thy people free. . . .
>
> Hark, the herald angels sing, glory to the new-born King. . . .
> Mild he lays His glory by, Born that man no more may die. . . .

5. Ibid., 7:113.

And also at Easter:

> Love's redeeming work is done,
> Fought the fight the battle won. . . .

Nowhere is the Wesleyan message of divine grace more powerfully expressed than in the greatest of Charles Wesley's hymns:

> And can it be that I should gain
> An interest in the Saviour's blood?
> Died he for me, who caused his pain?
> For me, who Him to death pursued?
> Amazing love, how can it be
> That thou, my God, shouldst die for me.

In short, the work of the Wesleys represents a turning point in the history of Christianity because they and their "methodist" colleagues renewed doctrines of God's grace that had grown stale in the English church.* They applied these doctrines with a fresh vigor to whole stretches of the population, like the working classes of Bristol, whom the churches had passed by. The Wesleys' work of revitalization, in effect, created modern evangelicalism out of the legacy of Reformation Protestantism.

To be sure, neither the Wesleys nor the English methodists acted alone. They were only the most visible English leaders in a more general movement of pietistic renewal that, beginning from the late seventeenth century, would eventually stretch from central Europe to North America. What they, along with other evangelicals and pietists, represented was a series of emphases that changed the face of Protestantism. In order to grasp the nature of that change, it is helpful to see how the shape of English evangelicalism followed similar currents at work among continental Protestantism, and then to consider in a little more detail how evangelical and pietist strands of Protestantism fit into broader developments within the Christian church during the seventeenth and eighteenth centuries.

---

* In Wesley's own day, "methodist" was a general word that included some who later became part of the Methodist denomination (like John Wesley), some who remained in the Church of England with their Arminian theology (like Charles Wesley), and some who advocated a strong Calvinist message whether in the Church of England (like George Whitefield) or in the Church of Wales (like Howell Harris) or in dissenting churches separated from the established church (like those who would eventually be called Welsh Methodists).

Pietism on the Continent

The methodism of the Wesleys and like-minded evangelists could be considered the British phase of a more general movement in the Protestant churches of Europe. The English historian W. R. Ward has been a leader in charting the thick web of connections and common interests that linked pietists on the Continent, evangelicals in Britain, and revivalists on the American frontier.[6] Chief among these links was a common thirst for a more directly personal religion and a common resistance to efforts by both Catholic and Protestant state-church regimes to exert tighter control over their local populations. So it is that a sketch of the pietist movement in Germany, which emerged in the generation before Wesley, features many of the themes, questions, problems, and solutions that also characterized the work of John Wesley, Charles Wesley, George Whitefield, and their associates in Britain.

"Pietism" is a contested term, but it can be traced historically to currents within German Lutheranism in the seventeenth century. At the start of that century the Lutheran churches in the German lands labored under many difficulties. Their work was tightly confined by the princes of Germany's many sovereign states. Their ministers seemed often more interested in philosophical wrangling and rhetorical ostentation than in encouraging their congregations. The quarrel with the Reformed-Calvinistic wing of Protestantism, which dated from Luther's lifetime, continued with considerable bitterness into the 1700s. Moreover, the devastating Thirty Years' War (1618–48), which was fought over a confused welter of religious, political, and economic matters, had enervated central European life in general, including the churches.

To be sure, the religious picture was not entirely bleak. Influences from beyond German-speaking lands were encouraging a more vital Christian faith and practice. A resurgence of godly living and wholesome theology in Holland spilled over into northern Germany. Devotional works by English Puritans like Richard Baxter (1615–91) and John Bunyan (1628–88) were being translated into German. There was also renewed interest in some of the mystical Christian writings of the Middle Ages. In Germany itself a more vigorous faith was promoted by the writings of Johann Arndt (1555–1621), whose *True Christianity* (1606) would become an important influence on later pietists, and the moving hymns of Philip Nicolai (1556–1608), like "Wake, Awake, for Night Is Flying."

6. Especially important is W. R. Ward, *The Protestant Evangelical Awakening* (New York: Cambridge University Press, 1992).

But in many places these signs of spiritual life were obscured by the formalism and insincerity of church leaders. This bleak general situation was the context for the unstinting work of Philipp Jakob Spener (1635–1705), who is often called the Father of Pietism. Born near Strasbourg and educated in that city and elsewhere on the Continent, he was called in 1666 to be the chief minister at Frankfurt am Main. There, beyond his heavy schedule of official duties, he renewed structures for educating and confirming young people. He called for moral reform in the city. And he initiated a far-flung correspondence with rulers and other leaders that eventually won him the title "spiritual counselor of all Germany."

Most important, Spener also promoted a major reform in the practical life of the churches. A sermon in 1669 mentioned the possibility of laymen meeting together, setting aside "glasses, cards, or dice," and encouraging each other in the Christian faith.[7] The next year Spener himself instituted such a *collegia pietatis* (pious assembly). The group met on Wednesdays and Sundays in Spener's home to pray, discuss the previous week's sermon, and apply passages from Scripture and devotional writings to their lives. Two generations later John Wesley would modify Spener's innovation as the basis for the class system (or interconnected small groups), which became the spiritual hallmark of methodism.

Spener's efforts reached a broader public when in 1675 he was asked to prepare a new preface for the published sermons of Johann Arndt. For this effort, Spener penned his famous *Pia Desideria* (The piety we desire). This brief work examined the sources of spiritual decline in Protestant Germany and offered proposals for reform. It was an immediate sensation. Spener criticized nobles and princes for exercising unauthorized control over the church, ministers for substituting cold doctrine for warm faith, and laypeople for disregarding proper Christian behavior.

Spener's six proposals for reform became a banner for Pietism in general. First, there should be "a more extensive use of the Word of God among us." The Bible, said Spener, "must be the chief means for reforming something." Second, Spener called also for a renewal of "the spiritual priesthood," the priesthood of all believers. Here he cited Luther's teaching as a way to urge all Christians to be active in the work of Christian ministry. Third, he appealed for Christian faith to be expressed in authentic practice, arguing that Christianity was more than

---

7. Theodore G. Tappert, introduction to Philip Jakob Spener, *Pia Desideria* (Philadelphia: Fortress, 1964), 13. All quotations from *Pia Desideria* in the next paragraphs are from this English translation.

Spener on Mutual Sharing in Christian Assemblies

In his *Pia Desideria* Spener proposed a conservative form of the small-group meeting that would (in many variations) become standard among pietists and evangelicals:

[I]t would perhaps not be inexpedient ... to reintroduce the ancient and apostolic kind of church meetings. In addition to our customary services with preaching, other assemblies would also be held in the manner in which Paul describes them in I Corinthians 14:26–40. One person would not rise to preach ... , but others who have been blessed with gifts and knowledge would ... speak and present their pious opinions on the proposed subject to the judgment of the rest, doing all this in such a way as to avoid disorder and strife. This might conveniently be done by having several ministers (in places where a number of them live in a town) meet together or by having several members of a congregation who have a fair knowledge of God or desire to increase their knowledge meet under the leadership of a minister, take up the Holy Scriptures, read aloud from them, and fraternally discuss each verse in order to discover its simple meaning and whatever may be useful for the edification of all. Anybody who is not satisfied with his understanding of a matter should be permitted to express his doubts and seek further explanation. . . . Then all that has been contributed, insofar as it accords with the sense of the Holy Spirit in the Scriptures, should be carefully considered by the rest, especially by the ordained ministers, and applied to the edification of the whole meeting. Everything should be arranged with an eye to the glory of God, to the spiritual growth of the participants, and therefore also to their limitations. Any threat of meddlesomeness, quarrelsomeness, self-seeking, or something else of this sort should be guarded against and tactfully cut off especially by the preachers who retain leadership in these meetings.[2]

a matter of simple knowledge. Fourth, Spener urged restraint and charity in religious controversies. He asked his readers to love and pray for unbelievers and the erring and to adopt a moderate tone in disputes. Fifth, he called for reform in the education of ministers. Here he stressed the need for training in piety and devotion as well as in academic subjects. Last, he implored ministers to preach edifying sermons, understandable by the people, rather than technical discourses, directed at other clergy.

These proposals provided an impetus for reform and renewal among many clergy and laity alike. They also posed two difficulties that continue to trouble pietistic and evangelical religion. First, they were opposed by some clergymen and professional theologians. Some were concerned only about preserving their traditional authority, but others saw dangers of rampant subjectivity and anti-intellectualism in the populism of Spener's proposals. Second, some laypeople took Spener's proposals as authorization for departing from the traditional churches altogether. While Spener firmly rejected the separatist, or sectarian, conclusions that others drew from his proposals, he was not always successful at reining in those who criticized the traditional churches. In a similar fashion, John Wesley hoped his methodist societies would be a fruitful assistance to the Church of England, but he lived to witness the formation of a new Methodist denomination that separated from the Church of England.

Spener's aim was to revive the concerns of Luther and the early Reformation. Yet he also altered Reformation theology in much the same way that Wesley would alter it. For example, Spener saw salvation much more as regeneration (the new birth) than as justification (being put right with God), even though the reformers had stressed the latter more than the former. Spener, along with later pietists and evangelicals, also regarded the sacraments more as occasions for fresh experiences of God within the heart than as the objective offering of grace, which had been the view of the major reformers. Such changes in Protestant doctrine were subtle, but as with similar changes from John Wesley, they represented important adjustments fitting the Christian message to their best understanding of the needs of the age.

Spener left Frankfurt for Dresden in 1686; from there he was called to Berlin in 1691. His time in Dresden was stormy and beset by controversy. Before the decade was out, the faculty of Luther's university, the University of Wittenberg, would charge Spener with 284 doctrinal errors. His stay in Dresden was not a loss, however, for there he met the individual who would become his successor, August Hermann Francke (1663–1727). Later, Spener helped found the University of Halle (near Berlin), to which Francke was called in 1691. Under Francke's guidance the University of Halle showed what Pietism could mean when put into practice. Francke's Halle, in fact, became an inspiration for Protestant renewal and Protestant service throughout Western society.

Francke began his extensive practical work by opening his own home in 1695 as a school for poor children. The next year he founded an orphanage that became world famous and established an institute for the training of teachers. Later he was influential in setting up a publishing house, a medical clinic, and other institutions. To understand the importance of these pietistic efforts in society, it is helpful to remember that when George Whitefield went to Georgia in 1738, the official task of this famous itinerant was to serve as director of an orphanage, a work inspired by Francke's example in Halle.

Francke himself had experienced a dramatic conversion in 1687. In turn, his extensive and pioneering missionary efforts flowed from the desire to make Christian conversion possible for others who had not yet heard the gospel. Under Francke's direction, pietists trained at Halle became the first Protestants to engage in extensive cross-cultural mission work. The university established a center for studying oriental languages and also promoted translations of the Bible into non-Western languages. Francke's missionary influence was felt both directly, through laborers who went from Halle to foreign fields, and indirectly, through groups like the Moravians and an active Danish mission that drew inspiration and guidance from the leaders of Pietism.

The pietistic renewal sponsored by Spener and Francke soon multiplied into other varieties of German Pietism during the age of Wesley. Count Ludwig Nicholas von Zinzendorf (1700–1760), head of the renewed Moravian church, was Spener's godson and Francke's student. Zinzendorf organized refugees from Moravia (in today's Czech Republic) into a kind of *collegia pietatis* within German Lutheranism. Later he shepherded this group in reviving the Czech Unity of the Brethren. These Moravians, as they came to be called, carried the pietistic concern for personal spirituality almost literally around the world, with important missions in India, the West Indies, North America, and elsewhere. It is of momentous significance for the history of English-speaking Christianity that John Wesley was thrown into a company of Moravians during his voyage to Georgia in 1735. What he saw of their behavior then and what he heard of their faith after returning to England contributed directly to his own evangelical awakening.

The Moravians were pietists who moved beyond Lutheranism. Another group, at Württemberg in Germany, remained within the Lutheran state church and became noteworthy for the nature of its biblical study. Its leading figure, Johann Albrecht Bengel (1687–1752), possessed an unusual combination of scholarly expertise and devotional commitment. Bengel was a pioneering student of the text of the New Testament as well as a careful and pious exegete. His *Gnomon Novi Testamenti* was used by Wesley for his own biblical works and remains in print today. Bengel's contention that the story of salvation constitutes the heart of all Scripture stimulated the work of many others. He also wrote several books on the millennium and the last days, which also led to a characteristic pietistic and evangelical fascination with the end of the age.

The influences radiating from Halle, Württemberg, and the Moravians profoundly affected Protestantism throughout Europe and the New World. Pietistic influences moved rapidly into Scandinavia. When soldiers from Sweden and Finland were captured in battle with Russia (1709), pietist concerns migrated with the captives to Siberia. Pietism was important in America too. The father of American Lutheranism, Henry Melchior Muhlenberg (1711–87), was sent to America by Francke's son in response to requests from German immigrants for spiritual leadership. Elsewhere in early America pietist influences were also present among the Mennonites, Moravians, Brethren, and Dutch Reformed.

As indicated above, Pietism had a formative influence on John Wesley, even though he would break with the Moravians in the early 1740s. During his stay in Georgia from 1735 to 1737 and after his return to England, Wesley's direct contacts with several Moravians played a key role in his discovery of God's active grace. Despite these connections, Wesley eventually came to feel that pietistic spirituality incorporated too much mysticism and that pietistic sensibility did not lead to sufficient activity in Christian causes. Yet despite later differences, Wesley's debt to the pietists—as shown by his visits to Germany and his translations of German hymns by Zinzendorf and other pietists—remained substantial.

Several movements of renewal in Europe throughout the nineteenth century can also be traced in part to the continuing influence of Spener, Francke, and their circle. In Germany the revival of interest in Luther and his theology is associated with pietistic impulses. The Basel Mission and the Inner Mission Society of Denmark, two active agencies for cross-cultural activity in the nineteenth century, also drew upon pietistic traditions. In Norway the revivalist Hans Nielsen Hauge (1771–1824) restored a pietistic presence to the Lutheran state church. In Sweden the recovery of pietistic concerns was one of the factors in the establishment of the Swedish Mission Covenant Church (1878). Especially when offshoots of Pietism migrated to North America, with its large English-language population, the merging of evangelical and pietistic influences was a common experience.

The movements of renewal on the Continent shared a great deal with the methodism promoted by John and Charles Wesley and exemplified in large measure by the hugely popular preaching of George Whitefield. The English and continental movements shared an emphasis on Scripture, a zeal for evangelism, a method of organization through small groups, and a dedication to practical social benevolence. It was not only what these commitments meant positively, however, but also what they entailed by way of negation that marked the rise of evangelicalism (and Pietism) as such important developments in the history of the church.

Evangelicalism and Pietism in the History of Christianity

Evangelicalism in the English-speaking world and Pietism on the Continent together represented a strategic shift in Christian energy, direction, assumptions, and associations. Some of that new direction came in response to altered conditions in Europe, some was more directly a response to conditions within the churches.

The world of eighteenth-century Europe was no longer the world in which the Protestant Reformation was born. Then, in the sixteenth century, it was simply assumed that for any one region there should be a single, unifying church. Now, in the eighteenth century, pressure was growing behind the idea that regimes could tolerate minority religions, and in the European colonies of the New World the radical idea could be heard that several churches could coexist with full civil rights in a single place.

Then almost all Europeans, except the most extreme Anabaptists, embraced the concept of Christendom and considered it only natural for the sphere of the church's influence to extend over all of society. Now Christendom was an increasingly beleaguered concept, beset on the one side by Christian sectarians who were willing to give up Christendom in order to save the church and on the other by a growing number of secularists who wanted to give up Christendom in order to escape the church.

Then intellectual life was instinctively conservative, oriented to the past for guidance, inspiration, and substance. Now far more of the laity were learned, far more rewards were being offered to those who could discover something new, and far less deference was automatically paid to the past.

Then Bible reading, even among Protestants who made the authority of Scripture preeminent over all other authorities, was almost universally regarded as a communal activity. Luther, Calvin, and the other early Protestants wanted laymen and laywomen to read the Bible themselves, but they still expected biblical interpretations from learned, pious clergy (like themselves) to be accepted by the faithful. Now Bible reading was rapidly becoming a solitary activity that divided, rather than united, communities. Already by 1700, innovative secular inter-

Although they were almost ceaselessly on the go, Charles and John Wesley are immobilized here in the stained glass of the Grace Methodist Church in Wilmington, North Carolina.

Christian History Archives

preters were beginning to question the unique divine authority of Scripture, while from another direction, more and more sectarian readers were rejecting the churches' historic patterns of interpretation.

Then European population was still overwhelmingly rural. Now great cities had become a magnet for spiritual, as well as economic, innovation, and the landscape was dotted with increased numbers of growing towns.

Then economic life, though beginning to expand at an accelerating speed, was still mostly local, still mostly under the authority of those who had inherited wealth, and still mostly oriented toward agriculture. Now the beginnings of modern economy could be glimpsed, where market forces were overtaking rural self-sufficiency and where large-scale developments in manufacturing, finance, and communication were beginning to draw previously isolated localities into ever larger circles of production and consumption.

Then the only part of the world that most Europeans knew or cared about was Europe. Now contacts with non-Europeans, efforts to colonize far-distant shores, and trade with several non-Western regions were multiplying on every side.

In other words, the differences between sixteenth-century Europe and eighteenth-century Europe were great. In these general circumstances evangelicals and pietists were busy with two tasks. They were retrieving elements of the Protestant past—especially *sola Scriptura*, an emphasis on grace, and the priesthood of all believers. With these elements they sought a more genuine Christianity, or what many throughout all of northern Europe and North America at the time called "true religion." But they were also creatively interpreting those religious commitments in social circumstances that differed greatly from the conditions in which Protestantism had been born.

In the wake of the Reformation, Protestant church–state establishments had replaced Catholic church–state establishments in much of Germany and Switzerland, the Netherlands, England, Scotland, Wales, the Scandinavian countries, and a few principalities in eastern Europe such as parts of Hungary. European settlements in the New World found it difficult to maintain European notions of religious establishment, but all early efforts at colonization except Rhode Island nonetheless preserved some form of church–state connection. These Protestant establishments had done much to instruct the people in new Protestant teachings, to make the Scriptures available in the European languages, to promote a Protestant hymnody, and to set up institutions for education from the earliest grades through seminary training for ministers.

But as the examples of Spener's Germany and Wesley's England suggest, the Protestant state churches also experienced many difficulties following the deaths of their first-generation leaders. Serious theological strife and strategic political reversals had confined Lutheranism to the German and Scandinavian lands. Anabaptists like the Mennonites remained a marginalized, often fugitive, people. Throughout the sixteenth and seventeenth centuries, Reformed varieties of Protestantism continued to expand in Holland, Switzerland, the British Isles, and for a time in France. But militant self-assurance of the Reformed meant that it was very difficult for Calvinists to act peacefully in winning over opponents or the indifferent. Militancy, which greatly inspired adherents, also greatly offended nonadherents. For example, there was much to admire in the zealous Puritans who worked from the 1580s to complete the Reformation in England. Puritans were patient preachers, dedicated shepherds to the grieving and to those wracked by sin, earnest promoters of discipline in family and at work. But Puritanism also proved disruptive. Along with the intransigence of the Anglican monarch Charles I, Puritan zeal drove England to civil war in the 1640s, to a benevolent dictatorship under Oliver Cromwell in the 1650s, and to exhaustion with religious strife in the 1660s.

The trials of Reformed Protestants in England were similar to the disasters experienced by Roman Catholics and Protestants on the Continent during the Thirty Years' War. This war unleashed a series of brutal conflicts that devastated central Europe with a ferocity that would not be witnessed again until the First World War three centuries later. Political strife, economic competition, and many other nonecclesiastical factors contributed to the Thirty Years' War. But Protestant and Catholic fears, jealousies, insecurities, and vengeance also added fuel to this violent conflagration. Recent historians have suggested that the churches may have been used as puppets by military imperialists in this struggle, but the war still led to a growing sense that it was necessary to reduce the visibility of religion in order to have peace in the day-to-day life of European nations.

The churches' failure in politics was matched by Protestant limitations in core areas of the faith. As indicated by the work in Germany of Johann Arndt, the labors in England of Richard Baxter and John Bunyan, and the hymn-writing of Philip Nicolai in Germany or of Thomas Ken in England (1637–1711, author of the "Doxology"), serious attention to spiritual life was not absent in the Protestant churches of the seventeenth century. But neither was such attention dominant or particularly dynamic. The Protestant state-church establishments were often more effective at nurturing parishioners through the ordinary crises of the life cycle than later reformers would admit. But throughout the seventeenth and into the eighteenth centuries—with some local exceptions (like the Czech educator Johannes Comenius [1592–1670])—they were not doing as well in Christian instruction as the Jesuits or other renewed Catholic orders. They were not successful in freeing themselves from the political restraints of their own establishments. And (again by comparison with the Roman Catholics) they showed almost no interest in taking the gospel into non-Christian cultures.

Pietism in German and evangelicalism in Britain were movements of Protestant renewal that responded to these weaknesses in the church, even as they also adjusted to the changing realities of European political, social, economic, and cultural life. In retrospect, several commitments by the leading representatives of Pietism and evangelicalism were especially important in their redirection of Christian energies.

Although Spener, Francke, Whitefield, and the Wesleys all were loyal, in at least some measure, to the Protestant state churches in which they had been born, all were also ready to experiment with religious practices that repudiated, or neglected, traditional church–state establishments. Thus, the pietists' *collegiae pietatis* were intended to strengthen the regular work of the state church, but they did so by forming an alternative to state-church structures. For the Moravians, it was a simple step to drop connections with the state church altogether. In Britain, the Wesleys and Whitefield likewise were entirely content with their Anglican ordinations. But in various ways their innovations also weakened ties to the traditional church, even as they exploited new conditions in eighteenth-century society. The early methodists soon became masters of procedures dictated more by the needs of their age than by the heritage of the church. For example, Charles Wesley wrote hymns for society meetings that were only loosely connected to the established church. John Wesley was zealous to establish religious and social-relief societies unconnected with the church. George Whitefield was more innovative yet. He was an absolute genius as a "salesman" for the gospel in the British Empire's new competitive marketplace, where ability to draw a crowd and attract attention for a "product" was beginning to count more than deference to traditional patterns of "consumption" as provided by the established church. In addition, Whitefield's ability to use his era's burgeoning public press as a vehicle to spread word about his preaching also represented an accommodation to the spirit of his times that the established church was not ready to make.[8]

The ways in which pietists and evangelicals renovated the gospel message for conditions in the eighteenth century were theological as well as social. Evangelical religion is sometimes considered the antithesis to the religion promoted by representatives of the eighteenth-century Enlightenment, and it is certainly true that some major figures of the European Enlightenment, like Voltaire and Rousseau in France, were decidedly anti-Christian. Yet, as illustrated by John Wesley, leaders of evangelicalism and Pietism often accentuated for Christian purposes many of the same currents that also defined the Enlightenment. Thus, Wesley—like spokesmen for the Enlightenment and in opposition to traditions of the Anglican establishment—was an innovator who readily gave up traditions that now seemed old-fashioned; he laid great stress on testing the reality of faith by its "experimental" (or experiential) nature rather than on its conformity with traditional dictates; he was intensely interested in practical, even utilitarian, effects of faith, rather than merely its conformity to inherited truths; and he made the decisions of the individual critical for the life of faith as opposed to stressing dictates handed down from the previous generation. In all of these ways, Wesley promoted a religious faith that resembled

---

8. See especially Harry S. Stout, *The Divine Dramatist: George Whitefield and the Rise of Modern Evangelicalism* (Grand Rapids: Eerdmans, 1991); and Frank Lambert, *Pedlar in Divinity: George Whitefield and the Transatlantic Revivals, 1737–1770* (Princeton: Princeton University Press, 1994).

the forms of the Enlightenment, even though his purpose in doing so was Christian in a way that many proponents of the Enlightenment had abandoned.[9]

Evangelicals and pietists also responded to unique possibilities of their age by being much more active in cross-cultural evangelism than any Protestants had ever been before their time. The missionary efforts of Spener, Francke, and the Moravians were major Protestant innovations. The zeal displayed by the Wesleys, Whitefield, and a host of unsung methodist itinerants for carrying the gospel message to Britain's miners, soldiers, industrial workers, and others whom the established church ignored was the beginning of massive evangelical efforts at carrying the gospel to the unreached. Evangelical preaching in the New World featured much more concerted outreach to Native Americans and African Americans than had taken place before. By the end of the eighteenth century, evangelicals in the English-speaking regions would be imitating their pietist colleagues from Germany and Scandinavia in beginning to send representatives overseas to preach the gospel. In some sense, such missionary exertions were a natural extension of hereditary Protestant beliefs about salvation and the potential dignity of all people. But in important ways, those missionary labors were also a distinctive adjustment to the realities of that age.

The ability of pietists and evangelicals to combine a message rooted in Protestant history with techniques, attitudes, sentiments, and innovations resonating with the realities of late seventeenth- and eighteenth-century Europe resulted in rapid, widespread success for these versions of the Christian faith. Before a century and a half had passed from the publication of Spener's *Pia Desideria* and less than a century from Wesley's Aldersgate experience, various forms of evangelicalism or Pietism had become the most important expression of Christian faith in many of the fringe regions of the eighteenth-century British Empire, including the United States (both north and south), the Scottish Highlands, the Canadian Maritimes, the northern part of Ireland, and Wales. In these regions, evangelical influences not only dominated in the Protestant churches but also exerted a powerful effect on society as a whole.

In many other regions, evangelicalism or Pietism, if not quite as dominant, had become an important component in the Protestant churches and often a significant influence in society. These places included Holland, England, Lowland Scotland, Upper Canada (now On-

9. On the Enlightenment connection to evangelicalism, I am following the interpretation of David W. Bebbington, *Evangelicalism in Britain: A History from the 1730s to the 1980s* (London: Unwin Hyman, 1989), 20–74.

tario), many areas of Germany and Scandinavia, some parts of Switzerland, and a few localities in eastern Europe.

These new forms of Protestantism shared the emphases that had inspired the pietist and evangelical movements, but because they were
movements adapting to local situations, they also differed dramatically
among themselves. In theology, evangelicals and pietists could embrace Lutheran, Calvinist, Arminian, or a bewildering variety of mediating positions on questions about the actions of God and of humans
in the process of salvation. In their views on the church, some supported traditional Anglican, Presbyterian, or Lutheran forms, while
others wanted to break free of all traditional ecclesiastical authorities.
In their politics, evangelicals in America tended to be republican and
often even democratic opponents of monarchy, but in Britain, Germany, Scandinavia, and Nova Scotia their religious peers were much
more likely to be found supporting inherited monarchies, or opting out
of politics altogether, than to favor either republicanism or democracy.
It is therefore not surprising that some evangelicals and pietists
thought their form of faith would rescue Christendom, while others
thought that it rendered Christendom superfluous. Similarly, in their
attitudes to the life of the mind, some were ardently intellectual while
others suspected formal reasoning of being a threat to the faith.

The important point to make about these differences is that they
arose largely from efforts to shape inherited features of Christianity to
the new realities defined by European social change and developments
in the European state churches. Yet despite a range of differences in
politics, social practices, attitudes toward the intellect, and other matters, evangelicals and pietists in fact shared a widely recognized set of
basic religious convictions. Two were most important. First, evangelicals and pietists were determinedly Protestant in their attachment to
Scripture. They could differ widely among themselves on the meaning
of the Bible, but the Scriptures remained an indisputable anchor.
Spener's ministry revolved around a lively application of the Bible to
the lives of ordinary people, while John Wesley prided himself on being
a *homo unius libri* (a man of one book). Second, evangelicals and pietists shared a conviction that true religion required the personal experience of God. They could offer many different norms for that experience and even more ways for aligning the experience of God with
reason, traditions, and hierarchies, but the experiential character of
faith remained central.

The intensity of these twin commitments—which flowed together in
what might be called an experiential biblicism—led to three other characteristics. In the first place, evangelicals and pietists were prejudiced

(sometimes only slightly, sometimes massively) against inherited institutions. As an example, only in the eighteenth century does the Protestant watchword *sola Scriptura,* or "the Bible alone," begin to mean "no authority except the Bible," instead of the meaning "no authority over the Bible," which had earlier prevailed in Protestantism. In the second place, evangelicals and pietists made flexibility with respect to intellectual, political, social, and economic conditions into a principle. Many traditions for church, politics, liturgy, hymnody, and prayer that had been treated as necessary pillars of faith in previous Protestant history now were open to negotiation. In the third place, evangelicals and pietists practiced what the historian Daniel Walker Howe has called discipline.[10] Their experiential biblicism might lead along many different paths to principles of conduct for self and others, but those principles were meant to be internalized, they were meant to foster personal holiness and appropriate social service.

On the foundation of their experiential biblicism, evangelicals and pietists thus erected a new form of Christian faith. It was a Protestantism clearly marked by the inheritance of the Reformation, but also one that in its willingness to discard tradition, its eagerness to adjust to widely diverse social realities, and its zeal for the practice of piety represented a significant new stage in the history of Christianity. The movement that began personally for the leaders of Pietism in Strasbourg, Frankfurt, and Dresden, and for leaders of English-speaking evangelicalism in society meetings like Aldersgate, eventually spread, and spread with massive effect, into all the world. If the renewal of Roman Catholicism in the second half of the sixteenth century was the most important development in Catholic history until the twentieth century, much the same can be said for Protestantism about the innovations symbolized so well by John Wesley's decision in April 1739 to preach in the fields.

If the evangelical and pietist revivals of the eighteenth century imparted immediacy to the Christian life, so also did they bestow heightened self-consciousness. No representative of evangelicalism felt the burden of that self-consciousness more than the poet William Cowper (1731–1800). Afflicted by mental disability that might today be called manic-depressive psychosis,

10. Daniel Walker Howe, "The Evangelical Movement and Political Culture in the North during the Second Party System," *Journal of American History* 77 (March 1991): 1216–39.

Cowper alternated between moments of serene faith and periods when he felt sure he had been predestined to eternal damnation. Notable evangelicals like the converted slave-trader and hymn-writer John Newton (1725–1807) patiently befriended him, but despite their efforts, Cowper gradually slid toward insanity. His poems were often prayers that reflected an exquisitely painful sense of self alongside a full experience of divine grace. The following one was called, with reference to Jeremiah 23:6, "Jehovah our Righteousness."

> My God, how perfect are thy ways!
>   But mine polluted are;
> Sin twines itself about my praise,
>   And slides into my pray'r.
>
> When I would speak what Thou hast done
>   To save me from my sin,
> I cannot make Thy mercies known,
>   But self-applause creeps in. . . .
>
> This heart, a fountain of vile thoughts,
>   How does it overflow,
> While self upon the surface floats,
>   Still bubbling from below!
>
> Let others in the gaudy dress
>   Of fancied merit shine;
> The Lord shall be my righteousness;
>   The Lord for ever mine.[11]

Further Reading

Baker, Frank, ed. *Representative Verse of Charles Wesley.* Nashville: Abingdon, 1962.

Bebbington, David W. *Evangelicalism in Modern Britain: A History from the 1730s to the 1980s.* London: Unwin Hyman, 1989.

Brown, Dale. *Understanding Pietism.* Grand Rapids: Eerdmans, 1978.

Erb, Peter C., ed. *Pietists: Selected Writings.* New York: Paulist, 1983.

Heitzenrater, Richard P. *Wesley and the People Called Methodists.* Nashville: Abingdon, 1995.

11. *The New Oxford Book of Christian Verse,* ed. Donald Davie (New York: Oxford University Press, 1981), 200–201.

Jeffrey, David Lyle, ed. *English Spirituality in the Age of Wesley*. Grand Rapids: Eerdmans, 1987.

Noll, Mark A., David W. Bebbington, and George A. Rawlyk, eds. *Evangelicalism: Comparative Studies of Popular Protestantism in North America, the British Isles, and Beyond, 1700–1990*. New York: Oxford University Press, 1994.

Outler, Albert C., ed. *John Wesley*. New York: Oxford University Press, 1964.

Pietism Re-examined [*Christian History*, no. 10]. 1986.

Rack, Henry D. *Reasonable Enthusiast: John Wesley and the Rise of Methodism*. New York: Trinity Press International, 1989.

Stoeffler, F. Ernst. *German Pietism during the Eighteenth Century*. Leiden: E. J. Brill, 1973.

———. *The Rise of Evangelical Pietism*. Leiden: E. J. Brill, 1970.

Whaling, Frank, ed. *John and Charles Wesley: Selected Prayers, Hymns, Journal Notes, Sermons, Letters, and Treatises*. New York: Paulist, 1981.

Zinzendorf and the Moravians [*Christian History*, no. 1]. 1982.

11

Discontents of the Modern West:
The French Revolution (1789)

One of the most popular hymns in English-language areas of the world was written shortly before the tumultuous events of the French Revolution. "All Hail the Power of Jesus' Name" was published in the April 1780 number of the *Gospel Magazine,* an English periodical committed to the values of the evangelical revival associated with the Wesleys, George Whitefield, and their various allies. The author was Edward Perronet (1726–92), whose biography, as well as the biblical material he put to use in the hymn, reflect important themes of the era. Perronet was descended from a Huguenot family that had been forced to flee from persecution in France; he was an ardent worker for reform but did so while shifting among Methodist, Anglican, and Congregational churches; and his vivid use of biblical imagery from the Prophets and the Book of Revelation stressed the dynamism, power, and worldwide scope of Jesus' reign. This hymn, therefore, speaks of the conflict, expansion, persecution, and reforming zeal that were so much a part of European Christian life in the tumultuous decades surrounding the French Revolution. The verses below are from Perronet's original text, which was modified shortly after it first appeared by a Baptist minister, John Rippon, whose edited version is the one usually found in hymnals today.

> *All hail the power of Jesus' Name;*
> *Let Angels prostrate fall,*
> *Bring forth the royal diadem*
> *To crown him Lord of all.*

Let highborn seraphs tune the lyre,
And as they tune it, fall
Before His face Who tunes their choir,
And crown Him Lord of all. . . .

Crown him, ye martyrs of your God,
Who from His altar call;
Extol the stem-of-Jesse's rod,
And crown him Lord of all. . . .

Let every tribe and every tongue
Before Him prostrate fall,
And shout in universal song
The crownèd Lord of all.[1]

On November 10, 1793, France's greatest church, the Cathedral of Notre Dame, witnessed an unprecedented spectacle. For over six hundred years, from the time this magnificent gothic structure began to be constructed in the mid-twelfth century, it had served as a symbol for the Christian identity of the nation. But now in the enthusiasm of revolution the cathedral had been renamed the Temple of Reason. A papier-mâché mountain with Greco-Roman motifs stood in the nave. Historian Simon Schama describes what happened next: "Liberty (played by a singer from the Opéra), dressed in white, wearing the Phrygian bonnet and holding a pike, bowed to the flame of Reason and seated herself on a bank of flowers and plants."[2] This inverted "worship service" was a high point in the French Revolution's program of dechristianization, whereby leaders of the Revolution attempted to throw off what they felt to be the heavy, dead hand of the church. In Paris, the revolutionaries renamed 1,400 streets in order to eliminate reference to saints as well as monarchs. Priests, bishops, and other religious were forced to leave their posts. A general effort was made to extirpate France's age-old connection with the Roman Catholic Church. As Al-

1. Text and background from *The Penguin Book of Hymns,* ed. Ian Bradley (London: Penguin, 1990), 19–21.
2. Simon Schama, *Citizens: A Chronicle of the French Revolution* (New York: Knopf, 1989), 778.

exis de Tocqueville later wrote, the animus against Christianity knew almost no bounds: "In France . . . Christianity was attacked with almost frenzied violence, there was no question of replacing it with another religion. Passionate and persistent efforts were made to wean men away from the faith of their fathers, but once they had lost it, nothing was supplied to fill the void within. . . . There is no question that the nationwide discredit of all forms of religious belief which prevailed at the end of the eighteenth century had a preponderant influence on the course of the French Revolution. This was, in fact, its most salient characteristic, and nothing did more to shock contemporary observers."[3]

A number of long-festering conditions had prepared the way for this attack on Christianity. Tensions before the beginning of Revolution in 1789 were manifold. Strain existed between political form (absolute monarchy) and political reality (the power of the king checked on every side by the hereditary privileges of nobles, corporations, and the Roman Catholic Church). Intellectual strain grew out of the tension between the traditional authoritarianism of Catholic Church and monarchical rule, on the one hand, and, on the other, a surging confidence in human reason and human capacities (exemplified in different ways by Voltaire [1694–1778], the philosophers who published the great *Encyclopédie* between 1751 and 1780, and the brilliant eccentric Jean-Jacques Rousseau [1712–78]). Social strain divided aristocrats from a rising "middle class" of commercial interests and both of those groups from a large peasant sector, which, although very poor, was required to bear the heaviest tax burden.

The events of 1789 represented the eruption of those tensions. In June the "Third Estate" (that part of France's States-General, or parliament, representing the bourgeoisie) formed a new National Assembly; on July 14 a popular uprising in Paris liberated the Bastille; these actions then set off riots throughout the countryside in which peasants destroyed records of their servitude and created a "Great Fear" among aristocrats; on August 26 the National Assembly issued the Declaration of Rights of Man and of the Citizen. This declaration held, among many other propositions, that "the source of all sovereignty is located in essence in the nation; no body, no individual can exercise authority which does not emanate from it expressly."[4] The European world as it once had been was beginning to pass away.

Surprisingly, there was a great deal of preliminary support for the Revolution from some stalwart Protestants. In America an initially fa-

---

3. Alexis de Tocqueville, *The Old Régime and the French Revolution*, trans. Stuart Gilbert (Garden City, N.Y.: Doubleday, 1955 [orig. 1856]), 149, 155–56.
4. Paul Harold Beik, ed., *The French Revolution* (New York: Walker, 1970), 95.

Bibliothèque Nationale

A contemporary print shows the actress posing as the Goddess of Reason who was "worshiped" by Jacobins in the Cathedral of Notre Dame.

vorable view came from Samuel Miller, a rising Presbyterian minister in New York City who would later become a conservative fixture at Princeton Theological Seminary. As late as July 1793, even after news had been received in New York about the execution of Louis XVI, Miller still hoped that Europe's "convulsive struggles" would hasten the spread of Christianity and human happiness. Miller remembered France's key role in helping American patriots in their War for Independence and wondered if it were possible to "view the interesting situation of our AFFECTIONATE ALLIES, without indulging the delightful hope, that the sparks, which are there seen rising toward heaven, though in tumultuous confusion, shall soon be the means of kindling a general flame, which shall illuminate the darkest and remotest corners of the earth, and pour upon them the effulgence of ten-fold glory?"[5]

Miller's positive view of the Revolution in France represented a Christian version of what was then a common sentiment among many sensitive Europeans. At last, it seemed, society was being directed toward the good of the whole community instead of toward the private

5. Samuel Miller, *Christianity the Grand Source, and the Surest Basis, of Political Liberty* (New York: Thomas Greenleaf, 1793), 30–31.

benefit of a tiny elite of kings, nobles, and bishops. At last "the people" had grasped the power that was theirs by right. "Bliss was it in that dawn to be alive," wrote the poet William Wordsworth, who lived in France during the early years of the Revolution,

> When Reason seemed the most to assert her rights
> When most intent on making of herself
> A prime enchantress—to assist the work,
> Which then was going forward in her name!
> Not favoured spots alone, but the whole Earth,
> The beauty wore of promise.[6]

But if this was the best of times, it was also, as Charles Dickens put it in the memorable first line of *A Tale of Two Cities*, the worst of times. Even before the Revolution turned to bloody excess, Edmund Burke looked across the channel from England with grave foreboding: "But what is liberty without wisdom, and without virtue? It is the greatest of all possible evils; for it is folly, vice, and madness, without tuition or restraint."[7] The course that the Revolution took in France soon disabused observers like Wordsworth and the American evangelicals of their earlier hopes. As control passed to ardent ideologues and as carnage ran wild, earlier friends of the Revolution recoiled in horror.

The record of events after 1789 was indeed a daunting one. Traumas and cataclysms followed with breathtaking speed. Escape from deference, traditions, and the rule of hereditary elites led to new sources of oppression rather than a flowering of liberty. Indiscriminate violence orchestrated by new rulers mocked visions of equality. A flourishing of ideology, especially from the left-wing Jacobins, lent a sinister meaning to notions of fraternity. Hundreds of the politically suspect were executed at one fell swoop in September 1792. Also in that year began wars carried out by France's "citizen armies" that changed the face of Europe forever. The execution in January 1793 of King Louis XVI and his queen, Marie-Antoinette, shocked Europeans almost as much as the Puritans' execution of England's Charles I had done 144 years before. From September 1793 to July 1794 the Committee of Public Safety ruled by means of "the Terror," which brought tens of thousands to their deaths. Maximilien Robespierre, who orchestrated this terror, used phrases like "love of the fatherland" and "the general inter-

6. *William Wordsworth: Selected Poems and Prefaces*, ed. Jack Stillinger (Boston: Houghton Mifflin, 1965), 332–33.
7. Edmund Burke, *Reflections on the Revolution in France* (New York: Prometheus, 1987 [orig. 1790]), 250.

Calendar of the French Revolution

1789   June 17, the Commons of the States-General declares itself to be *the* National Assembly
July 14, Storming of the Bastille
The Great Fear
August 26, Declaration of Rights

1790   Civil Constitution of the Clergy and other limitations on the Roman Catholic Church

1792   April 20, a new Legislative Assembly declares war on Austria (this is the first of the French Revolutionary Wars)
September 22, a Republic established, monarchy abolished

1793   January 21, execution of King Louis XVI
Left-wing *Jacobins* struggle against more moderate *Girondists;* revolutionary faction gains control and under Georges Danton and Maximilien Robespierre push *dechristianization* and make liberal use of the guillotine (this period comes to be known as the *Reign of Terror*)

1794   July 27, Robespierre overthrown; guillotined the next day

1794–95   *Thermidorean Reaction*—weak government, anarchy, inflation, riots

1795–99   *Directory* established—many coups and coup attempts against moderates

1799–1804   *Consulate*, with Napoleon as first consul

1804–15   First *Empire* under Napoleon

1815   Final defeat of Napoleon and restoration of the monarchy in France

est" to justify these actions. Charismatic leaders like Robespierre devoted themselves with Spartan zeal to the pursuit of virtue, but an ever-accelerating rush to the guillotine was the result. And the National Assembly passed reams of ambitious legislation, setting out literally to remodel the world. Part of that legislation involved the program of dechristianization.

In the face of such excess, reaction was inevitable. This reaction happened to coincide with the gargantuan ambition of a dashing young general. Soon that general was exalted as first consul, and then as the emperor Napoleon. Until his last defeat in 1815 by the combined armies of Europe, he would expand the unprecedented destruction and warfare begun by France's Revolutionary Army in 1792.

In our own century Arnold Toynbee summarized aptly the consequences of revolution and reaction: "In the Revolution a sinister ancient religion which had been dormant suddenly re-erupted with elemental violence. This revenant was the fanatical worship of collective human power. The Terror was only the first of the mass-crimes that have been committed [since the Revolution] in this evil religion's name."[8] Later this evil religion would be born again variously as "nationalism," "ideology," "the state," and "class warfare."

An even more pointed assessment has been made by Conor Cruise O'Brien, an Irish diplomat and writer who has witnessed many of the violent conflicts of the twentieth century. In his view, the growth of nationalistic or ideological spirit in the eighteenth century took place directly at the expense of traditional religion: "The older supernatural God had faded into the distance indeed, but it was not Reason, mostly, that took His place. It was new terrestrial creeds with new Revelations, and exponents who were often as arbitrary, as arrogant, and as fanatical as the worst of the old persecuting priests and monks."[9]

The turning point in the history of Christianity represented by the dechristianizing effort of the French Revolution was the end—or at least the beginning of the end—of European Christendom as the dominant expression of Christianity in the world. The ideal of Christendom had held sway in Europe for close to a millennium and a half. In that ideal the interests of Christianity and the interests of European civilization were regarded as two expressions of the same reality. But now at the end of the eighteenth century that ideal was very badly frayed. Both Catholic–Protestant competition and a constant series of inter-European wars had undermined notions of European unity. At least from the middle of the seventeenth century, an increasing number of European intellectuals used new ideas about the natural world, society, and the nature of things in general to attack the established churches, to question traditional views of divine revelation, and even (in an unprecedented step) to doubt the existence of God.

Less than one lifetime after the events of the French Revolution, the English literary figure Matthew Arnold wrote a famous poem, "Dover Beach," which likened the fate of traditional Christianity to

---

8. Arnold Toynbee, introduction to Christopher Dawson, *The Gods of Revolution* (New York: Minerva, 1978 [orig. 1972]), p. x.

9. Conor Cruise O'Brien, "A Last Chance to Save the Jews?" *New York Review*, April 27, 1989, p. 27.

the moon-lit spectacle of a tide receding at night from a great beach. In his rendering,

> The Sea of Faith
> Was once too, at the full, and round earth's shore
> Lay like the folds of a bright girdle furl'd.
> But now I only hear
> Its melancholy, long withdrawing roar,
> Retreating, to the breath
> Of the night-wind, down the vast edges drear
> And naked shingles of the world.[10]

As a description concerning the worldwide fate of Christianity in the nineteenth century, Arnold was simply mistaken. Even as he wrote these words, the nineteenth century was experiencing the greatest increase ever recorded in the number of Christian believers and a greater proportional increase than at any time since the fifth century. For Europe, however, Arnold's words rang true. The end of Christendom was at hand. The radical dechristianization practiced by France's ardent revolutionaries was a harbinger, not for how it went about displacing Christianity from the heart of European consciousness, but for the reality of that displacement.

This chapter sketches briefly several of the major forces that contributed to the end of European Christendom. It then expands at slightly greater length on major responses of the European churches. The chapter closes with a reminder that, while the preoccupations, traumas, and distresses of Christians in the West greatly affected the history of Christianity, that history was by no means limited to what was going on in Europe.

The Demise of Christendom

Students of European intellectual life often point to major developments at the end of the seventeenth century as marking a dramatic shift in the center of European cultural gravity. The publication of Sir Isaac Newton's *Principia Mathematica* in 1687 was one of these events. Although Newton himself was a painstaking student of the Bible (especially the apocalyptic parts) and although Newton's reputation at first inspired closer ties between formal religion and Europe's intellectual elite, the use of his work would eventually help revolutionize European intellectual life. Newton's ability to describe the apparently boundless

---

10. Matthew Arnold, "Dover Beach," in *Poetry and Criticism of Matthew Arnold*, ed. A. Dwight Culler (Boston: Houghton Mifflin, 1961), 162.

course of nature with precise mathematical formulas eventually led other intellectuals to claim that all of life could be understood with reference to itself, rather than with reference to God or the teachings of the churches.

C. S. Lewis once called the transition begun by such beliefs "the greatest of all divisions in the history of the West," and many others, like the French historian Paul Hazard in an influential book called *The Crisis of the European Mind*, have come to the same conclusion.[11] Yet the momentous shift underway among European intellectual elites by the early eighteenth century did not have a widespread general impact until considerably later. In a thought-provoking study entitled *The Secularization of the European Mind*, Owen Chadwick once suggested that "the years between 1650 and 1750"—that is, the years of Sir Isaac Newton, his English contemporary John Locke, Voltaire and the French philosophes, the creative pantheist Baruch Spinoza, and the Scottish skeptic David Hume—"were the seminal years of modern intellectual history." But for the results of these ideas to affect broader European society, it took another century and a half. "That is why," Chadwick explains, "the problem of secularization is not the same as the problem of Enlightenment. Enlightenment was of the few. Secularization is of the many."[12]

Another way of describing the secularization of which Chadwick writes is to call it the end of Christendom, or the end of that lengthy period of European history when the interests of church and society were thought to be the same and where it was almost universally assumed that Christian spiritual realities were more fundamental than realities of the temporal world. Of course, European Christendom did not die in a day. The continuing existence of state-supported churches in several European countries, as well as the prominence of Christian themes in the buildings, art, music, and literature of many European regions, attest to the lingering power of the ideal of Christendom. But the program of violent dechristianization carried out in the French Revolution is a fitting symbol for the evolving process whereby temporal realities began systematically to displace Christian realities as the center of European loyalty, preoccupation, and cultivation.

11. C. S. Lewis, "De Descriptione Temporum," in *Selected Literary Essays by C. S. Lewis* (Cambridge: Cambridge University Press, 1969), 7; Paul Hazard, *La Crise de la conscience européene*, published in translation as *The European Mind, 1680–1715* (London: Hollis & Carter, 1953 [orig. 1935]).

12. Owen Chadwick, *The Secularization of the European Mind in the Nineteenth Century* (New York: Cambridge University Press, 1975), 5, 9.

Over the course of the nineteenth century, a new post-Christian Europe began everywhere to be visible. Structural developments in economic and social life were probably the most obvious venues of change. Believers from different traditions continued to search for Christian perspective on, and Christian use of, the modern economy. Toward the start of the century, the Scottish Presbyterian Thomas Chalmers made a major effort to reinvigorate the urban parish as a way of meeting the human needs created by the new industrial society. At the end of the century, Pope Leo XIII issued a papal encyclical, *Rerum novarum* (1891), that offered well-considered guidance from Scripture and Catholic tradition concerning the same economic problems that Chalmers had addressed. But general economic trends, as well as the social effects of economic change, were running rapidly away from the churches. Increasingly, the production of wealth, the uses of wealth, the disparities in possession of wealth, and the application of wealth to social problems assumed a life of their own beyond the watch or guidance of the churches. Both the possibilities for hitherto undreamed of consumption and the proliferation of urban, industrial poverty became central features of nineteenth-century European life. They did so, moreover, in a secular landscape increasingly unaffected by Christian influences. By the second half of the century, Europe's traditional churches, after having already lost the intellectuals, were losing the working classes as well.

The great national crises of the era likewise unfolded in a secular setting. Warfare might cause a few people momentarily to think about God, but European national life was moving well beyond Christendom. Negotiations neutralizing the authority of the churches contributed to Bismark's strategy in unifying a German nation in 1871. The parallel movement that led to the unification of an Italian state at just about the same time moved more aggressively against traditional religion by forcefully pushing the pope aside. At the end of "the long nineteenth century," European nations experienced cataclysms that testified to the gulf separating them from their past, the centuries in which Christianity was integral to European self-definition. The carnage of the First World War overwhelmed any lingering sense of divine solicitude for Europe, at least among a very wide circle of cultural elites. The Russian Revolution of 1917 dropped any pretense of deference to Christianity and treated the institutions and leaders of the Orthodox Church as enemies of the people.

Long before these convulsive events of the early twentieth century, leaders of European thought had moved further and faster away from Christian faith. Metaphysical and ethical questions formulated during the Christian centuries may have continued to preoccupy European intellectuals. But the great philosophical influences of the nineteenth century—like Immanuel Kant and G. W. F. Hegel in Germany, or J. S. Mill in Britain—labored to replace traditional dependence upon revelation and religious tradition with what they held were more secure foundations of the good, the true, and the beautiful. Kant's argument in his 1793 work *Religion within the Limits of Reason Alone* became an intellectual charter for many great minds of the nineteenth century: "True religion is to consist not in the knowing or considering of what God does or has done for our salvation but in what we must do to become worthy of it . . . and of whose necessity every man can become wholly certain without any Scriptural learning whatever. . . . Man *himself* must make or have made himself into whatever, in a moral sense, whether good or evil, he is or is to become."[13]

The same drift characterized the development of science. While traditional cooperation between Christian faith and scientific endeavor actually survived longer and in many more forms than much twentieth-century historiography suggests, still the trend was toward a conception of the world in which traditional beliefs concerning God's power and creative wisdom were superfluous. Charles Darwin's *Origin of Species* (1859) was actually more ambiguous on these matters than later commentary admits, since Darwin retained the possibility of some kind of divine origin of life. Moreover, some of Darwin's early followers thought that his description of "natural selection" was compatible with God's purposeful design of the world. Yet Darwin's *Origin* soon became a symbol of science proceeding on its own without reference to a Creator. Furthermore, a new class of professional scientists employed by governments and universities worked energetically and rapidly to show why their systematic research qualified them to replace amateur naturalists, many of whom had been clergymen, in providing definitive information about what the natural world was really like.

By the middle of the nineteenth century, even the instinctive deference to Scripture as a divinely given book, a deference that had played a central role in European self-consciousness since time immemorial, was fading away. A growing array of publicly influential voices—resting on foundations constructed from eighteenth-century philosophical skepticism and nineteenth-century assertions about the centrality of the self—began to discard traditional attitudes toward the Bible. In 1835 David Strauss published his *Leben Jesu* (Life of Jesus), which de-

13. Immanuel Kant, *Reason within the Limits of Reason Alone*, trans. T. M. Greene and H. H. Hudson (New York: Harper & Row, 1960), 123, 40.

Contrasting English Views on Science and Christianity

In 1868 the clergyman Frederic William Farrar (1831–1903) published an attack on his fellow Anglicans for opposing the day's new science, like Darwin's evolutionary hypothesis, with crude, unreasonable reactions. All such noise was unnecessary, according to Farrar, since the best results of modern science must, in principle, be compatible with the truth found in Scripture, or anywhere else.

> Again and again I say that, if theology be only a true interpretation of the revelations of God, then *Science is itself one of the noblest forms of Theology*. It has deepened indefinitely our sense of the mysteries around us; it is the reading of that world which even Plato called 'God's epistle to man'; . . . Once more I must say that God, by the discoveries of science, has revealed more fresh truth respecting His own glory than all theology has declared for us since the last of the apostles.

By contrast, T. H. Huxley (1825–95) thought that the new science rendered many traditional Christian beliefs obsolete and their defenders reprehensible. For the vigor with which he promoted such views, he was called Darwin's Bulldog. This comment is from 1860:

> Another, and unfortunately a large class of persons take fight at the logical consequences of such a doctrine as that put forth by Mr. Darwin. If all species have arisen in this way [by natural selection operating randomly], say they—Man himself must have done so; and he and all the animated world must have had a common origin. Most assuredly. No question of it. . . . I would . . . point out that perhaps the very noblest use of science as a discipline is, that now and then she brings us face to face with difficulties like these. Laden with our idols, we follow her blithely—till a parting in the roads appears, and she turns, and with a stern face asks us whether we are men enough to cast them aside, and follow her up the steep? Men of science are such by virtue of having answered her with a hearty and unreserved, Yes; by virtue of having made their election to follow science withersoever she leads, and whatever lions be in the path.[1]

picted the Christ of the New Testament as a product of projection back in time from the early Christian community. The widely quoted Tübingen theologian Ferdinand Christian Baur (1792–1860) applied Hegel's dialectics to the New Testament in order to suggest that antithetical pictures of Christ and his work had been presented by a strain of writing influenced by Paul and another influenced by Peter, and that the appearance of cohesion in the New Testament came about only through creative editors in the late second century. Ernest Renan's *Vie de Jésus* (Life of Jesus) in 1863 presented Jesus as a simple Galilean preacher who would have been flabbergasted at what later generations said about his supposedly supernatural origins and powers. By the last third of the nineteenth century, formal academic study of the Old Testament had likewise been strongly influenced by views assuming that the Hebraic writings were the products of evolving Semitic experience rather than of revelations from God. Again, a whole host of more orthodox "lives of Jesus" and a small army of orthodox students of the Old Testament entered the lists in the nineteenth century to defend more traditional views of the Bible. Despite the intrinsic merit of much of that orthodox work, all who compared the nineteenth-century situation to what had existed only shortly before realized that things had greatly changed. When it had become necessary to *defend* the divine character of Scripture, the Christendom that once had given total (if often inattentive) loyalty to the Bible was no more.

Finally, a new sense of the self as God-like in heroic potential captured the imagination of more and more influential Europeans. This exalted view of human potential often goes under the name "Romanticism," but it extended well beyond the boundaries of identifiable literary or cultural movements. This sense of human boundlessness flourished in the English Romantic poets (Wordsworth and Coleridge early in their careers, Shelley and Byron throughout their brief lives), it inspired Goethe in early periods of his vastly influential writing career, it drove the musical compositions of Beethoven and Wagner, and it undergirded the spectacular rise of the novel as the dominant form of European literature. It is important to note that the Romantic sense of the self could be incorporated into Christian expressions, such as the German poet Novalis's depiction of the Middle Ages as an idyllic Christian arcadia, into some of Mendelssohn's music based on hymn tunes, or into the efforts of the heralded London preacher Edward Irving to found a new apostolic church. But the Romantic sensibility could also lead its advocates to despair, as in the case of Germany's Heinrich Heine. The importance of extreme Romantic views in the history of Christianity, as also of the extreme views of the Enlightenment from the generation before, was the relative absence of Christian revelation, practice, or piety in these broad cultural movements that came to mean so much for Europe.

These developments in European economic, social, national, intellectual, and cultural life spelled the end of an era. Christianity was not banished from Europe, but over the course of the nineteenth century it came to be marginalized. Since the fourth century and efforts by Roman emperors like Constantine and Theodosius to patronize the church, Christianity had been *the* major factor in European culture. Moreover, it was the major factor in public life precisely because it won the loyalty of so many Europeans in their private lives. Over the course of the nineteenth century, the religious influence of the various churches waned, and the ranks of the faithful were dramatically thinned. Christendom lingered in formal ways, such as the protected place of theological faculties in state-sponsored German universities, the deference in some historically Catholic countries to the papacy, or the church-sanctioned rituals of state occasions in England. But the tide had turned.

Christian Responses to the "Modern" Age

Christian reaction to the ebbing of Christendom took several forms. The churches were now faced with a "modern" world in which influential voices proclaimed matter in motion to be the most basic reality, the human mind as the arbiter of truth, and human happiness the ultimate social good. In the face of this new situation believers faced issues of preservation and advance. How can we keep the ancient faith alive? How can we, despite obstacles, spread the gospel?

Intellectual, Evangelistic, Social

European Christians, with their North American allies, succeeded better in this age at advancing the gospel in society and in evangelism than they did intellectually. To be sure, some estimable Christian intellectuals left a long-lasting imprint. One example was Søren Kierkegaard (1813–55), the intense, whimsical Danish writer who, while mounting the most rigorous intellectual critique of his age's dominant philosophical fashions, also insisted that Christianity was ultimately a life to be lived rather than a set of dogmas to affirm. A trio of English biblical scholars likewise showed what could still be done by traditional Christians who exploited the era's most formidable learning. The "Cambridge Triumvirate"—Brooke Foss Westcott (1825–1901), Joseph Barber Lightfoot (1828–89), and Fenton J. A. Hort (1828–92)—expertly deployed classical and contemporary learning to demonstrate the basic integrity of the New Testament text and the general reliability of subapostolic history. By so doing, they defused much of the alarm at the startling eurekas of contemporary biblical criticism. From youthful

America came at mid-century a surprisingly sturdy array of careful Christian thinkers who skillfully sifted European thought and the intellectual implications of living in a new world in order to preserve an intellectually vigorous Christian faith. These Americans included, among others, the Congregationalist biblical scholar Moses Stuart (1780–1852), the Presbyterian confessional theologians Charles Hodge (1797–1878) and Henry Boynton Smith (1815–77), the Reformed champion of organic, catholic Christianity John Williamson Nevin (1803–86), and Daniel Alexander Payne (1811–93) of the African Methodist Episcopal Church, who mediated subtle complexities of the ancient faith to the brutal realities of African American life. Yet even after such solid intellectual work has been duly noted, the fact remains that scholars working from orthodox, classically Christian convictions did not provide the intellectual firepower equal to the powerful cannonades of Comte, Darwin, Marx, Nietzsche, or Freud. That relative weakness, however, obscures the fact that in other spheres of Western life, Christians were busy exploiting widening opportunities.

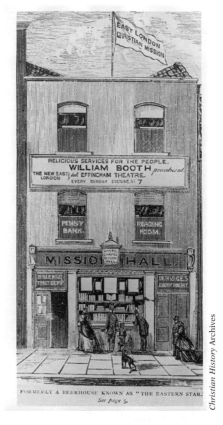

FORMERLY A BEERHOUSE KNOWN AS "THE EASTERN STAR.
See page 5.

Christian History Archives

William and Catherine Booth took the programs of the Salvation Army into the highways and byways that the older churches had come to neglect.

The next chapter highlights the non-Western expansion of Christianity in the nineteenth century, to which Western churches made an important contribution. Working against powerful secularizing forces, evangelists inside Western societies also witnessed significant advances as well. Leaders of such renewal movements included representatives from most of the major churches in most of the major Western nations. In Scandinavia, the Danish Lutheran minister Nikolai Grundtvig (1783–1872) and especially the Norwegian layman Hans Nielsen Hauge (1771–1824) established networks of revival that to this day support Scandinavians as leaders in Protestant missionary ventures. In Germany, Johann Christoph Blumhardt (1805–80) promoted evangelism, faith healing, and an interest in international missionary labors from his home base in Württemberg. Two other effective promoters of German renewal, Johannes Evangelista Gossner (1773–1858) and Aloys Henhöfer (1789–1862), were Roman Catholic priests who, for promoting what Henhöfer called "inner Christianity," eventually were forced out of Catholicism into the Lutheran Church.

A movement that drew some in the opposite direction was the Catholic evangelism sponsored by the Redemptorists, an order strong in Germany and then in the United States that for a time received a boost from the labors of Isaac Hecker (1819–88), the most prominent of many Americans to become Catholic converts during the middle decades of the nineteenth century.

In Scotland, the brothers Robert (1764–1842) and James Alexander (1768–1851) Haldane were both converted in 1795 and went on to promote many different missionary activities in Scotland, England, France, Switzerland, and around the world. Their work had some influence on another pair of brothers, the Frenchmen Frédéric (1794–1863) and Adolphe (1802–56) Monad, who were prime movers behind *Le Réveil* that energized the Reformed Protestant churches in France and Switzerland. Among many other effective promoters of Christian renewal in the nineteenth century, Izaak da Costa (1798–1860) of the Netherlands is among the most interesting, for he was not only an effective apologist who wrote against some of the major modernist books of his age but also a much-read poet whose poems reached a wide audience.

Evangelists in Western societies during the nineteenth century by no means agreed with each other on all points of doctrine or all questions of revivalist technique. But the visibility of their continued successes, which in turn paved the way for the later work of celebrated preachers like D. L. Moody, showed that the secularization of the West was not going to blot out the faith.

Similar innovation, in a similar diversity of forms, also marked Christian social outreach throughout the nineteenth century. During the first half of the nineteenth century, the most important sphere of Christian social activity was the fight against slavery. Led by William Wilberforce (1759–1833) in Britain and joined by a host of philanthropists elsewhere, slow but steady progress was made in promoting the conviction that Christianity was incompatible with slavery. Christian social conservatives who upheld some aspects of the status quo could still be active supporters of reform, as were Anthony Ashley Cooper, seventh earl of Shaftesbury (1801–85), who worked to regulate child labor in British industry, and Wilhelm von Ketteler (1811–77), the Catholic archbishop of Mainz, who defended the cause of German workers. From the other side of the political spectrum, earnest believers who looked to some variety of socialism for answers to Europe's crises of industrialism included Keir Hardie (1856–1915) in Britain, Christoph Blumhardt (1842–1919) in Germany, and Leonhard Ragaz (1868–1945) in Switzerland. Other Christian social reformers paid less immediate attention to politics but still managed to do much good. In England at the start of the nineteenth century the Quaker Elizabeth Fry (1780–1845) was an effective pioneer for a humane prison system; at the end of the century, William (1829–1912) and Catherine (1829–90) Booth founded the Salvation Army as a vehicle for meeting a whole range of urban social needs while still vigorously promoting a Holiness vision of the gospel. Earlier in the century, Theodor (1800–1864) and Friederike (1800–1842) Fliedner organized a movement for deaconesses within the German Lutheran church that also creatively addressed a wide range of practical social needs.

When regarding this range of active Christian social involvement, alongside the vigorous movements of revival and renewal, it is clear that even if, in Matthew Arnold's phrase, "the sea of faith" might be receding in Europe, even an outgoing tide could remain a vigorous force.

Conceptual and Institutional

The question of keeping belief alive among the humble faithful in the day-to-day realities of ordinary life, while remaining responsible guardians of inherited institutions, also elicited varied Christian responses. What might be called an accommodating, liberal strategy appeared mostly as the reaction of learned elites to a feeling of intellectual crisis. Much more important among ordinary Protestant believers were varieties of pietistic or sectarian strategies. In some Protestant state churches, as well as in the Roman Catholic Church as a whole, defensive efforts to restore Christendom were the order of the day.

Efforts to adjust an inherited faith by responding to the metaphysical assertions of "modernity" took place throughout Western societies, but the best known efforts were in Germany. In 1799, F. D. E. Schleiermacher (1768–1834) published a series of lectures entitled *Religion: Speeches to Its Cultured Despisers*. This book, and a lifetime of influential theologizing that followed, retained more emphases from Schleiermacher's pietist upbringing than his critics were willing to concede. But by moving the heart of belief toward human "God-consciousness," or, more generally, to "a sense of dependence," Schleiermacher opened the way for more radical redefinitions of what Christianity was supposed to mean.

The climax of a century of liberalizing European theology was reached in the lectures published by Adolf von Harnack (1851–1930) of Berlin in 1900. *Das Wesen des Christentums* (translated as *What Is Christianity?*) contended that the simple gospel preached by Jesus had been largely lost when it was translated into a Hellenistic idiom. Harnack, an immensely learned scholar whose works on the early history of Christianity are still read with profit, felt that the simple original gospel could be summarized as the fatherhood of God, the brotherhood of man, and the infinite value of the human soul.

A much smaller movement of theological liberalism eventually emerged in the Catholic Church, but only for a few short years around the beginning of the twentieth century. Promoted by biblical critics like the Frenchman Alfred Loisy (1857–1940) and theologians like the Englishman George Tyrrell (1861–1909), these self-confessed modernists hoped for the same kind of adjustments in Catholicism that they saw taking place in some Protestant churches. In a book from 1902 prompted by Harnack's *What Is Christianity?* Loisy's *L'Évangile et l'église* (The gospel and the church) drew an even sharper distinction between the pure altruism of Jesus and the hypocritical self-serving of the church. The course of Catholic modernism was cut short with ruthless efficiency by papal pronouncements in 1907 and then in 1910 by the institution of an "antimodernist oath" that was mandated for all church personnel. Among Catholics, such liberal theology would not reappear for another half century.

Harnack and Loisy's major statements of liberal Christianity appeared in the decade before the outbreak of World War I. Less than two decades after the end of that war, the American theologian H. Richard Niebuhr wrote a devastatingly succinct summary of what by that time had become a well-established tradition of liberal Christian theology: "A God without wrath brought men without sin into a kingdom without judgment through the ministrations of a Christ without a cross."[14] What Niebuhr felt was missing in theological liberalism was missed by most ordinary Christians as well. For them, the typical response to the end of Christendom was much more commonly flight or fight.

Over the course of the nineteenth century, several movements provided sectarian forms of Christian faith and practice as antidotes to the receding presence of Christendom. In the sense used here, "sectarian" means religion focused on the individual and on intentional groups made up of dedicated Christian individuals who, in order to find Christ,

14. H. Richard Niebuhr, *The Kingdom of God in America* (New York: Harper & Row, 1959 [orig. 1937]), 193.

more or less leave the world behind. The contrast is with the habits of Christendom, where it was assumed that private faith would naturally be expressed through public, society-wide influence. "Sectarian" movements of this sort existed within both Catholicism and Protestantism; they could be militantly doctrinal or predominately devotional; and they by no means promoted a common version of what ideal Christianity should look like. What they shared, however, was the conviction, often implicit, that, if only genuine Christian faith could be found, it was no great loss to give up worldly influence.

In Ireland, Poland, and smaller regions of other predominately Catholic countries, powerful devotional revivals moved many active Catholics in this direction. The devotions might feature renewed reverence for the Virgin Mary, new forms of meditation on the sufferings of Christ, or pilgrimages to the relics of venerated saints, but they had the common result of inspiring depths of Catholic faith relatively unconcerned about Catholic power. Among Protestants, some pietistic groups established entirely new structures, as did, for example, the Christian (or Plymouth) Brethren, who in the course of promoting a dispensational interpretation of Scripture and an apocalyptic judgment on the organized church separated from Anglicanism. Other movements of Protestant piety, like the "prayer houses" established by the ministry of Hans Nielsen Hauge in Norway, were careful to provoke no break with the traditional Lutheran Church. Later in the century, a series of Protestant renewal movements, often with connections to America, began to exert a larger influence in Europe. These included the Holiness revival arising out of Methodism and the Pentecostal movement, which stressed divine healing and speaking in tongues.

Where sectarian responses to the decline of Christendom tended to be more prominent among Protestants, the most vigorous effort to defend—and even to restore—Christendom came from the hierarchy of the Catholic Church. After the end of the German Empire in 1806 and the reorganization of German states, some of the new political units, such as Prussia, did create unified Protestant churches that would continue to exercise some of the traditional, society-wide authority of the Reformation magisterial churches. But the most ardent defenders of Christendom were Catholics, and the leader of that defensive effort was Pope Pius IX. When Archbishop Giovanni Maria Mastai-Ferretti became Pope Pius IX in 1846, he was considered a moderate. He seemed to be open to suggestions respecting toleration of other religions, liberty of the press and education, and the rights of constitutional government. Traumatic experiences in the European Revolution of 1848–49, however, drove such thoughts from his head. During these conflicts,

Declaration of the First Vatican Council on Papal Infallibility (1870)

Therefore, faithfully adhering to the tradition derived from the commencement of the Christian faith, to the glory of God our savior, to the exaltation of the Catholic religion, and to the salvation of Christian nations, *Sacro approbante Concilio* [with the holy consent of the Council], we teach and define that it is a divinely revealed dogma: that the Roman pontiff, when he speaks *Ex Cathedra*, that is, when in the discharge of his office of pastor and doctor of all Christians, he defines, in virtue of his supreme apostolic authority, a doctrine of faith or morals to be held by the universal Church, is endowed by the divine assistance promised to him in blessed Peter, with that infallibility with which our divine redeemer willed that the Church should be furnished in defining doctrine of faith or morals; and, therefore, that such definitions of the Roman pontiff are irreformable of themselves and not in virtue of the consent of the Church.[2]

the pope was forced to flee Rome when Italians fighting for the creation of a modern, constitutional Italy took the city. He was restored only through the support of the French army.

From this early point in his long pontificate, Pius IX (pope 1846–78) mobilized all of his considerable resources to fight, as one enemy, the drift of secularism and the reduction in power of the Catholic Church. To him, the papacy's thousand-year history as a significant ruler in the Italian peninsula represented a "robe of Jesus Christ" that sheltered the church's body. In 1854 he formally defined the immaculate conception of Mary in an effort to link the papacy with popular Marian devotions practiced by the church's ordinary faithful. Ten years later he issued a stunning encyclical that, even as it denounced modernizing changes in general, ended with a "Syllabus of Errors" that specified eighty widespread contemporary opinions as grievous mistakes. The last and most sweeping of these errors was the belief that "the Roman pontiff can and ought to reconcile and harmonize himself with progress, with liberalism, and with modern civilization."[15] Soon thereafter in 1869–70 followed the First Vatican Council, where, with papal representatives bearing down hard on the assembled bishops, a declaration was promulgated defining the pope's ex cathedra pronounce-

15. Colman J. Barry, ed., *Readings in Church History*, vol. 3, *The Modern Era, 1789 to the Present* (Westminster, Md.: Newman, 1965), 74.

ments as infallible.* Despite the vigor of his actions, however, Pius IX was forced to give up the last remnants of traditional papal power (with the exception of Vatican City) when the champions of Italian national unity finally achieved their goal in 1870. (In fact, the First Vatican Council had to be brought to an abrupt end when the armies of the unifying forces entered Rome.)

Although he was forced to give up his temporal power, Pius IX was successful in confirming the Catholic Church as Europe's most conservative institution. He was a firm champion of his church in Protestant countries like England and the Netherlands, and he succeeded in establishing concordats preserving the privileges of the Catholic Church in Spain, Austria, and other traditionally Catholic countries.

The long-term effect of Pius IX's actions has been the source of much interpretative debate. On the one side, it is clear that his actions lent great weight to Catholic efforts at confining the secularizing forces that were working powerfully in Europe. Yet from a perspective at the end of the twentieth century, even that struggle looks different than it appeared at the time. With knowledge of how rapidly the Catholic Church has changed in the decades since the Second Vatican Council (1962–65), it might seem that Pius IX succeeded more in bottling up, rather than wiping out, the forces of modernization, which, at the end of the twentieth century, are as evident within Catholicism as among Protestants.

Other memorable Christian efforts existed in nineteenth-century Europe to impede the course of dechristianization. In the 1830s a group of High Church Anglicans coalesced into an "Oxford Movement" to apply the lessons of the early church to the perils of the present. While one of the leaders of this movement, John Henry Newman (1801–90), eventually became a Roman Catholic, others like John Keble (1792–1866) and E. B. Pusey (1800–1882) carried on with their vision of a reconstituted godly English society. Later in the century, the Dutch Calvinist Abraham Kuyper (1837–1920) worked mightily as theologian, editor, and politician—among ordinary citizens, scholars, and representatives of government—to match institutional Christian vigor to the intelligent exposition of the faith. Kuyper's contemporary Leo XIII (pope 1878–1903) was just as vigorous in promoting a Catholic program of spiritual and social renewal.

In sum, liberal, sectarian, and traditionalist responses to the weakening of European Christendom all had considerable vigor, though of markedly different kinds. Yet despite much laudable faith and much ef-

---

* Since 1870, only one papal pronouncement has been strictly defined as infallible, the 1954 declaration that Mary was assumed bodily into heaven.

fective practice, the juggernaut of secularism rolled on. Nothing would so well—but also so tragically—sum up the "long century" of dechristianization that began with the French Revolution as the events that unfolded in World War I. In that war, candidates that had appeared over the course of the century as substitutes for Europe's traditional Christian faith combined with malignant effect. Critics of Christendom have, in fact, been correct to charge that when institutional Christianity dominated Europe, it often led to inhumane disaster. But nothing in Christendom's long, admittedly fallible history could match the depths of degradation to which the nineteenth century's new deities now led. From 1914 to 1918, supreme allegiance to nation, implicit reliance upon technology (which produced the marvels of poison gas, machine gun, tank, and bomber), and the triumphs of propaganda, erected with the marvels of mass communication—all joined forces to slaughter a full generation of European young people and lay waste the Continent as it had not been decimated since the fourteenth century and the scourge of the Black Death. Only this time the survivors did not tremble, as many of them had in the fourteenth century, for fear of their sins before God.

But just as earlier, when the trials of Christianity in its historic heartland did not spell the demise of the faith, so too over the course of the nineteenth century, the receding of European Christendom did not mean the collapse of Christianity. As before, when disruption of the Christian homeland in the eastern Mediterranean coincided with the planting of Christianity in Europe, so now the disruption of the Christian homeland in Europe coincided with the blossoming of Christianity well beyond Europe. Over the ocean in North America, the United States, the world's most "modern" nation, enjoyed surprisingly vigorous scenes of active faith. By the end of the nineteenth century, Canada, with its strong Catholic and Protestant communities, witnessed, if anything, even more vigorous Christian practice than the United States. And by the start of the twentieth century, the blooming of Christian faith throughout many other parts of the world anticipated a state of affairs that would have been unthinkable a mere century earlier. Even if European Christendom, the historic heart of Christianity for more than a millennium, was fading, worldwide Christianity was not.

The industrial revolution and resulting growth of cities during the nineteenth century posed a challenge to churches as well as to governments. How would believers respond to the degrading conditions of men, women, and children crowded into slums and laboring—sometimes in inhumane conditions—without education, without protection, and without hope? One response came from an English aristocrat, Anthony Ashley Cooper, the seventh earl of Shaftesbury. Educated at Harrow and Oxford and a member of the Conservative Party, Shaftesbury nonetheless worked diligently for parliamentary legislation to protect the rights of laborers, especially women and children. He founded schools for the poor and supported evangelism and social reforms both overseas and in Britain. The compassion and faith that motivated his life's work appear in this prayer:

> *O God, the father of the forsaken, the help of the weak, the supplier of the needy; you teach us that love towards the race of man is the bond of perfectness, and the imitation of your blessed self. Open and touch our hearts that we may see and do, both for this world and that which is to come, the things that belong to our peace. Strengthen us in the work which we have undertaken; give us wisdom, perseverance, faith, and zeal, and in your own time and according to your pleasure prosper the issue; for the love of your Son Jesus Christ.*[16]

Further Reading

Brooke, John Hedley. *Science and Religion: Some Historical Perspectives.* New York: Cambridge University Press, 1991.

Chadwick, Owen. *The Secularization of the European Mind in the Nineteenth Century.* New York: Cambridge University Press, 1975.

Clouse, Robert G., Richard V. Pierard, and Edwin M. Yamauchi. *Two Kingdoms: The Church and Culture through the Ages.* Chicago: Moody, 1993. Especially helpful on European movements of mission, evangelism, and social reform.

Conser, Walter H., Jr. *Church and Confession: Conservative Theologians in Germany, England, and America, 1815–1866.* Macon, Ga.: Mercer University Press, 1984.

Gay, Peter. *The Enlightenment.* Vol. 1, *The Rise of Modern Paganism;* vol. 2, *The Science of Freedom.* New York: Knopf, 1966–69.

Hope, Nicholas. *German and Scandinavian Protestantism, 1700 to 1918.* New York: Oxford University Press, 1995.

Lundin, Roger. *The Culture of Interpretation: Christian Faith and the Postmodern World.* Grand Rapids: Eerdmans, 1993. Helpful on the influence of Romanticism.

McLeod, Hugh. *Religion and the People of Western Europe.* New York: Oxford University Press, 1981.

16. *Eerdmans' Book of Famous Prayers,* comp. Veronica Zundel (Grand Rapids: Eerdmans, 1983), 72.

McManners, John. *The French Revolution and the Church.* London: SPCK, 1969.
Manuel, Frank E. *The Changing of the Gods.* Hanover, N.H.: University Press of New England, 1983.
Martin, David. *A General Theory of Secularization.* New York: Harper & Row, 1978.
Smart, Ninian, et al., eds. *Nineteenth-Century Religious Thought in the West.* 3 vols. New York: Cambridge University Press, 1985.

12

A Faith for All the World: The Edinburgh Missionary Conference (1910)

Throughout the history of Christianity, as the faith has spread into the world in the spirit of the Great Commission, the church has adopted local idioms in order to make the universal Christian message accessible in new environments. The missionary expansion of the twentieth century has been no exception. While some missionaries tried to transpose unaltered their Western hymnody into non-Western settings, others encouraged the development of lyrics and melodies more in harmony with local traditions. The following hymn from China, "Rise to Greet the Sun," is an example of the latter efforts. It also illuminates the fertilization from the mission field back to the Western church. Written by T. C. Chao in 1936 and set to a Chinese folk melody, this hymn was translated into English by Bless Wiant in 1946. Interestingly, its own Chinese idiom echoes the theme of Christ as light that inspired much of the first great hymnody of the church.

> Rise to greet the sun
> Red in the eastern sky,
> Like a glorious bridegroom
> His joyous race to run.
> Flying birds in heavens high,
> Fragrant flowers abloom
> Tell the gracious Father's nigh,
> Now His work assume.
>
> May this day be blest,
> Trusting in Jesus' care,

Heart and mind illumined
By heaven's radiance fair.
Thanks for raiment unadorned,
Rice and wholesome food;
These the Lord in mercy gives,
Neverfailing good.[1]

The 1910 World Missionary Conference was called to order on the evening of June 14 at the Assembly Hall of the United Free Church of Scotland, in the shadow of Edinburgh's famous castle.[2] After an opening prayer, the president of the conference, Lord Balfour of Burleigh, read greetings from the Imperial German Colonial Office, from former U.S. president Theodore Roosevelt (who had been named a delegate to the conference by the Dutch Reformed Church in America but was prevented by press of business from attending), and from King George V of England, the upright sovereign who only a month before had succeeded his dissolute father Edward VII to the British throne. After the last greeting, the delegates arose spontaneously to sing "God Save the King."

Speakers for the evening were Lord Burleigh, who voiced the hope that "a unity begun in the mission field may extend its influence, and react upon us at home and throughout the old civilisations"; the archbishop of Canterbury, who expressed the opinion that some at that meeting might "not taste death till they see the Kingdom of God come with power"; and the American missionary statesman Robert E. Speer, who challenged the delegates to remember that no one can follow Christ "without following Him *to the uttermost parts of the earth*" and urged them to believe that "living faith will make it possible for Him [Christ] to use us for the immediate conquest of the world."[3]

For the next ten days, dramatic speeches were interspersed with wide-ranging debate as the conference took up eight separate subjects. For each theme there was a full volume of published reports. The

---

1. William J. Reynolds and Milburn Price, *A Survey of Christian Hymnody*, 3rd ed. (Carol Stream, Ill.: Hope, 1987), 118, 241.

2. For general information, I have relied on W. H. T. Gairdner, *Echoes from Edinburgh, 1910: An Account and Interpretation of the World Missionary Conference* (New York: Fleming H. Revell, [1910]).

3. Ibid., 40–43.

authors of these reports drew liberally from over one thousand extensive questionnaires that had been returned by missionaries. The topics considered were (1) the transport of the gospel to the whole non-Christian world, (2) the church in the mission field, (3) the place of education in national Christian life, (4) the message of Christian missions in relation to non-Christian faiths, (5) the preparation of missionaries, (6) the home base of missions, (7) missions and governments, and (8) the promotion of Christian unity. Distinguished British, American, and European missionaries from around the globe led the discussions, which were often enlivened by recitations of missionary experience itself.

The conference ended with the shared conviction that the gathering was too important simply to let slip away. Discussions begun at Edinburgh in 1910 did in fact continue. Eventually they led to the establishment of the International Missionary Conference, and less directly in 1925 to the Universal Christian Conference on Life and Work and in 1927 to the World Conference on Faith and Order, two organizations that eventually merged in 1948 to create the World Council of Churches. The missionary conference in Edinburgh was, therefore, the beginning of the twentieth-century ecumenical movement.

It also represented the high tide of Western missionary expansion, which had gathered strength all throughout the nineteenth century. In that century—when first Britain filled a vacuum of worldwide leadership and then the United States emerged as a great economic power and shaper of civilization—the proportion of the world's population associated with Christian churches increased more rapidly than at any time since the fourth century. Where less than a quarter of the world

A postcard from Liverpool in the 1920s communicates something of the missionary vision that was reaching its peak in those years.

Courtesy of the Billy Graham Center Museum

could be identified as Christian in 1800, almost 35 percent could be so numbered at the time of the Edinburgh Conference.[4] The zeal of Robert Speer and the optimism of the archbishop of Canterbury were thus understandable. The delegates at Edinburgh had lived through an unprecedented expansion of the church, much of it the direct result of missionary efforts. It seemed as if they had a right to rejoice, to anticipate the speedy completion of the Great Commission, and even to assume that this great task would be brought to its end under the leadership of the Protestants responsible for the Edinburgh Conference.

But if Edinburgh marked a high point, it was also, in the phrase of mission historian Stephen Neill, "the end of an epoch."[5] From a perspective at the end of the twentieth century, the Edinburgh meeting looks as curious as it was remarkable. It was a conference on the worldwide mission of the "church," but only Protestants attended. (In 1900, there were approximately 520 million people worldwide affiliated with Christian churches; of these about 135 million were Protestant [including Anglican], 115 million Orthodox, and 265 million Roman Catholic.) Even more, it was a meeting to discuss the evangelization of *the world*, but over 80 percent of the approximately 1,200 delegates were from Britain and North America, with only 170 from the European Continent and only 18 representing the world beyond Europe and North America. The overwhelming British and American preponderance can be explained in part by the fact that missionaries from these regions were the major planners of the meeting. But another part of the explanation is that as of 1910 in Edinburgh—or New York, Chicago, Los Angeles, Toronto, Berlin, or Copenhagen—"worldwide Christianity" still meant a Christianity reaching out from Europe (and its North American extensions) to the rest of the globe.

The World Missionary Conference is a turning point in the history of Christianity because of its ecumenical significance. As it happens, at Edinburgh voices were heard speculating whether Christianity should be considered the *absolutely final* revelation from God or merely the *best* revelation from God. These were notes that, from the standpoint of traditional Protestants, Catholics, and Orthodox, would come back later to haunt the movement leading to the World Council of Churches. Even more, Edinburgh marked a turning point because it represented just about the last moment when "worldwide Christianity" could in any

4. Most of the statistics in this chapter are from David B. Barrett, ed., *World Christian Encyclopedia* (New York: Oxford University Press, 1982), or from Barrett's "Annual Statistical Table on Global Mission," found since 1985 in the January issue of the *International Bulletin of Missionary Research.*

5. Stephen Neill, *A History of Christian Missions* (New York: Penguin, 1964), 395.

Membership[a] by Ecclesiastical Bloc (in millions)

	1900	1970	1997
Roman Catholic	266	689	992
Protestant[b]	134	288	426
Orthodox	116	147	215
Other[c]	9	74	238

Membership[a] by Continent (in millions)

	1900	1970	1997
Africa	9	119	310
Asia	20	90	299
Europe	369	494	527
Latin America	60	268	451
North America	60	173	203
Oceania	4	15	20

522 mil   *1810 mil*

Source: Barrett, "Annual Statistical Table on Global Mission: 1997," *International Bulletin of Missionary Research* 21 (January 1997): 25.

[a]For Barrett, membership enumerates "affiliated" Christians who, however nominal in day-to-day practice, are called Christian by outside observers and who have some kind of connection to a Christian church.

[b]"Protestant" here combines Barrett's "Anglican" and "Protestant" categories.

[c]"Other" here combines Barrett's categories that are furthest removed from traditional Western churches: "Catholics (non-Roman)," "marginal Protestants," and "nonwhite indigenous Christians."

meaningful sense be equated with the Christianity of Europe and North America. The wave of the future was toward a world Christianity defined as much outside of Europe and North America as by Europe and North America; the wave of the future was the indigenization of Christianity in countless regional cultures around the world; the wave of the future pointed toward the Lausanne Conference on World Evangelization in 1974, when 2,700 delegates, including at least half from the Two-Thirds World, gathered from 151 different countries to discuss a theme that over the course of the twentieth century was becoming a reality.

Standing as it did between a Western definition of Christianity and the worldwide expansion of the faith, the Edinburgh Missionary Conference provides an excellent vantage point for examining the missionary tides that led up to it, as well as those that swept beyond 1910 to cover the world. Yet in the general history of Christianity, mission activity is incomplete without the local indigenization of the faith. During the nineteenth and twentieth centuries the transition from missionary expansion to local appropriation has taken place at different times in different ways. For the Christian history of recent centuries, that transition has been every bit as significant as it was in the dynamic explosion of the first three centuries after Christ.

A Revival of Mission Activity

For a number of reasons pertaining to life both inside and outside the churches, the expansion of Christianity beyond the West had slowed to a crawl during the eighteenth century. To be sure, missionary-minded Roman Catholics carried on the work of the Catholic Reformation that had witnessed Dominicans, Augustinians, and (preeminently) Jesuits fanning out with their message to many parts of the world. In addition, the renewal of European Protestantism by the pietist movement was also responsible for promoting considerable missionary vigor. But apart from efforts to stimulate the faith among the European colonists of North America, the eighteenth century was not a great age of Christian expansion. Some of the reasons for this situation were political. Quarreling between the Jesuits and several European monarchs, especially in France, led to the elimination of that premier missionary order in 1773. (The Jesuits would be restored in 1814 and would shortly thereafter become a major missionary force again.) In Russia, which had become the leader of the Orthodox world, heavy-handed interference in Orthodox affairs by rulers like Peter the Great (reigned 1682–1725) and Catherine II (reigned 1762–96) acted as a general drain on the energy of the church, including its concern for mission. For most of the eighteenth century, intermittent warfare between the two great European powers, France and England, created logistic barriers to missionary service and also undercut allegiance to Christ with allegiance to nation. At the end of the century, turmoil from the French Revolution and then the wave of national liberation movements fostered by Napoleon further diminished European concern for cross-cultural Christian expansion.

The external conditions were matched by serious problems within the churches themselves. Reaction to the seventeenth-century wars of religion included the rise of various forms of the Enlightenment, which promoted religious tolerance much more than Christian zeal. The major churches in Europe and North America were, in general, more concerned with maintaining the status quo than with expansion. On the Continent, Lutheran, Reformed, and Catholic Churches all faced problems of self-protection in conflict with the era's aspiring monarchs (who wished to be known as Enlightened Absolutists). From the mid-eighteenth century, Britain's established Anglican and Presbyterian Churches, as well as the dissenting denominations, were quickened by evangelical impulses, but they also were reeling from efforts to meet religious needs in burgeoning cities in the face of galloping industrialization. In North America the Protestants who predominated in the British colonies as well as the Catholics in French Quebec had all they could do simply to survive in a largely inhospitable wilderness.

Christian outreach revived in all of the historic Christian regions of Europe and North America as a by-product of more general Christian renewal. The rise of Pietism among European Protestants and of evangelicalism among British Protestants in both the Old World and the New soon fueled missionary expansion. The very humiliations that Pope Pius VII (1800–1823) suffered at the hands of Napoleon worked a spiritual purification in the Roman Catholic Church that soon bore missionary fruit. Also in Russia and the East the nineteenth century brought significant currents of spiritual renewal that soon spilled over into notable missionary labor among the Orthodox.

For Roman Catholics the first two-thirds of the nineteenth century witnessed another fertile period in the establishment of religious orders, which, as had also been the case in the sixteenth century, provided a great stimulus to missionary activity. Among the orders with longest-lasting significance was the Missionaries of Our Lady of Africa, founded in 1868 by Charles Lavigerie, the archbishop of Algeria. Soon known as the White Fathers, for the adoption of Arabic dress, and soon joined by an order of White Sisters, similarly clothed, Lavigerie's order remained stalwart in its dedication to Rome and a conservative vision of Catholic theology, but also stalwart in its dedication to evangelize the center of the continent around Lake Victoria and Africa's other great lakes.

Missionary renewal among the Orthodox was led by several dynamic Russian priests who exerted special labors in bringing Christianity to

Siberia and points even farther east. One of the most important of these missionaries was John Veniaminou (1797–1879), who was born in the Siberian province of Irkutsk. As a young priest, Veniaminou volunteered for service in the Aleutian Islands, where his preaching was received with great eagerness. Later he personally evangelized in, or sent out missionaries to, Alaska, Japan, the island of Sitka, and the far reaches of Russia's vast eastern empire. When at the age of seventy Veniaminou finally retired to a monastery, he thought his life's work was over, but the death of the patriarch of Moscow led to his election to that key post. For another decade this veteran—who, with his fellow missionaries, had been "forged by the experiences of life in Siberia" and came "back to Russia with their souls renewed, well-instructed and zealous"[6]—guided the Russian church and greatly expanded its missionary vision.

The awakening of a similar vision among Protestants calls for a fuller account in light of the fact that, with only a few exceptions, Protestants for more than two centuries after the Reformation displayed remarkably little interest in cross-cultural proclamation of the gospel.[7] When systematic Protestant missionary efforts finally began, they did so as a result of the expanding vision of a Protestant monarch. Just as earlier Roman Catholic mission was linked to awakening world-consciousness in Spain and Portugal, so now in the eighteenth century the world concerns of northern European Protestants began to make a difference. In this case it was the pietistic King Frederick IV of Denmark and Norway who early in the eighteenth century took steps to provide for the spiritual welfare of the people affected by his country's trading center in Tranquebar, South India. When Frederick could not find candidates in Denmark, he turned to August Hermann Francke in Halle, who commissioned two German pietists for the task, including Bartholomaus Ziegenbalg (1682–1719), who became the first widely recognized Protestant missionary statesman. Ziegenbalg's multifaceted work in Tranquebar was a particular inspiration in Britain, where the same mixture of religious and economic concerns that prevailed in pietistic Denmark were beginning to fuel interest in non-European areas of the world.

6. The comment is from a contemporary Russian account, as quoted in Neill, *History of Christian Mission*, 444.

7. This account of Protestant mission expansion is indebted especially to the noteworthy attention to missionary themes in Robert G. Clouse, Richard V. Pierard, and Edwin M. Yamauchi, *Two Kingdoms: The Church and Culture through the Ages* (Chicago: Moody, 1993), 351–513.

For most of the eighteenth century, however, German pietists, with the assistance of like-minded believers from other northern European Protestant states, remained the mainstay of Protestant missionary efforts. Johann Heinrich Callenberg (1694–1760), a professor at Halle, was an eager student of Arabic, Persian, and Turkish who hoped that the publication of Christian literature in these languages would effect the conversion of Muslims. Besides his interest in Islamic evangelism, moreover, Callenberg's concern for the Middle East led him to found the Jewish Institute in 1728, which promoted peaceful evangelistic practices in place of the violent coercion that had so often marked Christian outreach to Jews. Missionaries from Halle were also sent as ministers to the German-speaking populations migrating to the New World. Among these missionaries, Henry Melchior Muhlenberg (1711–87) was the leading figure. He arrived in Pennsylvania in 1742 and by 1748 had succeeded in establishing the Pennsylvania ministerium as the first Lutheran synod in North America.

The Moravians, who shared so many emphases with the Halle pietists, became the most dedicated Protestant missionaries in the whole of the eighteenth century. During the first century after the Moravians were reconstituted as a church under the leadership of Count von Zinzendorf in the early 1720s, approximately two thousand (one-fourth of them women) volunteered for cross-cultural missionary service. The first Moravian missionaries were J. L. Dober (1706–66) and David Nitschmann (1696–1772), who responded to Zinzendorf's appeal (itself spurred by a call from the Halle missionaries associated with the Danish mission) by establishing a self-supporting Christian work in the Danish Virgin Islands. Soon there followed significant Moravian missions to Greenland, Surinam, South Africa, Estonia, Labrador, the Nicobar Islands, and still other places in Asia, Africa, North America, and Central America. In the 1730s, Moravian missionaries began a work among North American Native Americans that proved more successful than any other such European venture. Themselves a marginalized people who eschewed connections with nationalistic power, the Moravians' very freedom from the ordinary concerns of politics lent special credibility to their message. Unfortunately, Moravians had more difficulty convincing the European settlers in North America of their Christian purposes than they did the Native Americans. Twice—in Pennsylvania as part of the French and Indian War of the 1750s and then in Ohio in the early 1780s after the American Revolution—Moravian Indian communities were attacked by American militia operating under the mistaken impression that the Indian converts were supporting the enemy. The longtime leader of North American Moravian mis-

Carey's Appeal for Foreign Missions

The following is from the first and last paragraphs of William Carey's *Enquiry:*

As our blessed Lord has required us to pray that his kingdom may come, and his will be done on earth as it is in heaven, it becomes us not only to express our desires of that event by words, but to use every lawful method to spread the knowledge of his name. . . . We are exhorted "to lay up treasure in heaven, where neither moth nor rust doth corrupt, nor thieves break through and steal." It is also declared that "whatsoever a man soweth, that shall he also reap." These Scriptures teach us that the enjoyments of the life to come, bear a near relation to that which now is; a relation similar to that of the harvest, and the seed. It is true all the reward is of mere grace, but it is nevertheless encouraging; what a "treasure," what an "harvest" must await such characters as PAUL, and ELLIOT, and BRAINERD [missionaries to North American Indians John Eliot and David Brainerd], and others, who have given themselves wholly to the work of the lord. What a heaven will it be to see the many myriads of poor heathens, of Britons amongst the rest, who by their labours have been brought to the knowledge of God. Surely a "crown of rejoicing" like this is worth aspiring to. Surely it is worth while to lay ourselves out with all our might, in promoting the cause, and kingdom of Christ.[1]

sions, David Zeisberger (1721–1808), finally found a refuge for his Delaware Indian converts in Ontario, where remnants of that community survive to this day.

The early pietist and Moravian missions promoted goals of Christian self-sufficiency for new converts that the most far-seeing missionaries of later generations also pursued. Thus, in Tranquebar, Bartholomaus Ziegenbalg learned Tamil so that he could translate the Bible into the indigenous language, he founded schools so that new believers could learn to read the Scriptures for themselves, he became a serious student of Indian culture and religions in order to make a credible presentation of the gospel in an appropriate idiom, he made medical assistance available, and he prepared Tamil converts for ordination to serve as pastors of Tamil congregations.

These were virtually the same tasks that William Carey (1761–1834) pursued when, at the end of the eighteenth century, he became the dynamic pioneer of English-speaking Protestant missions. To be sure, serious missionary attempts had earlier taken place among English colonists in North America, where John Eliot (1604–90) and the Mayhew family (first Thomas, Jr. [1621–57], and then his father, Thomas, Sr. [1593–1682]) had led to some Christian conversions among Algonquian-speaking Indians of Massachusetts and the Native Americans on Martha's Vineyard and Nantucket. But these earlier efforts were continually hamstrung by the need of Eliot and the Mayhews to placate white settlers as well as guide Indian converts. What began with William Carey was cross-cultural outreach with single-minded missionary purpose. Carey was a Baptist shoemaker whose dedication to missionary service grew out of the intense spirituality of Britain's evangelical revival. In 1792 his pamphlet *An Enquiry into the Obligations of Christians to use Means* [that is, human activity] *for the Conversion of the Heathens* sounded a clarion call for many who would follow in his train.

The next year Carey and his family embarked for India, never to return. At first they attempted to do their work under the aegis of the British East India Company, but when more propitious conditions became available under Danish auspices, they moved to Serampore, where Carey eagerly joined a teacher, Joshua Marshman (1768–1837), and a printer, William Ward (1764–1823), who had followed him to India under the sponsorship of the Baptist Missionary Society. Together, this "Serampore Trio" pursued evangelism and church planting, they carried out or sponsored the translation of Scripture into many Indian languages, they published Bibles and other Christian literature, they studied and published Bengali and Sanskrit books, they founded (and taught in) colleges, and they took an active role in social and agricultural reforms.

Carey became an inspiration who drew others to India, among whom the American Adoniram Judson (1788–1850) became one of the best known. Carey's work also was a factor in the broader missionary concern that soon was promoted by the Church of England and the Presbyterian Church of Scotland. And it paralleled an awakening of missionary interest throughout Protestant Europe. During the first third of the nineteenth century an unusual spirit of cooperation prevailed among the new missionaries. As an example, Johannes T. Vanderkemp (1747–1811), founder of the Netherlands Missionary Society, served for several years in South Africa under the London Missionary Society (interdenominational). After the formation of a mission society in Basel, Switzerland, in 1815, a number of these Swiss found service under the Church Missionary Society (Anglican). By the 1830s, most Protestant denominations in Britain, France, Denmark,

Sweden, Norway, Germany, the Netherlands, and the United States had joined the missionary tide.

During the first half of the nineteenth century, Protestant mission-ary movements occurred in concert with an accelerating worldwide ex-pansion of Western economic and political interests. Yet in this period the concurrence of missionary, trading, humanitarian, and political motives possessed an innocence that was later lost. For the British, as an example, early missionary efforts were tied closely to the campaign against slavery. Parliament's ban of the slave trade in 1807 realized a prime goal in William Wilberforce's evangelical aspiration for the moral reform of British society. But it also spurred British Protestants to carry the fight against slavery (and for Christianity) into Africa itself. Yet once the European scramble for non-Western colonies and advan-tage began with the opening of Japan in the 1850s, and then acceler-ated from the 1870s as nationalistic conflict in Europe fueled colonial conflict abroad, missionary effort became more and more difficult to disengage from imperial intent.

The earlier, relatively benign combination of imperial and Christian interests is well illustrated by the Niger Expedition of 1841. It was led by T. Fowell Buxton (1786–1845), Wilberforce's successor as an evan-gelical leader in Parliament and antislave crusader, who hoped that promotion of "Christianity, commerce, and civilization" in the Niger River Valley of West Africa would overcome the ravages of the slave in-dustry that still, despite the Parliament's abolition of slavery in British territories in 1834, went on. (The continuation of slavery in the United States sustained both a market and a justification for the African com-merce in human lives.) As it happened, Buxton's expedition failed mis-erably, but it did serve as an inspiration for David Livingstone (1813–73) of Scotland. Livingstone's lifetime of activity in sub-Saharan Af-rica—as missionary, explorer, scientist, consultant to European gov-ernments, and antislave zealot—was guided by a firm belief that mod-ern agriculture, energetic commerce, and serious Christianity could together end the slave trade and ennoble African society. If Living-stone's most serious difficulty in the early part of his career was to con-vince Africans of the merit of his goals, by its last years his main prob-lem was with Europeans who had begun to pull back from earlier principles supporting self-sufficiency for indigenous peoples.

Those principles, however, were well established by early leaders in the Protestant missionary surge, and they continued to be articulated, even when European and American imperialism bore down harder on the non-Western world at the end of the nineteenth century. Henry Venn (1796–1873), secretary of Britain's Church Missionary Society

(Anglican), and Rufus Anderson (1796–1880), foreign secretary of the American Board of Commissioners for Foreign Missions (an interdenominational agency in which Congregationalists predominated), were two of the leaders who thought missionary activity should lead directly, intentionally, and swiftly to indigenous leadership of the new Christian churches. In a work from 1869, Anderson summarized his understanding of New Testament missionary principles in words only slightly more compact than Venn had communicated to several generations of Anglican missionaries:

> Apostolic missions [meant] . . . gathering converts into churches at the centers of influence, and putting them under native pastoral inspection and care. The means employed were spiritual; namely, the Gospel of Christ. The power relied upon for giving efficacy to these means was divine; namely the promised aid of the Holy Spirit. The main success was among the members of the middle and lower classes of society; and the responsibilities for self-government, self-support, and self-propagation were thrown at once upon the several churches.[8]

Later in the century, two missionaries to China—the American Presbyterian John L. Nevius (1829–93) and the Anglican Roland Allen (1868–1947)—reiterated similar principles at a time when Western engagement in Asia could be very heavy-handed. Their contemporary J. Hudson Taylor (1832–1905), founder of the China Inland Mission and probably the most important early promoter of the "faith mission" strategy of missionary fund-raising, was not as articulate as a mission theorist, but his policies of wearing native Chinese dress and of sending missionaries into the Chinese backcountry far beyond the reach of Western protection likewise promoted the indigenization of newly established Christian churches.

From the start, a vitally important role in Protestant missions had been played by women, acting both as wives of missionary husbands and on their own. Ann Hasseltine Judson (1789–1826), the first wife of Adoniram, put a busy pen to use for promoting Christian devotion and for informing about missionary circumstances, especially while her husband was in a Burmese prison. Hudson Taylor's first wife, Maria, was a full partner in the founding of the China Inland Mission, and his second wife, Jennie, also took a full share in directing outreach in China as well as sustaining support in Britain, the United States, and Canada.

8. Rufus Anderson, *Foreign Missions: Their Relations and Claims* (New York: Scribners, 1869), 61.

Here are over sixty women missionaries who were studying Chinese in Yangzhou in 1931 as preparation for service with the China Inland Mission.

Also from the first, however, single women could be found in the thick of Protestant missionary activity. Mary Slessor (1848–1915), who came from a poor Scottish home, was one of the most energetic of such women, Inspired by the death of David Livingstone to volunteer for missionary service, she arrived in 1876 at the Presbyterian Calabar station (in what today is Nigeria), where she quickly learned the local language and immediately became a fixture as a teacher. From 1880 she was in charge of her own mission. Through several moves to new areas she combined religious instruction, medical assistance, and advocacy for the unprotected (like orphans or abandoned twins) in ways that made her beloved of the Africans and respected by the British. So far did she go in identifying with her new environment that, in a breach of common missionary practice, she regularly went hatless and shoeless, as did the Africans.

The career of Lottie Moon (1840–1912) illustrated how spunk as a missionary could have as large an impact on a Western sending church as in the mission field. In 1873 Lottie Moon arrived in China as a missionary for the Southern Baptist Convention. Her notable efforts in Shantung Province as an educator, evangelist, and advocate of women's ministry made a considerable mark in a region where missionaries were introducing the Chinese to various forms of Western life as well as to Christianity. But Lottie Moon's effect was even greater in the United States. Her 1888 appeal for added funds to support her mission labors led to the organizing of the Southern Baptists' Women Missionary Union and then in 1918 to the establishment of an annual of-

fering among Southern Baptists for missionary work. The former
agency has channeled immense energy into Southern Baptist mission
life, while the latter has led to the collection of more than a billion dol-
lars to support mission work from the Southern Baptist Convention.

As the century went on and the number of Western missionaries increased dramatically, the proportion of single women missionaries
leaving Western cultures for missionary service increased even more
dramatically. In the latter part of the nineteenth century, a number of
important missionary societies were founded, funded, and directed by
women acting on their own. These included the Female Education Society and the Church of England Zenana Missionary Society in Britain,
the Women's Union Missionary Society in the United States, and several orders of German Lutheran deaconesses.

When the expanding Protestant concern for mission was added to
the revival of missionary interest among Catholics and the Orthodox,
the result was that the nineteenth century witnessed a broader and
more diffuse expansion of Christianity than had happened since the
very first centuries of the church's existence. As preparation for the indigenous existence of significant Christian bodies on every continent,
the nineteenth century truly was, in the phrase of the noteworthy mission historian Kenneth Scott Latourette, "the Great Century."

Counting the Cost

The parallel with the early centuries is a reminder, however, that
such cross-cultural expansion does not take place without a cost. As in
the church's very earliest expansion, so also in the nineteenth century,
the cost for both missionaries and new believers was often high.

Western histories naturally stress first the premature death of missionaries, of which there could be a nearly endless recital: fifty men and
women dead in the Church Missionary Society's first two decades of
work in Sierra Leone (ca. 1805–25); or John Williams of the London
Missionary Society clubbed to death and eaten in 1839 on the island of
Erromanga in the South Pacific; or the Anglican Bishop Hannington
slain in 1885 as he attempted to move overland into modern Uganda;
and many, many more.

Yet if Western accounts are naturally attuned to the death of those
who brought the gospel into previously non-Christian regions, the mar-
tyrology of the nineteenth and twentieth centuries is in fact mostly a
story of new converts who, like the Japanese Catholics two centuries
before, were hounded to death while still young in the faith. To be sure,
some of the outrages committed against Christians in the nineteenth
century were a product of long-standing antagonisms, like the massa-

cre of 35,000 Greek and Turkish Christians by Muslims in 1821.[9] Still other martyrs suffered at the hands of other types of Christians, like the Protestant evangelicals harassed by Orthodox in Ukraine from the 1880s. But most of the century's occasions when Christians were faithful unto death took place where the entrance of Christianity was still a new thing. Thus, the death of perhaps 70,000 Roman Catholics in Viet Nam in 1851, of countless others in Madagascar during the century's middle decades, of 25,000 Catholics in Korea in 1866, of 100,000 Catholics in Indochina in 1885, of perhaps 50,000 Catholics and Protestants during the Boxer Rebellion in China in 1900, and still others in many other places of the globe testified to the enduring reality of Tertullian's saying, that the blood of the martyrs was the seed of the church. The personal dramas—whether heroic, pathetic, tragic, ennobling, or all at once—that lurk behind such numbers constitute an open invitation to the serious research they have not yet received.

One example must serve to convey something of the humanity latent in such rapid summaries. An event that helped precipitate an attack on new believers in Buganda, East Africa, occurred on May 22, 1885, when the mother of Princess Nalumansi presented her with her own umbilical cord as a symbol of the duty the princess owed to ancestral Bugandan religion. When the princess cut up the cord and threw it away, fuel was added to a fire already smoldering against the believers. The fire became gruesomely real less than two weeks later when thirty-one Christians, Catholics and Protestants together, were executed in a great conflagration at Namugongo, while at the same time Bugandan authorities ordered the execution of many others by sword and spear.[10]

The expansion of Christianity in the great age of missions was not, in other words, a bloodless triumph. Nonetheless, it was a triumph. Here are David Barrett's laconic summaries on the "Global Status" of Christianity in 1750 and 1900.

1750: 57 generations after Christ, world is 22.2% Christians (85.2% of them being Whites), 25.8% evangelized; with printed scriptures available in 60 languages.

1900: 62 generations after Christ, world is 34.4% Christian (81.1% of them being Whites), 51.3% evangelized; with printed scriptures available in 537 languages.[11]

9. These figures and the others in this paragraph are from Barrett, *World Christian Encyclopedia*, 28–29.

10. The story is set in a fuller context in Adrian Hastings, *The Church in Africa, 1450–1950* (New York: Oxford University Press, 1994), 379.

11. Barrett, *World Christian Encyclopedia*, 27, 29.

Local Indigenization

Missionary outreach from the West, which from the early nineteenth century has played such a large role in the world history of Christianity, became permanently significant, however, only when it led to the appropriation of Christianity by non-Western peoples. That appropriation, along with the expansion of the faith in numbers and cultural impact, represents the truly momentous development in Christian history of the last two centuries. The link between Western missions and indigenous appropriation, moreover, is complex. Sometimes new churches reflect quite directly the forms and emphases of mission Christianity. Much more frequently the faith experienced as churches emerge in the Two-Thirds World differs— sometimes in subtle ways, sometimes more manifestly—

Samuel Crowther, head of the Anglican mission to the Niger Territory, is shown here in a photograph from 1888, about thirty years before the photo on page 286 was taken of William Wadé Harris, the evangelist of West Africa whose preaching, baptizing, and attacks on fetish worship made him as important in his day as Crowther had been earlier.

from the faith brought by the missionaries. Additionally, in a growing number of places, indigenous Christian communities have emerged that display scant connection at all with Western Christianity. The number of believers whom missiologist David Barrett calls "nonwhite indigenous Christian" has simply sky-rocketed over the course of the twentieth century, from less than 10 million in 1900 to almost 200 million in 1997. The truly earth-shaking development heralded by the great mission conferences, like Edinburgh in 1910, is the varied process of appropriation. Whether leading to new adaptations of Roman Catholicism, new forms of Protestantism, or entirely new churches, however, is of less moment than recognizing how important the cross-cultural diffusion of the faith has become in the most recent epoch of world Christian history. Four examples from Africa suggest something of the variety of Christian indigenization over the last two centuries as well as about the various connections between missionary labor and indigenous appropriation.

William Wadé Harris

The life of Samuel Ajayi Crowther (ca. 1807–91) testifies to both the generosity and the petty-mindedness of Western missionaries, to both the potential and peril for Christianization in the nineteenth century.[12] Crowther was born in Yorubaland (modern western Nigeria), was captured by African slavers and sold to a Portuguese trader for transport over the Atlantic, but was rescued by a British naval squadron and put ashore in 1822 at Freetown, Sierra Leone. This West African country had been established by British evangelicals to serve as a haven for the enslaved, whether returning from America or before they could be exported. In Sierra Leone, Crowther was converted; he was educated there and in England, and in 1843 he was ordained as an Anglican minister for service with Henry Venn's Church Missionary Society (CMS). Crowther was one of the leaders of a successful missionary venture that took him and several other former slaves back to their native Yorubaland, where a vigorous Christianity soon arose. Yoruba Christian faith was distinctly Protestant in an evangelical Anglican style, but it also bore many evidences of successful connection to traditional Yoruba religion. Thus dreams, which had been an important part of Yoruba religion, functioned also as important elements in the conversion of many to Christ. Yoruba tolerance for deities of all sorts meant that the introduction of the Christian God—who was called Olurun, the traditional Yoruba name for the Creator—was never a problem. Under the skillful leadership of Crowther and a talented body of African clergy (many like him from Sierre Leone) the Yoruba who became Christians were allowed to proceed at

---

12. This section follows the relevant passages in Hastings, *The Church in Africa;* and Andrew F. Walls, "Samuel Ajayi Crowther, 1807–1891: Foremost African Christian of the Nineteenth Century," in *Mission Legacies: Biographical Studies of Leaders of the Modern Missionary Movement,* ed. G. H. Anderson et al. (Maryknoll, N.Y.: Orbis, 1994), 132–39.

their own pace in burying or destroying their traditional holy objects, the *Ifas* and *orisa*.

Crowther's manifest spiritual maturity as well as his capacity for leadership led Henry Venn in 1864 to secure Crowther's ordination as an Anglican bishop. Rather than place him in charge of the Yoruba church, however, the CMS directed Crowther to undertake a mission along the Niger River, although this assignment took him to tribes of diverse languages and to areas under the influence of Islam. Nonetheless, Crowther labored diligently in the assignment. Especially noteworthy was his cautious approach to Muslims: Crowther made much of common ground between the Koran and the Scriptures, he was careful about making biblical tracts and texts available until their users could be warned against using them like charms, and he also developed an apologetic grounded almost entirely on biblical quotations. In the end, however, Crowther failed in his work along the Niger because the task was all but impossible, because he could never find sufficient African helpers (European missionaries were no good since most who took up service along the Niger simply died), and because his forced reliance upon British traders put him at the mercy of individuals who eventually became more interested in selling gin than promoting civilization or Christianity. In a tragic denouement to a sterling career, Crowther in 1890 was stripped of his ecclesiastical authority by a band of young English missionaries who were inspired by a wooden vision of proper spirituality and an unthinking dedication to a British imperial ideal. Crowther had taken genuinely significant steps toward the Africanization of Christian faith, but his work remained more a promise of what would come than its realization.

Even as Crowther's effort to indigenize an evangelical Anglicanism was running aground, however, other movements were underway that proved more successful. One of the most important of these had its origins within fifteen years of Crowther's death. In South Africa shortly after the turn of the century, an unlikely, but potent, mix of confessional European Protestantism, newer forms of Holiness teaching, and Pentecostal healing were acting on each other in the creation of Zionist movements.[13] Early influences for Zionism were the devotional work of Andrew Murray, a Scottish pietist who had exercised a large ministry among the Dutch Reformed; P. L. Le Roux, an Afrikaner who carried Murray's ideas, including his belief in faith healing, in mission to the Zulus; and emissaries from John Alexander Dowie, founder of the Christian Catholic Apostolic Church in Zion City, Illinois, who was an

---

13. For a solid account, see Hastings, *The Church in Africa*, 499–504.

Anglican Bishop Crowther

The following is a part of the entry for October 19, 1854, from the published journal of Samuel Crowther, concerning an expedition along the Niger River and related territories in West Africa:

I asked him [Ogara of Yimmaha, king of Panda] whether, in case trade should be established with this country, he would like his people to be taught God's book, and how to worship God as we do in the white man's country; for it was these two things together, which made England great, and that they would bring peace and prosperity to any country who received and embraced them. I told him that the same thing was proposed to the chiefs of Aboh, to the Atta of Igara, their sovereign, and to Mohamma, king of Hamaru-wa, respecting the Baibai or Djuku people, and that they were all willing to trade, and that their people should be taught God's book: I wanted, therefore, to know what he would say to it also. He replied that trade was their chief employment, and that he was very desirous that war should cease, that his people might trade, and be taught God's book: he wished us many blessings and long life from the God whom we worship. He said that he was a trader himself.[2]

early pioneer of several practices that defined the modern Pentecostal movement. Soon, however, these missionary impulses were appropriated by African leaders, like Daniel Nkonyane, who in 1908 replaced Le Roux as the head of the self-styled Zionist movement. (The term "Zion" came originally from the use of a Moravian hymnbook, *The Songs of Zion*, but was inspired more directly by Dowie's restorationist theology, which pointed to charismatic practices as the herald of the appearance of the Heavenly City.) By 1920, and now completely under African leadership, the Zion movement was divided into several subgroups and had moved beyond the Zulus into Swaziland, Basutoland, and Southern Rhodesia (now Zimbabwe).

Zionism's power as a dynamic Christian movement has much to do with its ability to employ traditional aspects of African religion—like the exorcism of demons, ecstatic dance, the centrality of prophet-healers, as well as elaborate purification and initiation rites—in the service of a biblical, Christ-centered, Pentecostal form of Christianity. The contribution of the early Pentecostal, or Pentecostal-leaning, missionaries was critical in providing Western forms of the faith that bridged the gap to the world of African primal religions. But so thoroughly has that missionary contribution been integrated into a Christianity guided, organized, and proclaimed by Africans that the missionary connection is now almost completely irrelevant. Similarities to early Methodism in the English-speaking world are, however, striking, since Zionists encourage hard work, disdain the use of tobacco and alcohol (and also pork), sing vigorously, and, while encouraging solid citizenship, remain mostly apolitical. The numbers of Africans who belong to Zionist churches is contested, but they may today constitute as many as five million out of South Africa's population of forty million, plus two or three times that many outside of South Africa.[14] The Zion churches represent perhaps the most rapid and most complete example of transition from missionary Christianity to African Christianity. Delegates to the Edinburgh Missionary Conference in 1910 almost certainly had very little grasp of what was happening in South Africa, even as they deliberated the future of the Christianity, but the future largely belonged to the Africans who made their own sense out of missionary messages from Dowie, Murray, Le Roux, and other Westerners.

Not long after Zionism began to emerge as a distinctly African variety of Christianity in southern Africa, another important example of indigenization was taking place on the African west coast. In 1910 William Wadé Harris (ca. 1860–1929) was put into a Liberian prison for supporting an effort to replace the African American government of that country with leaders eager to enter the orbit of British rather than American influence.[15] Harris had been raised under Methodist teaching and had also done some teaching for an Episcopal church. While in prison he was visited by the angel Gabriel, who, in a great wave of pure light, told Harris to preach as a prophet of the last times, to destroy the fetishes that were a part of the region's traditional African religions, to baptize immediately all who would receive this Christian sacrament (it was customary for missionaries to require a long period of catechesis before baptizing converts), and to set aside Western dress in favor of a white robe.

After Harris was released from prison, he left Liberia to proclaim this new message in the Ivory Coast (lying eastward of Liberia). It was July 1913; his impact was sudden and dramatic. Thousands responded and eagerly followed his advice to organize their local Christian life around

14. These figures are from Bill Keller, "A Surprising Silent Majority in South Africa," *New York Times Magazine*, April 17, 1994, pp. 34–40, 54, 72, 78, 83 (numbers on p. 39). Helpful as a more general assessment is G. C. Oosthuizen, "Indigenous Christianity and the Future of the Church in South Africa," *International Bulletin of Missionary Research* 21 (January 1997): 8–12.

15. For an introduction, see Hastings, *The Church in Africa*, 443–47.

the twelve apostles that Harris regularly appointed in converted communities. But Harris also urged converts to connect with churches directed by European missionaries. Converts were impressed by the fervor of the Christ-centered message that Harris preached, but also by the power with which it was supported. Many healings were reported, and stories circulated of colonial administrators who died unexpectedly after they interfered with Harris and likewise of sudden death coming upon those who were baptized after claiming to have destroyed their fetishes but who had only buried them. Both Catholic and Protestant churches in the Ivory Coast, the Gold Coast, and surrounding regions were overwhelmed by the thousands of Africans who sought membership in their churches (converts who were not gathered into the European groups formed an autonomous Harrist church). Missionaries were, however, less pleased with Harris's toleration of polygamy. Mostly, however, they rejoiced at the harvest that Harris and his colleagues reaped so fully in regions where their own work had been mostly in vain.

William Wadé Harris's form of Christian faith was not as thoroughly indigenized as the Zionist movements of South Africa, since his self-conscious willingness to incorporate converts into missionary churches left a clear Western stamp on his movement. Nonetheless, what happened with his ministry was no less an illustration of the grounding of Christianity in new soil. David Shank, a leading authority on West African Christianity, summarized the "new indigenous lay religious movement" begun by Harris as "covering a dozen ethnic groups and involving new patterns of unity in the midst of diversity: one God, one theocentric law (the Ten Commandments), one day (Sunday), one book (the Bible), one symbol (the cross), one baptism (break with 'fetishes'), one place of worship, one institution (church leadership by 'twelve apostles')." The missionary churches to which Harris directed converts as well as the independent Église Harrist that emerged were marked, again in Shank's words, by "the distinct Harris stamp: strong anti-fetish accent on one God; prayer as a replacement for sacrifice; use of traditional music and dance; use of cross, Bible, calabash [a kind of gourd], and baptismal bowl as liturgical instruments; liturgical vestments following the model of Harris; traditional marriage practices, with preachers having only one wife; government by 'twelve apostles'; self-supporting preachers chosen from within the local congregation."[16] Harris's ways of connecting Christianity to Africa was not the only way to do it, but he left a remarkable legacy nonetheless.

16. David A. Shank, "William Wadé Harris, ca. 1860–1929: God Made His Soul a Soul of Fire," in *Mission Legacies*, 161, 162.

Yet another pattern of indigenization has taken place among the Bor Dinka on the east side of the White Nile River in southern Sudan.[17] Christian missions began in 1906 among this group, but for the first seventy years and more of its activity, the Anglican Church Missionary Society (CMS) experienced only scant results. From the 1970s, and with accelerating force in the '80s and '90s, however, Christianity under the guidance of the Episcopal Church of the Sudan has expanded with remarkable strength. The external circumstances of this expansion are tragic, for the Dinka have been caught in civil war with various Muslim factions from northern Sudan. The Dinka have suffered great loss of life. They have also been stripped of the cattle herds that were the backbone of their culture, and they have been forced in massive numbers to migrate from ancestral lands. Precisely in these circumstances the Christian faith has taken root.

But it has done so in a distinctively Bor Dinka manner. Everywhere in the new Dinka churches and among the burgeoning tide of converts is seen the cross. The display of the cross is particularly striking in massed processions on holy days, when, as described by Marc Nikkel, "their crosses [create] a thick forest, surging with the crowds, thrusting heavenward with every beat of the songs they sing."[18] In the first instance, the prominence of the cross in Bor Dinka life represents a Christianization of existing cultural forms, for the Dinka had historically put to use a wide variety of carved walking sticks, staffs, and clubs. Among Dinka converts, the Christian symbol has filled a form provided by traditional culture.

In the second instance, however, the Dinka appropriation of the cross has also become a powerful expression of pastoral theology. As revealed in a flourishing of fresh, indigenous hymnody, the cross is now a comprehensive reality of great power. The cross provides protection against hostile spirits, or *jak;* the cross figures large in the baptisms that mark conversions; in hymns the cross becomes an ensign or banner raised high for praise and protection; the cross brings the great God, *Nhialic,* close to the Dinka in the person of Christ, whose suffering is appropriated with striking subjectivity; the cross is spoken of as the *mën,* or the solid central post that supports the Dinka's large, thatched cattle sheds; and the cross becomes a symbol of the potent Spirit who replaces the ancestral *jak* (sing. *jok*), whose protective powers have so obviously failed in recent years. A song composed by Mary Nyanluaak

---

17. The following paragraphs rely on Marc R. Nikkel, "The Cross of Bor Dinka Christians: A Working Christology in the Face of Displacement and Death," *Studies in World Christianity* 1 (1995): 160–85

18. Ibid., 161.

Lem Bol illustrates the depth to which the cross has entered Dinka culture in desperate times:

> We will carry the cross. We will carry the cross.
> The cross is the gun for the evil *jok*.
> Let us chase the evil *jok* away with the cross.[19]

Bor Dinka appropriation of Christianity, along with the other African examples, represents only the smallest fraction of the incredibly diverse number of individual narratives that have appeared outside of the West over the past century and a half. The story of Roman Catholic adjustments to traditional religious patterns in Africa, Latin America, and Asia is a huge subject by itself, since Catholicism has been, by far, the most widely represented form of Christianity around the world in the twentieth century. Similarly, however, the new flourishing of Protestant groups in several areas of Latin America and Asia would also require a sensitive ability to chart a full spectrum of means by which the Christian faith has come to be "at home" in regions where two hundred or one hundred or even fifty years ago it did not exist. Missionary initiative is part of the picture in many of those individual stories, though not all of them. But even where missionary initiative has played a large role, the climax of the story in these newly Christianized regions is inevitably a story of local appropriation.

The Meaning of Mission for the History of Christianity

The Edinburgh Missionary Conference of 1910 represents a great turning point in the history of Christianity, not so much for what was done by its delegates, as for symbolizing a dawning consciousness concerning the worldwide extension of the faith. What has happened in the past century or two may mean just as much for the future of Christianity as early cross-cultural transmissions have meant. The main difference in the twentieth century is that earlier expansions of Christianity mostly involved single originating and single receiving cultures. To be sure, the ramifications were great indeed when the Jewish Christianity of the New Testament era was "translated" into the Hellenistic culture of the larger Mediterranean world, and then when the Hellenistic Christianity that resulted was translated into the tribal societies of northern Europe. The difference in recent centuries is that the church has been developing in several directions at once. Early Christian communities in Africa and Asia were seeds for this new expansion, but its

19. Ibid., 175.

great impetus has been the Western missionary efforts of the modern period. Mission, however, is always transitional, and it is the local appropriation of Christianity that makes a lasting difference. Given the situation of the past two centuries, where a process of local appropriation has been underway in many parts of the world at the same time, the implications for the history of Christianity are immense.

Such multiple translations of Christian faith at the same time in different parts of the globe can only appear chaotic, especially to those whose Christian experience is deeply rooted in the long Western appropriation of Christianity. What will come of the simultaneous translations of the Christian faith into so many of the world's cultures, God alone knows. But a long historical perspective can inspire considerable confidence. As expressed by the Scottish historian of missions Andrew Walls, "It is a delightful paradox that the more Christ is translated into the various thought forms and life systems which form our various national identities, the richer all of us will be in our common Christian identity."[20]

Hindsight shows that the delegates who met at Edinburgh in 1910 were foolish to think that Christian expansion throughout the world would replicate a faith that looked pretty much as it appeared in the precincts of Scotland's United Free Church Assembly Hall. But they were far from foolish in being optimistic about the reality of that expansion. The appeal of Western Christianity would soon be tarnished by World War I, the Russian Revolution, rampant commercial materialism, and other cultural calamities. Yet since the delegates at Edinburgh were themselves the product of a Christianity that had been translated culturally to their ancestors (however distant), their very existence illustrated the vitality that could arise from faith transmitted to still other cultures. While the Western missions represented at Edinburgh would do their part, it was the appropriation of Christianity by peoples literally around the world that marked the critical turning point.

The offering of thanks that follows presents the last of three prayers that are typically prayed during rites of communal conversion among the Bor Dinka of southern Sudan. The ritual includes a statement of intent to destroy ancestral spirits, or *jak*, and to trust in God, or *Nhialic*. Along with destruction of ancestral shrines, the ritual includes baptism, a procession featuring

20. Andrew F. Walls, *The Missionary Movement in Christian History: Studies in the Transmission of Faith* (Maryknoll, N.Y.: Orbis, 1996), 54.

crosses or banners marked with a cross, reading from the New Testament, a sermon, the singing of hymns, the placement of a cross on the site of the shrines that have been destroyed, the gift of a cross and a New Testament to the converts, and several other prayers. The whole service signals the beginning of new life under the protection and authority of the cross.

> *We thank you, O Nhialic, Father, Son, and Holy Spirit, for bringing this family into your flock. We now commend them into your care, asking that you endow them with your strength and assure them that you are continually present, abiding with them. By your power the jak have been uprooted and cast out. Now you have replaced those old powers with your Great and Holy Jok. Give these, your children, complete security and confidence in this fact. This homestead is now your dwelling place, since your cross, the sign of Christ, has been planted here.*[21]

Further Reading

Anderson, Gerald H., Robert T. Coote, Norman A. Horner, and James M. Phillips, eds. *Mission Legacies: Biographical Studies of Leaders of the Modern Missionary Movement.* Maryknoll, N.Y.: Orbis, 1994.

Clouse, Robert G., Richard V. Pierard, and Edwin M. Yamauchi. *Two Kingdoms: The Church and Culture through the Ages.* Chicago: Moody, 1993.

Hastings, Adrian. *The Church in Africa, 1450–1950.* New York: Oxford University Press, 1994.

Hudson Taylor and Missions to China. [*Christian History,* no. 52]. 1996.

Isichei, Elizabeth. *A History of Christianity in Africa.* Grand Rapids: Eerdmans, 1995.

Latourette, Kenneth Scott. *A History of the Expansion of Christianity.* 7 vols. New York: Harper & Bros., 1937–45.

Martin, David. *Tongues of Fire: The Explosion of Protestantism in Latin America.* Oxford: Blackwell, 1990.

Neill, Stephen. *A History of Christian Missions.* New York: Penguin, 1964.

Sanneh, Lamin O. *Encountering the West: Christianity and the Global Cultural Process, the African Dimension.* Maryknoll, N.Y.: Orbis, 1993.

Stanley, Brian. *The Bible and the Flag: Protestant Missions and British Imperialism in the Nineteenth and Twentieth Centuries.* Leicester, Eng.: Apollos, 1990.

Walls, Andrew F. *The Missionary Movement in Christian History: Studies in the Transmission of Faith.* Maryknoll, N.Y.: Orbis, 1996.

William Carey [*Christian History,* no. 36]. 1992.

---

21. A Dinka prayer recalled by Akurdit Ngong Akurdit, as quoted in Nikkel, "The Cross of Bor Dinka Christians," 179.

13

Further Turning Points of the Twentieth Century

One of the strongest signs of ferment in twentieth-century Christianity is the burst of hymn-writing that has been underway since the 1950s. The influence of charismatic worship, the provision of appropriate music in cultures and languages where Christianity is a new faith, a widespread return to Scripture as a source for hymnody, a concern in the West to reach individuals with no church background—these are only some of the factors that have made the current period one of the liveliest ever in the history of Christian hymnody. A danger arising from the upsurge of new music is that the incredibly rich treasure of the church's historic hymnody will be neglected. A strength is that the Lord's songs are being sung in idioms and with sensibilities addressing current situations.

The following example is one of thousands that could be presented to illustrate the late twentieth-century efflorescence of hymn-writing around the world. Its author is Lindomar Moreira da Silva, at the time of writing an eighteen-year-old member of an evangelical Protestant church in Buriticupu, Maranhão, deep in the interior of northeastern Brazil. This is a region with almost no economic opportunity and almost none of the comforts taken for granted in North America, Europe, and other developed parts of the world. When he wrote this song in the mid–1990s, the author was living with his mother and seven other children in a four-room house.

> *Não te desanimes nunca mais,*
> *Jesus Cristo já te deu*
> *a paz, o amor, a alegria,*

não o mundo de fantasia.
  Não olhe para trás,
  Jesus Cristo já te tirou do mal.
  Olhe para frente e nada mais.
Não te desanimes de cantar.
Com força e graça, tudo passa.
E a vitória Ele nos dará.
E juntos ganharemos o galardão.

(Don't be discouraged ever again.
Jesus Christ has already given you
Peace, love, and joy,
Not a fantasy world.
  Don't look back,
  Jesus Christ has taken you from sin.
  Just look ahead, nothing more.
Don't be discouraged from singing.
Through strength and grace all will pass.
And the victory he will give us.
And together we will win the crown.)[1]

Beside the Edinburgh Missionary Conference of 1910, what might later historians consider the twentieth century's most important turning points in the history of Christianity? As difficult and subjective as it may be to decide upon the major turning points in the long history of the church, it is even more difficult and much more dependent upon subjective judgment to discover major turning points in the recent past. In the search for Christian turning points, the soundest strategy is to look for those events and circumstances that led to the deepening of the Christian faith, to the expansion of Christianity, or to both. There have been many such events of varying character throughout the world, so the search could go in many directions.

Well-documented movements with high institutional visibility have certainly been important. For example, the establishment of the World Council of Churches in 1948, along with its subsequent development,

1. I am pleased to thank my friend Jim Ohlson for providing a copy of this song, which he obtained in 1995.

have marked signal efforts by mostly the older Protestant churches to cooperate in Christian thought and practice. Likewise, the emergence of "fundamentalist" movements in the United States and then (though the word becomes slippery) in Latin America, Africa, and elsewhere has also received serious attention from historians and, in recent years, from commentators of all sorts. Even loosely organized movements that have linked independent Christian groups, like the 1974 Lausanne Congress on World Evangelization, with its 2,750 participants from 150 countries, have received some attention, though not as much as they deserve. Unless, however, institutions related to such movements come to exert a deeper and a more sustained influence than they have exerted so far, it is doubtful that later historians will find their creation the most important events of the century.

Something of the same might be said of individuals. A whole host of Christian men and women have exercised unusual influence throughout the course of the twentieth century, in several different ways and several different spheres. Even to attempt a list of such ones brings the list-maker face-to-face with the full weight of his or her own biases. It can also obscure the Christian truth that great work for God is often done without recognition and out of the public eye. My list of figures who have made a significant difference comes from a North American and evangelical Protestant angle, but it may indicate what sort of people could be included. If this is deficient in figures not from the West, it is a problem of the author's limitations more than of the church's actual life:

from Russia the writer Aleksandr Solzhenitsyn (1918–), the Baptist dissident Georgi Vins (1928–), and the martyred Orthodox priest Aleksandr Menn (1935–90);

out of Russia as an emigré the Orthodox theologian Georges Florovsky (1893–1979);

from England the "mere Christians" G. K. Chesterton (1874–1936) and C. S. Lewis (1898–1963), the playwright and theologian Dorothy L. Sayers (1893–1957), and the scholarly Anglican evangelist John R. W. Stott (1921–);

from Albania Mother Teresa (1910–97), a nun who worked on behalf of the dying;

from the United States the evangelist Billy Graham (1918–), the civil rights leader Martin Luther King, Jr. (1929–68), and the Catholic editor and social reformer Dorothy Day (1897–1980);

from Switzerland two theologians, the Protestant Karl Barth (1886–1968) and the Catholic Hans Urs von Balthasar (1908–88);

for extraordinary leadership in the Roman Catholic Church, Popes
Leo XIII (1878–1903), John XXIII (1958–63), and John Paul II
(1978–);

the German pastor, theologian, and martyr Dietrich Bonhoeffer
(1906–45);

and as Christian political leaders, the nonecclesiastical Protestant
Tomás Masaryk (1850–1937) of Czechoslovakia, the Catholic
Konrad Adenauer (1876–1967) of Germany, and the Presbyterian
Woodrow Wilson (1856–1924) of the United States.

Giving all honor where honor is due, however, it would still be surprising if any one of these individuals, or others to be noticed in better-
balanced compilations, assumed global importance in telling the Christian story of the twentieth century.

For determining turning points of this century, a better case might
be made for Christian reactions to large-scale world events or large-
scale economic and social changes. The two World Wars, as the most
intensive instances in this most bloody century of warfare, were not
church historical events in a narrow sense. Yet these wars had much to
do with very important developments in the world history of Christianity (for example, destroying the moral legitimacy of "Christian Europe"
or hastening the rise to world dominance of the United States and its
particular expressions of Christianity). Something of the same could be
said for the Russian and Chinese Revolutions, since they greatly affected Christian life, not only in these two countries, but throughout
much of the rest of the world. The expansion of the world economy, the
more recent explosion of computer-driven communications, as well as
the development of radio, television, and the cinema may loom very
large in Christian histories of the twentieth century, depending on the
uses to which believers put these matters.

The five possibilities I describe below as turning points could also be
among the most significant. Even if they are not the most important developments of the century, describing them may help others discern
events or circumstances having even greater significance:

1. the rise and spread of Pentecostalism;
2. the Second Vatican Council of the Roman Catholic Church;
3. the emergence of women into greater public visibility;
4. the massive production of new Bible translations as an aspect,
   more generally, of the globalization of Christianity;
5. the survival of Christianity under Communist regimes.

The Rise and Spread of Pentecostalism

One of the most momentous developments in the twentieth-century history of Christianity must certainly be the emergence of Pentecostalism as a dynamic force around the world. In 1900 there were, at most, a bare handful of Christians who were experiencing special gifts of the Holy Spirit similar to those recorded in the New Testament. By the end of the century, as many as 500 million (or more than a quarter of the worldwide population of affiliated Christian adherents) could be identified as Pentecostal or charismatic.[2] (The usual difference in these terms is between Pentecostals who are organized in churches with a distinct emphasis on the sign gifts of the Holy Spirit and charismatics who practice those gifts within churches that do not formally endorse this understanding of the Holy Spirit's work.)

The beginnings of Pentecostalism, with its characteristic practice of speaking in tongues as evidence of baptism by the Holy Spirit, is often associated with a revival beginning in 1906 at the Apostolic Faith Gospel Mission on Azusa Street in Los Angeles, California. In that year a mild-mannered African American preacher, William J. Seymour (1870–1922), began a lengthy series of nightly meetings. Soon visitors from around the world were coming to Azusa Street and carrying back to Chicago, Toronto, New York, London, Australia, Scandinavia, South Africa, and many other places the message that the living presence of the Holy Spirit could be experienced as a reality in this age.[3]

As important as Azusa Street has loomed in the consciousness of historians, however, earlier leaders and movements had anticipated what Pentecostals call "the latter rain" or the "outpouring of the Spirit." The Scottish preacher Edward Irving (1792–1834) was only one of several nineteenth-century leaders whose ministry encouraged special spiritual gifts. Toward the end of the century, widespread longing for revival combined in several places with an equally great longing for Christian sanctification. Among zealous heirs of John Wesley's Methodism such longings were expressed in the language of "Christian perfection" or "Holiness," while Protestants of Calvinist background spoke more of "the higher Christian life." With their stress on the need for a special work of the Holy Spirit, these longings led to episodes where the Holy Spirit was thought

---

2. David B. Barrett, "Annual Statistic Table on Global Mission: 1997," *International Bulletin of Missionary Research* 21 (January 1997): 25.

3. On the early spread of Pentecostalism, I am following Edith L. Blumhofer, "Transatlantic Currents in North Atlantic Pentecostalism," in *Evangelicalism: Comparative Studies of Popular Protestantism in North America, the British Isles, and Beyond, 1700–1990*, ed. M. A. Noll, D. W. Bebbington, and G. A. Rawlyk (New York: Oxford, 1994), 351–64.

In Brazil, where this baptism is taking place, the number of Pentecostals increased from 18 members in 1911 to over 14 million in 1993.

Photo supplied by the Division of Foreign Missions, Assemblies of God

to descend in a special way. Before the turn of the century, Charles Fox Parham (1873–1929), who had been raised in Methodist and Holiness churches, was instructing students at his schools in Kansas and Texas that a baptism of "the Holy Ghost and fire" should be expected among those who had been converted and who were going on to the perfect sanctification that Holiness advocates proclaimed. (One of those students was William Seymour.) At the start of the twentieth century, a worldwide revival tour by Reuben A. Torrey (1856–1928), a younger associate of the famed American evangelist D. L. Moody, linked together many who would later participate in the Pentecostal movement (though Torrey himself did not become a Pentecostal). Then a well-reported revival in Wales (1903–4) fanned further hope for a special outpouring of the Spirit.

Once underway, the Pentecostal movement rapidly became a worldwide phenomenon. Over the last half of this century, the charismatic movement in Catholic, Lutheran, Presbyterian, Episcopal, and many other denominations expanded emphases on healing and other spiritual gifts borrowed from earlier Pentecostalism. Together, the Pentecostal and charismatic emphases upon *experiencing the grace of God*—especially upon sensing God through more intimate, less cognitive forms of worship—have influenced Protestants, Catholics, and even some Orthodox all over the world.

Also in the second half of the twentieth century, Pentecostal and charismatic currents have been central in the rapid expansion of Christianity outside the West, with most of the rapidly growing churches in Brazil, Nigeria, Korea, Russia, China, and many other nations either explicitly Pentecostal or heavily influenced by charismatic practices. In

A Pentecostal Healing

The Pentecostal movement arose from a conglomeration of experiences like those of Carrie Judd Montgomery (1858–1946). Montgomery eventually affiliated with the Assemblies of God denomination in 1914, but years before, an experience of healing had put her on the path that linked holiness and the special exercise of God's power in a typically Pentecostal pattern. The following comes from a work first published in 1880:

On the 6th of January, 1877, after a gradual decline in health, I was prostrated with an attack of fever proceeding from my spine, the result probably of a severe fall on a stone sidewalk several months before. . . . For eleven months I could not sit up at all. . . . Everything that the most skillful physicians could do for me had been done; only the "Great Physician" could restore me by His almighty power. I have no doubt that it was ordered by providence that just at this time there should appear in the daily paper a short account of the wonderful cures performed in answer to the prayers of Mrs. Edward Mix, a colored woman, of Wolcottville, Connecticut. . . . I waited a few hours, then requested my sister to write [to] her that I believed her great faith might avail for me if she would pray for my recovery. . . . [Mrs. Mix responded by reminding Carrie Judd of the biblical passage, "The prayer of faith shall save the sick, and the Lord shall raise him up."] I began to pray for an increase of faith. I left off all medicine at once, though I confess it was with a struggle. . . . At the hour appointed by Mrs. Mix, members of our own family also offered up prayer, though not in my room. Just before this, I seemed to have no power whatever to grasp the promise. Terrible darkness and powerful temptations from Satan rose to obscure even the little faith I had, but suddenly my soul was filled with a childlike peace and confidence, different from anything I had ever before experienced.

There was no excitement, but without the least fear or hesitation, I turned over and raised up alone for the first time in two years. . . . Directly after, with a little support from my nurse, I walked a few steps to my chair. During that same hour, a decided change was perceptible in my color, circulation, and pulse, and I could talk aloud with ease. . . . The more fully I cast myself upon [the Lord], the more I was supported, and often I felt borne up as if by some buoyancy in the air, while there was little or no effort of my own. Even more wonderful and . . . precious than being brought from death unto life physically is the renewed life which the soul experiences at the same time under the healing influence of the Holy Spirit.[1]

these situations, Pentecostal and charismatic forms of Christian faith flourish by directly confronting pagan gods and animistic spirits as well as by imparting the direct immediacy of God's presence.[4]

Most Pentecostals and charismatics hold to traditional Christian beliefs on the Trinity, human sinfulness, and the authority of the Bible. Many share a perspective on Christ in four interrelated roles as Savior, Healer, Baptizer in the Spirit, and Returning King. With such emphases, Pentecostals and charismatics have placed great stress on the supernatural power of God to defeat disease and to provide other miraculous interventions in ordinary life.

Should the trends of the twentieth century continue with Pentecostal and charismatic forces continuing to expand, especially in the Two-Thirds World, events around 1900 that precipitated identifiable Christian movements defined by belief in the special work of the Holy Spirit may loom as one of the most decisive turning points in the recent history of Christianity.

The Second Vatican Council

The Second Vatican Council, which met in four separate sessions from October 11, 1962, to December 8, 1965, signaled a new era for the Roman Catholic Church, the largest and most widely spread Christian organization in the world. On January 25, 1959, early in his pontificate, Pope John XXIII issued a first appeal for a council. Later in his official call, the pope expressed the hope that a council would "give the Church the possibility to contribute more efficaciously to the solution of the problems of the modern age."[5] As it actually unfolded, the council witnessed its full share of intrigue, suspense, and sometimes bitter controversy. Some Catholic conservatives hoped to reassert the kind of top-down papal supremacy that had characterized the decrees of the First Vatican Council of 1869–70. Some radicals wanted the church to embrace progressive movements of social renewal and theological modernism. But most of the approximately 2,300 cardinals, archbishops, and bishops who made up the council proper, along with a small army of advisers and invited guests, did not want changes inspired by either extreme Right or extreme Left but hoped that the necessary steps could be taken to preserve the church's traditions while making necessary adjustments to the modern world.

The sixteen official documents produced by the council included four "constitutions" (on the church, divine revelation, the sacred liturgy, and the church in the modern world), nine "decrees" (on subjects like ecumenism,

---

4. For preliminary discussion, see Karla Poewe, ed., *Charismatic Christianity as a Global Culture* (Columbia: University of South Carolina Press, 1994).

5. Walter Abbott, S.J., ed., *The Documents of Vatican II* (New York: Guild, 1966), 705.

the training and life of priests, and the functions of the laity), and three "declarations" (on Christian education, relationships with non-Christian religions, and religious freedom). Compared with the mood of the First Vatican Council, the tone of these documents was much more conciliatory to non–Roman Catholics, especially the Eastern Orthodox Church. Sophisticated biblical study informed much of the council's debate, but so also did sophisticated reliance on church tradition. As an indication of the many hands that contributed to the formulations, the council's documents reaffirmed a high doctrine of papal authority but also spoke extensively of the need for bishops to act collegially in guiding the church and also called upon the laity to become more active in all phases of the church's life.

In the wake of the council, Roman Catholicism could not remain the same. The ferment of Vatican II stimulated a profusion of Catholic special-interest groups—charismatic, socially active, modernist, biblical, conservative, ecumenical, and more. In fact, one of the most enduring features of the Catholic Church since the 1960s has been the intense debate over just what the council *really* intended. Merely to sample opinions is to note the wide range of conclusions on what the council was and accomplished.

A Lutheran, George Lindbeck, was impressed with how far the council moved the Catholic Church away from earlier habits. "All the major documents have clearly abandoned the classical framework of thought with its triumphalist and authoritarian view of the church, individualistic notion of worship and religious experience, and intellectualistic concept of revelation. . . . They display a unity which . . . constitutes a sphere of theological discourse and conceptualization which is sharply and definably different from that which has prevailed in Roman Catholic magisterial teaching ever since the Middle Ages."[6] A Protestant evangelical, David Wells, was more impressed with the potential for radical pluralism. "The pivot on which the future turns would seem to be the shift towards subjective religious experience and away from objective Church allegiance. . . . Sometime in the decade ahead, therefore, it may become impossible to speak any longer of *the* Catholic faith as a whole, since it will mean different things to different men in different places. . . . The intrusion of these factors on the shaping of Catholic belief will mean that, in the old sense and on the traditional basis, the unity of the Church will disappear."[7] An opinion that mattered even more was that of the Polish bishop Karol Wojtyla, who in 1978 became Pope John Paul II. In 1972 he commented in the following terms on the religious ideals of the council's work:

6. George A. Lindbeck, *The Future of Roman Catholic Theology: Vatican II—Catalyst for Change* (Philadelphia: Fortress, 1970), 116–17.
7. David F. Wells, *Revolution in Rome* (Downers Grove, Ill.: InterVarsity, 1972), 118–19.

The Council outlined the type of faith which corresponds to the life of the modern Christian, and the implementation of the Council consists first and foremost in enriching that faith. . . . [quoting from council documents] "Only the light of faith and meditation on the Word of God can enable us to find everywhere and always the God 'in whom we live and exist' (Acts 17:28); only thus can we seek his will in everything, see Christ in all men, acquaintance or stranger, make sound judgments on the true meaning and value of temporal realities both in themselves and in relation to man's end." [8]

Divergent as such opinions are, the one unquestioned judgment is that the Second Vatican Council ushered in a period of unusual movement and contention for the Catholic Church. Because of its very size and the weight of its traditions, what happens to the Catholic Church profoundly affects the direction of Christian history in general. When, in addition, leaders like John Paul II appear, whose preparation for the papacy included the ravages of war, the rigors of life under Communism, and intensive training as a philosopher, the prominence of the Catholic Church becomes even greater. How the Second Vatican Council comes to be judged, how its adjustments to Catholic tradition work out in the church's future course, may one day be viewed as a critical turning point in the twentieth-century history of Christianity.

New Visibility for Women

A twentieth-century development that has been too diffuse to associate with a single, discrete moment may yet be of momentous significance for the Christian future. This development is the emerging visibility of women in the church. The importance of this development has been suggested by the depth of controversy surrounding several different issues. Whether the commissioning of single women missionaries (which has been controversial in both Catholic and Protestants worlds), the ordination of women to pastoral office (which is still fiercely debated in the West at the end of the twentieth century), or the new social and economic roles opened to women in Western societies (which has engendered intense discussion over "family values"), attention to women's public Christian activities has been a source of friction and hope throughout the century.

Attention to the disputes, however, can hide a more important underlying reality. To be sure, it can be upsetting, liberating, scandalizing, and empowering—or all at once—for traditional gender roles to change in worship, organization, oversight, and public visibility. But the more en-

8. Karol Wojtyla (later John Paul II), *Sources of Renewal: The Implementation of Vatican II* (San Francisco: Harper & Row, 1980 [orig. 1972]), 420–21.

compassing reality of the twentieth century is the fresh awareness of how important women have been throughout the entire history of Christianity. Historical awareness of such larger realities makes possible a much more comprehensive awareness of gender issues today. Three of many possible instances of that awareness are the role of women in cross-cultural communication of the gospel, the importance of women's theological vision, and the preponderance of women as ordinary followers of Christ.

In the first instance, new significant literature has begun to show how absolutely integral women's work has been in the missionary enterprise. Books by scholars like R. Pierce Beaver, Jane Hunter, and Dana Robert, which concentrate on Protestant missionaries, show something of the dimension of those activities.[9] From the days of the Moravian pioneers through the burst of British-American activity at the start of the nineteenth century and the explosion of "faith missions" at the end of that century, on throughout the twentieth century, women (both married and single) have played a disproportionately large role in the activities of mission, including fund-raising, theologizing, and leadership. The Catholic picture is slightly different because of the long-standing significance of women's religious orders in missionary outreach. But for Catholics as well as Protestant missions, it is now clear that the expansion of Christianity has been for a very long time the work of women as well as, or even more than, men.

Second, breakthroughs in scholarship for a number of historical periods, especially the Middle Ages, have highlighted the critical place of women in the fuller expression of theology. Such breakthroughs do not alter the traditional picture of formal theology as primarily a male preserve. But a generation or more of careful work from historians whose work emerges from fresh attention to previously neglected sources,[10] along with extensive publication of works by women Christian writ-

---

9. R. Pierce Beaver, *American Protestant Women in World Mission*, rev. ed. (Grand Rapids: Eerdmans, 1980); Jane Hunter, *The Gospel of Gentility: American Women Missionaries in Turn-of-the-Century China* (New Haven: Yale University Press, 1984); Dana Robert, *American Women in Mission: A Social History of Their Thought and Practice* (Macon, Ga.: Mercer University Press, 1997).

10. Historians of the Middle Ages have led in this effort, but they have been joined by scholars on other periods as well. For only a hint of a great number of books, see Caroline Walker Bynum, *Holy Feast and Holy Fast: The Religious Significance of Food to Medieval Women* (Berkeley: University of California Press, 1987); Bynum, *Fragmentation and Redemption: Essays on Gender and the Human Body in Medieval Religion* (New York: Zone, 1991); Derek Baker, ed., *Medieval Women* (Oxford: Blackwell, 1978); Sherrin Marshall, ed., *Women in Reformation and Counter-Reformation Europe: Private and Public Worlds* (Bloomington: Indiana University Press, 1989); Lyndal Roper, *The Holy Household: Women and Morals in Reformation Augsburg* (New York: Oxford, 1989); and Patrica Crawford, *Women and Religion in England, 1500–1720* (London: Routledge, 1993).

ers,* has begun to expand the conception of theology. This full range of historical writing has shown that basic Christian truths like the incarnation and foundational Christian realities like communion with Christ take on a more affective, bodily, and domestic shape in the lives and writings of women. This awareness has contributed to the alteration of twentieth-century Christian reflection by pushing theologians, both men and women, to express the Christian faith with fuller attention to the expressive, contemplative, and mystical dimensions of the faith that have tended to predominate in the theological reflections of women. That twentieth-century development rests solidly on a historical foundation. As only one indication of the change that has taken place, a computerized database ("First Search") revealed in 1996 that in the hundred years before 1950, only 46 works were published by or on Hildegard von Bingen (1098–1179), the German abbess, theologian, musician, and mystic. In the last forty-five years there have been 239 such works.

The research results are similar for another question: Who have been the ordinary participants in the church's life throughout its history? Studies from almost every era of the church's past and from many regions have offered similar findings, namely, women have made up a larger proportion than men among church attenders, those practicing Christian devotion, and those maintaining orthodox beliefs. Whether speaking of the number of Roman Catholic religious, participants in the early methodist movement, church membership in colonial New England, Christian activity under Communist regimes in the Soviet Union and China, religious practices and beliefs as recorded by modern surveys, or healers among the African Independent Churches of South Africa, the results are similar. Where the business of the church can be counted, women normally show up more often than men.

The turning point with respect to women's activities does not concern primarily the activities themselves. Rather, the turning point includes public awareness of women's importance for ordinary Christian activities, the correction of perspective to include a fuller picture of women's work, and a growing awareness of how incomplete are theo-

---

* Women authors available in two series from Paulist Press (Mahwah, N.J.) suggest something of the texts now available: "Classics of Western Spirituality": Julian of Norwich, Catherine of Genoa, Teresa of Ávila, Catherine of Siena, Hildegard of Bingen, Birgitta of Sweden, Gertrude of Helfta, Angela of Foligno, Margaret Ebner, and Marguerite Porete; "Sources of American Spirituality": Anne Bradstreeet (in *Early New England Meditative Poetry*), Marie of the Incarnation, Phoebe Palmer, Rose Hawthorne Lathrop, Sisters of Mercy, and Elizabeth Seton.

Medieval Christian Women on Gender

The following summary paragraph from Caroline Walker Bynum's study on the religious use of food by women in the Middle Ages suggests some of the theological depth found in the recovery of women's Christian experience:

In the final analysis, it is wrong to see medieval women as internalizing the idea of their gender as inferior, because contrasts of male/female, superior/inferior, spirit/flesh seem, as *contrasts*, to have been less important to women than to men. If it is inaccurate to see late medieval asceticism as self-hating because it is wrong to think that medieval people saw flesh primarily as opposed to spirit, it is doubly inaccurate to see female asceticism as based in dualism, because all dualities were less important to women. Women saw themselves not as flesh opposed to spirit, female opposed to male, nurture opposed to authority; they saw themselves as human beings—fully spirit and fully flesh. And they saw all humanity as created in God's image, as capable of *imitatio Christi* through body as well as soul. Thus they gloried in the pain, the exudings, the somatic distortions that made their bodies parallel to the consecrated wafer on the altar and the man on the cross. In the blinding light of the ultimate dichotomy between God and humanity, all other dichotomies faded. Men and women might agree that female flesh was more fleshly than male flesh, but such agreement led both sexes to see themselves as in some sense female-human. For it was human beings as *human* (not as symbol of the divine) whom Christ saved in the Incarnation; it was body as flesh (not as spirit) that God became most graphically on the altar; it was human suffering (not human power) that Christ took on to redeem the world. Religious women in the later Middle Ages saw in their own female bodies not only a symbol of the humanness of both genders but also a symbol of—and a means of approach to—the humanity of God."[2]

logical, ecclesiastical, and historical accounts that do not reflect the perspectives of both men and women.

The future effect of the churches' expanded gender perspective is difficult to predict. Solid Christian reasoning, from both sexes, as well as male-dominated traditions, will no doubt continue to resist much radical secular feminism. Likewise, some Christian traditions that preserve strong gender roles may be shown to rest on solid biblical and theological grounds. Nonetheless, the change of perception over the course of the twentieth century is still dramatic. More clearly now than in 1900, many in the church see that, while men feature disproportionately large in the public achievements of Christianity, so too do they figure disproportionately large in its heresies, power grabs, schisms, and spectacular falls from grace. More clearly than in 1900, many more now recognize the indispensable contribution of women to the church. More clearly than in 1900, many in the church now also see that what matters most in the realities of Christian faith and life must be experienced and expressed by women and men together.

Bible Translation

The shift of Christianity's center of gravity from the Northern toward the Southern Hemisphere, which was a major theme of chapter 12, certainly must figure as a crucial development throughout the twentieth century. Since 1900, while the world's population has multiplied 3.6 times, the number of identifiable Christians in Europe has increased by a factor of only 1.4, and in North America by a factor of 3.4. By contrast, over those same ninety-plus years, the number of Christians in the Pacific islands has multiplied by 5.0, the number in Asia by 15.0, and the number in Africa an astounding 34.4 times. Where there were approximately 9 million identifiable Christians in Africa in 1900, there are now 310 million. On the basis of what has happened so far this century, missiologist David Barrett projects that within thirty years, the number of Christians in Africa and Asia *each* will outstrip the number in Europe, while the number of Christians in Africa alone will approach three times the number in North America.[11]

If it were necessary to find a single turning point symbolizing the movement of Christianity from the North to the South, a good candidate might be the founding of Wycliffe Bible Translators in 1934. This organization, which draws its workers mostly from North America and Europe, has been the most visible promoter of Bible translation in the twentieth century. The translation of the Scriptures, in turn, may be the most enduringly significant feature of the global expansion of Christianity that has been taking place since the start of the nineteenth century. Historians of Christianity take for granted that Jerome's translation of the Greek and Hebrew originals into Latin exerted an immense impact on Western society in the Middle Ages, as did Luther's translation on German language and literature, the King James Version and other translations on Britain and its colonies, and still more European versions in their regions. Similarly, much can be expected in cultures where the Bible has been rendered into the common language for the

---

11. Barrett, "Status of Global Mission, 1996," 25.

Archives of the Billy Graham Center, Wheaton, Illinois

This photo from the early 1960s shows a Vietnamese informant and a Western missionary at work on a translation of the Scriptures into Vietnamese.

first time in the twentieth century, for example (to mention only a few instances where a complete Bible has been published in this century), into isiZulu, Hausa, and KingyaRwanda in Africa, as well as Tibetan, Vietnamese, Tagalog (Philippines), and a number of Chinese versions.

To illustrate the magnitude of twentieth-century efforts at translating the Scriptures, two sets of figures are helpful. In 1989 the Gambian mission historian Lamin Sanneh enumerated 289 separate languages into which the complete Bible had been translated as of that date. Of those 289 translations, 170 had been published in the twentieth century.[12] Again, mission demographer David Barrett's *World Christian Encyclopedia* reported that in 1900 portions of the Bible were available in 537 different languages. By 1980 that total had risen to 1,811.[13] Both

12. Lamin Sanneh, *Translating the Message: The Missionary Impact on Culture* (Maryknoll, N.Y.: Orbis, 1989), 246–49. For the broader effects of translation, I am indebted to this book as well as to Lamin Sanneh, "Gospel and Culture: Ramifying Effects of Scriptural Translation," and Andrew F. Walls, "The Translation Principle in Christian History," both in *Bible Translation and the Spread of the Church*, ed. Philip C. Stine (Leiden: E. J. Brill, 1990).

13. David B. Barrett, *World Christian Encyclopedia* (New York: Oxford University Press, 1982), 29, 32.

Sanneh and Barrett admit imprecision in their figures. But even if they are only close, the implications are staggering. More—far more!—individual language groups, and the cultures that these languages define, have received the Scriptures during the twentieth century than in the preceding 1,900 years of the church's history.

The implications of this massive translation effort lie on several levels. Most obviously, the translation of the Bible brings the message of salvation through faith in Jesus Christ into the lives of individuals, families, and larger social contexts all throughout the world. In this sense, while the message of Christ that missionaries *brought* has been of great significance, even more important has been the message they *left* in the shape of vernacular Scriptures.

On another level, however, the profusion of Bible translations in the twentieth century speaks to the unfolding drama of Christianity itself. At Pentecost, "God-fearing Jews" from many tongues and nations were "utterly amazed" when all of them could hear "the wonders of God in our own tongues" (Acts 2:5–12). Almost as amazing is the powerful message communicated by this "twentieth-century Pentecost" of Bible translation. When people hear the Word of Life in their own languages, Christian affirmation about the universality of salvation comes closer to reality. Salvation is no longer an offering from an alien culture but an offering from within the culture. Likewise, the possession of the Bible in one's own vernacular often begins to effect a process of Christianization as the possession of the Bible in Latin, German, French, or English once did for the cultures of Christendom. Lamin Sanneh has put these matters well:

> There is a radical pluralism implied in vernacular translation wherein all languages and cultures are, in principle, equal in expressing the word of God. . . . Two general ideas stem from this analysis. First is the inclusive principle whereby no culture is excluded from the Christian dispensation or even judged solely or ultimately by Western cultural criteria. Second is the ethical principle of change as a check to cultural self-absolutization. Both of these ideas are rooted in what missionaries understood by God's universal truth as this was revealed in Jesus Christ, with the need and duty to work out this fact in the vernacular medium rather than in the uniform framework of cultural homogeneity.[14]

For these reasons and more, the founding by William Cameron Townsend (1896–1982) in 1934 of the Wycliffe Bible Translators may stand symbolically for one of the great Christian events of the age. The question that a Cakchiquel Indian of Guatemala once asked Townsend,

14. Sanneh, *Translating the Message*, 208–9.

Christian History Archives

Protestant congregations in Romania, where this photo was taken, suffered grievously during the Communist era, but nonetheless persevered.

who had come to that country in 1917 to distribute Spanish-language Bibles, has received a resounding response: "If your God is so smart, why doesn't he speak Cakchiquel?"[15]

Survival under Communism

Whether or not future historians will regard it as a grand turning point of the twentieth century, the survival of Christianity under Communist regimes is certainly a very important story. Among Lenin's first moves after the Russian Revolution of 1917 was to attack the Christian presence in the new Soviet Union. Stalin's multidecade campaign of terror against all traditional religions picked up where Lenin had left off. It relaxed only when the assistance of the Orthodox Church was required to hold off the Germans during the Second World War. In China, the Communist victory there (1949) as well as the Cultural Rev-

15. David J. Hesselgrave, "Townsend, William Cameron," in *Dictionary of Christianity in America* (Downers Grove, Ill.: InterVarsity, 1990), 1181. Camerson worked for ten years to produce a Cakchiquel translation of the New Testament, which was the first book ever in that language.

olution of 1966 and following years brought systematic oppression for the churches. Moreover, the efforts of Lenin, Stalin, and Mao were only the high points of the dedicated offensive against Christianity that occurred wherever Communist regimes took control.

The effect of these offenses was devastating. In a few states, like Albania, Christianity seemed, at least for many years, to be entirely wiped out. Massive loss of property accompanied massive loss of life. To take only the case of Orthodox Christians in the Soviet Union, during the first decades of Soviet control, the number of functioning Orthodox churches was reduced from about 55,000 to a few hundred, and the number of monasteries was reduced from 1,025 to 0. At the same time, at least 130 Orthodox bishops were slain (or perished in labor camps), along with tens of thousands of priests.[16]

Moreover, strife engendered by Communist attacks poisoned relations among Christians, as, for example, between Chinese Catholics who tried to remain loyal to the Vatican versus Chinese Catholics who obeyed their regime in breaking allegiance with the pope, Soviet Baptists who registered their churches with the state versus those who did not, Eastern European traditional churches who negotiated with regimes versus newer Protestant churches that would not, and so on.

Superlatives must be used with care in talking about the persecution of the church, since the long and varied history of Christianity has witnessed many bloody episodes, including more than a few in which Christians killed other Christians. Proper qualifications having been made, however, the twentieth-century assault of state-Communist regimes on Christianity still represents one of the most intense, one of the most purposeful, and one of the most thoroughly systematized periods of such activity in all of history.

The turning point in this situation is that Christianity survived. The story of how it survived will never in this life be fully known, for despite heroic efforts by a few chroniclers to preserve an account of oppression (like Aleksandr Solzhenitsyn in his three-volume *Gulag Archipelago*), most of the slain and much of what was destroyed passed away with no one to notice. What emerges as fragments, partial accounts, and occasionally with full documentation, however, is that the faith survived because traditional Christian words were refined, under deadly pressure, into a living reality of extraordinary purity.

If the survival of Christianity under Communist regimes comes to be regarded as a major turning point of the twentieth century, it will be be-

---

16. Timothy Ware, *The Orthodox Church*, new ed. (New York: Penguin, 1993), 148, 162.

cause the church as a whole takes to heart the witness of believers like Anatoly Vasilyevich Silin.[17] Aleksandr Solzhenitsyn was drawn to Silin during his own incarceration in the 1950s, because of the dedication to poetic composition he shared with Silin. Silin was raised with atheist instruction in an orphanage but then found Christian books while in a German prisoner-of-war camp during the Second World War. That slight acquaintance was enough to set him on a life of dedicated Christian witness. When Solzhenitsyn met him, Silin had spent his entire adult life in the camps. With no formal training, almost no access to religious books or even other believers, Silin went on writing and memorizing poems in his head, which he could recite at great length when he found a sympathetic listener like Solzhenitsyn. Untutored, untrained, persecuted, usually alone, Silin could yet rise to supernal heights of theological reasoning. He believed, for instance, that Christ suffered, not only to atone for human sins, but because God himself, out of pure love to his creatures, wanted to experience the full measure of human suffering. Silin could express a serene theodicy, or explanation for the existence of evil in the world:

> Does God, who is Perfect Love, allow
> This imperfection in our lives?
> The soul must suffer first, to know
> The perfect bliss of paradise. . . .
> Harsh is the law, but to obey
> Is for weak men the only way
> To win eternal peace.

According to Solzhenitsyn, Silin also displayed a gentle meekness to all who crossed his path, despite the extraordinary harshness of his lot.

When it is written as fully as possible, the story of Christian survival under Communist regimes will be an incredible story. It will include Polish Catholic determination, Russian Orthodox resilience, Baptist perseverance in Romania, Ukraine, and Russia, and everywhere the bearing up under grief and the shedding of blood. It will also somehow have to show how the number of Christians in China grew from less than one million Protestants and 3 million Catholics in 1949, when the Western missionaries were expelled and Mao unleashed his campaign against the churches, to the tens of millions that exist today (estimates range for Catholics from 6 to 12 million and for Protestants from 10 to 40 million).

17. The material on Silin is from Aleksandr I. Solzhenitsyn, *The Gulag Archipelago, Three* (New York: Harper & Row, 1978), 104–8.

A hint as to how Christianity survived under Communist oppression, as well as a suggestion why the reasons for that survival could define a turning point in the world history of Christianity, are contained in part of what Solzhenitsyn reported about his friend Anatoly Vasilyevich Silin.

> Before the war Anatoly Vasilyevich had graduated from a teachers' college, where he had specialized in literature. Like me, he now had about three years left before his "release" to a place of banishment. His only training was as a teacher of literature in schools. It seemed rather improbable that ex-prisoners like us would be allowed into schools. But if we were—what then.
>
> "I won't put lies into children's heads! I shall tell the children the truth about God and the life of the Spirit."
>
> "But they'll take you away after the first lesson."
>
> Silin lowered his head and answered quietly: "Let them."

At the end of a book on turning points in the history of Christianity, it is worth repeating the lessons that such an exercise illuminates.

The church survives by the mercy of God, not because of the wisdom, purity, or consistent faithfulness of Christians.

Nonetheless, many moments of unusual faithfulness can be found in the Christian past, both recent and ancient. It is important to note, however, that even when such moments turned out to make a dramatic difference for later history, they almost always resulted from gratitude to God rather than from a desire to influence the future.

Authentic Christian faith has taken many different shapes and can be expected to assume still other shapes in the future.

Finally, the promise of Jesus to be with his followers "always, to the very end of the age" (Matt. 28:20) provides not only a framework for studying the history of Christianity but also a fitting description of what Christian faith is, at its most essential level.

Like almost all other books, the destiny of this volume on turning points in the history of Christianity is to appear for a moment and then quietly disappear. It is, thus, most unlike the Scriptures and a very few other writings, like the Nicene and Chalcedonian creeds, that live on from age to age. However transient and inadequate these chapters may prove to be, readers perhaps may still find them consistent with the inspired one-sentence summary of the history of Christianity that Paul spoke to Roman Christians at the very beginning of the church's story: "Therefore I want you to know that God's salvation has been sent to the Gentiles, *and they will listen!*" (Acts 28:28)

During the twentieth century, contributions from Christians around the world have added significantly to the treasure of recorded prayer. The ones that follow are, first, the prayer of a Muslim who became a Christian and, second, the prayer of an Indian Christian.

> *O God, I am Mustafah the tailor and I work at the shop of Muhammad Ali. The whole day long I sit and pull the needle and the thread through the cloth. O God, you are the needle and I am the thread. I am attached to you and I follow you. When the thread tries to slip away from the needle it becomes tangled and must be cut so that it can be put back in the right place. O God, help me to follow you wherever you may lead me. For I am really only Mustafah the tailor, and I work at the shop of Muhammad Ali on the great square.[18]*

> *O Lord, let me rest the ladder of gratitude against thy cross and, mounting, kiss thy feet.[19]*

Further Reading

Alberigo, Giuseppe, and Joseph A. Komonchak, eds. *History of Vatican II.* Maryknoll, N.Y.: Orbis. Vol. 1 appeared in 1995; four more volumes are planned.

Bays, Daniel H., ed. *Christianity in China from the Eighteenth Century to the Present.* Stanford, Calif.: Stanford University Press, 1996.

Bediako, Kwame. *Christianity in Africa: The Renewal of a Non-Western Religion.* Maryknoll, N.Y.: Orbis, 1995.

Bergman, Susan, ed. *Martyrs: Contemporary Writers on Modern Lives of Faith.* San Francisco: HarperCollins, 1996.

Blumhofer, Edith. *Restoring the Faith: The Assemblies of God, Pentecostalism, and American Culture.* Urbana: University of Illinois Press, 1993.

Broun, Janice. *Conscience and Captivity: Religion in Eastern Europe.* Washington, D.C.: Ethics and Public Policy Center, 1988.

18. George Appleton, ed., *The Oxford Book of Prayer* (New York: Oxford University Press, 1985), 88.

19. Ibid., 143.

Burgess, Stanley M., and Gary B. McGee, eds. *Dictionary of Pentecostal and Charismatic Movements*. Grand Rapids: Zondervan, 1988.

Dyrness, William A., ed. *Emerging Voices in Global Theology*. Grand Rapids: Zondervan, 1994.

Keeley, Robin, ed. *Christianity in Today's World*. Grand Rapids: Eerdmans, 1985.

Martin, David. *Tongues of Fire: The Explosion of Protestantism in Latin America*. Oxford: Blackwell, 1990.

Newbigin, Lesslie. *The Gospel in a Pluralist Society*. Grand Rapids: Eerdmans, 1989.

Sanneh, Lamin O. *Translating the Message: The Missionary Impact on Culture*. Maryknoll, N.Y.: Orbis, 1989.

Studies in World Christianity. A twice-yearly journal from the Centre for the Study of Christianity in the Non-Western World, University of Edinburgh. First issues 1995. Available in the United States from Orbis Books, Maryknoll, N.Y.

Walls, Andrew F. *The Missionary Movement in Christian History: Studies in the Transmission of Faith*. Maryknoll, N.Y.: Orbis, 1996.

Box Notes

Chapter 1: *The Church Pushed Out on Its Own: The Fall of Jerusalem (70)*

1. "Easter Letter 39," in *St. Athanasius: Select Works and Letters,* ed. Archibald Robertson, vol. 4 of *The Nicene and Post-Nicene Fathers* (Grand Rapids: Eerdmans, 1978 [orig. 1891]), 551–52.

2. Henry Bettenson, ed., *Documents of the Christian Church,* 2nd ed. (New York: Oxford University Press, 1963), 68–69.

3. "Letter to the Trallians," in *The Early Christian Fathers,* ed. Henry Bettenson (London: Oxford University Press, 1956), 60–61.

4. Bettenson, *Documents of the Christian Church,* 23–24.

5. John H. Leith, ed., *Creeds of the Churches,* 3rd ed. (Atlanta: John Knox, 1982), 24–25.

Chapter 2: *Realities of Empire: The Council of Nicaea (325)*

1. Quoted in Robert Payne, *The Holy Fire: The Story of the Fathers of the Eastern Church* (Crestwood, N.Y.: St. Vladimir's Seminary Press, 1980 [orig. 1957]), 82–83.

2. Cited in *St. Athanasius on the Incarnation: The Treatise "De Incarnatione Verbi Dei,"* trans. and ed. A Religious of C.S.M.V. (Crestwood, N.Y.: St. Vladimir's Seminary Press, 1953 [orig. 1944]), 33–34.

3. Philip Schaff, *The Creeds of Christendom,* 3 vols., 6th ed. (New York: Harper, 1919), 1:28–29.

Chapter 3: *Doctrine, Politics, and Life in the Word: The Council of Chalcedon (451)*

1. Richard A. Norris, trans. and ed., *The Christological Controversy* (Philadelphia: Fortress, 1980), 132, 134.

2. Ibid., 135, 137–38.

Chapter 4: *The Monastic Rescue of the Church: Benedict's Rule (530)*

1. *The Rule of St. Benedict in English,* ed. Timothy Fry, O.S.B. (Collegeville, Minn.: Liturgical, 1981), 86–88.

2. Anne Boyd, *The Monks of Durham* (Cambridge: Cambridge University Press, 1975), 16.

3. Hildegard of Bingen, *Scivias,* trans. Mother Columba Hart and Jane Bishop (New York: Paulist, 1990), 479.

4. Hadewijch, *The Complete Works*, trans. Mother Columba Hart, O.S.B. (New York: Paulist, 1980), 209.

5. Quoted in Evelyn Underhill, *The Mystics of the Church* (Cambridge: James Clarke, 1925; reprint, Wilton, Conn.: Morehouse-Barlow, 1988), 158–59.

Chapter 5: *The Culmination of Christendom: The Coronation of Charlemagne (800)*

1. Quoted in the introduction to St. Gregory the Great, *Pastoral Care*, trans. Henry Davis, S.J., Ancient Christian Writers Series, vol. 11 (Westminster, Md.: Newman, 1950), 10–11.

2. Ibid., 66–67.

3. Thomas Aquinas, *Summa of Theology* III, q. 60, a. 6, c, from *An Aquinas Reader*, ed. Mary T. Clark (Garden City, N.Y.: Doubleday, 1972), 483.

Chapter 6: *Division between East and West: The Great Schism (1054)*

1. John H. Leith, ed., *Creeds of the Churches*, 3rd ed. (Atlanta: John Knox, 1982), 55–56.

2. Walter M. Abbott, S.J., ed., *The Documents of Vatican II* (New York: Guild, 1966), 725–26.

Chapter 7: *The Beginnings of Protestantism: The Diet of Worms (1521)*

1. Luther, "Preface to Latin Writings," in *Luther's Works*, 55 vols. (St. Louis: Concordia; Philadelphia: Fortress, 1955–76), 34:336–37.

2. *The Book of Concord: The Confessions of the Evangelical Lutheran Church*, ed. T. G. Tappert (Philadelphia: Fortress, 1959), 344–45.

Chapter 8: *A New Europe: The English Act of Supremacy (1534)*

1. From Roland H. Bainton, *Erasmus of Christendom* (New York: Scribner, 1969), 106, 108.

2. From Donald J. Ziegler, ed., *Great Debates of the Reformation* (New York: Random House, 1969), 342–43.

Chapter 9: *Catholic Reform and Worldwide Outreach: The Founding of the Jesuits (1540)*

1. *The Spiritual Exercises of St. Ignatius Loyola*, trans. Elisabeth Meier Tetlow (Lanham, Md.: University Press of America and The College Theology Society, 1987), 67.

2. Philip Schaff, ed., *The Creeds of Christendom*, 3 vols., 6th ed. (New York: Harper & Brothers, 1931), 1:96–99.

3. Ray R. Noll, ed., *100 Roman Documents concerning the Chinese Rites Controversy (1645–1941)* (San Francisco: Ricci Institute for Chinese-Western Cultural History, 1992), 22.

Chapter 10: *The New Piety: The Conversion of the Wesleys (1738)*

1. Edward H. Sugden, ed., *The Works of Wesley*, vol. 1, *Wesley's Standard Sermons* (Grand Rapids: Zondervan, 1955 [orig. 1921]), 40–41.

2. Philip Jakob Spener, *Pia Desideria* (Philadelphia: Fortress, 1964), 89–90.

Chapter 11: *Discontents of the Modern West: The French Revolution (1789)*

1. James R. Moore, ed., *Religion in Victorian Britain*, vol. 3, *Sources* (Manchester: University of Manchester Press, 1988), 443, 415.

2. Colman J. Barry, ed., *Readings in Church History*, vol. 3, *The Modern Era, 1789 to the Present* (Westminster, Md.: Newman, 1965), 78–79.

Chapter 12: *A Faith for All the World: The Edinburgh Missionary Conference (1910)*

1. William Carey, *An Enquiry into the obligations of Christians, to use means for the conversion of the heathens: in which the religious state of the different nations of the world, the success of former undertakings, and the practicability of further undertakings, are considered* (Leicester, Eng.: Henderson & Spalding, 1934 [orig. 1792]), 3, 86–87.

2. Samuel Crowther, *Journal of an Expedition up the Niger and Tshada Rivers* ([Portland, Oreg.]: Frank Cass, 1970, reprinting the London edition of 1854), 158–59.

Chapter 13: *Further Turning Points of the Twentieth Century*

1. Edith L. Blumhofer, ed., *"Pentecost in My Soul": Exploration in the Meaning of Pentecostal Experience in the Assemblies of God* (Springfield, Mo.: Gospel Publishing, 1989), 67–72.

2. Caroline Walker Bynum, *Holy Feast and Holy Fast: The Religious Significance of Food to Medieval Women* (Berkeley: University of California Press, 1987), 296.

Index

Mark A. Noll is the McManis Professor of Christian Thought and professor of history at Wheaton College. He is a church historian whose books include *A History of Christianity in the United States and Canada* and *The Scandal of the Evangelical Mind*.